Decoding Gender

Decoding Gender

Law and Practice in Contemporary Mexico

EDITED BY
HELGA BAITENMANN
VICTORIA CHENAUT
ANN VARLEY

FOREWORD BY
MAXINE MOLYNEUX

RUTGERS UNIVERSITY PRESS
NEW BRUNSWICK, NEW JERSEY, AND LONDON

LIBRARY OF CONGRESS CATALOGING-IN-PUBLICATION DATA

Decoding gender : law and practice in contemporary Mexico / edited by Helga Baitenmann, Victoria Chenaut, and Ann Varley.
 p.   cm.
Includes bibliographical references and index.
ISBN-13: 978-0-8135-4050-4 (hardcover : alk. paper)
ISBN-13: 978-0-8135-4051-1 (pbk. : alk. paper)
 I. Women—Legal status, laws, etc.—Mexico. 2. Sex and law—Mexico. 3. Indians of Mexico—Legal status, laws, etc.—Mexico. I. Baitenmann, Helga. II. Chenaut, Victoria. III. Varley, Ann
 KGF462.W62D43 2007
 346.7201'34—dc22   2006031255

A British Cataloging-in-Publication record for this book is available
from the British Library.

This collection copyright © 2007 by Rutgers, The State University

Individual chapters copyright © 2007 in the names of their authors

Manufactured in the United States of America

CONTENTS

Tables   vii

Foreword   ix
    MAXINE MOLYNEUX

Acknowledgments   xv

Introduction. Law and Gender in Mexico:
Defining the Field   1
    HELGA BAITENMANN, VICTORIA CHENAUT,
    AND ANN VARLEY

PART ONE
Discourses on Law and Sexuality

1   Love, Sex, and Gossip in Legal Cases from
    Namiquipa, Chihuahua   43
    ANA M. ALONSO

2   Sins, Abnormalities, and Rights: Gender and
    Sexuality in Mexican Penal Codes   59
    IVONNE SZASZ

3   The Realm outside the Law: Transvestite Sex
    Work in Xalapa, Veracruz   75
    ROSÍO CÓRDOVA PLAZA

PART TWO
Gender at the Intersection of Law and Custom

4   Women's Land Rights and Indigenous Autonomy in
    Chiapas: Interlegality and the Gendered Dynamics of
    National and Alternative Popular Legal Systems   93
    LYNN STEPHEN

5   Indigenous Women, Law, and Custom: Gender
       Ideologies in the Practice of Justice   109
           MARÍA TERESA SIERRA

6   Indigenous Women and the Law: Prison as a Gendered
       Experience   125
           VICTORIA CHENAUT

PART THREE
Legal Constructions of Marriage and the Family

7   Domesticating the Law   145
           ANN VARLEY

8   Conflictive Marriage and Separation in a Rural
       Municipality in Central Mexico, 1970–2000   162
           SOLEDAD GONZÁLEZ MONTES

9   The Archaeology of Gender in the New
       Agrarian Court Rulings   180
           HELGA BAITENMANN

PART FOUR
Legal Reform and the Politics of Gender

10 Law and the Politics of Abortion   197
           ADRIANA ORTIZ-ORTEGA

11 Married Women's Property Rights in Mexico: A Comparative
       Latin American Perspective and Research Agenda   213
           CARMEN DIANA DEERE

       Afterword. Thinking about
       Gender and Law in Mexico   231
           JANE F. COLLIER
       Bibliography   239
       Notes on Contributors   265
       Index   271

TABLES

7.1.	Comparing the 1884 and 1917 Legislation	150
7.2.	The 1961 *Tesis de Jurisprudencia* on the Marital Home	152
8.1.	Marital Conflicts in Xalatlaco's Court Records, 1970–2000	166
10.1.	Legal Status of Abortion in Latin America	198
11.1.	Choice of Marital Regimes in Selected Latin American Countries	215
11.2.	The Dual-Headed Household and Recognition of Consensual Unions in Selected Latin American Countries	218
11.3.	Inheritance Rights of Widows: Rules Governing Testaments	222
11.4.	Inheritance Rights of Widows: Rules If Deceased Dies Intestate	223

FOREWORD

MAXINE MOLYNEUX

Scholarly work on law and gender in Latin America has begun to gather pace in recent years, after a period of relative neglect. This revival has proceeded in tandem with efforts by women's movements during the period of democratic transition to advance programs of reform aimed at securing gender equality in the spheres of law, politics, and social rights. Nourished in part by this interaction, a growing literature is to be found on the social, political, and historical aspects of law and gender relations, as well as a sizeable quantity of policy-related work on specific aspects of legal reform. This output is, however, dispersed across discipline and region; some of it is ephemeral; and there are still only a handful of book-length studies dedicated to this important area of scholarship. *Decoding Gender: Law and Practice in Contemporary Mexico* is therefore to be welcomed both for bringing together a quality collection of studies spanning more than one hundred years of Mexican history, and for its coverage of issues of contemporary scholarly debate.

Mexico is in many respects an ideal case study for exploring the intricate associations between law and gender in Latin America. A history of state formation marked by colonialism, revolution, and a "perfect dictatorship" of seventy-one years, together with uneven progress to join the dozen largest economies in the world, were and remain consequential on women's rights, in unexpected and sometimes conflicting ways. Today Mexico is a country with a population of over one hundred million people, more than half of whom are of indigenous or mestizo descent. Mexican society is riven by deep inequalities along class, gender, and ethnic lines, with these divisions refracted across social and cultural forms unevenly incorporated into the market economy. Three centuries of Spanish rule left its imprint on Mexico's justice systems, religion, language, demography, and economy, but this institutional apparatus always existed in a dual relationship, part coercion, part accommodation, with indigenous society. The colonial state was founded on the Greco-Roman tradition of law, its jurisprudence modified over the centuries, but more decisively transformed in the modern epoch by the influence of the Napoleonic Codes, by independence, and by the influence of liberalism and Enlightenment thought.

From the mid-nineteenth century, Mexican rulers embarked on a process of modern state formation, inspired by liberal principles of governance and justice, albeit adapted to and insecurely implanted in the formation over which they presided. If the modern history of law and gender in Mexico is that of state formation and re-formation, it is also a history of national and local discontinuities and of a complex articulation of state and customary modes of social regulation. Thus, despite the apparently unifying instance of law in the institutions and codes of the state, there is no singular account of law and gender, and even today in some regions of Mexico legal regulation is conducted through a plurality of parallel, overlapping, or syncretic systems. Common to much of the region, these features endured in some parts of Mexico despite the upheavals of the revolution of 1910 to 1920 and the creation of a modern corporatist state.

Such continuities existing within the broader currents of social change are central themes in analyses of law and gender in Latin America. Post-independence liberal governments sought to promote structural and institutional changes as part of their modernizing projects, and treated law as an accompaniment to, and instrument of, social change. Legal and constitutional reform and the creation of new regulatory instruments subjected the diverse forms of social life to a central authority, which defined itself according to prevailing liberal principles. Yet gender relations were only partially transformed in this process, and not always to women's advantage.

Luso-Hispanic colonial laws had accorded women rights and status different from men's, imposing on married women the obligation to serve and obey their husbands. This principle was reiterated in Article 213 of the Napoleonic Civil Code, and, although early liberalism proclaimed itself committed to freedom from servitude, its laws did little for what John Stuart Mill described as the slavery within marriage. At the heart of liberal legal reasoning about the gender order lay elements of earlier systems of patriarchal right. Although postcolonial state makers in Latin America sought to shift the principles of legal regulation from what has been called "colonial patriarchalism" to liberal contractarianism, and while there were some significant reforms in women's rights, masculine authority and privilege continued to prevail in the domestic and public sphere.

Mexican modernity, whether in its liberal, revolutionary, or corporatist moments, incorporated women selectively, on far from equal terms, and with a surprising degree of inconsistency. Mexico led the way in Latin America when it in 1870 established the principle of separation of marital property and in 1884 allowed testamentary freedom. But for much of the twentieth century, citizens' rights rested on deeply rooted notions of gender difference that accorded with an idealized view of the asymmetric social roles occupied by the sexes. In this ordering, men were naturally assumed to be the primary breadwinners, while women's duties lay in the home. The influence of the Catholic Church, although diminished in the revolutionary years, remained a powerful moralizing force, particularly in matters pertaining to the family and to women's sexual and reproductive roles. Even today, some of the most restrictive and punitive abortion laws can be found in Mexico.

From their earliest manifestations, women's movements in Mexico had to confront a complex field of engagement in their struggle for citizenship. The revolutionary years, with their radical dynamic influenced by socialist currents, made some positive though limited impact on women's status. Revolutions tend to be state-strengthening and centralizing forces, but they are also paradoxically both conservative and modernizing, fixing certain social relations in the moment of their apparent transformation. The revolutionary government's project of accelerated development and nation building was premised on a bureaucratic one-party state, corporatist in form and selective in interest representation. The government's program of social modernization was also partial in that patriarchal authority and the sociolegal relations that underpinned it remained resilient and, to a significant degree, encoded in state law and practice.

The Constitution of 1917 and the Civil Code of 1928 accorded women legal equality and gave them some new rights, notably through removing *potestad marital,* yet denied them full civil and political rights. Women's right to contract remained limited, and married women, charged with legal responsibility for domestic matters, could only work outside the home with their husband's permission. Most surprisingly, perhaps, universal female franchise was not granted until 1953—later than in most Latin American states. Masculine privilege endured in these codes despite its transformation and resignification and the weakening of many of its institutional supports as a result of the profound changes in Mexican society.

This unevenness in women's acquisition of citizenship rights was particularly evident in judicial rulings that assumed male prerogatives and sexual rights over women's bodies. The old division between public and private matters of legal jurisdiction allowed the "private" sphere of the family to be left "outside justice," as in the case of marital rape and domestic violence, which were often treated as a private matter, with lenient sentencing of husbands even for serious cases of assault. Only gradually did the law place limits on men's authority over their wives, with women remaining subject to what has been called a "fraternal sexual contract," through which they acquired some rights in the public sphere but were denied others in the private sphere and by virtue of their "difference."

Violations of equality principles were not easily reformed, but those who opposed them appeared to have moral right on their side in an age when universalist principles prevailed in matters of justice. Other types of bias against women were more subtle and could be deeply divisive among women themselves. Although formal legal equality might be a desirable ideal, and an advance on subjection, there was a risk that women's rights might simply be assimilated to what was, in effect, a masculine norm. This was a false equality in that, in erasing pertinent differences (such as childbearing), it assumed a level playing field for both sexes. In treating women as men, simple equality ignored inequalities of circumstance and opportunity, and could have the perverse effect of reproducing inequality through hidden forms of discrimination. Conservative maternalist lobbies, supported by Catholic traditionalists, had argued against equality on these as well as on moral grounds. They believed that women and men should be treated differently in accordance with their biological functions and temperamental dispositions, and that women should be accorded special dispensations on account of childbearing and child-rearing. Mexican laws, like those elsewhere in Latin America, had long recognized the special status of motherhood, framed in part as a concern for the well-being of children, with mothers and children seen as in need of "protection" rather than full citizenship. Equality feminists worried that lack of legal equality would only confirm women's second-class status, and would disadvantage them in employment, but at the same time they were aware that the failure to recognize the implications of the sexual division of labor and responsibility for childcare placed women at a disadvantage in relation to men in the competitive marketplace. Women, they argued, paid twice for the failure to equalize domestic responsibilities: in having fewer opportunities, and in bearing the cost in the form of lower pay, promotion prospects, and long-term financial security.

If the "difference question" remained as unresolved in law as among women's movements, more agreement could be reached over the treatment meted out to women in the courts. This form of discrimination, within the practice of the law, attracted the attention of scholars and activists alike and revealed the double standards to which women were all too often subject. Women's testimony often counted as less than men's, and courts were shown to be biased against women, especially in cases of domestic conflict and sex crimes. The most telling example of this last was the treatment of rape cases, where female victims were routinely subject to a range of pejorative assumptions situating them as colluding with the perpetrator or acting provocatively.

Campaigns for gender justice across the last century or more have therefore been directed at achieving reform in these three broad areas. Most evidently, they have sought to remove patriarchal and masculine privilege in the legal codes regulating the public and private spheres. This has involved tackling discrimination against women in public life, individuating women's rights from family or marriage status, and removing spurious forms of protection from employment, civil, and family laws. In recent times campaigns have challenged masculine right in matters of private conduct, demanding the reform of laws concerning domestic violence.

Equal-rights campaigners have also challenged the assimilation of women to the masculine norm where this is clearly at variance with justice. They have argued for laws that respect difference without surrendering the principle of equality, a demand that has characterized the historical struggle for women's citizenship rights across the world. In Latin America, feminist movements have supported entitlements for women that derive from their role as childbearers and mothers (such as paid maternity leave and job retention for pregnant women), as well as a range of restitutive measures designed to take account of the fact that equality of opportunity does not guarantee equality of outcome if conditions among competitors are unequal. Positive discrimination, targets, and quota systems are measures informed by this position, and their adoption in some areas of public life, notably in the political realm, have helped to shift the balance of representation in women's favor.

Reform efforts have also been directed at the judicial process itself, to make it more responsive to criticisms of its practice and more accountable to the principle of equal treatment. Concern over the prejudice routinely displayed in the courts against women has been challenged by campaigns to raise awareness of its nature and extent and to demand that women be treated as moral equals in the judicial process. Women's organizations have had some success in securing reforms in the law and the practice of justice in cases of domestic violence and in rape trials, and in drawing attention to the need for the training of the police and judiciary to create greater sensitivity to women's situation in these cases. Yet, as the tragic murders of young women in Ciudad Juárez and elsewhere show, the difficulties of securing justice for women remain formidable in contexts where weak institutionality, corruption, and violence routinely undermine the rule of law.

Taken together, there can be little doubt that the reforms of the last thirty or so years have brought striking advances in women's rights and legal treatment not only in Mexico but across Latin America. The wave of legal reforms that attended democratization was unusual in its scale, and derived some of its momentum from the strength of second wave feminism, both in its regional and international forms, and from international human rights legislation. In a politically favorable context, these elements combined to liberalize, modify, and transform gender relations as inscribed in law, with reforms governing the transmission of property, political representation, marriage, and sexuality serving as important levers of social change. Such changes represent significant steps towards gender justice, but law does not simply determine social relations, and, to the disappointment of some who participated in the reform movements, the hierarchical ordering of society along gender lines has seemed little altered.

It is through exploring the multiple interactions between law and gender that the chapters in this volume cast light on this question of the limits of law. In revealing the many dimensions of legality, these writings underline the point that while the law is itself a social relation, and is to an important degree constitutive of social relations, it does not simply determine social life. The law exists in a relationship of reflexivity with society: it adapts to change; it is constantly contested and is subject to a degree of interpretation by those who exercise authority, with reference to presumed social norms.

The relationship between law and gender is therefore not simply one of unmitigated female victimhood. Even aspects of colonial, patriarchal, and indigenous laws gave women some rights that could serve, in sometimes surprising ways, to their advantage. Women from all social groups, from the poorest and most disadvantaged to those in more privileged circumstances, have been adept at challenging legal rulings, strategizing over which rights to appeal to in securing their diverse goals. As gender also cross-cuts other forms of social positioning that produce differences of interests and conceptions of justice, the idea that there is one account of "gender and law" is further unsettled.

The law thus does not exercise a direct and unambiguous mode of regulation over women. As the chapters in this book show, "the law" is not a unitary instance, and, in a context of interlegality, parallel and overlapping systems of regulation may prevail. Formal codes and the lived reality of social practice may also diverge significantly and have little bearing on how people negotiate their rights and entitlements and their social conduct within the social worlds which they inhabit. Transforming social relations to achieve equality and justice has provided feminism with a difficult and uncompleted task, one that depends not only on legal reform but on a multidimensional process of social change. Legal reform is a necessary condition for this change to occur, but is clearly not sufficient for the achievement of gender justice, as the discussions contained in this rich collection, *Decoding Gender: Law and Practice in Contemporary Mexico*, so convincingly illustrate.

ACKNOWLEDGMENTS

This book originated in a research workshop held at the Institute of Latin American Studies (now the Institute for the Study of the Americas, or ISA) in February 2004. Discussions benefited from the participation of, in addition to the contributors to this volume: Elizabeth Dore, Diane Elson, Juan Guillermo Figueroa, Jane Hindley, Fiona Macaulay, Kevin J. Middlebrook, Caterina Pizzigoni, Patricia Ravelo-Blancas, Sergio Sánchez, Patience A. Schell, Line Scholden, Rachel Sieder, and Katie Willis. We would like to thank Director James Dunkerley, Karen Perkins, and Olga Jiménez from ISA for all their hospitality and support. We gratefully acknowledge funding from ISA, the Embassy of Mexico in the United Kingdom, and the Society for Latin American Studies. Other institutions that have generously supported our work throughout the years include the Centro de Investigaciones y Estudios Superiores en Antropología Social (CIESAS–Golfo) and the Economic and Social Research Council (UK).

Revised versions of workshop papers were presented at the 2006 Latin American Studies Association (LASA) congress in San Juan, Puerto Rico. We gratefully acknowledge the support of Viviana Kluger, cochair of the Law and Society Section of LASA. LASA panel participants included Mary Goldsmith and Matthew Gutmann.

We owe special thanks to Adi Hovav, editor at Rutgers University Press, who encouraged us enormously by her enthusiastic support of the project from the very start. Thanks also to Marilyn Campbell for guidance during the production process, and to Paula Friedman for her superb copyediting. The volume benefited from the helpful and detailed comments made by two anonymous Rutgers University Press reviewers.

As social scientists (rather than lawyers), grappling with complex and often changing laws was perhaps the greatest single challenge we faced in this collective endeavor. In searching for clarifications, we benefited from the counsel of numerous friends and colleagues, including Carmen Diana Deere, Ana Gamboa Rosas, Gilbert E. Haakh, and Juan Carlos Pérez Castañeda. Any errors remaining are our own responsibility.

We are very grateful to Olimpia Gracia, Regina Henríquez Morales, and María del Rocío Ochoa García for research assistance. We also wish to thank the staffs at the CIESAS–Xalapa and Mexico City libraries, the British Library, and the many legal archives consulted in Mexico; staff at each provided unfaltering support in response to our continued queries and requests.

Special thanks goes to all the Mexican *funcionarios judiciales* who shared their experiences with us, and to the women and men who opened the doors of their homes, told us their stories, and allowed us to learn from their difficult experiences.

Cover art for the paperback edition is by Álvaro Santiago (1953, Oaxaca City). Santiago's artistic work is part of major international collections, including that of the Irish Museum of Modern Art (Dublin), the Museum of Latin American Art (Long Beach, Calif.), and the Mexican Cultural Center (Paris). We thank him kindly for graciously allowing us to use his artwork for this cover design. We found his fragmented (and largely androgynous) human figures distributed among a number of panels in a mosaic-like form particularly fitting for the title *Decoding Gender*. As with the construction of gender, the faces in the painting are, in the words of the artist, "composites of many masks."

As editors, we wish to thank our contributors for their patience with our seemingly unending requests and for the dedication that they showed throughout the process. One contributor characterized our exchanges as a "small seminar on legal matters," and we have indeed learned much together. We are especially grateful to Maxine Molyneux and Jane F. Collier for their essays framing the volume— but particularly for having been an integral part of the project from the very start.

On a more personal level, Helga would like to thank Kevin Middlebrook for his extensive scholarly (and personal) support and advice, and Mariel Baitenmann-Middlebrook, who (at age seven) chose Mary Kingsley for her school project on explorers "because it had to do with women's rights." Together, they made my share of the work a little easier and much more meaningful.

On her behalf, Victoria would like to thank Valentina and Magdalena Gatti, whose presence and cheerfulness supported the long process of bringing this project to completion.

Similarly, Ann would like to thank Alan Mosley for all his encouragement and support (and his good-humored patience about not being able to get near the computer *yet again*). The editing of this book has coincided with particularly difficult times for my family, and the understanding and practical support, both of Alan and of my former head of department, Richard Munton, have made a major contribution to enabling me to complete my share of the work.

For us as editors, it has been a novel experience to work as a team of three scholars from different disciplines living on two continents. We would like to acknowledge one another for the ongoing confidence, support, and learning we have encountered during this long and difficult four-year process. The enthusiasm we have shared has both reinforced our sense of the value of the project and renewed our commitment to bringing it to a successful completion.

Decoding Gender

INTRODUCTION

Law and Gender in Mexico

Defining the Field

HELGA BAITENMANN
VICTORIA CHENAUT
ANN VARLEY

An extensive literature links the subjects of law and gender in Mexico, but only rarely is the connection itself the focus of attention. This book demonstrates that the linkage is complex and, at times, contradictory. Law (written corpus, legal procedures, and everyday practices) frequently reproduces and perpetuates exclusion, discrimination, and inequality on the basis of gender (idealized notions of femininity, masculinity, and heteronormativity), but also is often malleable and provides spaces for agency, negotiation, and redress. Moreover, law and gender cut across traditional social science dichotomies (state–popular, hegemonic–subaltern, and so forth) in interesting and complex ways. Thus, this collective endeavor takes as its point of departure the idea that law and gender is not a narrow and specialized concept, but rather an important means through which to analyze a broader range of power relations in contemporary Mexico.

This introductory chapter has three main goals. First, it briefly highlights the central concerns this book shares with contemporary international debates about gender justice. Second, it provides a comprehensive overview of studies of law and gender in Mexico, which both sets the stage for the chapters that follow and traces the contours of a field that has heretofore been disparate and largely implicit. Third, this chapter considers contributors' essays in the light of theoretical and empirical advances in the field more generally, drawing special attention to Mexico's particularities with regard to law and gender.

Law and Gender in International Perspective

The contributors to this volume engage in a dialogue with both international debates about gender studies and a rich scholarship on law and gender in

Mexico. They share a number of questions and methodologies with the expanding international literature on gender justice. The first of these common concerns is a methodological focus (to a greater or lesser extent) on discourse analysis. Because state laws are based on the written word, and because legal procedures are recorded in documents, many of our contributors share with international legal feminism an interest in how legal discourse constructs gender. Indeed, a number of studies on law and gender (including the essays in this volume) are concerned with identifying in the law forms of either overt or indirect discrimination. The latter case involves laws that appear gender-neutral but that, upon closer examination, actually exclude or disempower individuals on the basis of gender (for Latin America, see, for example: Birgin 2000; Cabal, Roa, and Lemaitre 2001; Cabal and Motta 2006; Facio and Fries 1999; Mehrotra 1998).

Contributors also share with the international human rights community the basic principle that gender-based abuses and discrimination are human rights violations. Conceptualizations of human rights are not gender-neutral if they do not address such matters as the right to autonomous decisions regarding sexuality and to freedom from violence against women, including domestic violence (Agosín 2001; Knop 2004; Petchesky and Judd 2006). Many recent studies explore how international gender rights concepts move from transnational to diverse local settings (Banda 2005; Chan-Tiberghien 2004; Galeana 2004; Kardam 2005; Merry 2006).

Together with other recent studies of gender justice, the essays in this volume are anchored in close empirical research on legal processes. This approach necessarily leads scholars to consider more closely social divisions such as age, marital status, economic condition, sexual orientation, and ethnic identity. Contributors combine the study of legal concepts with detailed empirical work on the everyday practices of law. Whether they focus on law and gender from an institutional or state-centered perspective (the historical development of a specific law, court decisions, rulings, judicial ideologies, and so forth), or whether they address the effects of laws in specific regions and contexts (*ejidos*, indigenous communities, urban spaces, and so forth), the contributors undertake fine-grained explorations of the subject matter, based on detailed empirical or archival materials.

Finally, this book shares with the broader literature on gender justice an interest in studying empirical particularities as part of such phenomena as liberalism and neoliberalism (Molyneux and Razavi 2002; Deere and León 2001; Razavi 2003), social movements (Stephen 1997), and partisan alternation in power (Htun 2003), as well as of the larger historical processes of state formation (Dore and Molyneux 2000) and democratization (Craske and Molyneux 2002). Thus, the contributors to this volume consider such topics as the impact of the Mexican Revolution and postrevolutionary state formation on law and gender, Mexico's particular history of collective rights embedded in a liberal system, the gendered effects of the 1994 North American Free Trade Agreement (NAFTA) and accompanying neoliberal legal reforms, and the 1994 Zapatista uprising and subsequent indigenous mobilizations in demand of collective rights within a neoliberal system.

The Study of Law and Gender in Mexico

Since the 1990s, there has been a boom in gender studies in Mexico. Some of the most recent collaborative projects (with extensive bibliographies that attest to the magnitude of interest in this topic) examine phenomena such as changes in family relations (Ariza and de Oliveira 2004); women's participation in government (Barrera Bassols 2000); maternity and reproductive rights (Torres Falcón 2005), including male reproductive sexuality (Figueroa, Jiménez, and Tena 2006); the politics of sexual difference (McKee Irwin, McCaughan, and Nasser 2003); women in rural areas (Fowler-Salamini and Vaughan 1994, González Montes and Salles 1995); violence against women in both rural and urban contexts (Torres Falcón 2004); women's role in shaping the legal process (Pérez-Gil Romo and Ravelo Blancas 2004); indigenous women's activism (Speed, Hernández Castillo, and Stephen 2006); labor studies from a gendered perspective (Mummert and Carrillo 1998), and gender and state formation in historical context (Olcott, Vaughan, and Cano 2006). Other authors have analyzed gender studies in Mexico as a disciplinary field (Gutiérrez Castañeda 2002b; Urrutia 2002b).

Although a number of studies have undertaken gendered analyses of law in Mexico, none explicitly addressed the links between the study of law and research on gender. Many of the debates in these areas thus have remained unconnected. This introduction seeks to delimit the field of study and establish some connections.

The existing scholarship on law from a gendered perspective comes largely from three disciplines: history, law, and anthropology. First, there is a branch of Mexican history touching on law and gender; although much of this research has focused on colonial and nineteenth-century Mexico, this branch of Mexican history has also made important contributions to the study of the less well-researched twentieth century. Second, there is a division of legal scholarship concerned with the legal status of women in Mexico; with roots in the nineteenth century, this scholarship now provides cutting-edge analyses in dialogue with the international human rights community. And third, there is a branch of legal anthropology that only recently developed an explicit gender focus, but which is already a vibrant subfield in law-and-gender studies in Latin America.

We can only fully appreciate the contributions of these three subdisciplines when we understand the development of these very separate strands. We learn (among other insights) about women's and men's agency as litigants, as legal scholars, and as activists, and that men and women often use the legal system in different ways. We are reminded that discrimination on the basis of gender and sexual preference is particularly evident in laws that regulate family matters, sexuality, and marriage, but that the implications of such discrimination go beyond the "private" sphere to include economic, political, and human rights. Moreover, we find that the law operates to women's and men's advantage and disadvantage. We also learn that the construction and reform of gendered and gendering laws are closely tied to the political history of Mexico. And we begin to recognize the complexity of rights in a multicultural society, as well as how the debate over rights occurs within different and gendered spheres of legal authority.

The following sections provide a detailed analysis of these three subfields, highlighting their theoretical and empirical contributions to the study of law and gender in Mexico—one of the Latin American countries with the longest and most dynamic traditions of scholarship on the legal system from a gendered perspective.

Historical Studies, Law, and Gender in Mexico

Judicial records make a vital contribution to the historical literature, since they permit "normally voiceless people to speak" (Kellogg 1995, 35). This section reviews scholarship on gender in Mexico that analyzes legislation and court records and documents women's agency as litigants. It then summarizes some of the main findings concerning the relationship between law and gender in Mexico, asking to what extent the law has operated to women's advantage or to women's disadvantage.

Legislation and Legal Records as Historical Sources

Much work on the history of gender is embedded in studies of the family, sexuality, and marriage (Caulfield 2001). This is true of many of the Mexican studies using colonial legal records, particularly the work of the Seminario de Historia de las Mentalidades.[1] As church and crown played complementary roles in the regulation of marriage, researchers have examined both the royal and the ecclesiastical courts (Lavrin 1989a). The unusually complete Mexican Inquisition records also provide a rich source of insight into everyday life (Boyer 1995). Judicial records have therefore been used to study many aspects of marital and family life and sexuality in New Spain, including consensual union, interracial partnerships, conflicts over choice of marital partner, bigamy, adultery and divorce, illegitimacy, childhood and parenting, property inheritance, homosexuality, sexual witchcraft, prostitution, sexual abuse, and domestic violence or murder.[2]

Some of these themes reappear in studies of the period after independence and through to the present time, particularly those concerning violence against women and marital conflict.[3] For the nineteenth century, Silvia Arrom's pathbreaking work on divorce uses the ecclesiastical records as an "unequaled source" for the study of domestic life until the state asserted control over marriage in 1859 (Arrom 1976, 13).[4] The second half of the century witnessed the codification of Mexico's legal system in the modernizing search to "regulate practically all areas and events of social life" (Speckman Guerra 2001, 243–244). The expansion of government intervention and social engineering commenced anew after the Revolution (Knight 1994), encompassing what Mary Kay Vaughan (2000, 196) terms a "rationalization of domesticity." The process expanded the sources available to historians, as is evident in the literature on criminality. Although authors in this field continue to use case records, they also survey crime statistics, the work of criminologists, social workers and public health officials, and the published law reports.[5]

Perhaps in part as a result of the alternative sources available, the number of historical studies examining legislation or court records drops as we move closer to the present day, although the range of topics addressed has widened. There is greater emphasis on income generation—for example, how legal regulation shaped the lives of women engaged in domestic service, street vending, and prostitution—but there is otherwise little work using legislation or court records for the 1930s to 1990s.[6] Interest in the gender consequences of the 1992 dismantling of Mexico's agrarian reform has recently led to the inclusion, however, of new types of legislation and archives: those concerning agrarian property rights and their transformation.[7]

A noteworthy recent trend is a move away from central Mexico as the reference point, with studies focusing on Chihuahua (Alonso 1995a, 1995b), Sonora (Shelton 2004), Oaxaca (Stern 1995; Sousa 1997), Veracruz (Chenaut 1997, 2001b, 2002; Baitenmann 1997), and Yucatán (Gill 2001; Smith 2006).

As historical sources, legislation and legal records have a number of limitations. The pitfalls of relying on legislation are summarized in the title of the Seminario de Historia de las Mentalidades collection *Del dicho al hecho*. In early colonial times, inefficient bureaucracy compounded the effects of geography to create tension between "what was said"—the laws of Spain and the Catholic Church—and "what was done" (Guzmán Vázquez and Martínez O. 1989a, 9). A mobile population and gender imbalance in the Hispanic population hindered the imposition of imported norms, and a mestizo group emerged for which there was no specific legal provision (Alberro 1982). The result was an extraordinary contradiction between formal gender ideologies and the social reality of concubinage and illegitimacy (Kuznesof 1992; Gonzalbo Aizpuru 1998; Margadant 1991). It would, then, "be a mistake to assume that one can determine women's status on the basis of formal codes of law" (Kellogg 1995, 105).

This does not mean that laws are of no assistance. Arrom (1985b, 11) argues that they may be closer to actual experience than are the writings of pamphleteers or journalists. Their limitations can be countered by using other sources, such as legal commentaries and court proceedings.

Judicial records also have their limitations. Court records have little to say about people who abide by the norms the courts are supposed to defend (Alberro 1982). The emphasis is on deviance: the marriages that appear, for example, are those that exceeded the usual levels of subordination of women. Some degree of "corrective" physical punishment of wives was acceptable to ecclesiastical and legal commentators and seemingly tolerated by many women across the centuries.[8] Consequently, marriages displaying only "a politics of skirmishing" do not appear in the records (Boyer 1989, 259).[9] We can nonetheless "learn something of marriage by looking at troubled ones" (ibid., 279; Lipsett-Rivera 2001).

Straightforward readings of (non)compliance with legal norms should in any case be double-checked. For instance, in New Spain, bigamy did not necessarily entail rejection of the norm of marriage. Some people married twice, however, to avoid denunciation for "illicit friendship" (Boyer 1995, 111; Enciso Rojas 1982). "Violating the norm in order to adhere to it" could, then, be either a sincere or a superficial strategy (Enciso Rojas 1989, 106; Alberro 1982). One example of the latter is perhaps offered by the woman who excused her bigamy on the grounds that it was "Better to live in one sin [as a bigamist] than as a single woman in many" (Boyer 1995, 103). Conversely, a man accused of fornication claimed that "living with one [woman] was a mortal sin, but knowing one today and another tomorrow, was not a mortal sin but venial" (Atondo Rodríguez 1986, 149). Whether naïvely or manipulatively, such men echoed the church's ambivalence in defining fornication as a mortal sin while turning a blind eye to prostitution. They upheld the sanctity of marriage and feminine chastity while asserting their own right to sexual gratification. Extramarital sex was, therefore, not a sin if the woman was a prostitute or "single" (unmarried but not a virgin). Some men added that it was acceptable to sleep with an *india,* and one argued that in "deflowering" a slave he had committed only a venial sin (ibid.).

We should be wary, in short, of reading compliance simply as acceptance or oppositional discourses or practices, as resistance (Lewis 1996; Owensby 2005).

Women as Litigants

Within years of the conquest, indigenous women were engaging with the Spanish courts. In 1540, Doña Ana, wife of the ruler of Iguala, joined two men in denouncing her husband to the Inquisition. She complained of his sexual excesses, detailing his incestuous relationships, to get away from him (Gruzinski 1982). He had forced his attentions on her sisters and aunt, she said, and treated her "like a dog" (Archivo General de la Nación 1912, 202).

The most striking evidence of women's litigiousness comes from Susan Kellogg's (1995) study of how Spanish law changed Nahua culture. Kellogg is one of several authors to observe how avidly indigenous groups in Mexico took up litigation (see also Borah 1983; Cline 1986). Tenocha Mexica women were particularly active litigants, as likely as men to start a case (Kellogg 1997). In property suits, two-thirds of the cases featured a woman as plaintiff or defendant (Kellogg 1995, 32). What is more, women apparently played a leading role in cases involving their family. A judicial officer observed in 1599:

> When some Indian has a dispute, though the Indian may be very impor-
> tant, able and skilled, he will not appear before the court without bring-
> ing his wife with him, and they inform and speak that which by reason of
> the lawsuit it is necessary to say, and the husbands are very timid and
> quiet. (quoted in Kellogg 1995, 108)

Nahua women are also described as active litigants in seventeenth-century Cuernavaca (Haskett 1997), and Lisa Sousa (1997) notes a willingness on the part of Mixtec and Zapotec women to take disputes to Oaxaca's colonial courts, where the women acted on their own behalf rather than being represented by men. The Mixteca Juana López, for instance, accused a Spanish merchant of battery after he knocked her to the ground in a dispute over the price of hay.

In some cases, even black and mulatto women turned to the colonial legal system. These were extremely unusual litigants; the slaves who succeeded in getting their cases heard were likely to be urban-based, educated, and pos-sessed of remarkable determination (Alberro 1980; Palmer 1976). In 1633, María Negra went to a Mexico City magistrate to seek redress for mistreatment of her husband by his owner. Other women complained that their owners were deny-ing them their legal right to spend time with their husbands. In doing so, these women articulated a sense of having at least some rights (Boyer 1998, 163). Petronila Ruiz told the Inquisition that her master had forced her to marry a fel-low slave who branded, beat, and starved her. That she used legal arguments—"stressing that lack of consent, not bad treatment as such, invalidated the marriage"—suggests she had considerable knowledge of both the law and lawyers (Boyer 1995, 112; see also Owensby 2005).

Slaves also managed to get themselves denounced to the Inquisition for blasphemy, to escape their owners (McKnight 1999). One swore that "she did not love God" but found the devil "handsome." She later admitted she had said this "so that they will throw her out of the convent where she serves a nun she doesn't like" (Alberro 1979, 150).

Mexica women's status as litigants appears to have declined after the mid-seventeenth century (Kellogg 1995). In a very different social context, Patricia Seed (1988a, 1988b) shows that, whereas declarations by middle- or upper-class women concerning their engagements were treated with respect by ecclesiastical courts in early seventeenth century Mexico City, their testimony was regarded, by the late colonial period, with suspicion, requiring corroboration by men.

This is not to say that women ceased to use the courts. Caterina Pizzigoni (2005) notes how actively Nahua women in the Valley of Toluca sought to defend themselves against violence from their spouses or breach of promise in the mid-eighteenth century. They represented themselves rather than waiting for male relatives to do so (ibid., 506).

Property disputes also continued to spark litigation by women "of all social classes" (Lavrin 1978, 43). In the Valley of Toluca, population growth led to men threatening indigenous women's access to land in the late eighteenth century (Kanter 1995). Widows threatened with dispossession by a brother-in-law or other relatives turned to the courts for help.

Later evidence of women's willingness to engage with the legal system spans the late colonial period and early years of independence. In Sonora in the early nineteenth century, women, and particularly widows, routinely defended their financial interests in court (Shelton 2004). Sonya Lipsett-Rivera (2001) documents women turning to the courts to find a solution for marital breakdown. Lower-class rural women tended to bring criminal cases against their husbands for *malos tratos* (mistreatment—from economic desertion to violence), whereas wealthier women were more likely to seek separation of bed and board in the ecclesiastical courts. It was usually the wife who initiated the case, generally on the grounds of cruelty and physical abuse (Arrom 1985a, 210, 234; Dávila Mendoza 2005; García Peña 2006).[10]

Litigation initiated over the years by women shows that some at least have been able to access the legal system and, at least at the outset, have thought it worth their while to do so. To uphold state legitimacy and religious or moral norms, the courts were obliged to act with a modicum of concern for the less powerful; without it, they would be unlikely to attract such a response (Alberro 1979; Scardaville 2000).

Relating Law and Gender

Law has also operated to women's disadvantage. It seems always to have been difficult, for instance, for women to denounce sexual abuse.[11] The standard response of a man accused of sexual crimes—to impugn the woman's morals—often found a receptive audience in court (Giraud 1988; Gutiérrez 1991; Lavrin 1989c; Seed 1988a). Carmen Castañeda (1989) reports that women who had been raped or "deflowered" in late colonial Nueva Galicia were often given less credence than witnesses for the accused. The victims were not "recompensed" by marriage or a dowry, as required by law, prompting the author to question Asunción Lavrin's (1978, 48) identification of "protection" as "the key word for understanding the relation of male to female and of society to women." The treatment received by some victims resembled punishment more than protection. One indigenous girl of fourteen who had been impregnated by her father spent six years in the women's reformatory before being set free but banned from the town where he lived.

Courts have also generally been lenient to men who murdered their wives.[12] A light sentence could apply even where the wife's "provocation" had amounted to no more than refusing to stop weaving, put on a shawl, or hand over money for drink.

Judicial lenience to men who beat or killed their wives can be interpreted as collusion in the (re)assertion of masculine authority.[13] Arrom (1976) comes to a similar conclusion about the ecclesiastical courts' role in reinforcing men's authority from 1800 to 1857. Although women generally initiated a case, many did so only as a last resort, given the hardships they would face. They were placed in a *depósito:* respectable lodgings where they would be protected from their husband but where their conduct would be scrutinized—"a substitute for the control exercised by the husband" (ibid., 44). Ecclesiastical divorce itself was "a mechanism to control the wife," since "a married woman on the loose" was something to be avoided (ibid., 62). One husband was quite explicit about this: "How can we expect that a woman who has enjoyed and enjoys the benefits of a free existence would ever allow herself to be reduced to conjugal subjection?" (Arrom 1985b, 216; see also Penyak 1999). Even if the wife was the innocent party, her behavior continued to be subject to scrutiny, whereas even a guilty husband was free to do as he pleased (other than remarry).[14] A wife whose behavior was less than impeccable had no hope of succeeding in her petition, whatever her husband had done. An increasing acceptance of separation and the right to seek individual happiness and escape abuses of authority were nonetheless positive trends for women (Arrom 1976).

Thus the legal system has worked at times to (some) women's advantage, but at other times to their disadvantage. Although showing differences of circumstance, class, color, region, and time that make generalization difficult, the literature does address the direction of change over particular periods. The impact of colonization attracts a perhaps surprising range of opinions. For some authors, gender inequality was aggravated by colonization, with women's legal status declining (Kellogg 1995, 1997; Wood and Haskett 1997). Other authors take a more positive view on specific issues, such as a woman's freedom to choose a partner (Cortés 1988). The tridentine reforms required that believers be allowed to marry as an expression of free will, so marriage was a basis from which even women at the bottom of the social hierarchy could claim at least some rights (Boyer 1995, 1998; Legros 1982; Pizzigoni 2004).[15]

Ironically, marriage has also been described as central to the restrictions in women's legal status. It is important to distinguish between married women and single or widowed women, who enjoyed more rights in Hispanic law. A husband effectively stood as guardian to his wife and controlled most of her legal undertakings and property (Arrom 1985b, 65); he could, however, permit his wife to conduct her own transactions, and Lavrin (1978, 30) stresses that white women were "either active legal partners of their husbands or acted independently," buying and selling property and taking part in lawsuits. Lavrin views the colonial legislation as "restrictive [but] not repressive" (ibid., 47).

At the beginning of the nineteenth century, Mexican women enjoyed greater rights, in some ways, than their counterparts in Europe and the United States—in relation to property, for example. Independence did not bring about clear improvements in women's legal status (Deere and León 2001; Ramos Escandon 2005). Deborah Kanter (1995, 613) argues that one consequence was to dilute official paternalism toward "subjects whom colonial authorities had considered 'miserables,' in need of protection, such as Indians, the poor, and widows." For instance, whereas colonial judges had sided with widows defending their land rights in the Valley of Toluca, the loss of a protective judiciary disadvantaged rural women.

As elsewhere in Latin America, the major legal changes affecting gender relations date from the second half of the nineteenth century. The civil codes enacted at this time have been described as an "assault on the privileges of women" (Dore 2000, 6), placing them "in a situation of strict legal subordination vis-à-vis men" (Aguirre and Salvatore 2001, 23).

Ana Lidia García Peña (2006, 51) argues that, in Mexico, nineteenth-century liberalism deprived women of many legal advantages they had enjoyed during the colonial period, leaving them "in a highly disadvantageous position, faced with individualist laws marked by clear gender differences." With some exceptions, they lost protection but were unable to construct themselves as individual subjects with rights equal to those of men (ibid., 237). She regards the consequences of one modernizing reform, for instance, as "devastating" for some women (García Peña 2004, 668). In 1857, paternity investigations were prohibited to protect men's privacy (i.e., it was now *men* who were to benefit from the law's protection: García Peña 2006, 227). In Mexico City, single women abandoned by their lovers had previously sought maintenance orders almost routinely, and generally enjoyed the courts' protection. Now, they automatically lost if the man denied paternity. Women compensated for their new legal vulnerability by negotiating settlements, using the tacit threat of embarrassing the father, generally a married or higher-status man.

The Civil Codes of 1870 and 1884 introduced divorce by mutual consent (but not remarriage), reductions in paternal authority (*patria potestad*), and testamentary freedom (Arrom 1985a). These changes reflected liberal endorsement of individual freedom and benefited some women, but "wives were excluded from the general expansion in personal rights" (Dore 2000, 18). Patria potestad was granted to widows and separated or single women, but this ability to exercise authority over others did not extend to married women (Arrom 1985a). In marriage, women continued to be legal minors, as a result of the patriarchal parallel between the liberal state order and family order (Ramos Escandón 2001b, 2001c). To encourage legal equality between husbands and wives would, according to a nineteenth-century legal commentary, risk a "continual mutiny of the subjects against the established authority" (*Nuevo Febrero Mexicano* 1850, quoted in Arrom 1985a, 310).

Another expression of the search to bolster individual liberty was couples' new ability to choose whether to hold their property in common or separately. The implications of separate property depended on class, but Arrom (1985a, 312) queries its attractions even for wealthy women. A wife needed her husband's consent to dispose of even her own property.

It should be noted that the pursuit of individual freedom did not put an end to concern over questions of honor; the combination increased gender inequality in some areas (Arrom 1985b; Chenaut 2001b; Speckman Guerra 2002).[16] Whereas adultery by either spouse had previously constituted grounds for divorce, male infidelity (only) was now generally condoned (Arrom 1985a).[17] Adultery was classified as a crime in the 1871 Penal Code, but an adulterous wife was more severely penalized (Chenaut 2001b). Judicial practice was also biased, as Elisa Speckman Guerra (2002) demonstrates by analyzing cases from the Federal District. She argues that a moral panic about the effects on women of social and economic modernization found expression in greater severity toward female criminals, who served as scapegoats for those whose behavior did not adhere to feminine stereotypes. Unlike men, they were judged as much for social as for legal transgression (see also Buffington 2000).[18]

Judges' views on appropriate feminine behavior also affected the implementation of legal reforms with the potential to benefit women. One example concerns the criminalization of domestic violence. Whereas "moderate" violence used to "correct" wives had previously been overlooked, wife beating was now incorporated into general categories of assault and punished without regard to its severity (Alonso 1995a, 31–32). However, in turn-of-the-century cases from Chihuahua, the women most likely to win their case against a violent husband were "those who abided by the norms and values of honorable femininity" (ibid., 41). Other women—especially those with economic resources or family support—resisted the disadvantages resulting from the "individualist reform," in ways that slowly and unevenly incorporated them into the discourse of individual rights and responsibilities (García Peña 2006, 237–239). Single mothers abandoned by their lovers, for instance, stopped presenting themselves to the courts as the passive victims of male seducers (ibid., 239).

Fewer studies address the period after the Revolution, and the coverage is more uneven. Legislative change, particularly in the 1917 Law of Family Relations and the 1928 Civil Code, has attracted the attention of authors documenting the rise of the feminist movement (Buck 2000; Lau Jaiven and Ramos Escandón 1993; Macías 1982; Soto 1990). Although feminists had foregrounded revisions to the civil code in their demands, they gave a mixed reception to the legal reforms after the Revolution; historians share their ambivalence. In view of the restrictions on married women's legal capacity, it is perhaps unsurprising that most changes focused on wives, removing the requirement that they obey their husbands and granting them guardianship and child custody rights.

However, legislators failed to remove the double standard in adultery and the gender bias in divorce and paternity investigations. At best, therefore, the reforms constituted "a limited victory" (Macías 1982, 121).

Some state legislators, particularly in the southeast, showed greater enthusiasm for women's concerns. Limited advances in suffrage were made in states with progressive governors, decades before the 1953 extension of the right to vote in national elections (Soto 1990). As early as 1915, the governor of Yucatán introduced reforms improving working conditions for domestic servants and relieving some of the burdens that state regulation imposed on prostitutes (Pérez 1988). He adopted the family law reforms promoted by Venustiano Carranza, including absolute divorce. In practice, however, divorce became primarily a male-initiated process, particularly after a 1923 reform, later repealed, made it possible to divorce a spouse without the latter's knowledge or consent (Smith 2006).

In Veracruz, the 1932 Civil Code went further in giving married women equality with men, and even included measures to prevent ambiguities of gendered language undermining the principle of equality: "When for reasons of grammatical construction, or enumeration . . . the text of the law uses or gives preference to the masculine gender, or makes reference to [a person's] sex that could be interpreted in an exclusionary sense against women, the authorities, judges and courts shall interpret the ambiguous text in an egalitarian sense for both men and women, so that the latter are considered on the same basis as the former" (quoted in Chenaut 2001b, 118). Reforms were, nonetheless, undermined by a persistence of "older ideas about gender, sexuality, and the individual, which clashed with the Revolution's emphasis on social change and community improvement" (Bliss 2001, 215). The liberal commitment to individual freedom has arguably continued to shape law and judicial practice. In the 1950s, for example, Supreme Court judges defined the practice of married couples sharing accommodation with the man's parents as failing to constitute an acceptable marital home. In doing so, they helped free younger women from traditional subordination to a mother-in-law, and endorsed the nuclear family as the model for a modernizing nation (Varley 2000b). Such changes gradually led to women acquiring "an increasingly individualistically oriented legal status" (Buck 2000, 10). The emphasis on the individual still has its perils for women, however, despite growing equality. Although the 1971 Federal Agrarian Reform Law gave women equal rights to acquire land, the 1992 counterreform privileged existing landholders, usually male, in allowing them to sell individualized holdings, leaving spouses and children merely the right of first refusal (Baitenmann 2000).

Future Challenges

As the focus of attention moves closer to the present, other disciplinary approaches—such as those we address in the next two sections—increasingly enter discussions about the relationship between law and gender in Mexico. It seems unfortunate that such approaches have not generally made use of some of the sources that historians have explored to such effect. Where problems of access can be resolved, judicial records have no less to tell us about gender ide-ologies and relations simply because other sources of information are available. One of our aims in this book, therefore, is to contribute to understanding of law and gender, through studies of judicial records, in the period from the Revolu-tion to the present day.

Two other avenues for further development in historical research from a gender perspective are regional differences and the workings of law in practice. The potential for significant variation between states is overlooked by studies that unquestioningly take Federal District legislation as the norm for Mexico. However, this is not a call for an arid regionalism, a mere accumulation of excep-tions. As Steve Stern (1995, 220) argues, "the uniqueness of a region may reside in particular twists placed on a recognizable them. . . . The challenge . . . is to draw out consistency and variation simultaneously." Laura Shelton (2004, 245) has observed, for example, that in the early nineteenth century, a recognizable regional identity did not prevent "familial experiences in Sonora, as understood through the courts, shar[ing] similarities with the rest of Latin America, as well as Europe."

The case for greater emphasis on the workings of law as practice has recently been made by Brian Owensby (2005, 39):

> Historians have feasted on the content of cases . . . to satisfy a hunger for insight into the social worlds that gave rise to them. Only rarely have scholars savored the record for the intricacies of procedure, the use of language, the burden of proof, the presentation of evidence, or the modes of legal reasoning—the stuff of law in practice.

Paying more attention to the interaction between the people—lay and profes-sional—brought together by court proceedings will help counteract any ten-dency to read power "as merely a projection from above" (ibid., 78). As Owensby observes, one key insight of recent work in sociocultural history and legal stud-ies has been "the recognition that law and legality represent an arena of contes-tation, a place where common people may voice their concerns and even win out over superiors" (ibid., 43). The challenge is to take forward that insight in work on gender in Mexico, past and present.

Legal Scholarship on the Status of Women in Mexico

There is a substantial and longstanding body of legal scholarship and commentary concerned with the relationship between law and gender in Mexico. This scholar-ship, with roots in the nineteenth century, has had for its central concern the legal status of women (*la condición jurídica de la mujer*). This section deals with the historical development of these legal studies, and highlights several trends in the literature over time.

Nineteenth-Century Legal Scholarship and the Origins of Equality

In nineteenth-century Mexico, most legal commentators took for granted the unequal status of women. However, debates about the fundamental political principles of the newly independent state included the abolition of slavery and the proclamation of equality of all citizens. This nineteenth-century legal concept of equality before the law (*el concepto jurídico decimonónico de igualdad ante la ley*) allowed a few legal scholars to begin questioning at least some—if not all—discrimination in Mexican law (see, for example, Nieto Castillo 2001, 842). A growing belief in women's competence and the growing prestige of motherhood, for example, allowed some commentators to question restrictions on a mother's legal authority over her children (Arrom 1985b, 85–86).

Silvia Arrom (1985b, 97) points out that "it is easy to overlook the egalitarian trend in legal reform because it was so tentative and manifested itself so sparingly." Moreover, legal scholars debating women's inequality characteristically did so in some areas only, while supporting discrimination in others. For instance, the author of the introduction to the *Nuevo Febrero Mexicano* (1850), a Mexican adaptation of a famous Spanish legal dictionary, recognized a woman's "full capacity to govern herself," refuting allegations of mental weakness, yet at the same time tried to justify a wife's inferior position (quoted in Arrom 1985b, 94–95).

One of the first persons to explore the idea of legal equality for women was lawyer Manuel Dublán, who in 1876 wrote an essay entitled "The Condition of Women in Modern Legislation" (*El Foro*, 3 May 1876). Although cautious about questioning men's legal power over women, his work reflected a subtle change in traditional legal discourse on women's rights (Muñoz de Alba Medrano 1988, 818–819). By 1891, legal scholar and Porfirian statesman Genaro García had written a university thesis (and later a book) entitled *Notes on the Status of Women* (*Apuntes sobre la condición de la mujer*). Stating that "equality is the first condition of liberty," García analyzed the Civil Code of 1884 and explained in what ways it curtailed women's rights, especially with regard to marriage (Soto 1990, 10–11).[19]

Legal Scholarship during the 1910–1920 Revolution

Debates about democracy and citizenship at the time of the Mexican Revolution (1910–1920), an incipient "first wave" feminist movement, and the fixation of (General and President) Venustiano Carranza's revolutionary faction on law-making, all created a space for the continued discussion of women's rights.[20]

As in the nineteenth century, legal commentators focused mainly on the status of married women. Although some women already were demanding

greater rights in all types of law, early feminist postrevolutionary legal analysis—
consistent with its liberal roots—focused more on civil rights issues (marriage,
the household, and so forth) than on the social rights (such as labor and agrarian rights) addressed in the 1917 Constitution. For example, two of the early
postrevolutionary essays on women's rights, Sofía Villa de Buentello's *Women
and the Law* (1921) and Adela Hernández's (1926) study on women's ability to
represent themselves in court, focused strictly on reforms to the civil code, as
did work by Elodia Cruz y F. (1931) and Francesco Consentini (1930). Although
most of the women's national congresses (starting with the first 1916 Yucatán
congress) had demanded labor rights for working women and equal agrarian
rights for *campesinas* (peasant women), it was not until the 1950s that legal
scholars began scrutinizing the corresponding laws in terms of women's rights.

Surprisingly, early legal tracts on the status of women in Mexico usually did
not deal with suffrage. The demand for voting rights had become more of a
political issue and, with some notable exceptions, much less part of a detailed
analysis of existing laws (at least not until the 1930s).[21] For the most part, it was
activists, journalists, and politicians, rather than legal scholars, who were involved
in debating women's suffrage.

The general concern with equality allowed some legal scholars to think
about broader systems of domination based on gender. For example, Rafael
Enríquez Vidal's (1938) law thesis, "The Legal Status of Women in our New Legislation," analyzed the 1928 Civil Code in terms of the concept of *potestad marital*
(the principle of a wife's legal subordination to her husband). Similarly, Feliciano
Vidales Macouzet noted in his law thesis (1938) that married women in Mexico
had fewer rights than men, and he explained that this "unjust situation" was a
form of potestad marital in which married women had fewer rights than single
women. The analysis of potestad marital as a broader system of domination based
on gender foreshadowed future debates on law and gender.

Women's Equality at the National School of Law

The first major legal debate about women's rights flourished at the School of
Law of the Autonomous National University of Mexico (UNAM) in the 1950s and
1960s, years before the "second wave" of feminism in Mexico that began in the
1970s. Both women and men engaged in these discussions, which involved feminist as well as nonfeminist arguments about women's equality before the law.
Moreover, legal scholars would at this time embark upon the novel task of exploring women's rights not only in the civil and penal codes but also in postrevolutionary social law.

There are several factors that might have led to this small boom in Mexican
legal studies on the status of women. First, by the 1950s, women had entered
law schools in greater numbers. Second, legal scholars at the time were greatly
influenced by the 1953 reforms that gave women full suffrage rights. It was no

coincidence that in that same year the Alliance of Women in Mexico sponsored a study on the legal status of women (Alianza de Mujeres de México 1953). Written by a group of Supreme Court ministers, professors, and lawyers, this association foreshadowed by several decades the now numerous multiprofession coalitions of women (and men) writing on gender justice.

In the period leading up to and following the amendment of Article 34 of the Mexican Constitution (the amendment giving women full suffrage rights), authors argued that, if women were to become fully fledged citizens, they also had to have equal rights in all other Mexican laws. For example, in his law thesis "The Mexican Campesina Woman," Álvaro Morales Jurado (1954, 73) proposed urgent reforms to the Agrarian Code to make it "consonant with Article 34 of the Constitution." [22]

One novelty of this literature was that, for the first time, it included legal analyses of postrevolutionary social rights. For instance, in 1956 the influential law journal *Filosofía y Letras* published a double issue containing papers presented at a conference on "Women in National Life." One of the *Filosofía y Letras* articles touched on the heart of the debate surrounding the two major social landmarks from the Revolution: labor rights and agrarian reform. In an essay on "Women and Politics," María Esther Talamantes argued that, although agrarian legislation blatantly discriminated against women, labor laws were beneficial for women and only required proper implementation (1956, 113–114).[23] Indeed, scholars forcefully condemned women's unequal agrarian rights. Stating that as a woman and a jurist she had the responsibility to argue for equal citizenship rights, Martha Chávez Padrón in her article in the same issue of *Filosofía y Letras* offered a scathing critique of agrarian law. Claiming that existing laws left campesinas like "unredeemed Cinderellas," she gave detailed examples of the ways agrarian laws discriminated against rural women, and argued for a thorough revision of the Agrarian Code (Chávez Padrón 1956, 235).[24]

The debate about women's legal equality was for a time probably contained within university halls. In the late 1960s, however, studies of these issues began to circulate more broadly. One such example is Alma Spota Valencia's 1967 book on *Legal and Social Equality of the Sexes*. Publishing a book with a leading Mexican press (Porrúa) on a topic that had thus far circulated mainly in the form of theses and reports was a pathbreaking achievement. Similarly, in the late 1960s the Mexican Congress organized a symposium and book project entitled *Rights of Mexican Women* (Congreso de la Unión 1969). Written by nine female federal deputies and a number of lawyers and other professional women, the text analyzed the status of women in Mexican civil, penal, agrarian, and labor law. Some one hundred thousand copies of the one-hundred-page text were printed and distributed on a complimentary basis.

As a whole, the debate in the 1950s and 1960s about women's status in Mexican law was important because it legitimized the analysis of this subject based on the principle of equality. The tone was, however, more celebratory than critical. After universal suffrage rights in 1953, most authors (with the exception of writers of texts analyzing agrarian law) found the Mexican legal system to be equitable, if not outright beneficial for women. Moreover, the idea of an ongoing, almost evolutionary, progress toward equality within the established legal system was widely shared in these debates of the 1950s and 1960s.

Law and Gender in the Debates surrounding the 1975 International Women's Year

When in the 1970s President Luis Echeverría amended several laws and the Constitution to establish the principle of legal equality for men and women (and offered Mexico City as the host city for the First World Conference on Women in 1975), conservative scholars expressed outrage at laws they considered divorced from reality. At the same time, the nascent feminist movement accused the government of imposing a women's agenda without women's participation. Yet the history of legal scholarship on law and gender in Mexico shows clearly that, at least in the university halls where lawyer-presidents like Echeverría had trained, the debate was well advanced.

One work that symbolized the maturity of the discourse on equality was *The Legal Status of Women in Mexico,* a compilation of essays written by professors and students at the UNAM Faculty of Law (Bialostosky et al. 1975). Presented as UNAM's contribution to the International Women's Year (1975), the book combined historical analyses of women's legal status in Mexico with contemporary analysis of the civil, administrative, and labor codes.[25] The contributors to this volume engaged national and international law from a well-established perspective that accepted as a given the liberal legal concept of women's and men's equality.

A number of other texts produced during this decade hailed women's equal rights in Mexico. As in the 1950s, when scholars saw women's suffrage as progress toward equality, legal scholars in the 1970s adopted a celebratory tone. There were at least two reasons why more critical studies were late in coming. One was that many young scholars and activists came from the Left and/or had been part of the 1968 student movement, and they rejected political negotiation with the established regime (Lamas 2002, 72–73).[26] For some of these activists, analyzing existing laws and proposing amendments represented an implicit acceptance of the state—or, at the very least, recognizing the possibility of achieving justice within a system they rejected. Moreover, Marxist analytic frameworks adopted in Mexico at the time were largely not conducive to legal analysis (Gutiérrez Castañeda 2002a, 208).

But there was another reason why such critiques failed to appear at this time. Echeverría's legal reforms were, indeed, progressive.[27] As Patricia Kurczyn Villalobos (1975, 18) shows, several codes were modified in 1974 to give women greater equality in Mexican law. In her pioneering study on the Federal Labor Law and the Federal Law for Public Workers, Kurczyn Villalobos carefully shows how the new laws abolished legal "protections" for women that were deemed discriminatory (for example, limits to working overtime), and added a number of clauses on hiring and promotion policies that forbade discrimination against workers with families (ibid., 25–31). Indeed, seen in proper historical context, the amendments to labor law with regard to gender justice were very significant.[28]

The Search for Law and Gender in the 1980s: Challenging the Public–Private Divide

In the 1980s, one finds relatively little written or published on law and gender in Mexico. During this decade, scholars created what would become important women's and gender studies centers in academia, but at the time these institutions did not focus on the status of women in Mexican law or on a more gendered analysis of the legal system (see, for example, Urrutia 2002a). The few studies available basically fall into two types.

One trend was an outgrowth of earlier work on the status of women in Mexico. Sara Montero Duhalt (1984), for example, published an important book on women's rights in family law from an equality perspective. Other texts included overviews or compendia of women's rights in Mexico, with such titles as *Women's Rights in Mexican Legislation* (Sentíes 1984), *Agenda of Women's Rights and Obligations* (Gastelum Gaxiola 1987), and *Legal Guide for Women: Information Manual so that the Weaker Sex Understands and Defends Her Rights* (Martínez 1983). The goal was to identify those laws that affected women and men differently, to inform women of their rights.

A second trend (closely linked to the feminist movement and debates at the time) radically altered the terms of discourse on law and gender. In 1976, the National Movement of Women and the Mexican Feminist Movement, concerned that laws were being amended without their participation, created the Coalition of Feminist Women. As activists, they first focused on the legislation dealing with what they considered the most urgent issues of the moment, such as rape, abortion, and violence toward women (Toto Gutiérrez 2002, 402). Violence toward women became a paradigmatic case. This topic was engaged in 1979 by a varied group of professionals (inspired by the European and U.S. feminist movements) who formed small study groups (*grupos de reflexión*). The combination of new topics (violence toward women) and feminist theory that questioned the public–private divide (i.e., expounded the idea that one must politicize so-called private affairs) allowed for a radically new discourse on women's rights. Violence, previously considered a private matter, became a social and public issue (González Ascencio and Duarte Sánchez 1996, 168–169).

Lawyer and activist Mireya Toto Gutiérrez was one of the pioneers who linked law and violence toward women. In 1983, she wrote a historical legal analysis of the federal penal code in which she showed that concepts from the mid-nineteenth century were used to determine whether a woman had "actu-ally" been raped. Using statistics, she prefaced the analysis with a characteriza-tion of the typical rapist. Toto Gutiérrez showed that most rapists were not exceptional men (they were not jobless or single, for example). Similarly, she explained that rapes took place at any time of the day and in all kinds of places (Instituto Francés de América Latina 1983, 27). That is, to find more systemic causes of violence against women, Toto Gutiérrez first dissociated rape from the abnormal or exceptional. Only by bringing the criminal "home" could one properly analyze the penal code with regard to rape.

Legal Analysis, Gender Justice, and Human Rights in the 1990s

As the international women's movement in the 1990s intensified its engage-ment with rights and citizenship (Molyneux 2001, 196–197), so did research on law and gender in Mexico. Following broader Latin American and global trends, the 1990s in Mexico were characterized by feminists' greater involvement in the growing nongovernmental and human rights sector (both national and United Nations–affiliated) and in all branches of the bureaucracy, labor unions, and political parties (Cardaci 2002, 86; Espinosa 2002, 159; Molyneux 2001, 195).[29] Scholars, activists, and government officials joined forces in publishing educa-tional material on women's rights in Mexican legislation,[30] analyzed Mexican law in light of international human and gender rights conventions,[31] and engaged a long-standing but formerly nongendered tradition of constitutional commentary.[32] Earlier scholarship on the status of women in Mexico had mostly focused on federal legislation, but starting in the 1990s state laws were analyzed as well.[33] Changes in national legislation produced a flurry of additional studies, and laws that had not been reformed to current gender justice standards attracted important activism and scholarship.[34]

From the 1990s onward, there are at least two trends in legal analysis engaged with gender rights. First, studies intended for international conferences and government-sponsored reports became important spaces for the analysis of Mexican law in terms of gender justice. Second, as international agreements have transformed the concept of human rights from one based upon the male citizen to one that considers women's rights as "an inalienable, integral and indivisible part of universal human rights" (World Conference on Human Rights 1993), scholars and activists in Mexico, too, have expanded their conception of rights.

Among those public institutions that directly address law and gender are the Gender and Equity Commissions in Congress. The first of these bodies was created in 1997 by a number of congresswomen in the LVII Legislature (1997–2000). Women from all political parties joined together to establish a com-mission in charge of networking with other government branches, scholars, and activists, and were responsible for proposing a number of legislative initiatives aimed at reforming existing laws on the basis of gender equality and human rights. These reports include valuable lists of successful reforms as well as of the laws needing reform, with short yet incisive rationales for revisions (see, for example, Comisión de Equidad y Género 2000).

One example of the expansion of the conception of gender rights can be found in the document "Women's Reproductive Rights in Mexico: A Shadow Report," written by U.S. and Mexican nongovernmental organizations to supplement (or "shadow") the Mexican government's report to the Convention on the Elimination of All Forms of Discrimination against Women (CEDAW). The paper draws upon international conventions on women's rights to offer a critique of Mexican laws and Supreme Court decisions, with a heavy emphasis on those areas that had been left out of the human rights paradigm (such as sexual and reproductive rights, family law, and violence toward women) (Centro Legal para Derechos Reproductivos y Políticas Públicas 1997).

This global and national emphasis on human rights in general, and women's rights in particular, coincided with the boom in academic gender studies. As gender studies in (and about) Mexico flourished, social scientists engaged what had previously been only a topic for legal scholars. They searched for more sociological and political understandings of why women's legal status differed from that of men's.[35] One outstanding example is a pamphlet published in 1993 on the treatment of rape victims within the Mexican penal justice system. Written by Gerardo González Ascencio, a researcher at the Metropolitan Autonomous University's department of law and a long-time activist, this paper presents the results of a survey taken by ninety volunteer students at almost fifty police stations in Mexico City. Combining material from the surveys with an analysis of the penal code, the study offers an insightful examination of the ideology that devalues women as citizens and rape as a crime. For instance, in a section titled "The Penis: The Magic Wand," González Ascencio shows that—despite the fact that in 1989 the penal code had criminalized rape with a foreign object (albeit with less severity than rape with a penis)—police agents were not aware of the reforms. Moreover, 20 percent of the interviewees shared the idea that sexual aggression was more serious when rape occurred with "the protagonistic participation of the penis" (even if the consequences for the victim were the same) (González Ascencio 1993a, 23). The author thus highlights one more in the series of misconceptions that make it so difficult to attain justice in rape cases.

Future Trends in Legal Scholarship on Law and Gender in Mexico

In the early twenty-first century, legal scholars continue to publish a number of innovative studies. Some have refined and deepened earlier questions about law and gender (Bialostosky 2005), while others are pursuing new and important avenues of inquiry. One important example is Kurczyn Villalobos's study of discrimination in the workplace (2004). Her work is a response to employers' practice of performing pregnancy tests on potential employees (mainly, but not exclusively, in the *maquiladora* industry). Based on an analysis of existing laws, the study expands the concept of sexual harassment to include not only verbal or physical violence toward women, but *any* discrimination in employment, or in work rights and practices, based on sex, maternity, family responsibilities, or civil status (ibid., 43; see also Pérez Contreras 2004).

One characteristic of earlier legal scholarship on law and gender in Mexico is that, for many urban lawyers, indigenous women were invisible. However, groundbreaking studies by lawyers María Magdalena Gómez Rivera (1994, 1997) and Alicia Elena Pérez Duarte y Noroña (1997) have begun building bridges between legal scholarship and recent appeals by indigenous women. Most recently, the prestigious Institute for Legal Research (Instituto de Investigaciones Jurídicas) at the UNAM published its first book on indigenous rights. Its contents included an essay by lawyer Rosa María Álvarez de Lara (2002) on the relationship between state laws and indigenous women's rights. She began her essay by noting that the Chiapas rebellion of 1994 had brought to national attention topics that social scientists had discussed for years, but which had been altogether ignored by legal scholars (ibid., 111–112).

Another important topic beginning to receive some attention from legal scholars is discrimination in Mexican law and legal procedures on the grounds of sexual preference and heteronormativity.[36] María de Montserrat Pérez Contreras, another lawyer–scholar who has actively pursued the analysis of law and gender in Mexico, wrote a pioneering manual in which she analyzed homosexual rights within an international and national legal context (2000). Much more is needed, however, particularly with regard to law and the rights to sexual difference, to even begin to "decenter heterosexuality as the measure of evaluation and the origin of all definitions" (Hinojosa 2002, 185).

Legal Anthropology and Gender in Mexico

Legal anthropology (a subfield in anthropology that in Mexico has focused primarily on the study of indigenous law and justice systems in multicultural societies) only developed an explicit gender focus in Mexico in the 1990s. This was the result of the convergence of a number of trends. These included the movement for indigenous rights, the increasing influence of gender studies in academia, and the growing interest in Latin America in the subject of the rule of law. This section examines the factors that came together in Mexico to create a vibrant discipline that is today at the cutting edge of law and gender studies.

The Early Years of Legal Anthropology in Mexico

There have been two main phases in the study of legal anthropology in Mexico. The first began in the 1930s and 1940s, when foreign and Mexican anthropologists

began to explore legal practices and the administration of justice in the indigenous societies they studied.[37] The second phase began in the late 1980s, when a
growing interest in law and legal matters coincided with the indigenous rights
movements.

Although early legal anthropology in Mexico did not focus on women or
explicitly analyze societies in terms of gender, many ethnographies and anthropological studies described with great insight how indigenous women were
actively involved in family, neighborhood, and community conflicts.[38]

Laura Nader, for example, conducted field and archival work in the Zapotec
town of Talea, Oaxaca, during the 1950s and 1960s. One of her pioneering contributions to legal anthropology was her observation that "the user, in particular the plaintiff—not an abstraction like the courts or judicial decision, or even
variables like urbanization and industrialization—is the driving force in law"
(1990, 159). If users shape the law, then in what way did women contribute to
the construction of indigenous law? Analyzing court documents, Nader made at
least two important contributions to the future study of law and gender in
Mexico. First, she demonstrated that the women of Talea actively participated in
legal processes at the local and district level. Second, men and women used the
legal system in different ways; for example, although women generally became
defendants in property-related matters, the men appearing in court were commonly accused of having caused physical harm to someone. Both insights continue to be important in recent legal anthropological work on gender.

The research of legal anthropologist Jane F. Collier on indigenous law in the
municipality of Zinacantán, Chiapas, during the 1960s (and, in her later research,
the 1990s) was also influential. Analyzing marital disputes in Zinacantán, Collier described how men and women had different roles, rights, and obligations.
For example, she found that conflicts often stemmed from the patrivirilocal
character of Zinacanteco society (that is, a young couple must reside—at least
during the first years of their marriage—with the husband's family, turning the
daughter-in-law into an outsider under the authority of the mother-in-law).
Collier (1973) also analyzed the relationship between types of disputes and social
relations (conflicts between relatives, spouses, during courtship, and so forth).

The work of these authors was pioneering for at least three reasons. First,
women appeared for the first time as active participants in a social life that had
norms, rights and obligations, and conflicts. Women actively challenged roles
and hierarchies, and they demanded redress for the violation of their rights.
Second, by analyzing disputes that involved both men and women, albeit often
in different ways, these authors prepared the ground for gendered studies of law
focusing on the differential treatment and behavior of indigenous men and
women in courts. And third, the authors demonstrated in their studies the legal
pluralism prevalent in much of rural Mexico (different laws, courts, and justice

systems), and how women used the different levels of the legal system to demand their rights or seek redress.

Perhaps because the field of legal anthropology was not yet well established in Mexico, the original English versions of these works did not have a great impact on Mexican scholars. The work was only translated into Spanish in the late 1990s, when growing interest in the subject of law in multicultural societies provided the impetus to translate and publish these works in Mexico. However, these studies are now recognized as major contributions to the field.

Anthropology, Law, and Gender in Mexico

Starting in the 1970s with Lourdes Arizpe's (1975) pioneering work on migrant indigenous women in Mexico City, social anthropologists began focusing on campesinas and indigenous women. These studies initially aimed at making women's lives and work visible. Later studies would focus more on gender hierarchies and relations of power (Alberti Manzanares 2004).

Scholars would start to study indigenous women in Mexico mainly from one of two perspectives. On the one hand, they focused on patriarchal structures of domination, like the work in Oaxaca of Beverly Chiñas (1973). Other scholars broached the subject from a political economy perspective, analyzing the gendered effects of capitalist relations in campesino and indigenous communities (Gall and Hernández Castillo 2004).

One reason why the legal systems of indigenous peoples received relatively little attention before the 1990s was that Marxist theory greatly influenced the discipline of anthropology in Mexico (Toto Gutiérrez 2002). Especially in the 1970s and the early 1980s, Marxist approaches privileged a number of topics while excluding others—including both law and gender. One important exception was the work of social anthropologist Soledad González Montes (1988). Noting that most studies on campesinas in the preceding ten or fifteen years had focused almost exclusively on economic factors (family survival strategies and women's economic participation, for example), González Montes's pioneering essay on indigenous inheritance practices and ideology in Xalatlaco, State of Mexico, concluded that land was not equally bequeathed among offspring. In essence, men favored their sons (González Montes 1988). In a community in which women worked as much as men, including in agricultural tasks, how could one explain this inheritance pattern? González Montes analyzed the discourse of Xalatlaco residents based on interviews, and found that women's work was profoundly devalued and that this "constituted an indispensable element in the reproduction of relations of inequity between the sexes" (ibid., 73).

It was precisely at this time that the discourse on indigenous peoples qua indigenous peoples, and their rights, would begin to gain wider acceptance in academia, largely as a result of the indigenous rights movements, discussed in the following section.

The Indigenous Rights Movement

One important influence on the shaping of legal anthropology in Mexico was the growing concern of lawyers, sociologists, and anthropologists in Mexico (and Latin America more broadly) with human rights and the collective rights of indigenous peoples. Rodolfo Stavenhagen was one of the first advocates of indigenous rights. In 1988 he published a book that denounced violations of indigenous peoples' rights in various Latin American countries, in the context of the existing international legal framework. In subsequent years, he promoted seminars and research projects on indigenous law and indigenous legal practices in Mexico and elsewhere in Latin America (see, for example, Stavenhagen and Iturralde 1990).

Preparatory activities leading up to the commemoration in 1992 of the fifth centenary of the Spaniards' arrival in the Americas prompted the Mexican government to ratify Covenant 169 of the International Labor Organization (*Diario Oficial de la Federación,* August 3, 1990) and to reform the 1917 Constitution to recognize cultural plurality (*Diario Oficial de la Federación,* January 28, 1992).[39] These legislative changes gave a major impetus to debates about indigenous law and rights. Not long thereafter, the 1994 uprising of the Zapatista National Liberation Army (EZLN) in Chiapas profoundly shook the academic and political worlds. The armed rebellion advanced a series of well-articulated demands that questioned the entire system of justice and the concept of citizenship in Mexico.

These events (and parallel developments in other parts of Latin America) promoted what has been termed "a process of judicialization" of the relationship between indigenous peoples and national states, as a series of legal reforms began to address issues of justice for indigenous peoples (Gómez Rivera 1994). This process, in turn, has encouraged intense academic and political debates.[40] Academic analysts have, for instance, done research and taught courses on the legal systems of indigenous peoples, the concept of legal pluralism, and the legal practices that link indigenous peoples' law and state law.

By the 1990s, legal anthropology had gained increasing relevance as a field in Mexico. Major topics of research included analyzing relations of articulation, conflict, and negotiation between indigenous law and state law. However, the intense debate and politicization of Latin American anthropology with regard to indigenous movements, constitutional reforms, indigenous rights, and legal reforms in recognition of multicultural societies, took precedence over studies of law and gender in such societies. For instance, in the last four international congresses of the Latin American Network of Legal Anthropology (Red Latinoamericana de Antropología Jurídica, RELAJU), there were relatively few panels on the topic of gender and law, compared to those dealing with topics such as legislation, justice, and state reforms.[41]

Nevertheless, in the early twenty-first century, Mexico is probably the Latin American country in which the convergence of legal anthropology and gender has gained greatest momentum. This is largely the result of three developments, described in the following sections. First, the growing concern about violence toward women in general, and indigenous women in particular, has stimulated the study of law and gender from an anthropological perspective. Second, beginning in the 1990s, indigenous women began actively to shape the debates about their own rights in a multicultural society. And third, even though many legal anthropologists influenced by the indigenous rights movement and the growing debates about law in Latin America did not have an explicit gender focus, researchers increasingly felt the need to address gender theory to understand better the legal contexts in which women played central roles (as in the work Nader and Collier had conducted several decades earlier).

Violence toward Indigenous Women and the Court Systems

Beginning in the 1980s, violence toward women became a central concern for scholars and activists throughout the world. By the 1990s, a number of studies had addressed the phenomenon of violence against indigenous women.[42] Scholars have written on the "structural violence" that marginalizes indigenous women (higher indices of illiteracy, monolingualism, poverty, and malnutrition, as well as high indices of maternal death).[43] And researchers have described the political, psychological, and armed violence exercised by the armed forces of Mexico (Hernández Castillo 2002b).[44]

A number of authors have pointed to the fact that many indigenous women are subjected to daily forms of domestic violence.[45] These authors find that marital violence is related to alcoholism, male adultery, and the custom of patrivirilocal residence, which is a source of numerous conflicts and aggression. Indigenous women involved in these types of conflict often resort to the justice system, whether at the community level or in state (mostly municipal) courts. Studying indigenous women's claims has allowed scholars to understand the gendered nature of these proceedings. For example, husbands tend to justify violent acts on the grounds that their spouses do not fulfill their responsibilities as wives and mothers. In turn, indigenous women usually try to renegotiate gender roles so as to live a more dignified life, free of violence. Scholars have found that domestic violence toward women constitutes an integral part of the gendered and hierarchical power relations existing in indigenous families in Mexico.

It is worth highlighting the work on domestic violence undertaken since 1989 by the San Cristóbal Women's Group in San Cristóbal de las Casas (Chiapas). The group was founded as a civil association by professional women, women from the *colonias populares* (low-income urban housing areas), organized indigenous women, and women from ecclesiastical base communities. Through their Support Center for Women and Children, the group provided medical and legal assistance to women victims of sexual and domestic violence; on the basis of individual testimonies, these scholars and activists documented the circumstances in which gender violence and male power were expressed in the daily lives of indigenous families. This intercultural dialogue between advisors and victims allowed anthropologists to develop a number of innovative theoretical propositions with regard to law and gender. For example, scholars recognized the existence of different legal systems (both state and indigenous) operating at the same time and constituting what Santos (1987) has termed "situations of interlegality." They discovered that the systems of justice available to indigenous women (both state and indigenous) shared an ideology of asymmetrical gender relations in which women were in a subordinate position (Hernández Castillo and Garza Caligaris 1995). Another interesting finding was that, for abused women to file charges and request the intervention of state or indigenous authorities, the women had no choice but to play the role of victim. In other words, both legal systems required that indigenous women reaffirm stereotypical gender roles in order to demand their rights as citizens (Hernández Castillo 2002d).

Indigenous Women's Movements and Their Influence on Legal Anthropology

There is a large body of literature that explains, from differing perspectives, women's participation in indigenous movements and organizations. Here we highlight those aspects of the history of women's indigenous movements that have directly influenced the study of law and gender in the anthropology of Mexico.

Although indigenous women throughout Mexico have mobilized in demand of their rights, the indigenous region of the highlands of Chiapas is a paradigmatic example of how indigenous women's organizations have influenced legal anthropology in Mexico. Indigenous women from the area began organizing in the 1980s, but their participation in political, workplace, ecclesiastical, and community organizations, as well as in the EZLN's armed movement, became more visible at a national level during the 1994 Zapatista uprising. Particularly interesting for academics was the Women's Revolutionary Law, promulgated by the EZLN in 1994. In this historic document, indigenous women set forth a number of demands.[46] These and other demands made by indigenous women's organizations have since become important sources for studies on law and gender.[47]

Márgara Millán (1996), for example, noted that the Women's Revolutionary Law combined two sets of demands and each addressed a different sphere of legal authority. One set of demands (including those categorized as civil and economic rights) was directed to the national state; the second set (related to local political participation, human rights, and sexual and reproductive rights) was directed to the EZLN and indigenous authorities at the community level. According to Millán, indigenous women's demands were part and parcel of the indigenous movement's struggle for autonomy; it is the quest for autonomy that ties men's and women's struggles together.

With regard to indigenous women's claims for greater rights at the community level, Nellys Palomo, Yolanda Castro, and Cristina Orci (1997) analyzed the demands made by indigenous women in different arenas. They showed that indigenous women sought the elimination of practices such as forced marriage, marriage at an early age, domestic violence, lack of inheritance rights, and exclusion from elected community positions (*cargos*). Indigenous women's claims pointed to broader questions about relations of power and gender asymmetry in their communities.

However, scholars have also noted indigenous women's demands for protecting and preserving some collective rights and customs particular to their community or ethnic group, including the right to be treated with respect, to preserving their handicraft traditions, and to retaining community rituals like fiestas (Lovera and Palomo 1997; Rojas 1999). Therefore, these scholars note, indigenous women are not arguing for changes in all aspects of their lives in their communities. Rather, they seek to alter only those practices that violate their human rights. This point has prompted academics to reflect upon women's rights in multicultural societies, greatly contributing to broader international debates on the subject (Hernández Castillo 2001, 2002a; Hernández Castillo and Sierra 2005; Sierra 2004b). Hernández Castillo and Sierra (2005), for instance, join those who question a hegemonic feminism based on a liberal and universal conception of human rights, proposing instead a feminist perspective based on understanding women's rights in relation to indigenous human rights in an intercultural dialogue that takes into account the historical and cultural contexts of each ethnic group.

Renewed Interest in Legal Anthropology from a Gender Perspective in Mexico

The discussion among organized indigenous women, activists, and academics was accompanied by a renewed interest in the research methods pioneered by Laura Nader and Jane Collier. Starting in the 1990s, legal anthropologists recovered the tradition of undertaking fieldwork and archival research to understand the use made of courts, the interaction between court users and court officials, and the mechanisms available to resolve conflicts in indigenous regions. A number of legal anthropologists have (re)discovered judicial archives as ethnographic resources, a source also widely used by historians (see the section on history in this introduction). In addition, fieldwork is proving invaluable for understanding indigenous legal practices at the local level, because indigenous conciliation procedures are usually carried out by local authorities in oral trials that do not leave documentary evidence. For the most part, there are no written records of this type of community interaction, although María Teresa Sierra (2004e) and Ivette Rossana Vallejo Real (2000) found archives on conciliation and appearance (*comparecencias*) proceedings in indigenous communities of the Sierra Norte de Puebla, archives that proved a valuable source for learning about women's recourse to the indigenous justice system.

Legal anthropologists are beginning to unravel how the judicial system is organized in different Mexican states, starting with the local courts in rural communities and continuing upward toward municipal seats, judicial district seats, state capitals, and major cities with federal courts. Several authors have noted that there is a procedural continuum through which men and women transit, reaching from rural communities to the highest tribunals (Chenaut 1999, Sierra 2004c). Women appear as users of the legal system at all levels (although mostly at the community and municipal levels), making it possible to appreciate how the women claim their rights and negotiate gender roles in both indigenous and state justice systems.

Comparative studies on different indigenous regions in Mexico show that indigenous women frequently take their grievances to courts (indigenous and state) to denounce offenses that undermine their dignity, as well as to demand redress for the rights they consider violated (Sierra 2004d). It is more often the case that women file suits against men than the other way around. Nevertheless, there are many instances in which women have been taken to court because they did not adopt passive roles in the disputes in which they were involved (Chenaut 2004).

Indigenous women's recourse to law varies according to the social and economic conditions in the different regions, as well as the structure of the judicial system in different states. For example, Sierra (2004e) and Vallejo Real (2004a, 2004b) report that indigenous courts operate in the communities of the municipality of Cuetzalan (Puebla) and that women bring their grievances there rather than to municipal authorities. There are also many human rights organizations and socially committed lawyers who provide legal services to the indigenous population in Cuetzalan. In contrast, in the Totonac communities of the judicial district of Papantla (Veracruz), the indigenous justice system works unevenly and unreliably. As a result, indigenous women in the area tend to take their grievances to municipal courts (Chenaut 1999, 2004).

Apart from learning more about how indigenous women use different levels and types of courts, scholars continue to provide insights into gender ideologies. Beatriz Martínez Corona and Susana Mejía Flores (1997) have contributed to a gendered understanding of the Mexican judicial system by examining the ideologies and practices of the players involved in community, municipal, and district courts in the Sierra Norte de Puebla. They found that the court system is not only composed of the application of laws and norms, and negotiations based on legal procedures, but that the procedures are also permeated by the values and ideologies of the judges and lawyers—and that these most often undervalue indigenous women, adding ethnic prejudices to those of class. For example, in cases of sexual harassment (usually committed by acquaintances or family members), women have to prove that they did not provoke the crime, and judges often give their verdict on the basis of the woman's reputation in her community.

Similarly, Sierra (2004c) observed that the ideologies of officials in indigenous courts as well as in the national justice system are permeated by gender ideologies that reproduce patriarchal conceptions and interactions. For example, court proceedings often favor men, most commonly in marital disputes in which women tend to denounce their spouses for such abuses as mistreatment, unfulfilled duties as spouse and father, alcoholism, and adultery. Scholars have shown that, in such circumstances, both indigenous and state authorities encourage the reconciliation of the couple and the maintenance of family life—even if this is against the woman's wishes. These findings are supported by more recent work in Zinacantán, Chiapas, by Collier (2004), which found evidence of gender bias in indigenous legal proceedings. In cases involving adultery, for example, she found that when women were found guilty of adultery, both they and their lovers were punished. However, when men were caught in an adulterous relationship, they were not punished unless their lovers were married women whose husbands accused them of adultery.

The pervasiveness of gendered inequities in court rulings is perhaps most surprising in regions that are experimenting with more democratic forms of self-governance. For example, Anna María Garza Caligaris (2002) analyzed disputes between men and women in the courts of the so-called autonomous Zapatista municipalities of Chiapas. She found that, even where alternative forms of justice are being constructed vis-à-vis the hegemonic culture, law is permeated by gendered relations of inequality.

Future Challenges

Since the mid-1990s, a renewed interest in legal anthropology from a gender perspective has flourished in Mexico, fueled by the impassioned debate that has taken place internationally about indigenous law, legal reform in relation to indigenous groups, and individual and collective rights. This new body of research has kept up the tradition, inherited from Nader and Collier, among others, of paying careful attention to the question of women's rights. It has made great advances in analyzing not only indigenous women's participation in the court system but also the gendered ideologies and practices found in courts of different kinds and at differing levels of the judicial system.

Revealing how gender is constructed through law (both indigenous and state law) is one of the achievements of legal anthropology in Mexico; but more work is required. Future research from a gender perspective has a key contribution to make to broader debates about democratic transformations, the rule of law, individual and collective rights of indigenous population, and the administration of justice. One item on the agenda, for example, concerns the demands made by indigenous women's organizations; the impact of their proposals on law and citizenship rights in Mexico requires serious consideration.

It is also important to analyze more closely the concept of citizenship with regard to migration to the United States, and the transnationalization of daily forms of legal practice, as well as to explore how migration and globalization are transforming the relationship between law and gender throughout the Americas. These processes challenge legal anthropology to investigate how globalization affects gender relations and the practice of law, not only in indigenous regions of Mexico, but also among the urban and nonindigenous groups, including peoples of African descent. We need to open up the field in this way in order to gain a better grasp on the subject of law and gender in the changing social, political, and economic context of multicultural societies.

The Contributions to This Volume

The goal of this book is to bring together a significant number of studies on law and gender in twentieth-century Mexico that begin to bridge the subdisciplinary divides described in this introduction. The essays fall into four thematic groups.

The first set of essays, based on court records, current ethnographic work, and legal discourse analysis, explores the relationship between law and sexuality. In Ana Alonso's chapter, for instance, law becomes the site of discursive struggle when judges, plaintiffs, and the accused negotiate constructions of love, gender, and sexuality in the early twentieth-century Chihuahua courts. We learn from Ivonne Szasz's analysis of Mexican penal codes how sexual acts that are physiologically similar may have different social and subjective meanings, depending on the historical and cultural context and on the social relations involved. And Rosío Córdova Plaza's ethnographic study of transvestite prostitutes in the city of Xalapa shows how these individuals fall outside the dichotomized vision of society found in most Veracruz state laws, while the lack of up-to-date legislation regulating the trade leaves sex workers unprotected with regard to their rights and obligations as workers.

The second set of essays makes innovative, gendered contributions to the already booming field of "interlegality" (the relationship between national and indigenous law). Here, indigenous women become visible not only as the victims (as they often are) of a gendered legal system, but also as dynamic actors who increasingly influence the legal systems under which they live. Lynn Stephen focuses on land rights in Chiapas, arguing that indigenous women's best chance of obtaining land is through emerging popular legal systems that are a hybrid of national, indigenous, and revolutionary laws. María Teresa Sierra's detailed case study of the multitiered court system available to indigenous women illustrates how gender ideologies at the intersection of hegemonic legal discourse and indigenous laws do not necessarily contradict each other. Victoria Chenaut's chapter demonstrates, in turn, how the gendered construction of criminality in a Veracruz jail affects indigenous women, whose poverty, monolingualism, and illiteracy make them exceptionally vulnerable to criminal charges that can end in years of imprisonment.

In the third section, authors analyze from different angles the role law and legal processes play in the construction of family and marital rights and responsibilities. Ann Varley's study of legislation from the revolutionary era finds contradictions between revolutionary laws that decreed equality within the home and subsequent legislation that made women legally responsible for domestic labor. We learn from Soledad González Montes's essay that women in rural Mexico frequently abandon their home and seek assistance from local judges in renegotiating their marital contract in the hope of improving their daily life. Finally, Helga Baitenmann's analysis of recent agrarian court records from the state of Veracruz shows how judges and plaintiffs have internalized the construction of the "agrarian family" (nuclear, monogamous, and male-headed), which has underpinned Mexican agrarian property rights for almost a century.

The fourth and final section of the book problematizes questions about whether a nation's legal system is comparatively progressive with regard to gender justice. Carmen Diana Deere's analysis of women's property rights shows how legal change is a long-term process, its outcome often difficult to characterize. Although Mexico has been a pioneer in Latin America with respect to married women's property rights, the jury is still out concerning such questions as how far innovations in family law have promoted greater gender justice. Finally, Adriana Ortiz-Ortega's historical study of the treatment of abortion rights in Mexico's penal code demonstrates how the content of the law can reflect feminist demands, but its implementation be controlled by more conservative groups.

Framing this volume are a foreword and an afterword by two prominent figures in, respectively, the fields of gender studies and legal anthropology. Maxine Molyneux's foreword adopts a broadly comparative perspective, from which she makes pointed observations about the specificity of the intersection between law and gender in contemporary Mexico. In considering this subject from the colonial era to the present, she suggests that we should analyze the intersection between law and gender in terms of more general processes of gender and state formation. In turn, Jane Collier's afterword reflects meaningfully on why the relationship between law and gender in contemporary Mexico must be understood within the context of eighteenth-century liberal law and in terms of the constraints and possibilities that this legal legacy offers. In the course of her essay, she considers broader questions about the content of citizenship and the rule of law in present-day Mexico, and she fittingly reminds us that all attempts to analyze laws or legal institutions carry political implications.

Deconstructing Law and Gender

The essays in this volume clearly show that the connection between law and gender in contemporary Mexico is more complex, contradictory, and indeterminate than one might have assumed. We are only now beginning to understand the multidimensionality of law from a gendered perspective.

The chapters of this book show that discourses of law and gender are often regionally and historically specific. However, such considerations are not sufficient to understand the complexity of law with regard to gender relations. The linkage between law and gender is as multifaceted as the Mexican legal system itself—with its manifold legal frameworks (labor, agrarian, civil, penal, and so forth), its different types of legislation at state and federal levels (laws, codes, regulations, and so on), and its great variety and levels of courts (Supreme Court, state and federal appellate courts, agrarian courts, judicial district courts, municipal courts, indigenous procedures for conflict resolution, and so forth). Ortiz-Ortega analyzes, for example, the legislation of the thirty-one states and Federal District, and explains why the case of Mexico presents such a variety of positions on abortion. There is enough variation among the codes to allow her to divide them into "advanced," "intermediate," and "conservative" legislation with regard to the number of extenuating circumstances permitting abortion.

Given such change and variation with regard to the gendered nature of law, it is not surprising to learn that Mexico is more advanced than many other Latin American countries in some respects, yet more conservative in others. Moreover, although those Mexican states most liberal with regard to abortion are among the most liberal, in this regard, in Latin America, the least liberal Mexican states have adopted legislation in this area that is more conservative than such laws in any other Latin American country except Chile, Nicaragua, and El Salvador. Mexico's contradictory position is particularly clear in Deere's chapter, in which we learn that Mexico led the way in instituting the legal construct of the dual-headed household and in introducing complete testamentary freedom, yet "remains one of the retrogrades . . . with respect to the inheritance rights of spouses" when someone dies intestate. To complicate matters further, state-level legislation can be progressive on one topic and retrograde on another. For example, one of the states with the most conservative legislation on abortion is also one of the most progressive when it comes to extending married women's property rights to women living in consensual unions.

States not only have differing legal codes, but also diverge from one another with regard to the nature of their court systems. In the indigenous Sierra Norte de Puebla, the justice system has multiple levels, including an Indigenous Court, created in response to new federal policies aimed at recognizing cultural diversity (Sierra). Similarly, increasing numbers of indigenous communities are revitalizing and redefining what they regard as their "traditional" legal systems. Each such arena of justice—federal, state, and indigenous—is gendered in its structure and interpretation (Stephen). In addition to the justice system established in response to indigenous movements, a new agrarian justice system was set up to deal with the disputes arising from the 1992 constitutional reforms ending Mexico's postrevolutionary agrarian reform. These agrarian courts, functioning under the gendered constraints of agrarian law, constitute a legal system that operates in parallel with civil and criminal courts (Baitenmann).

Discovering variation in the legal system includes taking into consideration sources generally overlooked by social scientists, including legal discourse such as jurisprudence and extralegal genres such as gossip. In this volume, Varley explores how Supreme Court jurisprudence codifies interpretations that can persist even when the original legislation has been repealed. She shows how the overlapping processes of legislation and interpretation can, sometimes paradoxically, benefit women. Alonso shows how the articulation of law and gossip comes into play in early twentieth-century Chihuahua court cases, where criminal cases would depend on the reputation of litigants and defendants alike.

As many scholars have already noted, gender overlaps with other analytic categories such as class and ethnicity. Nowhere is this clearer than in Chenaut's essay on the prison system in rural Mexico. Gender ideologies not only "create the conditions in which women are accused of certain crimes," but indigenous women's extreme poverty and illiteracy, and their consequent lack of ability to understand the legal system, also become the conditions through which the judicial system criminalizes them.

Enduring Subtleties of Law and Gender

The contributions to this volume illustrate that, in spite of important changes in legislation and in the use of the legal system, discrimination, exclusion, and disempowerment on the basis of gender persist. Many naturalized gender ideologies prove remarkably resilient in the face of legal reform. Possibly more than any other of the institutions and practices that comprise the state, the legal system is permeated by gendered essentialisms that shape (and are shaped by) power relations in society. The chapters in this book illustrate the many dimensions of this phenomenon.

Collier, for instance, argues that the relationship between gender and law in Mexico must be understood within the context of the legal concepts and practices that developed in eighteenth-century Europe with regard to the protection of men's property. In her study of state and Federal District penal codes, Szasz finds important continuities between the medical and scientific discourse on sexuality and the religious ideas that preceded it. For example, both have viewed sexuality as a basic impulse that requires social controls, is inherently different in men and women, and should be practiced only within the bonds of marriage. Similarly, Ortiz-Ortega finds that the Catholic Church still influences which laws are passed, how they are worded, and how they are implemented.

The essays in this volume also show, in different ways, that a number of double standards and naturalized concepts seem constantly to reappear in laws and legal processes. For example, when Mexican revolutionaries proposed laws that would grant husbands and wives equality before the law, Supreme Court justices re-established, in translated form, the concept that a man should protect his wife and a woman obey her husband (Varley). Similarly, court documents from one municipality show remarkable continuity over the course of three decades, both in the kinds of marital conflicts presented and in the arguments that men and women have made (González Montes). And gendered agrarian concepts have persisted for almost a century in Mexico, despite profound changes in the nature of agrarian reform (Baitenmann).

Naturalized ideas about gendered relations are profound because they are often widely shared. For instance, gender ideologies found in both community and municipal legal institutions seem to respond to logics that do not greatly differ (Sierra). In the case of indigenous women in prison, both state and community sanctions are based on gendered double standards, standards that could have different effects on the postprison experiences of men and women (Chenaut). In agrarian court proceedings, plaintiffs and defendants, judges and witnesses, court officials and court users all employ the same gendered agrarian concepts (Baitenmann). Moreover, legal discrimination on the basis of sexual orientation is congruent with many people's perception that sexual orientations other than heterosexuality are abnormal, perverse, and dangerous (Córdova Plaza).

Spaces for Agency and Negotiation

Although the legal system is permeated by gendered essentialisms, law is not, as Htun states, "weighty tomes passed from one generation to the next" (2003, 2).

First, laws can have unintended gendered consequences, such that the outcome cannot be read directly from the letter of the law (Varley). Moreover, "abstract principles are interpreted in more or less flexible ways according to the contexts and constraints of legal practice, and deployed strategically" (Alonso).

Second, the chapters in this book collectively confirm that there is much variation in the roles that individuals can and do play in the Mexican legal system. Whereas laws are made by men (and, more and more, by men *and* women), there are plenty of men and women eager to have their say in state and federal legislatures. Indeed, in some cases, Mexican state legislatures are changing the civil and penal codes with remarkable frequency, in order to stamp their party imprint on sensitive social issues such as abortion rights. The frequency of legal change has increased since the 1990s, in conjunction with changes in the political system, with decentralization, and with partisan alternation in power.

Activists and socially engaged politicians have played key roles in reforming laws that discriminate on the basis of gender and sexual preference, and in bringing legislation in line with international gender justice standards. One of the feminist movement's accomplishments involves the recent inclusion of the crime of sexual harassment in more than half of the country's penal codes (Szasz). Similarly, recent reforms in abortion legislation in the Federal District bring Mexican law more in line with international gender-rights standards (Ortíz-Ortega). Activists fighting for legal reforms to fight homophobia are also making important headway (Córdova Plaza); nevertheless, even if successful, they will probably still have to confront the gap between law and implementation.

Some of Mexico's most socially marginal groups, such as indigenous women, are also active participants in legal disputes. In parts of rural Mexico, not only have women changed the way in which they respond to marital conflicts, but judges' and relatives' responses to such conflicts have also changed (González Montes). Indigenous jurisdiction and indigenous legal authorities continue to be the main reference points for resolving disputes in many communities, but in some regions women are resorting more frequently to the state's judicial institutions when the local ones do not provide solutions to their demands (Sierra). Moreover, there is now a national indigenous women's network dedicated to ensuring that women's rights are enforced in the process of granting indigenous autonomy (Stephen).

A principal message that emerges from this volume is the importance of fully grasping the content and application of the law. Deere underscores this point when she concludes that what is required is eternal vigilance on the part of those committed to gender equality, and actions to promote legal literacy so that individuals "become aware of their rights, demand these in practice, and find themselves capable of defending them when they are challenged."

A Note on Legal Citations

The complexity of Mexico's legal system, described in this introduction, poses a challenge to those wishing to cite the legislation. There is a considerable variety of laws, codes, and regulations at both federal and state level, as well as judicial rulings that in some cases establish required readings of the law (Zamora et al. 2004, 76–95). We follow the usual practice in Mexico of referring to a law by the year in which it was approved (rather than published, or brought into force), but this presents a certain difficulty when discussing specific sections within the civil and penal codes. Although the code continues to be known by the year in which it was issued until it is revised in its entirety (as has been the case with many of the states' civil or penal codes since the 1990s), it is common for individual articles to be reformed. The code may therefore change as much as several times a year. For this reason, we have preferred to cite the laws as primary sources in notes rather than by referring to the book versions produced by publishing companies, so as not to introduce confusion between the date of the book and the date the legislation or article in question was issued or reformed. Where we wish to draw attention to a particular reform, we have included in the text a reference to the date of publication of the reform in the official daily bulletin published at federal level (*Diario Oficial de la Federación*) or by individual states (*Gaceta* or *Periódico Oficial*). We have tried to ensure that quotations from the laws are appropriate to the period to which the text, at any given point, refers.

A further source of potential confusion is that the civil and penal codes for the Federal District (the core of Mexico City) also used to serve as federal codes in certain matters; however, since 2000 and 1999, the Federal District has acquired its own civil and penal codes, respectively; a new penal code for the Federal District was then issued in 2002. The pre-existing codes survived to become the Federal Civil and Penal Codes.

Electronic media and the internet have made a significant difference to the ease with which laws and judicial rulings can be consulted by those with access to the technology (Zamora et al. 2004, 97). Readers wishing to pursue this subject matter are recommended to consult the websites of the Suprema Corte de Justicia de la Nación (http://www.scjn.gob.mx) (for federal and state legislation, with details of individual reforms, and jurisprudence); the Cámara de Diputados of the H. Congreso de la Unión (http://www.diputados.gob.mx) or individual state government, Tribunal Superior de Justicia, and legislative websites (via links from the Cámara de Diputados's site); and the Instituto de Investigaciones Jurídicas of the Universidad Nacional Autónoma de México (http://juridicas. unam.mx) (which also provides access to many of the institute's publications online).

Where relevant, we also refer in the notes to individual case files in judicial archives. The notes generally include the name of the archive, the number of the file, and the date on which the suit was filed or a ruling issued. Given the variety of practices involved and of circumstances in individual archives, we have not tried to standardize beyond these basic elements.

NOTES

1. See Gonzalbo Aizpuru (1991), Guzmán Vázquez and Martínez O. (1989b, 1992), Ortega Noriega (1986), and Seminario de Historia de las Mentalidades (1982, 1985, 1988, 1994, 2000).

2. Where not otherwise mentioned: on conflicts over choice of marital partner, see Villafuerte García (1989); adultery and divorce, Lavrin (1978) and Pita Moreda (1996); bigamy, Pizzigoni (2004); illegitimacy, Twinam (1999); homosexuality, De Los Reyes-Heredia (2004) and Garza Carvajal (2003); sexual witchcraft, Behar (1987, 1989) and Lewis (2003); prostitution, Atondo Rodríguez (1992); "deflowering," rape, or other sexual abuse, González Marmolejo (1982); domestic violence or murder, Boyer (1989), Castro Gutiérrez (1998), Haslip-Viera (1996), Lozano Armendares (1987), Pescador (1996), Sousa (1997), Stern (1995), and Taylor (1979).

3. See Alonso (1995a, 1995b), Gill (2001), González Montes and Iracheta (1987), Lipsett-Rivera (1996, 2001), Piccato (2001), and Shelton (2004). Conflictive marriages, adultery, and divorce reappear in historical studies using court records for these later periods; see, in addition, Arrom (1976, 1985b), Chenaut (1997, 2002), Smith (2006), and Varley (2000b).

4. Where not otherwise specified, all translations from Spanish are by the contributors to this book.

5. For work using case records, see Azaola Garrido (1996a), Bliss (2001), and Piccato (2001). The work of criminologists, social workers, and public health officials is examined by Buffington (2000), Piccato (2001), Núñez Becerra (2002), and Rivera-Garza (2001).

6. On domestic service, see Blum (2004, 2006) and Pérez (1988); street vending, Porter (2000); prostitution, Bliss (2001) and Pérez (1988).

7. See, for example, Baitenmann (2000), Deere and León (2001), Hamilton (2002), and Nuijten (2003b). Varley (2000a) concerns the transformation of agrarian into urban property rights.

8. See, for example, Alonso (1995a), Arrom (1976, 1985b), Boyer (1995), Castro Gutiérrez (1998), García Peña (2006), Lipsett-Rivera (2001), Shelton (2004), and Stern (1995).

9. This perhaps overstates the case. Plaintiffs sometimes used the courts strategically, to persuade a partner to mend his or her ways (Alonso 1995b; Arrom 1985b; Pita Moreda 1996; Scardaville 2000).

10. Similar findings have been reached for the early twentieth century by Gill (2001) and Smith (2006) for Yucatán, and by Chenaut (1997, 2002) for northern Veracruz.

11. See, for example, Castro Gutiérrez (1998), Gill (2001), González Marmolejo (1982), González Montes and Iracheta (1987), and Piccato (2001).

12. See, for example, Azaola Garrido (1996a), Buffington (2000), González Montes and Iracheta (1987), Pescador (1996), Pizzigoni (2005), Stern (1995), and Taylor (1979).

13. Most studies interpret male violence as punishment for women's disobedience or their questioning men's freedom of action. Less attention is given to women's violence (Piccato 2001, 111). Some men in eighteenth- and nineteenth-century Mexico City complained of violent treatment by their spouses, albeit less frequently than women did (Dávila Mendoza 2005, 189; García Peña 2006, 100). Dávila Mendoza (2005, 268–269) suggests that the difference reflects the strategic deployment of gender stereotypes by litigants in divorce cases.

14. García Peña (2006, 135–138) notes, however, that as the state assumed control over marriage, the practice of *depósito* became more favorable to women. If the wife was the innocent party, she could now decide whether or not to accept depósito as a protective measure, and could now exercise her existing right to choose where she was to be housed. On the ambivalent nature of depósito, see also Penyak (1999).

15. The decrees of the Council of Trent, which ended in 1563, were adopted for Mexico by the Third Mexican Provincial Council in 1585 (Ortega 1989). These upheld freedom of choice of marital partner—for women and for men, and for slaves and the indigenous population as well as for those of Spanish descent (Cortés 1988; Kuznesof 1992).

16. For nineteenth-century Latin America as a whole, however, Putnam, Chambers, and Caulfield (2005, 17) stress that the outcome varied according to context. In some cases, women began to "push the boundaries of respectability," and occasionally men accused of sexual abuse could "find their own reputations tied partially to their sexual conduct" (ibid.).

17. This change can also be seen in the move from the 1868 Veracruz Civil Code—the first in the country—to the 1896 one (Chenaut 2001b). (Most references to the civil or penal codes are to those for the Federal District.)

18. Elena Azaola Garrido (1996a) makes a similar argument to explain greater judicial severity toward women murderers (especially those who kill children), compared with men, in contemporary Mexico City.

19. Carmen Ramos Escandón believes that, although García was not the only one debating women's rights, he was probably the first within the political elite who openly argued in favor of women's suffrage and equal civil rights (2001a, 98–103).

20. The gendered history of this time period has been amply discussed elsewhere. See, for example, the bibliography in Olcott, Vaughan, and Cano (2006).

21. One of these exceptions was the study sponsored by the Lawyer's Socialist Front (Bremauntz 1937).

22. Also see, in order of publication, Solís Cámara (1956), Guzmán Lazo (1957), Gómez Lara (1965), Graue (1965), Ochoa Flores (1968), González Salazar (1969), and Vallejo Azuela (1969).

23. Women's work was usually the only topic about which law students and scholars would stray from the principle of equality before the law to support women's (different) rights as mothers. Virginia Ortega Ramos (1955) was not alone in supporting protections for women in her thesis, nor was Xóchitl Mazadiego López (1966) when she considered protective legislation for working women as part of a larger struggle for women's rights. (This attitude would change in the 1970s, when the main thrust of debate was to eliminate labor "protections" or restrictions for women.)

24. For theses dealing with agrarian rights, see, for example, in chronological order, Morales Jurado (1954), Pedrero (1959), Ávila Osorio (1963), Romo Chávez Mejía (1963), and Mantilla López (1965).

25. The International Women's Year also sparked a flurry of legal theses on women's rights. See, for example, Bedolla Guzmán (1976), Bernal Gómez (1984), Dueñas (1980), Gómez González (1975), Hernández Bautista (1976), Palacios Escobar (1977), Pérez Carbajal y Campuzano (1975), Pérez Guerrero (1976), and Yee Verduzco (1975).

26. For insights on feminism and the Left in the 1970s, see Espinosa (2002), Gutiérrez Castañeda (2002a), Hinojosa (2002), and Toto Gutiérrez (2002).

27. An analysis of the Echeverría laws is beyond the scope of the text. For a brief overview, see, for example, Payán (1975).

28. Another important example of Echeverría's legal reforms was his 1971 Federal Agrarian Reform Law giving campesina women equal agrarian rights (see Baitenmann, n/d).

29. For example, women in Congress were behind the 1989 Chamber of Deputies Justice Commission's "Forum for the Discussion of Sexual Crimes" ("Foro de consulta sobre delitos sexuales"), where participants presented over one hundred essays on the subject (de Barbieri and Cano 1990, 348–349). An important precedent was the Alianza de Mujeres de México's 1959 "Reuniones de mesa redonda sobre la situación jurídica de la mujer mexicana en el código agrario," which included women government officials.

30. See, for instance, Begné (1990), Kurczyn Villalobos (2000), and Olamendi Torres (1998).

31. As with early women's rights in general, nationality rights (of Mexican women married to foreigners) became one of the first topics to be linked to the new human rights discourse (Jastrow Becerra 1982).

32. Some examples are Bernal Gómez (1984), Galeana (1998), and González de Pazos (1987).

33. Although almost all civil, penal, and procedural codes in Mexican states are modeled on federal codes, each state (and the Federal District) has its own codes (Zamora et al. 2004, 120). Some early studies on state laws, like Solís Marcin (1939), were conducted at state universities. The detailed comparison of the different states' penal codes in Porte Petit Candaudap (1966) was exceptional for its time. Although the text does not analyze women's rights, the gendered analysis is implicit when talking about the topic of "rape as a crime." For a sample of these texts, see, in order of publication, González Salazar (1989), Gobierno del Estado de México (1992), Guevara and Begné (1993), Pérez Duarte y Noroña (1995), Martínez Sánchez (1996), Torres Medina (1997), Ávila Godoy and Aguirre Angulo (1998), Hernández Franco (2000), and Aragón Salcido (2004).

34. Some important examples from the new literature on gendered labor rights include Fernández Muñoz (1990), Kurczyn Villalobos (1998, 2004), and Pérez Contreras (2001).

35. Some early examples include de Barbieri (1992) and Muñozcano Skidmore (1995).

36. Heteronormativity is the belief that human beings fall into two distinct and complementary categories, male and female, and that sexual and marital relations are normal only when they involve two people of different genders.

37. See the monographs of Aguirre Beltrán (1953), Foster (1967), Lewis (1960), Villa Rojas (1945), and Vogt (1969), among others.

38. See Collier (1966, 1973), Nader (1964a, 1964 b, 1969, 1990), Nader and Metzger (1963), Nash (1972) and Parnell (1988).

39. Other state and federal laws were modified during these years, to include some indigenous human rights (such as the right to have a translator during trial hearings).

40. For studies on this topic published during the 1990s, see among others, Assies, van der Haar, and Hoekema (1999); Chenaut and Sierra (1995); Clavero (1994); Gómez Rivera (1997); Instituto de Investigaciones Jurídicas (1994); Sierra (1998); and Stavenhagen (1992).

41. These congresses were held in Ecuador (1997), Chile (2000), Guatemala (2002), and again in Ecuador (2004).

42. See, for example, González Montes (1998); Hernández Castillo (1998); Martínez Corona and Mejía Flores (1997); Muñiz and Corona (1996); and Torres Falcón (2003).

43. See, among others, Bonfil Sánchez and Marcó del Pont Lalli (1999); Bonfil Sánchez and Martínez Medrano (2003); Freyermuth Enciso (2003); and González Montes (1999b).

44. This includes fratricidal struggles and political factionalism, such as the one that occurred in Acteal (Chiapas), in which a group of armed men assassinated in cold blood twenty-nine indigenous women and twelve indigenous men (Eber 2002, Hernández Castillo 1998).

45. See, for example, Collier (2004); Chenaut (1999, 2001a, 2004); Garza Caligaris (2002); Hernández Castillo (2004); Martínez Corona and Mejía Flores (1997); Mejía Flores, Villa Hernández, and Oyorzabal (2003); Sierra (2000, 2004a, 2004c, 2004e); Vallejo Real (2000, 2004a, 2004b); and Villa Hernández (2003).

46. The Ley Revolucionaria de Mujeres can be found in "El Despertador Mexicano" (EZLN 1993), Lovera and Palomo (1997), and Rojas (1999). For an analysis of this law, see Millán (1996).

47. In 1996, indigenous women wrote a controversial Proposal to Extend the Zapatista Women's Revolutionary Law (Propuesta de Ampliación de la Ley Revolucionaria de Mujeres Zapatistas) to coincide with International Women's Day. See Lovera and Palomo (1997) and Rojas (1999) for this and other documents by indigenous women's groups.

PART ONE

Discourses on
Law and Sexuality

1

Love, Sex, and Gossip in Legal Cases from Namiquipa, Chihuahua

ANA M. ALONSO

In 1923, Andrés, a son of the pueblo of Namiquipa, Chihuahua, brought a civil suit against his brother-in-law José. José, Andrés complained, had been "living scandalously with a señora who is not his wife," setting his son Juan such a "bad example" that the poor youth had had to move out of his home.[1] Andrés told the judge that "this young man . . . wishes to take a road that is straighter than his father's and to be a man who is not a libertine." The case was resolved when José gave his son formal permission to live with his maternal grandfather.

This case flies in the face of stereotypes about machismo in Mexico. But it is not unusual for this pueblo, where excesses of virility that threatened family order were censured. What were Namiquipans' notions of gender, love, and sexuality, and how did these come into play in legal cases? Why did individuals take sexual offenses (which, if not suitably avenged, could dishonor an entire family) to the local judge instead of resorting to violence? What was the relationship between legal discourse and extralegal genres such as gossip for sanctioning behavior? In this chapter, I explore the gendered operations of law and the legal regulation of sexuality by analyzing criminal cases concerning "the order of families" prosecuted in the pueblo of Namiquipa, Chihuahua, during the 1920s. This is a particularly interesting decade because the state lacked a monopoly of force, and law was only one of several resources for dealing with interpersonal conflict.

Legal testimonies from judicial archives have been an important source in feminist historiography. Yet using this rich evidence is by no means straightforward. Women's testimonies appear in the legal record as reported speech; the meaning of such speech is mediated by the reporter as well as by the reporting context. Here, I develop an analytical method designed to deal with the problem of voice in legal cases and to grasp how multiple dimensions of the context in which law operates—historical, social, cultural, and linguistic—shape the meaning and outcome of gendered legal processes.

Modernization of Patriarchy and Regulation of Sexuality in Mexico

The Liberal Revolution of the mid-nineteenth century set in motion political reforms that attempted to ground public as well as domestic authority in legal–rational rather than patrimonial norms. Nineteenth-century legal codes represented new forms of governmentality that defined and regulated the sexuality of women and men in gender-specific ways.[2] Judicial ideology represented normative femininity as sexually passive. At the same time, women's sexual virtue was considered essential to social order, guaranteeing paternity rights and the intergenerational transmission of property. Hence, the 1871 Penal Code penalized antisocial expressions of virility and "protected" those who were considered its passive victims.

Estupro, rapto of women as well as *violación* of either women or men, corruption of minors, and adultery were defined and classified as "Crimes against Family Order, Public Morality and Good Customs" in the 1871 Penal Code.[3] Estupro (generally translated "statutory rape") was defined as sexual intercourse with "a chaste and honest woman" not of legal age, employing "seduction and deceit" to obtain her consent.[4] Rapto (which can be translated as "abduction") was colloquially known as *robo de mujeres* ("theft of women").

Women and minors of both sexes were given some guarantees against the worst abuses of patriarchal power. The home was opened up to a series of state interventions, as "private life" became a matter of public order, not only of patriarchal discretion (see Varley 2000a, and Varley, this volume). The 1871 Penal Code permitted the prosecution of wife-beating as a punishable crime and provided for the arrest of violent husbands (Alonso 1995a). In contrast, wife-beating was largely regarded as a private matter in the United States until the 1970s; Congress did not pass the Violence against Women Act until 1994.

Legislation on estupro, rapto, and adultery represented a compromise between the reach of law into the domestic sphere, and patriarchal sovereignty (see also Szasz, this volume). Making the prosecution of these crimes hinge on the complaint of victims or the victims' representatives gave the offended parties and their immediate relatives the choice of keeping matters quiet and avoiding any additional wounds to honor that publicity might entail (Porte Petit Candaudap 1972, 60–61). Moreover, parties were given the option of settling out of court, cleansing honor either through marriage or through monetary indemnification.

The provisions of legal codes are never mechanically applied as rules. Abstract principles are interpreted in more or less flexible ways according to the contexts and constraints of legal practice, and deployed strategically in the course of cases. Hence, it is not enough to study legal codes; we must also analyze legal practices. Consider, for instance, the prosecution of crimes against "family order and public morality" in the *serrano* community of Namiquipa.

Gender and Sexuality in the Serrano Community of Namiquipa

Serranos, or "people of the mountains," are the non-Indian inhabitants of the Sierra Madre of the state of Chihuahua, Mexico. They received land and other concessions from the state in return for fighting the Apache in the eighteenth and nineteenth centuries (Alonso 1995b; Nugent 1993). Founded in 1778, by 1900 the serrano town of Namiquipa was the political center of a rural municipality with a total population of roughly three thousand souls.

Brought to Mexico by the Spanish, the Mediterranean rhetoric of honor acquired new meanings as the social value of men on the Northern frontier became linked to the defense of "civilized" women (Gutiérrez 1991). One of the sources of Namiquipans' legal ideology was the gendered contrast between lawless *bárbaros* and law-abiding *gente de razón*. Being a man in Namiquipa involved exercising razón (reason) to temper instincts and passions. Yet a man could still lose all reason, especially if drunk, and regress to an animal-like state in which he might insult others, get into fights, or commit sexual crimes, as numerous cases in the local judicial archive attest (Alonso 1995b).

As tamers of the beast in men, nonindigenous women came to be valued as reproducers of the crucial boundary between "civilization" and "barbarism" (ibid.; Rubio Goldsmith 1998). *Pudor*, the basis for women's "good conduct," was a sensibility that defined normative femininity and fostered adherence to norms of sexual propriety. In contrast to other Mexican communities where consensual unions were common (Ramos Escandón 1987), marriage was the norm in Namiquipa. Women who lost their virginity outside of marriage, or wives who committed adultery, dishonored themselves and their families, forfeiting rights to men's respect and protection; they were often forced into domestic service, concubinage, or prostitution to support themselves and their children. Namiquipan judges favored women who conformed to normative femininity (Alonso 1995b); hence local gender ideology shaped and was shaped by legal practice.

Namiquipa became one of the main centers of Villismo (that is, of the followers of northern revolutionary leader Pancho Villa) during the Revolution of 1910–1920. The local court (Juzgado Menor) continued to function, though sporadically, during these decades. Although men did use violence to avenge honor, this behavior was viewed, somewhat ambivalently, as "taking the law into one's own hands." Use of the law for negotiating offenses to family order was tied to a belief, reinforced by revolutionary ideals, that the law was the true fount of justice, as well as to notions of gender honor that privileged the mediation of nature by reason.

Gossip and Legal Discourse in Namiquipa: Points of Suture

Although legal discourse was regarded as impartial, the law provided points of suture with other, more partial, genres. Regarding the crime of estupro, for example, the 1871 Penal Code declared that two conditions had to be met for an offense to be so classified. First, the man had to proceed by "deceit" and "seduction." Second, the young woman had to be "chaste and honest."[5] As the legal commentator Mariano Jiménez Huerta (1968, 253–254) points out: "A woman is chaste and honest in accordance with the values of a community." Not only did local values come into play but, importantly, so did gossip, one of the key genres for negotiating reputation in Namiquipa.

Genres of discourse are relatively stable, normative forms of utterance that "correspond to typical situations of speech communication, typical themes, and consequently, also to particular contacts between the meanings of words and actual concrete reality" (Bakhtin 1986, 87). Bakhtin notes that secondary speech genres such as legal discourse "arise in more complex and comparatively highly developed and organized cultural communication (primarily written). . . . During the process of their formation, they absorb and digest various primary (simple) genres that have taken form in unmediated speech communion" (ibid., 62). In face-to-face corporate communities such as Namiquipa, the secondary genre of legal discourse exists in continual tension with the primary genre of gossip.

At first glance, the genres of legal discourse and gossip appear to be opposites. Gossip, after all, is telling stories out of rather than in court. Moreover, gossip, in Mexico is considered a feminine genre (even though men too gossip), and legal discourse, a masculine one. Legal discourse is authorized by the state, gossip by the reputation of the speaker who claims the moral high ground. Gossip is characterized by informal, colloquial, expressive speech; legal discourse is marked by a formal, impartial, "high" style of language (Bourdieu 1991, 125).

Gossip is generally an oral genre; legal discourse is both oral and written. The written legal record remains a permanent (and accessible) attestation of the "facts of the matter." By contrast, once a story is circulated as gossip, it is altered and embellished, its circuit cannot be traced, and who said what to whom cannot be reliably recalled. In legal cases, however, there is a paper trail: each declaration is ratified, witnesses are read their statements and asked to validate them, and statements can be reliably reproduced since they are written down. If the court of gossip is private, subjective, and directly accountable to no one, the court of law is public, impartial (in principle), and accountable to society.

The truth status of gossip is always ambiguous. By contrast, legal discourse does its best to dispel ambiguity; it is rationalistic and referent-analyzing (Bakhtin 1973, 115–140). It has a protocol for eliciting truth, corroborating testimony, and punishing those who are caught lying. It does not assume that people will tell the truth or that language is a transparent medium of reference—precisely the opposite. Namiquipan cases make some of their intertextuality explicit, through typical modes of citation such as references to legitimating texts or the use of reported speech. Rendered explicit, sources can be checked and crosschecked. Legal decisions can be appealed and can be reversed. But dirt, true or false, sticks.

Nevertheless, legal discourse has important characteristics in common with gossip: both genres are explicitly judgmental; the thematic focus of discourse is on what people have done wrong; and judgments are rendered meaningful in relation to narratives (Delgado and Stefanancic 2000). Both law and gossip are disciplinary forms through which social norms and values are policed and disputes mediated (Cloete 2003). In small towns where communication is largely face to face, gossip is a key genre through which reputation is negotiated; as such, gossip can become relevant to those legal cases, such as the criminal prosecution of estupro, in which testimony about the parties' reputations comes into play. Although the penalties for infringement of norms and values imposed by gossip and by the law differ, they do have one thing in common: they can turn a community member into a persona non grata.

Law and gossip's personal stories are shaped by broader, generic cultural narratives that are told and retold across genres (though not in identical ways). The law criminalizing estupro and the local prosecution of cases tacitly engage with such generic narratives. As I show in this chapter, judicial verdicts depend on how fragments of people's stories are interpreted in the light of several plausible standardized plots. Indeed, even the most erudite legal commentary can rest on such generic plots. For example, writing about the crime of estupro, and referring to the notion of masculine seduction, Jiménez Huerta (1968, 262–263) says: "possible hypotheses as to its typical realization should be contemplated with extreme caution in order to prevent the law from becoming a go-between for infamous feminine plans to hunt inexpert young men during their first flight, with a false tale." It is clear which cultural narrative he found most credible.

An In-Depth Analysis of a Case of Estupro in Namiquipa

Summary of the Case

This criminal case opens on May 31, 1926, when Don Francisco, in his capacity as the father of a nineteen-year-old illegitimate daughter, authors a written complaint (*querella formal*) that he presents to the judge of the local court (Juez Menor).[6] Don Francisco was a highly respected community elder who had gained military distinction in the Apache Wars and had held local political offices. He had left his legal wife and legitimate children to live in Namiquipa with his concubine, with whom he had several more children, before she ran off with another man. Don Francisco was a wealthy and beneficent rancher. He embodied many local notions of honorable manhood.

On May 31, Don Francisco accuses a young man of having had sexual relations with his daughter, Teresa, in 1924, "Seducing her by means of deceit and offering to fulfill his commitment." As proof he presents letters signed with the alleged seducer's name and addressed to his daughter. He asks that the man in question marry his daughter or pay the penalty the law demands. The judge has the secretary read Don Francisco's complaint back to him and asks him to ratify it. The case is then forwarded to the *sub-agente del Ministerio Público* (sub-agent of the Public Prosecution Agency), whose function it is to decide whether or not there are sufficient grounds to prosecute the accused. The secretary writes "that the judge reports . . . that the sub-agent says . . . that the declaration of the estuprada is necessary" (probably because the woman's father cannot prove his status as her parent since he has not followed the legal procedure to recognize her as his daughter).

The court personnel proceed to her home, accompanied by Don Francisco. There the judge takes Teresa's *protesta de la ley*, an oath that commits her to tell the truth or incur stiff legal penalties. He also takes her *generales*—name, age, civil status, place of birth, and residence. A question and answer session then takes place between the judge and Teresa. The legal secretary reports their speech in formal legal discourse using the third person. Teresa states that she has had "amorous relations" with the young man since 1923 and that the estupro committed upon her person in April of 1924 led to the birth of a child. Since she is nineteen now, she was around sixteen or seventeen when the estupro occurred. She asks, ratifying her father's complaint and becoming a party to it, that her lover fulfill his promise to marry her or pay the penalties the law establishes.

On June 4, the public prosecutor, upon reading Teresa's declaration and seeing the documents presented as evidence, responds: "that he opines (for it is not possible to opine otherwise due to the accumulation of probatory antecedents which have been placed in my view) to proceed to the preventive declaration of the accused." This is a key moment in the case since, by "framing" (Bakhtin 1981, 1986) the letters and photos as "probatory antecedents" so numerous that further investigation is warranted, the prosecutor indicates a strong suspicion that the accused is guilty.

Jesús María, the accused young man, was at this time a legal adult, described as five feet three and one-quarter inches tall, having white skin, with brown eyes and black hair. He wore brown striped cashmere pants, a striped shirt, and yellow spats with his shoes—a very fancy outfit for a son of the pueblo—when he presented himself to the judge on June 8.

Jesús's story is that he went to Bisbee, Arizona, wishing to make money to pay off debts in Namiquipa (and not to flee either his responsibilities to Teresa or the wrath of her father). He wanted to make a better life for himself. Although he admits to having had "amorous relations" with Teresa about four years previously, he says that these were "light" (*lisitas*) and that he has never touched her or made her any promises. He denies being Teresa's child's father.

When the signed love letters are shown to him, he denies that he wrote them. In response, the prosecutor tells the judge that this denial by the accused is "contradicted by the documents or letters which have been appended to the complaint," and that the accused should be shown the letters again, and, if he continues to deny he wrote them, expert witnesses should be appointed to analyze the handwriting. This is another turning point in the case, since the public prosecutor is indicating that the "probatory antecedents" are more convincing than the denials of the accused.

On June 10, the judge declares the formal imprisonment of the accused and notifies him of his rights to appeal and to name a defender. In a writ probably prepared by his defender, Jesús appeals his imprisonment. He alleges that Don Francisco has no legal standing to bring a complaint on the part of Teresa since she is now of legal age to represent herself and, furthermore, is not even his daughter.[7] Don Francisco, the writ argues, has only one daughter—Sra. X—his legitimate child. This is a huge insult to the honor of both Don Francisco (who is apprised of the appeal's contents) and Teresa. Legally, however, this allegation has little merit since Teresa has already acquired the status of a *querellante* in the case. Nevertheless, by questioning the standing of the father, Jesús María's defender is creating a point of suture between the case and the gossip that had circulated about this family for years, putting into question the virtue of Teresa's mother and the correctness of her father's behavior, and, hence, Teresa's chastity and honesty (a legal requirement to proving estupro). Insinuating that there was "talk" about the girl's tarnished reputation and immoral conduct made her in effect "unmarriageable"; this was a time-tested masculine strategy for avoiding marriage, common since colonial times (Gutiérrez 1991, 218–219).

A day later, the judge decides that the case exceeds his faculties, and that he will forward it, along with the prisoner, to the Court of First Instance (Juzgado de Primera Instancia) in nearby Ciudad Guerrero, the district capital. This really seems to worry the accused; prisoners did not always survive a journey that provided opportunities for aggrieved relatives or their agents to murder them. He tells the judge, on June 12, "that having thought of marrying the lady . . . even though more recently he has denied everything . . . today he has realized that what he had [most recently] thought of doing is an ingratitude and now he is convinced of the error of his ways . . . offering to marry the lady." Don Francisco and his daughter are notified of his offer on the same day, and agree to withdraw their complaint as long as he fulfills his promise of marriage (which he does).

Discussion

Legal cases are "rites of institution" that redefine identities and statuses and, hence, impact the various forms of capital of the parties involved, shaping their future behavior (Bourdieu 1991, 118). At stake in a case of estupro is the symbolic capital or honor of both the offended woman and her alleged seducer and thus each party's marriageability and social future. If the woman is deemed to be "chaste and honest," she can only redeem her reputation by marrying the man (or by accepting some form of financial compensation). If the man is deemed a "seducer," he can only redeem his reputation by marrying the woman (or compensating her for the loss of her maidenhead). Such cases restore the order of particular families by reaffirming the categorical order of "the Family," imposing specific obligations of gender conformity on both men and women, and obliging them to "stay on the right side of the line" (ibid., 122)

How do the linguistic attributes of the legal discourse in this case shape the outcome? In Mexico, cases are largely conducted orally, but, as they are processed, a written record is formulated and subsequently archived; this written record weaves in and out of the oral proceedings—transcriptions of testimonies are read out loud, for example. The narrator is the legal secretary, a member of the community appointed, and hence authorized, by the judge. His reliability is established through a number of textual devices. For example, his signature and that of the judge, the public prosecutor, or any party whose speech he is reporting, appear at the end of every entry, attesting to its veracity. The immediate addressees in written accounts of oral legal cases include judicial personnel such as the public prosecutor or the judge, and the potential audience includes defenders of guilty parties, those involved in the case, and higher order judicial personnel. The "higher addressee" (Bakhtin 1986, xviii) is Justice, to whom judicial personnel, narrators, and witnesses are accountable.

A chronological order of presentation of episodes (discrete narrated events) structures the case, in accordance with the strictures of the Code of Penal Procedures (Código de Procedimientos Penales). References to this code are used to identify steps in the legal process; the code's instructions are cited and followed in a highly formal, impersonal way, endowing legal procedure with a ritualized character and the "sacred" aura of justice.

The encompassing legal narrative contains other genres of discourse such as: (1) reported speech (testimonies of witnesses, narratives of parties, instructions and deliberations of judicial personnel); (2) expository discourse; (3) hortatory discourse; and (4) other discourses cited as evidence, such as love letters. Moreover, legal narrative is in tension with extralegal genres such as gossip. Hence, legal discourse is *dialogic* in Bakhtin's (1981) sense of the term—it is produced in intertextual relation to other discourses that can be rendered explicit (through conventions such as citation or reported speech) or remain implicit. How the relations among different genres of discourse in a case are established can have a huge impact on the verdict. For example, as described in the previous summary, a key turning point in the case comes about when the public prosecutor frames the personal documents appended to the case as "probatory antecedents" supporting the legal complaint made by Don Francisco and his daughter.

In this legal case, a formal, impartial, "high" style of language governs lexical choice, syntax, and other conventions for reporting speech, such as the use of honorifics. The speech of parties and witnesses is generally reported indirectly, and is characterized by what Bakhtin calls a rationalistic and referent-analyzing style (1973, 115–140). The salient characteristics of this style are: (1) the reported speech is clearly marked off as a compact block from the authorial context (namely, the legal secretary's narrative); (2) however, there is generally a harmonization of verb tense and no shift of person between the authorial and the reported speech (though there are exceptions to this tendency); (3) the speech is reported from the third-person objective point of view and the focus is on the "analytical transmission" of content rather than on forms of speech; and (4) the reported speech is largely devoid of emotive or individual stylistic features. These characteristics point to the "impartial" quality of speech reporting in this legal style, attesting to its focalization from the perspectives of the witnesses, of the parties to the case, and of legal authorities, rather than from the standpoint of the reporter (the legal secretary).

Although this style discourages the expression of the narrator's evaluations and judgments, these can come across both at the level of content (where there are numerous ways of coloring the transcription) and at the level of linguistic form (where opportunities are more restricted). How the secretary reports others' speech can have a subtle impact on the case, especially since his narrative is available to the judge, the prosecutor, and the parties to the case. Conscious or unconscious strategies such as lexical choice can tacitly shape legal proceedings. One example of how lexical choice can color legal proceedings early in a case is provided by the use of "estuprada" to describe Teresa before estupro had been proven (see the summary). Once introduced, this descriptor cues others who read the case and lends credibility to Teresa's story.

Colonial justices placed great importance on the *prenda,* or love token, as proof of a commitment to marriage (Gutiérrez 1991, 219). As literacy spread during the Porfiriato, the exchange of love letters partially replaced the exchange of prendas as signs of marital commitment; written proof of seduction and deceit became the preferred form of evidence in estupro cases. The first love letter presented as evidence—addressed to Teresa and signed "Jesús María"—is typed in its entirety. It appears to have been written some time after "amorous relations" began but before intercourse occurred. The genre of this letter is intimate. Unlike most lovers or even husbands, Jesús María uses the familiar form *tú* to address his beloved.

The letter has a repetitive, insistent character; Jesús reiterates his feelings over and over again, anticipating Teresa's objections to "becoming his."

A high style of speech, removed from that of everyday life and consistent with the elevated character of romantic love, characterizes lexical choice and syntax in the letters. Jesús's romanticism echoes the sentiments and language of popular revolutionary *corridos* such as "Adelita." Prior notions of romantic and passionate love (see French 1994; Gutiérrez 1991) may have acquired revolutionary accents during the charismatic period of the armed insurgency. Young women, including those whose fathers were associated with the ancien régime, fell in love with romantic revolutionary officers and soldiers (Calzadíaz Barrera 1975, 99–100). The revolutionary officer Pedro Rascón from Namiquipa took time to pen love poetry (along with prayers) in the midst of a revolutionary campaign.[8] Young revolutionaries, once confined to their town and region, traveled all over Mexico; compared to their predecessors, they may have been more willing to take sexual risks or challenge parental authority, since they could leave town if they got a lover pregnant or ran afoul of her family.

Jesús's prose is very romantic. He exalts his beloved. He jokingly declares himself to be an unworthy object of her love. He declares that "we find our-selves in one of the last places on Earth, maybe, almost in the abyss, where only fierce wild beasts should live and not us"; but he will be a "happy man" if only he can be with her. *Amor,* or passionate love, is represented as an "affliction" of the soul, heart, and body, which impacts the lovers to such a great degree that it causes extreme suffering, proof itself of the "true and faithful" character of their love. She should love him, he pleads, if only out of pity, and, rather than losing respect for her, he will only love her more: "Even if I felt passionate about a loose woman, as I feel now about you, I could *fulfill [cumplir]* everything, every-thing. One day you will cease to doubt me on this matter, so that when you see this my letter, remember that by loving me, stroking me, adoring me, laughing with me, kissing me, embracing me, . . . you will make me yours and never any other woman's, in this sad world, full of suffering and mistaken impressions."

Significantly, he does not formally promise marriage; he only promises to be hers—and to "fulfill," without specifying exactly what. Here the discourse of seduction works by implicature. An implicature is "anything that is inferred from an utterance but that is not a condition for the truth of the utterance" (Loos et al. 1999); a potential implicature of "fulfill" in this context is "fulfill a promise of marriage." Many of Jesús's other declarations of undying devotion have the same implicature, and this is probably how Teresa interpreted them, though she had her doubts. But her lover anticipates these and responds cagily, using fictive reported speech, declaring that he will always be true to her, "even if you say, your words are lies, die of suffering, I . . . am not yours, not now, nor ever, nor a thousand times ever." A potential implicature of this and other sim-ilar statements is "What I am saying is true and you are cruel not to believe me."

A second, handwritten letter responds to her answer to his first. He reproaches her for avoiding him and for asking him to stop coming to talk to her at night. He declares that her aunt (who is her chaperone) has nothing to do with either of them and that, if things are going to continue so, "it would be better for us to get married whenever you wish than for me to suffer disap-pointments like this one." He dismisses her worries about gossip and concern with "what people will say," arguing that she will lose her "judgment" by worry-ing about others': amor is a personal experience that one should be true to, even in the face of social disapproval. But, if he exalts romance, he has a very worldly plan to consummate it, suggesting that they bribe her aunt to look the other way. He makes an assignation to come to her house that very night.

The last love letter, sent from Bisbee, Arizona, is dated January 26, 1925, and is a response to her letter of January 15, in which she tells him about the birth of their son. He jokes: "I see that you have recovered from your illness thanks be to God. I also am informed that we have one more servant [*criado*] to boss about and that he is my picture, according to Adela, as well as that you are confident that I will keep my word as I have done all my life." Again the implicature here is that he acknowledges the child and will keep his promise of marriage, but he does not say so directly. The intimacy of Jesús's letters is an invitation to mutual trust that is at odds with his caginess, and it puts Teresa in a double bind. Is he committing himself to marriage? Or is he just taking advantage of her innocence? Which story is the right one?

The persuasiveness of the fragmented and ambiguous stories told by individuals involved in legal cases does not depend on facts alone but relies also on the linkages such tales can evoke to presupposed, generic cultural narratives about the same themes and events. Such generic stories are told and retold, albeit in different forms, and to distinct ends, across genres (e.g., gossip, letters, corridos, ballads, legal discourse, folklore, novels, poetry, plays). By filling in the holes in personal stories, such cultural narratives contribute to judicial sensemaking. Generic narratives presupposed in the example presented include: the story of the fallen woman engaged in entrapping a young man into marrying her; and that of the deceitful seducer using the discourse of passionate love to arouse desire so as to take advantage of feminine innocence. Which of these was more persuasive in this case?

Jesús's discourse of seduction functions by implicature; hence, its interpretation is highly contextual and situational. However, his equivocal rhetorical strategies fit well with the definition of "deception" (*engaño*) given in legal commentary: "Deception in statutory rape consists in a tendentious mutation or alteration of the truth—presenting false things or false promises as true—which produces a state of error, confusion or mistakenness in a woman that leads her to accede to the erotic pretensions of her seducer" (González de la Vega 1970, 371).

Likewise, the flattering expressions and declarations of passionate love in Jesús's letters fit the definition of "seduction": "We understand by seduction, in its strict judicial sense: malicious, lascivious conduct whose goal is to sexually overexcite a woman, or flattery paid to a woman designed to conquer her resistance" (ibid., 373). Hence, the weak point in Jesús's story is that his rhetoric can plausibly be interpreted as deceptive and seductive.

The weakness in Teresa's case is whether she can reliably be described as "chaste and honest." Her mother's extramarital relations would have put her own sexual virtue into question. Doubtless, there was gossip circulating about her and her mother's virtue, and Jesús's defense evoked this talk. The judicial personnel could have probed these insinuations; this certainly happened in other cases, where witnesses were asked directly what talk they had heard about the woman involved. (For example, during a case brought to the court in 1936 by a widow against a young man for rapto and estupro of her twenty-year-old daughter, one witness, "asked what he knows of the prior conduct" of the young woman, answers that "in the time that he has known her she has always observed good conduct and he never knew nor heard say anything bad about her.") Yet Don Francisco was a respected, rich, and powerful man; further investigation would have insulted his honor.

No official verdict had to be reached in this case, since Jesús offered to marry Teresa. However, the framing of the letters as "probatory antecedents," the arrest of the young man, and nuances of legal expression indicate that the public prosecutor and the judge were most persuaded by Teresa's version, the generic story of the seducer who takes advantage of a naïve young woman through flattery and false promises. Their pressure was one factor in Jesús's decision to do the right thing. Ironically, in doing the right thing he evoked yet a third generic narrative, that of the repentant seducer who recognizes that he has done wrong and marries the woman he has deflowered.

Overview of Legal Cases of Estupro

Cases of rapto and estupro from the archive of the local court (1880s–1930s) shed light not only on the gender but also on the generational dimension of patriarchy.[9] Young men like Jesús who wished to acquire sexual experience rebelled against the strictures imposed by the older generation. Young people who wished to marry but who could not get the necessary parental consent had the option of committing rapto. Abduction of a woman followed by sexual relations was an old strategy for getting around parental objections (Gutiérrez 1991; French 1994). Legal penalties would be extinguished if the abductor married the abductee.

Parents, usually fathers, brought complaints of rapto and estupro before the judge. The sexual virtue of a daughter was part of family patrimony; this explains why the crime of rapto was colloquially labeled theft. In the majority of these cases, a judicial decision and legal penalties were not imposed; rather, the parties reached an agreement among themselves. Although parents generally demanded that *raptadores* and/or *estupradores* marry their daughters (Gutiérrez 1991, 216), in some cases they settled for a monetary payment to indemnify the loss of female virtue (see French 1994).

Estupro was difficult to prove or disprove. Gossip about the woman was crucial to the resolution of the case, since in Namiquipa, as in eighteenth-century New Mexico, the man's standard defense was generally that the woman had no virtue to lose (Gutiérrez 1991). For example, in one case brought by the father of an underage girl, the accused alleged that she was "a woman who has licentious customs" since she had had sexual relations with at least four other men; he demanded a physical "inspection" of the girl (generally done by an expert woman).[10] And there the story ended, for no more was done by the judicial personnel.

Local judges generally used their power to support women who presented themselves as sexually passive. Hence, mechanisms of censorship were doubtlessly brought into play by the offended women; as French notes, "only certain stories could . . . be told to judicial officials, stories in which women may have felt constrained to portray themselves as acted upon rather than as actors" (French 1994).

Outcomes also hinged on the quality of the evidence in play. For example, a case of estupro prosecuted later in 1926 by the same judicial personnel involved in Teresa's case had a different outcome.[11] Estrella, a young woman, made "contradictory" allegations, accusing her offender of more than one crime—"attempt against pudor" as well as "estupro." She kept changing her story. On one occasion, she claimed that sexual intercourse had not occurred; on another, she said it had occurred by force (which would make this a case of violación). Like Teresa, Estrella presented love letters as proof, but these had been written for the accused by a friend and only contained generic, certainly not explicitly sexual, expressions of love. In addition, her witnesses claimed to have been able to see the rape occur at a distance of 200 meters, which was not very credible.

The young man's story was that Estrella and her mother had attacked him in a field and that he was only just able to get free of them, and that, though he had been her boyfriend (novio) in the past, he had never had carnal relations with her. His story was corroborated by a witness who had seen the events at a distance of 25 meters. Doubts expressed by the prosecutor and the judge indicated that they thought the case was an instance of the generic story of the fallen woman engaged in entrapping a young man into marrying her. That her mother rather than her father stood up for her may also have shaped events (most likely, her mother was either widowed or unmarried, and gossip about her virtue may have negatively affected her daughter's reputation). The outcome of the case did not look promising for the young woman. She withdrew her querella, though it is possible that she received some compensation from the youth's family (if he had indeed got her pregnant some years before, as she alleged).

If it were functioning as it should, law would allow the less powerful a venue in which to defend themselves against the abuses of caciques or the aggression of the rich. At times, cases were brought by women who had considerably less power than the accused party. For example, on September 8, 1924, a widowed woman brought an accusation of estupro against her daughter's boss's son. Her fifteen-year-old daughter, María, had been working as a servant in "Sr. Pedro's" home for over a year. One night while María was sleeping in the same room as Sr. Pedro's offspring, the son got into her bed and took advantage of her without her consent. He continued to do this every night, but he made her no promises and she did not know if the family was ever aware of his behavior. The son denied everything. (Note that, according to the provisions of the 1871 Penal Code, this should have been classified as a case of rape. By classifying it as estupro, judicial personnel left an opening for a local resolution of the conflict.) Sr. Pedro, who was responsible for the safety of Maria's virtue as a servant in his home, decided to "come to an arrangement" with her mother, paying her the sum of 200 pesos—a huge amount of money in those days, when workers at the local mine made only 2 or 3 pesos per day.

Cases of estupro and rapto are more common than cases of violación in the archive of the local court. Estupro and rapto were crimes prosecuted only at the behest of the offended party or his/her representative, but this was not the case with violación. Classifying sexual acts negatively sanctioned by the local community as crimes that could only be prosecuted via a formal complaint brought by the victim or her representatives allowed the community greater flexibility in its use of the judicial system for cleansing family and personal honor. A legal penalty was not imposed in most cases of estupro, rapto, or *adulterio*. Instead, the court was one venue among others (including interpersonal violence) for conflict resolution. More frequently than not, parties to such cases came to an agreement that they formally communicated to the judge, and the accuser withdrew her or his complaint.

Local justice was more remedial and conciliatory than punitive. Justice, if it could be achieved, was the outcome of a process of negotiation in which local values and social relations came into play. For example, in the case of Teresa, the standing of her father had an impact on the way the case was conducted. The court did not investigate Jesús's insinuations about the young woman's illegitimacy, her father's adultery, or her mother's sexual waywardness. Nor did the court order a physical examination—an affront to her pudor—or bring in witnesses to testify about her sexual reputation. By countering the usual strategy of men accused of sexual offenses—namely, to allege that there was gossip about the woman's virtue—judicial personnel were more able to pressure Jesús to "do the right thing."

Conclusion

The relation between gossip and law merits more exploration than it has received. Introducing the concept of interrelated speech genres has allowed me not only to characterize legal discourse with some precision but also to examine how it is linked to gossip. Although, putatively, opposed discourses, law and gossip are articulated in a number of ways. Gossip can feed into legal cases; it can "become part of the legal record through insinuation" (Cloete 2003, 406; Gutiérrez 1991). However, a legal case, if satisfactorily resolved, can also put an end to gossip, and sometimes this was overtly stated as a reason for going to court.

Moreover, a legal verdict can be kinder than the verdict of gossip. For example, in the case of Teresa and Jesús, gossip may well have assigned some responsibility to her or to her family for her disgrace. (Was she really a virtuous young woman or did she take after her mother? Did her family guard her adequately? Why did her aunt and father not put a stop to Jesús's importunities?). Significantly, local judges, in their role as conciliators, could sometimes accomplish what the sanctions of gossip had failed to do: pressure men to marry women of good repute with whom they had had amorous relations, or lead wayward spouses to return home. But not all men were willing to subject themselves to the privations and discipline it took to be an *hombre de bien*; some were happy to live on the edge of the law and of community norms, using violence to earn fear if not respect.

Namiquipan legal ideology made the court a legitimate venue for conflict resolution, a place where honor could be cleansed and wrongdoing avenged, where harm might be compensated for, where dirt could be shed, where people could be successfully pressured to conform to the categorical order of gender, sexuality, and family. Sensemaking in legal cases rested not only on the evidence but also on how it was presented and interpreted. As I have argued, generic cultural narratives of love, sex, and gender were key to constructing the plausibility of fractured personal stories and, hence, had a bearing on legal process.

"The institution of an identity," Pierre Bourdieu (1991, 120) comments, "is the imposition of a name, i.e. of a social essence. To institute, to assign an essence . . . is to impose a right to be that is an obligation." As rites of institution, cases of estupro and rapto ratified categorical distinctions between "marriageable" and "unmarriageable" women, on the one hand, and between "seducers" and honest men on the other, locating the parties to the case in relation to a gendered and sexualized system of classification, and obliging them to behave accordingly. Yet, though it ratified the categorical order, legal practice also allowed women to renegotiate their locations relative to that order. Use of legal discourse by Namiquipan women had the potential not only to render their claims both intelligible and legitimate, but also to oblige men to respond to them. Law is not only a tool of domination but also a means for the less powerful to assert rights and claims, however limited, over the more powerful.

Although a state institution, law operates in various fields of action (such as the local court in Namiquipa). Genre conventions are re-accented in each field, and even in particular cases, due to a myriad of factors, including the distribution of symbolic, social, economic, political, and cultural capital among the actors involved. The legal ideologies in different fields also have a role in this process of re-accentuation. Perhaps the hegemony of law depends on the very possibility of its re-accentuation within a set of constraints; it is this possibility that allows law to be appropriated by a range of social groups situated in distinct social and historical contexts.

NOTES

1. Archivo del Juzgado Menor de Namiquipa (AJMN), "Civil promovido por X" (June 1, 1925). I use pseudonyms when discussing this and all subsequent cases, to protect the identities of those involved.

2. The 1871 Penal Code was adopted with almost no modification by most states. A revised version was in force until 1929 (Porte Petit Candaudap 1972, 59).

3. Código Penal paral el Distrito Federal y Territorio de la Baja California sobre Delitos del Fuero Común, y para toda la República sobre Delitos contra la Federación, 1871 (CC 1871), Título Sexto: Delitos contra el orden de las familias, la moral pública ó las buenas costumbres.

4. CC 1871, arts. 793–794.

5. CC 1871, art. 793.

6. AJMN, "Criminal por Estupro Contra de X." The case begins on May 31, 1926, and is resolved by June 12.

7. Significantly, French (1994), in his paper on cases of estupro and rapto in the Hidalgo district of Chihuahua during the Porfiriato and the Revolution, comments that some cases were dismissed when the person who initiated the proceedings could not legally prove parenthood or guardianship of the offended woman.

8. My thanks to his relatives in Sonora who let us see his diary.

9. The overview offered here is based on notes and photocopies of about fifteen cases. The archive had been partially destroyed, so I have no idea of the total number of complaints brought or actually investigated during these decades.

10. AJMN, "Criminal Contra X Promovido Por Y" (February 6, 1908). In this case, no crime is identified in the title of the case; the girl's father alleged that she was "*violada a la fuerza* [violated by force]" but the case was never classified as one of rape.

11. AJMN, "Criminal por Estupro contra de X" (October 4, 1926).

2

Sins, Abnormalities, and Rights

Gender and Sexuality in Mexican Penal Codes

IVONNE SZASZ

This chapter examines the gender constructions present in the normative discourse that defines which sexual practices are considered crimes in Mexico. The goal is to contribute to debates about the right to make decisions about one's own body and about gender equity.

The chapter begins with a brief review of crimes against individuals' sexual freedoms, examining in detail the definitions of some crimes characterized not as affronts against those liberties but as crimes against family order (including estupro, consensual sexual intercourse with an honest woman under the age of eighteen or seventeen; rapto, kidnapping with the intention to have sexual intercourse and/or to marry; and adultery). The discussion continues with a critical analysis of these penal norms from a gendered perspective, comparing the current legislation in Mexico's thirty-one states and in the Federal District and Federal Penal Codes. This analysis permits inferences about social constructions of feminine and masculine identities, social relations between men and women, and sexuality—constructions that underpin the formulations of criminal law in contemporary Mexico. The goal is to identify problematic aspects of these formulations, and the tensions that exist between legislators' constructions and the visions of the women's movement and of gender studies. Before turning to an examination of legal texts, however, the chapter briefly overviews international discourses on sexuality in order to situate the influence that these discourses have on formulations in Mexican penal codes.

Contemporary Discourses on Sexualities

The subject of sexuality emerged as a specific object of study and as an explicit topic in normative and public discourses in Western societies at the end of the nineteenth century. Since then, it has been considered an area of expertise in the clinical disciplines, including psychology, psychiatry, pedagogy, sexology, and medicine, that work with individuals. These disciplines have as their objective the study of forms of individual behavior considered dependent on the overall functioning of the mind or the biological systems (Bozon and Leridon 1993). For these schools of thought, individuals and sexual impulses exist prior to social order (Gagnon and Parker 1995).

This scientific discourse on sexuality is not totally separate from the religious ideas that preceded it—ideas still hegemonic in Latin America. Both Christian religions and Western medicine have viewed sexuality as a basic impulse that requires social controls, something that is different in men and women, and the appropriate expressions of which are sexual relations between adult men and adult women within the bonds of marriage. Positivist scientific discourse on this subject was viewed in Mexico as a liberating influence because it constituted a modernist reaction against traditional moralities. Traditional Catholic discourse characterizes nonprocreative sexual relations as sinful, considering that the carnal pleasure produced by sexual intercourse should not be sought as an end but rather as a means of procreation. Thus, Catholic discourse advises the moderation of pleasure and of the acts that lead to and accompany procreative intercourse; at the same time, it proscribes "perverse" (nonprocreative) forms of erotic pleasure (such as masturbation, bestiality, anal penetration, erotic activities with persons of the same sex, and coitus interruptus) and "lewd" fantasies or thoughts (Ortega Noriega 1988).

In contrast, positivist scientific thought has offered a different normative framework, one that considers erotic desires natural in all stages of life. It labels "normal" those heterosexual practices among adults (married, if possible) aimed toward erotic pleasure, whether or not they have procreation as the goal. This perspective assumes that science is capable of arriving at an impartial, universal notion of sexuality that, if known to and exercised by everyone, is capable of contributing to human well-being (Gagnon and Parker 1995).

Throughout the twentieth century, but especially in the post–World War II period, both traditional moralities and modern disciplines have presumed to offer legitimate understandings or "true discourses" on sexual and reproductive practices through such means as health care programs, policies concerning the human body, and normative systems. The "true discourses" of positivist scientific thought have intermingled with moralities on sexuality imparted by religious institutions. Although religious normative discourse has focused on prohibiting sexual practices that endangered the familial order or blocked procreation, scientific discourse has been more concerned with "deviant" erotic desires and adolescent sexuality.

The discourses on sexuality in feminist thought and in the critical social sciences recognize the historicity and the relational and cultural character both of sexual practices and of discourses about sexuality. From this perspective, to understand sexuality it is necessary to take into account class and gender relations and to consider the importance of cultures and forms of social control. Physiologically similar sexual acts can have different social and subjective meanings depending upon the historical period, cultural differences, and the way the acts are inserted in distinct social relations. Sexual acts do not carry any universal meaning, and the relation between acts and meanings is not fixed (Vance 1991). In this perspective on social matters, decontextualized individual behaviors do not exist. All action constitutes a social practice and is relational and historically produced. Practices and meanings—more than behaviors—are the object of study in the social sciences. Social contexts are not only socioeconomic in character, but are also historical, cultural, and discursive (Gagnon and Parker 1995; Vance 1991; Dowsett 2003).

A central characteristic of this discourse is its reflexive and critical quality. It questions false links established between actions and meanings, and between practices and identities. In particular, it challenges the presumed existence of an objective, value-free scientific discourse on sexuality. Instead, it argues that all discourse about sexualities is informed by values, and that all forms of categorizing or classifying sexualities are problematic and must be examined critically, especially when it is a matter of establishing dichotomous criteria of normality/abnormality.

From this perspective, normativities express relations that are historically and culturally specific, and they powerfully contribute to the social organization of sexualities. To the extent to which juridical norms are articulated in language, the examination of legal texts helps clarify the complexity of the links between power and meanings found in the formulation of norms making specific references to sexuality.

Rights Holders and Objects of Juridical Protection in Mexican Penal Legislation on Sexuality

The sexual interests protected by Mexico's federal and state penal codes differ.[1] Some actions are defined as crimes against persons' sexual freedom; other provisions protect the inexperience of minors and individuals considered "incapable." A third group of actions classified as crimes concern the familial order and sexual "correct customs" (*buenas costumbres*).

Offenses against the Freedom to Decide over One's Own Body

Among the penal code provisions that defend individuals' erotic freedom are those concerning the offenses of sexual violation (rape), sexual abuse, and sexual harassment. These are grouped in a section entitled crimes "*contra la libertad sexual*" ("against sexual freedom") or crimes "*contra la libertad y el normal desarrollo sexual (o psico-sexual)*" ("against the freedom and normal sexual [or pyscho-sexual] development" of individuals).[2]

In the case of these offenses, what is punishable is the attack on the freedom to decide about one's own body. Although the specific section that addresses these offenses varies from one federal or state penal code to another, references to sexual freedom predominate.[3] Such references to freedom constitute an achievement of the Mexican feminist movement, and a legal incorporation of advances in scientific thinking and international agreements on human rights and women's rights. In particular, the term "sexual freedom" was introduced into penal codes in response to proposals made by the feminist movement in 1990. Before that date, this section of the law was titled "Sexual Crimes" (Pérez Duarte y Noroña 2002).

In this section of Mexico's penal codes, what is being protected is consent and the freedom or will of a person to choose, accept, or decide. What is being punished is coercion and imposition. The defense of each person's right to decide about her or his own body and erotic desires constitutes a clear victory for the women's movement. The protection is specifically of individual liberties, not social customs, and it includes perspectives on gender relations that admit the possibility of erotic desires and sexual activity among women.

In the early 1990s the Mexican feminist movement, basing its position in international debates and agreements, won an increase in the penalties for rape. However, the feminist movement remains critical of the fact that marital rape is not expressly considered a crime, and that the penalties for rape are less when the assailant is the victim's spouse (Pérez Duarte y Noroña 2002). The absence of this explicit reference was the source of contradictory jurisprudence, with some judges ruling marital rape a crime and others not (Gallo Campos 2002). Nevertheless, one further achievement of feminist organizations is the initial movement toward classifying the circumstances under which marital rape occurs. Since 1997, the Federal Penal Code has specified that the penalty for rape applies in cases in which the victim of the violation is the assailant's wife or mistress (*concubina*).[4] Although the code does not establish a more severe penalty in such cases, and legal sanction depends upon the victim filing a formal complaint against her attacker, this provision is without doubt one of the most advanced provisions in Mexican law in relation to women's rights. It legally confirms an adult woman's freedom to decide over her own body even when her own spouse is who violates that freedom, thus abolishing women's so-called marital duty implicit in the marriage contract. The example set by the Federal Penal Code was followed in the penal codes of Coahuila (art. 385), Guanajuato (art. 183), Querétaro (art. 164), and San Luis Potosí (art. 151).

Another of the feminist movement's accomplishments concerning the right to decide over one's own body involves the recent inclusion of the crime of sexual harassment in more than half of state penal codes.[5] Most novel is the idea that relationships involve hierarchy and subordination, thus giving explicit recognition to the view that social relations generate inequalities in erotic interactions among adults. Legislators thereby recognized that, in addition to such factors as coercion, sexual inexperience, or being under the legal age for informed consent, the vulnerability of one of the parties in an erotic interchange can be the product of social relations. Criminal law, then, protects not only the right not to be violated, but also the right not to be pressured in erotic terms when in a position of social subordination.

The confirmation of this type of rights establishes a very important principle of equity in erotic interchanges. It constitutes the beginning of the defense of freedom to decide over one's own body in contexts of social inequality and gender asymmetries. In this sense, this development broadly coincides with the goals of movements for women's human rights.

Offenses against Minors and "Incapable" Individuals

The section of Mexican penal codes that addresses crimes against sexual freedom and "normal" pyschosexual development includes other kinds of offenses in which the right being protected is sexual security (something that is occasionally called "sexual inexperience"). Sexual security refers primarily to prepubescent individuals or to minors in general (González de la Vega 1998). Crimes against sexual security include consensual intercourse with minors or with persons incapable of exercising free will (*violación equiparada*) and sexual intercourse with anyone under the legal age for informed consent. These crimes involve introducing for lascivious purposes either the penis or another object into the vagina or anus of a prepubescent minor or a person deemed incapable of exercising free will. In these cases, even if there is nominal consent, the law's position is that consent is called into question by the victim's age or incapacity. One of the most problematic issues in the definition of this crime is imprecision regarding the age at which a minor can validly give her or his consent. Some state codes set fourteen years as the minimum age for informed consent (Chihuahua, Durango, Veracruz); the Nayarit code sets the age at thirteen years. However, the Federal Penal Code and the majority of state codes (Aguascalientes, Baja California Sur, Campeche, Coahuila, Colima, the Federal District, Guerrero, Hidalgo, México, Morelos, Oaxaca, Puebla, San Luis Potosí, Sinaloa, Sonora, Tamaulipas, Yucatán, Zacatecas) set twelve years as the minimum age for informed consent. Still other state codes (Guanajuato, Jalisco, Querétaro, Quintana Roo, Tlaxcala) speak of "prepubescent persons" without defining the age at all.

The age at which a person acquires freedom to decide about the use of the erotic potentialities of her or his own body should be related to the age at which individuals can enter into marriage. In Mexican penal codes, ideas about the age at which one can exercise one's own will with regard to bodily pleasures are linked to the term "normal pyschosexual development," introduced in 1991.

This expression reveals the predominance of medical–scientific conceptions of sexual normality, abnormality, and perversion. Nevertheless, the term is also closely related to religious conceptions that proscribe nonprocreative female sexuality. Mexican penal codes equate voluntary sexual activities by those under the age of fourteen years with the ideas of abnormality, corruption, or perversion. The penologist Francisco González de la Vega proposes that the idea of abnormality in this context be based upon the psychological or physiological limitations of minors. Thus, their young age supposedly prevents them from understanding (or causes them to ignore in rational terms) the meaning, implications, and consequences of sexual practices. At the same time, minors have supposedly not yet reached a stage of physiological development at which the "excretive sexual function of the genital glands" occurs (González de la Vega 1998, 351–352). The same author adds that premature sexual activity ("prematurity") can cause "psycho-physiological harm" and "moral degradation" by giving a child "irregular fixations or aberrant displacements of the sexual instinct" (ibid., 355).

The idea of "normal" sexual development presumes that those who initiate erotic bodily practices "prematurely" (that is, before the development of certain physiological signs) have a "development" other than "normal." Thus, the sexual security of minors consists of protecting them against premature sexual practices, not because these violate their freedom but because the practices endanger sexual "normality." The penal code of Tamaulipas establishes as an aggravating circumstance in such crimes "copulation that is against the natural order" (art. 277). Although this formulation is an exception (the Tamaulipas code is the only state law to include it), it reaffirms the idea of some natural order in sexuality—and the view that anything that varies from this is against nature, abnormal, corrupt, or perverse.

The principal tension related to the description of this crime concerns its consistency with civil legislation on the age at which minors can give their consent to contract marriage. The civil codes of twenty-four Mexican states set the legal age for marriage at fourteen years for women and sixteen years for men. However, a number of state codes recognize exceptions in which a judge can authorize marriage of young women under the age of fourteen years.[6] Thus, the marriage contract or judicial authorization suddenly transforms the "development" or "prematurity" of girls, who automatically acquire the biological or psychological maturity or the experience necessary to consent to sexual acts. At the same time, by virtue of the act of marrying them, males cease to cause girls "psycho-physiological damage," because they no longer endanger their sexual "normality"—and thus having sexual relations with them is no longer perverse, corrupting, or criminal. If sexual activities with underage girls occur within marriage, there is thus no offense against their freedom, and their biological "immaturity" disappears.

Offenses against the Family's Right to Control the Sexuality of Young Women

It is in the classification of offenses against the family order that one sees with greatest clarity a differentiated social normativity regarding the desires and erotic practices of men and women; this is especially clear in the case of sexual kidnapping (rapto) and consensual sexual intercourse with an honest woman under a given age (eighteen or seventeen) (estupro).

In Mexican penal codes, the crime of estupro appears in the same section as offenses "against the sexual freedom and normal psychosexual development," against "security," or against "inexperience." It is a crime that can only be committed by men against women. Indeed, in the majority of state penal codes, estupro consists of "copulating with a chaste and honest woman older than twelve [or thirteen, or fourteen] years, and younger than eighteen [or seventeen], obtaining her consent by means of seduction or deceit."[7]

There is great variation among Mexican penal codes in the ages specified in cases of estupro. It is between fourteen and eighteen years of age in Chihuahua, Durango, and México; between twelve and eighteen years in the Federal Penal Code and in the codes of Campeche, the Federal District, Guerrero, Hidalgo, Michoacán, Morelos, Oaxaca, Puebla, Sinaloa, Tamaulipas, and Zacatecas; between twelve and seventeen years in Tabasco; between thirteen and eighteen years in Nuevo León; between fourteen and sixteen years in Veracruz; between puberty and seventeen years of age in Querétaro; and simply under the age of sixteen in Baja California Sur and Guanajuato, and under the age of eighteen in Colima, Jalisco, Nayarit, and Sonora. The penal codes of Tabasco (art. 153) and Morelos (art. 159) explicitly state that the woman has not "reached normal psychosexual development" because she is under the age of, respectively, seventeen or eighteen years.

However, this vision of women's sexual "normality" becomes problematic given that the age at which a woman achieves "natural maturity" appears to vary substantially more in criminal legislation than in biological terms—and, moreover, this is a view that only applies to women. In the majority of Mexican codes, the age at which an individual reaches "normal development" is eighteen years, and civil codes in Mexico authorize the marriage of young people much earlier. (As noted above, in the civil code in twenty-five states, women can marry at fourteen years of age, or, with judicial authorization, even before fourteen.) These contradictions between criminal and civil legislation make clear that, when Mexican penal codes use science-like language in an attempt to define a biological or psychological fundamental, in reality they are referring to a social situation and a moral order: the authorization given by parents or by society for a young woman to have voluntary sexual relations, an authorization acquired via marriage even among girls under the age of fourteen years.

González de la Vega (1998, 426) indicates that, under the age of eighteen years, the value of a woman's consent would be reduced because she lacks the experience or is insufficiently knowing to confront "life's problems," because she would have insufficient "somatic and psychic development," and because at that age she would "not understand the true meaning" of eroticism. The logical opposite would be that women, by marrying (even at fourteen years or less, by special judicial authorization) or by turning eighteen, automatically acquire those attributes—deviousness, experience, or bodily or psychic development—that provide mature judgment and an understanding of the "true" meaning of eroticism. On the other hand, men (who, according to legislators, cannot be victims of estupro) possess these attributes independently of age (or since puberty).

González de la Vega (1998, 369) argues that there is a familial and social interest in preserving full control over young women's erotic freedom because of the consequences that premarital sexual relations can have for them. These consequences include "the corruption of their manners" (which could lead them into sexual commerce), inappropriate social typing (being labeled an "easy" woman, which could affect their future possibilities of marriage), possible separation from family, and the risks of illegitimate maternity, abortion, or infanticide (see also Alonso, this volume). It is also implicit in this position that, in the case of women, the "corruption of manners" consists of sexual commerce, but in the case of underage males it involves homosexual practices, identified as "abnormal," aberrant, deviant, or perverted. "Normality" and "corruption," then, are different for women and men; only young women (not young men) must be "protected" from the exercise of their erotic freedom with persons of the other sex.

Another argument that permits one to demonstrate the fallacy of presumed biological normality is that sexual practices that do not include vaginal intercourse are not punished as estupro. Young women under the age of eighteen years would be considered sufficiently developed to decide whether to engage in erotic contact, with men or women of any age, without vaginal penetration (including oral and anal sex). Yet practices of this kind are not considered offenses against the women's "security" or psychosexual "normal development."[8] The security that is being protected is the possibility that young women can contract a socially meaningful marriage in the future.

One also sees the gender inequality in views of female sexuality that require that consent be obtained via seduction or deceit, and that the woman be chaste and honest.[9] The state of Jalisco's penal code defines chastity as "the attribute of a woman who maintains a conduct in sexual matters that accords with what is socially considered correct" (art. 174). González de la Vega himself (1998, 378) describes chastity as abstinence, and differentiates chastity from virginity, which is "vaginal purity" free from all sexual contact. However, he places the emphasis on inexperience because it is that lack of experience that makes young women "easy prey to criminal salacious activities" (ibid., 426). To him, the crime of estupro occurs at the moment that the penis is introduced into "the natural path or ideal vessel for venereal copulation." In his opinion, estupro is not committed in cases of anal penetration, because a young woman who accepts such "lubricious abnormality" lacks sexual honesty (ibid., 378), and sexual honesty requires—in addition to abstinence—"a materially and morally correct attitude," as defined by the general cultural norms of the time and place (ibid.).

While "chastity" alludes to abstinence or sexual inexperience, "honesty" refers more to a public attitude. Honest young women live in their homes; they avoid vices and worldly knowledge; they are hidden away. The penal code of Jalisco defines honesty as "referring to the reputation that a woman obtains by her good material and moral conduct with regard to the erotic" (art. 174). The definition of chastity and of honesty as exclusively female attributes is clear evidence of the presence of a double standard concerning the sexuality of men and women, as well as of the overlapping of moral judgments with the juridical principles in Mexican penal codes.

Among the examples of deceit contained in Mexican and Spanish jurisprudence González de la Vega (1998, 376) mentions are: a false promise of marriage that is offered formally and with apparent sincerity; a married man giving the impression that he is single and promising marriage; simulated marriage; and causing the young woman to believe that she will receive employment or other benefits if she agrees to have sexual relations with an influential male. Such deceit produces a state of error, confusion, or misunderstanding without which the young woman would not have consented to have sexual relations. It is clear that, here, "error" involves social error and not bodily practices. The error consists not in the woman's having sexual relations, but in her belief that such activity would lead to marriage or would bring a material benefit. Such expressions clearly contain the notion that erotic desires are absent in "chaste and honest" women, who only desire copulation so as to receive, in exchange, some benefit other than erotic enjoyment.

The crime of estupro is not prosecuted as a matter of official obligation; rather, prosecution occurs only in response to the filing of an official complaint by the victim, her parents, or her legal representatives. With the exception of the penal codes of four states (the Federal District, Morelos, San Luis Potosí, and Tabasco) and the Federal Penal Code, criminal prosecution ends if the aggrieved party marries the perpetrator. The fact that the crime can be pardoned by the marriage of the offender and the victim demonstrates that the object being protected by law is not the "security" or the psychological or biological "development" of the young woman, but rather her social possibilities of contracting marriage. Estupro is a transgression of the social order, not of an individual right. The rights holders can be the young woman, her parents, or her guardians, but that right ceases to exist if the woman marries the author of the crime. This characteristic clearly shows that it is not the young woman's "development" that is being protected, and that her "normality" consists of her being a correct part of a family-based social order (see also Alonso, this volume).

The protection of the familial and social order embodied in the classification of this crime seems completely removed from an affirmation of the sexual rights of women. The protection of very young individuals from the possible abuses that can result from their erotic inexperience should extend to both young women and young men, and it might be part of a definition of sexual harassment or of a right to the necessary social conditions that would permit young people to make free and informed decisions. Considering all the issues covered by the penal code section on offenses against sexual freedom, only in the crimes of rape, harassment, and abuse is there a convergence between penal legislation and the sexual rights of women. In these instances, the right corresponds only to the affected individual, and the object of protection is the freedom of personal choice. The legislative provisions on these matters clearly involve individual rights; they recognize that what is being protected is freedom of decision over one's own body.

In the case of estupro, however, the rights holders are sometimes the young woman's parents or legal representatives, and the object of juridical protection involves more the familial order than individual rights. That order seeks to ensure that young women only have sexual relations within the context of marriage, of a marriage proposal, or to obtain some benefit. This same order depicts as "dishonest" any female sexual activity oriented exclusively toward erotic pleasure. In contrast, it considers a woman "honest" if she seeks a material benefit in exchange for a coupling that she would not consent to without such a benefit.

This is an order that establishes a differentiated social normativity between men and women, based upon two biological assumptions: the assumption of the biopsychological immaturity of women under the age of eighteen years (or, in some states, seventeen years, sixteen years, or fifteen years) who are not married—and the contrary assumption that young women automatically acquire such maturity at marriage (and that it is legitimate for women to have sexual relations in exchange for benefits other than erotic pleasure), as well as the assumption that males "naturally" exercise sexuality beginning at puberty (unless of course those sexual activities involve other males). Moreover, this is an order that maintains reminiscences of a traditional Catholic morality that considered unclean and perverse women's erotic desires and pleasure when these were not strictly oriented toward procreation within the bonds of marriage (Ortega Noriega 1988). The fact that marriage is considered compensation for the social harm caused to an honest woman who has consented to sexual intercourse before eighteen (or seventeen) years of age and before marriage reaffirms the traditional notion that a woman's body belongs to society and to the family.

Sexual kidnapping (rapto) is a crime included in twenty-five Mexican penal codes. It is defined as stealing, holding, or seizing control of a person by means of force (physical or moral), or by seduction or deceit, for the purpose of satisfying some erotic desire, engaging in a sexual act, or for marriage.[10] Note that there is a presumed equivalence between the intention of engaging in sexual activity (or satisfying a desire) and the intention of marrying. This is a crime that can only be committed by males, and the victims can only be women. (The exception occurs in the penal code of Zacatecas, which establishes a small penalty if an adult woman kidnaps a man under eighteen years of age: art. 270.)

Rapto is an offense prosecuted only if there is a formal complaint filed by the victim or by her legal representatives. In all instances criminal action ceases when the kidnapper contracts marriage with the offended person. There is no minimum age set for the woman, in cases in which the crime is cancelled following marriage. Some codes increase the sanction if the woman is under a specified age (fourteen years in Puebla and fifteen years in Oaxaca), and one code (Chihuahua) only increases the criminal penalty if the woman is under fourteen years of age and "lacks the maturity needed to dispose freely of her sexual patrimony" (art. 250).

The characteristics of a crime that requires no corporal action—especially the references to "sexual patrimony" and the maturity needed to freely dispose of it, and the fact that the offense is extinguished by marriage—reveal once again that the protected object is a social order. This is consistent with the protection of young women's possibilities of contracting, or uniting in, marriage. The freedom to decide over one's body is not protected, except in the case of "holding by force"; rather, in the cases of seduction or deception, the goal is to prevent the young woman from losing her marriageable status. Single women possess a "sexual patrimony" based in their inexperience (their chastity, their honesty), but they would need to attain a state of maturity (acquired through marriage or through having reached a certain age) to freely dispose of that possession. Before attaining such maturity, it is the young woman's parents or legal representatives who can decide about (or defend) her "patrimony." If it is threatened, the disposition of a young woman's "sexual patrimony" is resolved—even before she achieves the maturity to dispose of it herself—by her marriage to the delinquent.

The reference to the sexual "desires" of the kidnapper, and the absence of any reference to the desires of the kidnap victim, are noteworthy. In some cases the criminal statutes speak of voluntarily "consenting" or "following" the kidnapper, but they do not use the word "desire." Once again, this is a clear allusion to the sexual desires of men and a clear attribution to women of sexual passivity.

More than affronts to the juridical order, a sexual kidnapping and estupro can consist of the voluntary actions of a young couple to have sexual relations or to secure consent to marry, a social practice known in Mexico as *robo de la novia* (D'Aubeterre Buznego 2000a). However, sexual kidnapping and estupro can also consist of a man's coercions to force a young woman to marry him or cohabit with him, or strategems undertaken by a young woman or her parents to pressure a young man (or the young couple) into marriage or cohabitation. A bad move involving any of the pieces in this kind of chess game can result in a lengthy jail sentence for the man, or the loss of the woman's "sexual patrimony" or prestige in the marriage market. If all works out, the game can end in a marriage that possibly neither the man nor the woman desires. All these social controls have little to do with women's rights or freedom to choose.

The Crime of Adultery

Adultery is another sexual practice designated, to protect the familial order, a criminal offense. Fourteen of Mexico's penal codes (the Federal Penal Code and state codes in Aguascalientes, Chihuahua, Coahuila, Durango, Hidalgo, Jalisco, México, Morelos, Oaxaca, San Luis Potosí, Tabasco, Tamaulipas, and Zacatecas) list adultery as a crime. Only two codes (the federal code and the state code in Oaxaca) include it in the section on crimes against sexual freedom and normal psychosexual development. In the rest, it is listed among offenses against the family, the familial order, the institution of marriage, or the sexual order. What makes adultery a crime in Mexico is not the sexual relationship but the public scandal. The crime is prosecuted when the offended spouse files a formal complaint, and the criminal action is dropped when the guilty party is pardoned. It is clear that the designation of this kind of activity as a criminal offense is beginning to disappear in Mexico, and that it refers to the social order and not to individual freedoms and rights.

In crimes of estupro, sexual kidnapping, and adultery, the juridical objects of protection are situated within the familial order. Rights are social, not individual. In the latter two cases, the location of these crimes in penal codes is precisely among offenses against the familial order. The continued presence of the crime of estupro in the section on offenses against sexual freedom—and, in some codes, the continued presence of sexual kidnapping and adultery in this section—are remnants of earlier eras in which the norms shaping penal codes focused on protecting patrimony and sought to prevent all forms of genital contact by women outside the bonds of marriage. Such remnants convey the need to debate whether erotic practices are of a public or private character, whether there exists a differentiated social normativity between men and women with regard to sexual freedom, and whether parents should control the right to the sexual "patrimony" of "honest" young women. The way these practices are criminalized is entirely unrelated to the feminist movement's contemporary goals concerning the sexual rights of women.

Finally, it is worth noting that Mexican penal legislation does not punish either the practice of sexual commerce or homosexual practices among adults.

The only references to these matters in the criminal codes appear in the section concerning crimes involving the corruption of minors, where it is a punishable offense to induce, facilitate, or oblige a minor to engage in sexual commerce or homosexual acts. In the case of pimping, it is not sexual commerce that is punishable; what is sanctioned, rather, is the exploitation of sexual commerce by someone other than the person who practices it.

The Secular State and the Separation between Moral and Juridical Norms

The principal contribution made by the preceding examination of crimes is to define the boundaries between the realm of moral norms (corresponding to individual consciences) and the realm of criminal laws (which establish limits necessary for the respect of other people's rights and the bases for social coexistence). Penal legislation should only protect those individual or collective juridical objects that, if harmed, endanger either individuals (their lives, freedom, or property) or the general social order. Their point of placement in penal codes shows that the criminal offenses examined above are considered among those in which infractions threaten individual freedoms, even though the content of penal provisions concerning estupro, sexual kidnapping, and adultery does not always safeguard such liberties. The formulation concerning these offenses is imprecise, and they constantly make reference to a moral order that, in a secular state, should be a matter of individual conscience and not the subject of penal legislation. Criminal law, which must be based upon a social consensus about an ethical minimum permitting social coexistence, should maintain its autonomy vis-à-vis religious norms and moralities, thus accepting the diversity of beliefs and opinions in such matters.

The ambiguities that Mexican criminal law presents in this regard reflect its origins. Latin American penal codes are based upon nineteenth-century codes influenced by the French tradition, which in turn were mainly based upon Roman law. Pre-Christian Roman law established penalties for those sexual practices that harmed patrimonial interests or, to a lesser degree, individual freedoms. For example, rape and violent kidnapping were punished as forms of coercion against individual will. However, other "sexual" offenses (such as sexual kidnapping with the consent of the woman, adultery by married women, and consensual sexual intercourse with a young woman under the legal age for informed consent) were punished as acts of theft committed against the male head of family, who was considered the owner of the sexual patrimony of the women and girls in his family group. Pederasty was also considered an offense of "male robbery" committed against the head of a family. The daily practices of societies organized around patriarchical families established clear differences between the erotic comportment after puberty of men and of unmarried women, permitting extramarital sexuality for the former and limiting the latter's sexuality to the familial sphere. The erotic faculties of dependents and of slaves of both sexes depended on the decisions of male heads of family (Ariès and Duby 1987).

Christian–Roman law emerged in the second century A.D. It was characterized by a confusion of secular legislation with Christian morality. From its origins, Christianity was an ascetic doctrine that sought to forbid erotic pleasure and that was oriented toward limiting all sexual practice to the marital sphere (Ariès and Duby 1987). The Christian ascetic paradigm signified a profound modification of criminal legislation concerning sexual practices. Its purpose was to punish extramarital erotic practices, which created confusion between sins involving lewdness and sexual crimes. This link between crime and sin meant that nonmatrimonial sexual practices were repressed with great severity, including by capital punishment (González de la Vega 1998; Ortega Noriega 1988).

Three traditions of criminal law emerged out of Christian–Roman law, all characterized by the intromission of penal laws into matters of individual morality. These traditions were the Germanic and Anglo-Saxon codes, the French codes and Latin American codes drawing on the French tradition, and the Iberian tradition. The Germanic and Anglo-Saxon codes protected very severely the institution of matrimony, establishing a more extensive range of punishable offenses and more severe penalties than did the other two traditions. For example, these codes criminalized homosexual practices, bestiality, and, in some cases, even cohabitation and simple fornication. Latin codes were more indulgent in terms of penalties, and they did not punish fornication. In turn, the Iberian tradition (which also directly influenced Mexican penal codes) was characterized by the defense of family patrimony found in Roman criminal law; offenses against the modesty or honesty of women were defined as crimes against the family, and the objective of penal norms was to protect a family's women from vices and worldly knowledge (González de la Vega 1998).

With the emergence of national states, from the nineteenth century onward, the tendency in Western societies has been the formation of secular states in which a clear distinction is drawn between moral norms and the realm of laws. Moralities are concerned with behaviors that are matters of individual conscience; penal legislation concerns itself with sexual practices only in exceptional circumstances. In a secular state, erotic conduct is a matter of individual conscience. The law intervenes residually in those instances in which individual freedoms are clearly harmed or when the life of the collectivity is endangered (González de la Vega 1998, 177, 179, 324). The individual and collective juridical objects that penal norms should protect in a secular state are the individual's freedom from violence, the incapacity of some persons to give valid consent, and serious offenses against the basic elements of social order. In defining the interests that require the protection of penal law, legislators in a secular state should bear in mind the cultural characteristics of the social context as a whole, thereby ensuring the minimum ethical consensus necessary for collective social life. As a general norm, criminal law in a secular state must be autonomous vis-à-vis religions, moralities, and individual consciences; sexual practices are only to be regulated by criminal legislation if they harm or seriously endanger the legitimate interests of another person or the bases of collective coexistence.

The content of Mexican penal codes has evolved over time, from a focus closely linked to the Iberian tradition, rooted in Roman and canonic law, and with an emphasis on the vigorous defense of the family and the sexual modesty of the family's female members, gradually toward efforts to distinguish between the realm of Catholicism and the realm of criminal law inserted in a secular tradition. These penal codes never criminalized sodomy or homosexual practices among men, unless they involved minors or provoked scandal, thus differing from the Germanic and Anglo-Saxon tradition. In general, Mexican codes have been indifferent to sexual "disorder" except when it offends public morality or "correct" customs. Sexual commerce has not been considered a criminal offense, but Mexican codes have sought to regulate associated practices (including pimping, the corruption of minors, scandals, and the transmission of illnesses by sexual means) that might do harm to society as a whole.

The tendencies observed in Mexican criminal law—especially the reforms introduced beginning in the 1990s on the basis of proposals from the feminist movement—point toward greater gender equity and better protection of individual freedoms in sexual matters, particularly in comparison with the penal codes in effect before 1990 (Pérez Duarte y Noroña 2002). Nevertheless, this chapter has shown, what still prevails in these codes is a biologic and universalist vision of sexual practices and a gendered vision that is discriminatory against women. Finally, this analysis provides a basis for reflecting upon the limited bases of scientific knowledge that have informed Mexican penal legislation, as well as the value of incorporating into the law recent advances in social theory and social research provided by feminist thought and critical social science.

Translated by Kevin J. Middlebrook.

NOTES

1. This analysis is based upon the author's review of the Federal Penal Code and the penal codes of Mexico's thirty-one states and Federal District that were in effect on October 26, 2003.

2. The term "normal psycho-sexual development" appeared in Mexican penal codes beginning in 1991 (*Diario Oficial de la Federación*, January 21, 1991). It reflects medical-scientific perspectives on sexuality that include ideas of "normality" and "abnormality," as well as the conviction that sexuality has universal and singular (unitary) meanings.

3. In the Federal Penal Code and that of the Federal District, and in the codes of the
    states of Aguascalientes, Campeche, Hidalgo, Morelos, Quintana Roo, San Luis Potosí,
    Sinaloa, and Tabasco, the section is titled "crimes against psychosexual [or sexual]
    liberty and normal development." In the states of Chihuahua, Coahuila, Colima,
    Durango, Jalisco, Michoacán, Querétaro, Tamaulipas, and Veracruz, the section is
    titled "crimes against sexual liberty and security [or inexperience]." In the states of
    Baja California Sur, Guanajuato, Guerrero, México, and Zacatecas, the section is titled
    "crimes against sexual liberty" or "crimes against sexual liberty and the integrity of
    the person," and in the states of Nayarit, Puebla, Sonora, Tlaxcala, and Yucatán, the
    old term "sexual crimes" is employed.

4. Art. 265 (bis), incorporated into what subsequently became the Federal Penal Code in
    December 1997 (*Diario Oficial de la Federación*, December 30, 1997).

5. Sexual harassment is regarded as a criminal offense in the codes of Aguascalientes, Baja
    California, Colima, Chiapas, Chihuahua, the Federal District, Guerrero, Hidalgo, Jalisco,
    México, Morelos, Nuevo León, Oaxaca, Sinaloa, Sonora, Yucatán, and Zacatecas.

6. These include the civil codes of Aguascalientes, Baja California, Campeche, Coahuila,
    Chiapas, Chihuahua, Durango, Guanajuato, México, Michoacán, Morelos, Nayarit,
    Nuevo León, Oaxaca, Querétaro, Quintana Roo, San Luis Potosí, Sonora, Tabasco,
    Tamaulipas, Tlaxcala, Veracruz, Yucatán, and Zacatecas.

7. This is the language employed in the penal codes of Baja California Sur, Campeche,
    Durango, Jalisco, México, Michoacán, Nayarit, Nuevo León, Oaxaca, Puebla, Queré-
    taro, Sinaloa, Sonora, and Veracruz.

8. Nevertheless, if the partner is above the legal age of consent, the young woman could
    be considered a victim of the crime of corrupting a minor (as could a young man of
    the same age).

9. Only one of Mexico's penal codes (Aguascalientes) requires that the woman be
    chaste; others (Colima, Sonora, Veracruz) simply mention that she should be honest.
    Nayarit's code presumes chastity and honesty unless there is evidence to the con-
    trary. Some codes (the Federal Penal Code and the codes in the Federal District,
    Tamaulipas, Yucatán, and Zacatecas) recognize a crime only in the case of trickery
    (*engaño*), but do not require that the case involve seduction, chastity, or honesty. The
    State of México's code requires seduction, chastity, and honesty, but does not refer to
    trickery. Others presume that seduction or trickery is involved if the young woman is
    under the age of fourteen (Puebla), fifteen (Hidalgo and Oaxaca), or sixteen (Colima
    and Sinaloa). Still others (Guerrero, Durango, Michoacán, and San Luis Potosí)
    require the presence of seduction or trickery, but not of chastity or honesty.

10. This, or similar, language appears in the penal codes of Aguascalientes, Baja California
    Sur, Campeche, Chiapas, Chihuahua, Coahuila, Colima, Durango, Hidalgo, Jalisco,
    México, Michoacán, Nayarit, Nuevo León, Oaxaca, Puebla, Querétaro, Quintana Roo,
    San Luis Potosí, Sinaloa, Sonora, Tabasco, Tamaulipas, Veracruz, and Zacatecas.

3

The Realm outside the Law

Transvestite Sex Work in Xalapa, Veracruz

ROSÍO CÓRDOVA PLAZA

In this chapter, I examine the ways in which laws fail to recognize the rights of transvestite sex workers in Xalapa, Veracruz. On the one hand, the normative model of sexuality inherent in the laws is based on dichotomized categories linked to gender. In these laws, the gender system is presented as consisting of two mutually exclusive categories (women and men), often with complementary roles. Transvestites (and all persons who do not conform to an exclusively heterosexual model of sexual orientation) fall outside the dichotomized vision of society found in most Veracruz state laws. On the other hand, although sex work is not illegal in Mexico, the lack of up-to-date legislation regulating the trade leaves sex workers unprotected with regard to their rights and obligations as workers. Moreover, the existing laws on prostitution, procurement (pimping, on which see also Szasz, this volume), and child prostitution indirectly criminalize commercial sex work. Thus, transvestite sex workers' rights remain doubly unprotected by Veracruz state legislation.

The ethnographic data presented here shows that transvestite sex work is widely understood as something practiced by an abnormal, perverse male who assigns himself a gender that is not his, takes a subordinate position that does not belong to him, and engages in an activity associated with crime and vice. This social perception makes transvestites vulnerable to human rights abuses. Activists have claimed that abuses cannot be fought without changing existing legislation. Legal recognition of a variety of sexual orientations is a first (although not a sufficient) step to help transvestites and activists fight against ideas that feed into the social imaginary on homosexuality and transvestism—ideas such as abnormality, perversion, and dangerousness. Legal recognition of commercial sex workers could help dispel myths surrounding the perception of sexual services as a dishonorable activity linked to crime and addiction to alcohol and drugs, and provide tools to protect these individuals from the violence they are often subjected to.

The fieldwork presented in this chapter was gathered as part of a broader anthropological study of male sex work in the city of Xalapa, carried out over periods between the years 2000 and 2003. In the course of the research, I conducted field observation as well as countless nonrecorded conversations and eleven in-depth interviews with transgendered sex workers (known as transvestites or *vestidas*), and two interviews with consumers of their services.[1]

Transgendered Individuals and the Law

The Mexican Constitution fails to recognize alternative sexual orientations in general and transgendered individuals in particular. Article 1 states clearly that no one may suffer discrimination for any reason: "All discrimination motivated by ethnic or national origin, gender, age, ability, social condition, health conditions, religion, opinions, preferences, or marital status is prohibited, as is any other discrimination that harms human dignity and aims to cancel or diminish the rights and freedoms of persons."[2] However, the Constitution does not make explicit reference to sexual orientation with regard to rights and obligations in any of its first twenty-nine articles, contained in its section on individual guarantees (Pérez Contreras 2000, 62), and therefore remains largely underpinned by dichotomized, essentialist concepts of gender and by a reductionist view of the type of association that can happen between and within genders. For example, since 1974, Article 4 has stated: "Men and women are equal before the law. The law will protect the organization and development of the family." In this statement of principle, there is no room for diversified gender identities, either transgendered or transsexual, nor does the article cover couple relationships other than those between a man and a woman for the purpose of forming a family.

Some recent legal reforms are more progressive. In 2003, a new Federal Law to Prevent and Eliminate Discrimination listed sexual preference as one of the grounds on which discrimination was to be discouraged in a wide range of public and private arenas.[3] The new law prohibits "practicing or promoting physical or psychological abuse on the basis of physical appearance, manner of dressing, speaking, or gesturing, or for the public presentation of one's sexual preference."[4]

Some state-level legislation is also picking up on the theme of discrimination, and making it a criminal offense. For example, in 1999 the Penal Code of the Federal District included a new article, "Crimes against the Dignity of People." This article established penalties (prison terms of one to three years, or mandatory community service) for anyone found guilty of discrimination on the basis of age, gender, pregnancy, marital status, race, language, religion, ideology, sexual orientation, skin color, nationality, place of origin or social position, kind of employment or profession, economic position, physical characteristics, incapacity, or state of health (*Gaceta Oficial del Distrito Federal,* September 17, 1999). The section specifically prohibited actions provoking or inciting hatred or violence;

the exercise of professional, commercial, or entrepreneurial activities in such a way as to deny a service or a benefit to anyone with a right to such services or benefits; actions that offend or exclude any person, or group of persons, so as to cause material or moral damage; and actions that deny or restrict a person's labor rights.[5] Veracruz legislators followed suit in a new penal code enacted in 2003; in the section "Discrimination against Persons," Article 196 imposes sanctions (including prison terms) against various forms of discrimination in precisely the same language adopted by the Federal District Legislative Assembly.[6]

Federal District legislators also took an important step when they reformed the Penal Code's chapter "Corruption of Minors," eliminating earlier associations between the corruption of minors and homosexuality (Pérez Contreras 2000, 61). In Veracruz, however, laws still discriminate indirectly on the basis of sexual orientation. For example, the 1998 State of Veracruz Law of Social Assistance and Protection of Boys and Girls prohibits the incarceration of juvenile delinquents. Instead, the legislature created centers of social adaptation for boys and girls. The law stipulates that these centers should be run by a director who must be a Mexican national without a criminal record and "preferably married with children."[7] By focusing on the director's marital status (and not on his or her professional training and experience), the legislature is once again equating the nonheterosexual individual with depravity.

Sex Workers and the Law

Law regarding commercial sex work in Mexico must be understood in historical context. Basing his action on the idea that government had to develop hygienic measures to protect society from mostly incurable sexually transmitted diseases, Maximilian I (emperor of Mexico from 1864 to 1867) began what would become a series of decrees meant to regulate prostitution (Núñez Becerra 2002). In the twentieth century, the most important decree regulating prostitution was Mexico City's 1926 Reglamento para el Ejercicio de la Prostitución (Regulatory Law for the Practice of Prostitution). Katherine E. Bliss (2001, 2–3) argues that the law was ambiguous in its attitude toward prostitution:

> The registration, inspection, and surveillance of sexually active prostitutes was based on the modern science of hygiene, but the Reglamento's spirit of tolerating male sexual promiscuity and continuing disease among a group of "deviant" women resonated with older Catholic beliefs that prostitution, although a sin, was also a "necessary evil" that could prevent greater problems like rape or seduction from threatening the moral order.

The Federal District law was suspended in 1940, but two years later the state of Veracruz issued its 1942 Law on Prostitution and Social Prophylaxis. This law expects the state to "resolve the sexual problem in an integrated manner," and regulates activities related directly or indirectly to sexual commerce.[8] For example, it regulates "houses of assignation," "zones of tolerance," and "prostitutes" (*meretrices*).[9] Prostitution may be carried out only in precincts located in the zones of tolerance, to be demarcated by the state's directorate of public health on municipal or state-owned land and outside the city perimeter, by common agreement with the political authorities of each locality.[10] The houses should be monitored according to the Sanitary Code, and their interiors should not be visible from neighboring houses or from the street; at the same time, the houses were to maintain complete orderliness and discretion, so the sale and consumption of alcohol, games of chance, dancing and musical instruments, and the consumption of drugs were all to be prohibited.[11]

This state law reproduces the rigid, pathologizing models of gender and sex work still dominant today. One can draw attention to several points in this respect: first, the idea that sexuality is not only a problem of public interest to be solved but is also a dirty activity, susceptible to medical and social pathologies from which the rest of society has to be safeguarded by isolating and concealing it; second, the gender bias that assumes that the subject of sexual services is always a woman, never a man; third, the class bias that supposes that this activity is carried out by poor women, since high-class prostitution, not being restricted to the "zones of tolerance," is not subject to the mandates of this law; fourth, the lack of recognition of a visible mode of prostitution carried out in the streets, which takes place in the most central areas of the city; fifth, the association of prostitution with other "dangerous vices" such as drinking and gaming; and sixth, the notion of prostitution as a dishonest activity proscribed by society.

This last point is made clearly in Article 30 of the 1942 law, instructing the director of health to investigate the kinds of activity that may be carried out by individual prostitutes, "so that, as particular industries and sources of work are established by the state, it will be those [women] who are called upon for preference to work in those industries, in order to remove them from the kind of life into which they have fallen and reintegrate them into the bosom of society by means of honest toil."[12]

The implementation of this law depends on the individual municipal governments. Although municipal authorities established zones of tolerance in the city of Veracruz (and presently continue to suggest possible variants to the idea of special zones for prostitutes—often promoted by the prostitutes themselves), municipal authorities in the city of Xalapa did not (*Diario de Xalapa*, March 1, 2005; San Martín 2003).

Many moral connotations found in the 1942 Law on Prostitution and Social Prophylaxis are reproduced in more current legislation. In the 2003 Penal Code of the State of Veracruz, for example, outrages to public morals (including obscene images or displays), the corruption of minors and the disabled, and procuring are punishable by a prison sentence. The code also sanctions child pornography and trafficking in persons. What is penalized are exploitation and obtaining money from trade using the bodies of third persons (not one's own), and possessing or administering meeting places where prostitution may be practiced—independently of whether or not benefit is gained from the product of the sexual trade of others. The text of the code states that: "sanctions will be applied . . . against anyone who . . . induces a person to use their body for sexual trade or facilitates the means for this," but it does not mention the profit motive.[13]

Similarly, the 2004 Edict of Policing and Government (Bando de Policía y Gobierno) issued by the city council of Xalapa revokes the licenses of establishments where procuring, the use of pornography, child prostitution, or the use of children in sexual shows is practiced, and obliges the owner to advise the authorities if such activities are carried out either inside the premises or outside and adjacent to them.[14] It also outlaws: the enticement of minors or disabled people to carry out sexual acts or to prostitute themselves; immoral acts inside vehicles in public places; obscene acts of exhibitionism in public places, green spaces, wasteland, and performance spaces; and the trade in pornography.[15]

Although human rights activists fully support protections for minors, there are several legal arguments made against the way these regulations are formulated. First, they conflate the protection of minors and the disabled with those of adult commercial sex workers, reinforcing the sex workers' status as victims rather than giving them the legal status required for them to negotiate better working conditions and rights. Second, the idea of special zones of tolerance indirectly characterizes commercial sex work as immoral and dangerous, not for male and female sex workers but for society. Legalization would, on the contrary, mean considering sexual services as an ordinary job, governed by the rules of the market and subject to labor legislation (Brants 1998, 622–623). Indeed, in 1998, the International Labor Organization sponsored a study recommending governments to include commercial sex work in labor legislation (Lim 1988).

Article 5 of the Mexican Constitution already establishes that "no one can be prevented from practicing the profession, business, or job that he wishes, so long as the activity in question is not proscribed." Activists have suggested reforming the Federal Labor Law to include, in its section on service providers, the figure of the male and female commercial sex worker defined as "the individual who provides other individuals accidental, occasional, or regular sexual services through commercial establishments, which must provide a work contract for the service provider because a worker–employer relationship has been established and must therefore be regulated by the Federal Labor Law" (Madrid Romero 2002, 237).

Conceptions of Abnormality, Perversion, and Dangerousness

Legal discrimination on the basis of sexual orientation is congruent with many people's perceptions (including those of transvestites themselves) about sexual orientations other than heterosexuality as abnormal, perverse, and dangerous. On the one hand, effeminacy—and chiefly its most conspicuous modality, embodied in transvestism—is widely perceived as a danger to social order because it blurs the boundaries between genders, transgresses corporal limits, and introduces an internal contradiction by denying the basic postulates of the gender model (see Douglas 1966, 121–122). But, on the other hand, it also constitutes the condition for the system's survival, in the sense that it sums up all that is undesirable, dishonest, and punishable and symbolizes that which society rejects. Hence it is circumscribed in niches of stigmatization and high social vulnerability, such as prostitution.

Male sex work involves different forms of transgression against the dominant model of sexuality—heterosexual, based on romantic love, with bodily practices that are exclusive and hierarchic—and such transgression situates it at the margins of the margins: sex is bought and sold; the uses of the body overlap; hierarchies dissolve; identities invent other points of anchorage (Córdova Plaza 2005; Prieur 1998). If we add to this the connection between sex work and criminality, addictions, and the violence of the milieu in which sex workers lead their lives, we can understand the condition of social pariah to which the rest of society consigns them.

In the city of Xalapa, it is common to find that the popular sectors feel that homosexuality is a "sickness" with a cause that is vague and imprecise, or a problem of birth (for instance, the result of the child's having been conceived while the mother was menstruating). Some people even think that homosexuality could come from having been born under the *luna tierna*—during the first quarter of the moon—in the case of men, or under the *luna recia*—the last quarter—in the case of women. However, most of the interviewees give nonspecific explanations of their homosexual orientation, or they limit themselves to saying "it was God's will."[16] In this region, popular beliefs include the idea that it is possible to detect an inclination toward persons of the same sex from a very early age in boys, when an infant appears effeminate or excessively delicate. Girls, on the other hand, can enjoy rough games without this being taken as evidence of a future tendency to be "dykes." In any case, the roots of homosexuality are considered either congenital or the result of some "error," "problem," or "sickness" that affects the person's "nature" from birth. The dichotomous, excluding model of the anatomical sexes (Laqueur 1990) is affected at some moment in the process of gestation, through the influence of internal and/or external factors that sometimes can be identified and sometimes appear incomprehensible. As some transvestites remark:

> Well, they inject lots of hormones into chickens. So when the woman is pregnant she eats lots of chicken, and then she takes in this hormonal substance and that's how we come out [homosexual]. (Pretelín 2002, 51, citing interview with Claudia)

I think it's wrong, but I can't see any solution for it. God just made us like this and we have to accept how we are—what else can we do? My brothers used to say to me, "Why are you like that?" I was always discreet, so that they'd never realize. So they thought that when I was fifteen, sixteen, I became like this, but no. And later my brothers would say, "He got like this because he was corrupted." But no, it wasn't like that with me. (Yesenia, 24)

The outcome is a manifestation of the culturally assigned traits considered characteristic of one gender in a body whose dominant basic attributes are its conceptual opposite. But, on the other hand, there are also social or environmental factors in the popular etiology of homosexuality.

With me it's hormonal. There are people who are changed because of rape, because of their family, because they grow up in a home environment full of women, or of course because their parents only had boys and then they wanted a girl, so they treated them like girls. I realized it when I was in primary school, but I kept quiet about it at home because I was confused—you say to yourself, "what's this, what's happening to me?" So I tried to keep up appearances as far as I could. I didn't declare myself a homosexual until high school. I thought, "I want to lead my life and not be frustrated." So I came out, as we say. (La Güicha, 33)

The cultural protocols that underpin the binary anatomy-based system of gender allow for an intelligible explanation of homosexual orientation, encouraging a notion of "abnormality"—"abnormality" produced by biological or social circumstances, but beyond the will of the subject and manifesting itself both in erotic desire for individuals of the same sex and in a need to assume or affirm a different gender identity.

Because sexuality is an area inextricably bound up with power (Foucault 1978; Wrinkler 1990; Weeks 1986), where control mechanisms operate so as to obtain the subjects' adhesion to the prevailing social order (Foucault 1977), those who do not bow to its dictates are often the targets of various kinds of violence (Wilets 1997, 990). The idea of *abnormality* tends to give rise to an idea that links nonconformity with gender imperatives to violation not only of the laws of nature but also of social norms, and assumes that the given nonconformity is a perverse, incorrigible pathology. Sexual deviance, therefore, sums up the essential problem of anomaly, shaping subjects' perceptions of the transgressive character of their own experience. Some interviewees affirm this:

I believe in God and I know it's going against . . . know I'm going against him. . . . I'm going against everything (Viridiana, 21).

I know I'm not a normal person . . . but I'm not mad, I'm not crazy. (Yesenia, 24)

Homophobia, understood as fear or hatred of homosexuals and homosexuality, is accepted as the principal tool of control from the early stages of the process of socialization. Plummer (2001, 68) has studied the role played from infancy onward by homophobic expressions among peer groups in obtaining the subjects' adhesion to the norms of "correct" masculinity by demonizing deviations from stereotypical masculine behavior. Homophobia is a complex phenomenon that divides "real men" from "the others," the "abnormals," or the "deviants." All the subjects of this study affirmed that they had suffered conflict in the family or had been subjected to some kind of violence in adolescence or even earlier because of their sexual orientation, and in most cases this reinforced their feelings of abnormality:

> Ever since primary school my homosexual inclinations were obvious. And, well, to be honest, it embarrassed me a bit and started to make me feel reluctant to keep going to school, frankly . . . because the kids laughed at me, you know. There's never any shortage of people getting at you. (Bella, 25)

> I was scared of my family and even more so of my brother. When they found out, there was a huge row and, you know, it's even worse on the farm (*rancho*). My brother beat me up over and over again because he wanted me to change. He said he didn't want a faggot (*puto*) in the family. So I started to live an awful life. I didn't care about criticism, about people pointing at me, about what society thought. The hardest thing was that, instead of giving me moral support, my own family rejected me, because [they said] I was a disgrace to the family. (Jade, 34)

This violence can also be seen in the families' efforts to "correct" the interviewees and try to channel them in the "normal" direction of heterosexuality. The bosom of the family turns into a place where, because it is private, hostility can be hidden and aggression carried out with impunity (Wilets 1997). Hostility is disguised as concern or worry:

> I tried to please the family, to be a normal person, I did all I could to make them happy, to make them accept me. My brothers took me to bars where there were women. But I was just going 'round there like a dyke dressed as a man, trying to pretend to be what I wasn't and feeling uncomfortable, when what I wanted was to be an attractive woman, to look pretty. So that I'd change, my brother paid for me to go with prostitutes, and I'd say "What am I going to do with her? Make tortillas?[17] No way, I'm a woman!" What I had to do was to come clean with the girl, say, "Look, you know, I'm gay, but do me a favor, let's stay here a bit talking, you'll get paid, and you do me the favor of telling them I've been with you." (Mireya, 27)

The first attempts to invert assigned gender roles, conspicuous effeminacy, and sexual desire for persons of the same sex led most of the interviewees to leave home to avoid family pressures:

> I used to steal my sisters' makeup. I liked to do myself up the way I am now, right? That's how I feel: like a woman. Always trying to imitate them. Right from the start I felt like a woman. I liked putting on my sisters' dresses, because I wanted to be one of them. But I did it in secret because my family were very *machista* and I was scared. When they found out that I was like this, I started to drink, and in the heat of the drink I plucked up my courage and was open about it. I thought, "Why should I hide who I am? If I accept myself, what's it matter what other people say?" The problem is that in order to accept myself I had to confront my family. (Coral, 36)

Once the need to assert one's own identity and admit to homoerotic attraction is accepted, the process of transformation to a feminine appearance begins. "Being made up"—that is, "fabricated, manufactured, created"—is an exercise in creativity achieved through the use of external prostheses; hormonal treatments, used by some of the interviewees to lighten the voice and reduce body hair, or injections of cooking oil, which some others prefer to use to increase the size of their breasts, buttocks, and thighs:

> Imagine that I was a boy[18] and that I started to take hormones. . . . It changes you, your bust starts to grow, and, well, in the university it was a scandal. That is, everyone in the whole campus knew I was taking hormones. . . . Later I dressed [as a woman] and went to the library dressed like that. When I started to dress as a woman I'd been taking hormones for like half a year. . . . I changed a lot. (Stephanie, 22)

> I've never fancied women and even less the idea of penetrating a man. I feel 100 percent female. I've never liked my partners to see my breasts, and if it happens that I bathe with them, with a *tanga* or naked, I always turn my back. I like them to see my breasts and my body if possible when there's some trust; but I feel that if they see that part it'll break the spell, and then I think my partner will go and leave me. (Coral, 36)

The act of cross-dressing and the desire to be penetrated during intercourse are presented, then, as a perverse challenge to the laws of nature and the social order, incomprehensible to a spectator—a challenge that implies transgression not only against "correct" sexuality but also against naturalized patterns of understanding of sexual difference. Consequently, transvestism introduces elements of ambiguity and confusion that are reprehensible and dangerous for the rest of society, by putting the objectivity of gender in question.[19] The way society conceives gender roles determines the attitudes it exhibits toward sexual minorities. "As a general rule, to the extent a society does not assume a connection between same-gender sexual behavior and violation of gender *roles* (and the power relationships reinforced by gender roles), that same-gendered sexual behavior will be accepted" (Wilets 1997, 1007). Consequently, it is understandable that the emotional/affective, psychological, and social costs for the subjects are very high if they would fit into a conceptual scheme so dichotomized and excluding.

Violence against Sex Workers in Xalapa

Several studies have pointed out the increase in the number of male sex workers in the world, which suggests that prostitution is an expanding activity for large sectors of the population who are poorly qualified for other jobs and find themselves outside the labor market, and who see in prostitution an ever-present possibility of getting an income (Aggleton 1998). Although sex work can be attractive for transvestites, being better paid than the rest of the limited range of activities in which they can get employment, it is highly risky because it does not enjoy any kind of legal protection.

As the interviewees became increasingly involved in the practice of transvestism and made their gender identities public, they tended to leave the family home and try to settle somewhere less hostile. To gain their independence, it was essential to find paid employment; however, jobs where they could be occupied as transgendered individuals are quite rare, and in such circumstances prostitution becomes an almost inevitable activity.[20]

There is no doubt that entry into sex work is permeated by conditions related to class, although not all the interviewees belong socioeconomically to the least privileged urban strata.[21] Before they embarked on a public life as transgendered persons they had a variety of occupations: store attendants, students, agriculturalists (campesinos), kitchen staff, milk vendors. Some interviewees said that they were exploited but had to endure the exploitation because their obvious effeminacy made it difficult to obtain work. Also, once they had taken the decision to become transvestites, many of the changes they underwent were relatively permanent, or at least lasted for some time—for example, growing their hair long, dyeing it, or changing the size of various parts of the body (one effect of hormone therapy)—and this limited the jobs they could do. It tended to restrict them to jobs in places of night-time entertainment, jobs such as waiters, bargirls, or drag artists:

> I was working in this dive for like two and a half years as a barman. But I
> left because I used to get there at ten in the morning and leave at three,
> four in the morning, and it was very tiring. Because I asked for a higher

wage and more time to sleep, that's why I left. Then I was working in a toyshop for only three months, [and I left] over that issue of being personally accepted, because apparently they had customers who got upset about me serving them. Just now I've been working for about a year and a half in sexual services and I like it a lot better, I really do. Though you do get insults from passersby, aggression. But I feel more accepted here than in any other work. (Yesenia, 24)

Given the poor remuneration that tends to come with other job possibilities, sexual services becomes the logical choice for those individuals who have no other means of survival except to sell their labor power, and it becomes a space for free expression of their transgendered condition.[22]

There were some other gays I knew and they helped me start in what they called *fichar* (to hustle) in bars, prostituting my body at the tender age of fourteen. Some people I knew came by and asked me what I was doing there; but when you're this way, it's obvious from ten miles off what you are. I explained [that I'd left home] and they put me up. I was really grateful because I hadn't eaten for days. I always wanted to work in a decent job, but I never found one because society always discriminates against homosexuals. So I had no other choice but to start going 'round bars and bars, young as I was, and finally having to sell my body to the highest bidder, having to put up with them when they were drunk, because if not, there'd be no bread. You do it out of necessity. (Coral, 36)

I started working at this when I was twenty and I love it. First it was for the money and out of curiosity, to know what you feel like when you start to wear women's clothes, and I started to go with the older guys who hung around there. I started to see some money and I decided to work, I took the plunge. I've worked in a pizzeria, cutting hair, helping out in a kitchen. I've done the lowest jobs, and worked all day for very little money, because people only consider you a stylist or a chef, which pays little. We're not allowed to carry on our trade openly, but here you can earn plenty. (Bella, 25)

Similarly, the research has confirmed the existence of a small number of persons who engage in sex work for motives other than economic reasons: the possibility of having multiple partners, the acting out of fantasies, or the conspicuous expression of their orientation. For all these reasons, prostitution is almost the only public sphere where transgendered persons can exercise their preferences and earn a living by exhibiting them.

One feature that makes sexual services a highly risky occupation is the frequency with which sex workers are the butt of verbal abuse or physical attacks from people who feel threatened by their presence. During their nightly rounds, they are exposed to robbery, rape, or beatings. Sometimes they are attacked by groups of young men who act out their homophobia using the shelter of numbers.

> Look, they attack us physically and verbally, they pass by in cars and insult us. I can tell you that they've even beaten me up, many times. (Glenda, 49)

> Some people are aggressive. The other day, two guys beat me up in the street because I didn't want to go with them. My face was all covered with blood. I went to take a taxi, but no one would stop for me when they saw the state I was in. I've already been beaten up other times just for being gay. (Jade, 34)

Most of the interviewees expressed their perception of the dangers their profession entails simply by being practiced on the streets and by night, and because it is marginal. Sometimes their daily lives are full of insecurity and anxiety.

> You run a lot of risks in this job. Just thinking that I've got myself dressed up, I'm going out, but I don't know how I'm going to return [home], or whether I'm going to return or not. One time, I ran into several boys, around five. One of them came over as if to chat to me and the others went 'round behind me and threw stones at me. The first boy tried to snatch my bag but couldn't, because I had it rolled up in my hand. A taxi came along and they ran off, but they'd hit me with the stones and I had bruises for four or five days. I didn't go out for several days because I was receiving treatment. (Dulce, 23)

> Sometimes I go with a stranger, but, look, I've got something to defend myself with, because afterwards they try to take advantage of me [he shows a knife and puts it away again]. (La Güicha, 33)

Not infrequently, also, police officers extort money from them, abuse them, and demand sexual services in return for not arresting them (for real or nonexistent offenses).

> One time the police arrived and found me with a client in his car. I told them we weren't doing anything wrong. So they said, "Let's check in case you're carrying any drugs." I gave them my bag so they could look in it and they took out my money. I thought. "Now it's no use my even talking to them, they'll take me to the patrol and who knows what they'll invent at the police station." Since then I don't agree to go in a car or in the street, not any longer. (Dulce, 23)

> When a policeman wanted something from us, we had to pay him with sex as well [as the money] they'd already taken from us, and if not, they'd

take us to prison. So if we wanted not to be locked up, we always had to obey their whims, we had to put up with them although they were horrible, and, . . . when it came down to it, we were scared of them. (Coral, 36)

The absence of up-to-date regulation clarifying the letter of the codes contributes to the criminalization of sex workers by not recognizing them as workers with rights and obligations, and it also masks the abuses they suffer from police authorities. If we add to this the gender transgression that joins anomaly and perversion to the other ingredients that fuel social condemnation, it is understandable that violence is a common denominator in the life of transgendered workers, where a sort of traffic between medico-legal and criminological analysis is at work (Mendiara 2002). In other words, the component of perversion is privileged over that of abnormality.

This legislative void contributes to the fact that the transvestites themselves do not believe that the law protects their rights as individuals. Some were led into prostitution as minors, as was the case with Coral, quoted above, yet people like her do not consider themselves victims of the crime of procurement or feel they could have sought the protection of the law.

The situation is similar in regard to the protection of their health. Sexual service is a high-risk occupation because of the workers' constant exposure to sexually transmitted diseases, but the interviewees were not aware of legal provisions designed to reduce the risk of contagion, provisions that could protect them or penalize them according to whether they are the transmitters or recipients of infections. Although the 1942 law on prostitution prohibited, at risk of prosecution, the practice of prostitution by sufferers of diseases classified as contagious (placing the emphasis on the female prostitute) the sanction is applied these days to "anyone who suffers from a serious disease and deceitfully puts another person in danger of infection, [who] will receive a prison sentence lasting from six months to five years, and a fine equivalent to fifty days' salary."[23] This means that the user of the service is now also included as an object of legal sanction, but, as long as these sanctions are not more widely enforced, sex workers remain individually responsible for using precaution to avoid contagion. Such precaution varies.

Well, when drunk, I'm not going to tell you I've never done it without a condom, you know, when you are drunk you do not give a damn, and I charge the same amount. (Vanesa, 35)

I don't do anything without a condom, including oral. [Among clients] there's always someone who'll refuse to use a condom but you try to explain it to them, don't you? "I can tell you I'm not ill and you can tell me the same, but why should you believe me or I believe you? Better to use it, otherwise I don't work." When I first started work, the first few times, I took the risk of not using a condom, for money, but later, in the meetings we held, that's when we started to open our eyes and see the situations of other people who'd got ill, and that's when you start to say, "yes, you've got to take care." (Yazmin, 24)

Nevertheless, and regardless of the high risks of their line of work and the lack of legal instruments to protect sex workers, the city's transvestites are not necessarily passive beings who submissively accept the devalued meanings that hegemonic values impose on them. They have developed significant weapons for opposing the constant violence of which they are the target. Among these, robbery, assault, and, chiefly, "making a scene" are weapons that transvestite sex workers can use against their clients. Since the stigma rests on their "usurpation" of the "defining" traits of gender understood as a dichotomous system, the possibility of making a scene that will attract public attention to the masculinity of their person and the fact that the client, an apparently heterosexual (or "closeted") man, has had sexual relations with another man, puts them in a situation they can turn to advantage (see also Kulick 1996).

Concluding Reflections on Gender, Sexuality, and Sex Work

Legal codes regulating social relations in general and prostitution in particular, are permeated by naturalized conceptions of gender. On the one hand, the Constitution recognizes only a bipolar and purportedly equitable gender system and denies the existence of alternative gender identities. On the other hand, the Constitution, which guarantees citizenship to those men and women who carry out "honest" occupations, does not explicitly penalize commercial sex work, but, by not giving sex workers labor rights, it implicitly characterizes such work as "dishonest." In the background is implicit a concept of masculinized sexuality that leaves the door open for the practice of sex work that serves men. By extension, prostitution is understood as a "female" activity by means of which the hierarchical relations between genders are reinforced. This double legal vacuum makes transvestite sexual workers highly vulnerable, because as transgendered individuals they remain legally unrecognized, and the systematic human rights violations and individual guarantees concerning them remain masked.

In the last few years, government officials and activists have searched for legal ways to fight prejudice and exclusion, demanding the revision of state laws to include protection of sexual diversity and to protect the rights of sex workers. Efforts regarding sexual diversity include a 2006 legal initiative titled "Law of Gender Identity," which would guarantee the right of individuals to adjust their anatomy to their lived sexual identity, the right to have their government-issued identifications rectified (whether or not the individual has had sex-change surgery), and an extension of the right to marry and adopt (Meza Escorza 2006).

The adoption of these reforms would require changes in Article 4 of the Constitution and in the civil codes.

Similarly, activists have demanded legal reforms that (while protecting minors from sexual exploitation) include the right to free association and the right to engage in sex work free of violence. Activists have proposed several state and federal initiatives for a sexual labor code (González 2000; CIMAC 2003; Soria 2004). This would remove transgendered sexual commerce from the legal limbo in which it is now, where it is implicitly criminalized and characterized as pathological, and instead place it in a legal sphere where these sex workers' labor and human rights are protected.

Translated by Mandy Macdonald.

NOTES

1. Unless otherwise indicated, all interviews were conducted by the author. The names of the interviewees have been changed to protect their anonymity.
2. Constitución Política de los Estados Unidos Mexicanos, 1917, art. 1.
3. Ley Federal para Prevenir y Eliminar la Discriminación, 2003, art. 4.
4. Ibid., art. 9.
5. Código Penal para el Distrito Federal, 1999, art. 281 (bis).
6. Código Penal para el Estado Libre y Soberano de Veracruz de Ignacio de la Llave, 2003, art. 196.
7. Ley de Asistencia Social y Protección de Niños y Niñas del Estado de Veracruz, 1998, art. 79.
8. Ley Relativa a la Prostitución y de Profilaxis Social, 1942, art. 1.
9. Ibid., arts. 3–12, 13–20, and 21–28, respectively.
10. Ibid., arts. 3 and 13.
11. Ibid., arts. 5–7.
12. Ibid., art. 30.
13. Código Penal para el Estado Libre y Soberano de Veracruz de Ignacio de la Llave, 2003, art. 292.
14. Bando de Policía y Gobierno para el Ayuntamiento de Xalapa-Enríquez, 2004, art. 38.
15. Ibid., art. 49.
16. For a description of the different notions of the causes of homosexuality, see Boswell (1982–1983, 96–113).
17. This refers to the term *tortilleras* (tortilla makers), a slang word applied to lesbians.
18. He means that he maintained a masculine appearance.
19. Douglas (1966) has examined the relation between danger, anomaly, and dirt in things that are considered culturally out of place, confused, and susceptible to several interpretations.
20. As Richard G. Parker (1993, 91) observes, with respect to marginal zones where there is tolerance toward transgendered people in Rio de Janeiro, "within this world (which is also the world of female prostitution, drug trafficking, homosexuality and . . . the more sporadic prostitution of the *michês*), given pervasive prejudice and discrimination, almost no options other than prostitution are open to the *travesti* for earning a living; as a result, almost all *travestis* quickly become involved in prostitution as their primary

activity." (Michês are "hypermasculine figures who are stereotypically believed to perform the active role with their homosexually identifed clients": ibid., 89.)

21. Tolerance toward effeminacy (whether or not accompanied by transvestism) varies according to the region or ethnic group in which it occurs, and the existence of other work options for transgendered people depends on such tolerance (Alonso and Koreck 1999, 274; Miano Borruso 1999).

22. Although male sex work is on offer in other places in the city, such as discotheques, massage parlors, or escort agencies, none of these advertise for transgendered staff, so the street trade seems the only one in which transvestite sex workers operate.

23. Código Penal para el Estado Libre y Soberano de Veracruz de Ignacio de la Llave, 2003, art. 158. As Katherine Bliss (2001, 3) has pointed out in relation to the 1926 regulations in Mexico City, this law "rested on older arguments regarding the prostitute's deviancy and the client's normalcy that modern hygienists and sexologists used to justify public health concerns and place the burden of disease prophylaxis on women."

PART TWO

Gender at the Intersection of Law and Custom

4

Women's Land Rights and Indigenous Autonomy in Chiapas

Interlegality and the Gendered Dynamics of National and Alternative Popular Legal Systems

LYNN STEPHEN

The indigenous peoples of Mexico are currently living in a fluid legal and political period. Increasing numbers of indigenous communities are revitalizing and redefining their local legal systems,[1] while living under shifting federal and state legal systems that for the most part are moving toward more strictly defining indigenous rights and focusing on the granting of universal, individual rights rather than collective rights. At the federal level, the most important legal reform for indigenous peoples has been the 1992 agrarian legislation,[2] which has encouraged, but not required, the privatization of *ejidos* and agrarian communities.[3] In addition, in 2001 the Mexican congress and the legislatures of seventeen states approved a series of constitutional amendments known as the Indigenous Law (*Ley Indígena*), which severely limit the recognition of collective rights to land and natural resources, and the right of indigenous communities to regional affiliation.[4]

Nevertheless, in Chiapas, thirty Municipios Autónomos Rebeldes Zapatistas (Zapatista Autonomous Municipalities in Rebellion) have existed since the mid-1990s, and elsewhere in Mexico other indigenous communities and organizations are experimenting with ways to carry out the spirit of the 1996 San Andrés Accords on Indigenous Rights and Culture.[5] These communities are declaring control over territories, implementing their own justice systems, and attempting to rebuild cultural, educational, and health institutions. Even communities that have not declared themselves autonomous are experimenting locally and regionally with ways to increase their autonomy over their justice systems (see Sierra, this volume).

Each of these arenas of justice—federal, state, and local indigenous—is gendered in its structure and interpretation. During the 1990s, many women and some men were deeply involved in questioning the gender inequalities reflected in federal, state, and local law in relation to indigenous peoples. Women were

93

involved in the process of formulating the San Andrés Accords, in attempting to operationalize autonomous municipalities in Chiapas, and in the revitalization and interpretation of local indigenous rights. The women's questioning of the reforms to the federal and state constitutions, as well as debates about what local indigenous rights should be allowed to continue, has covered a wide range of issues including domestic violence, forced marriage, equal participation in political arenas, housing, education, jobs, medical care, and land rights.

Although these areas are important and have been documented by an ever-increasing crop of feminist anthropologists and others, here I shall focus on women's land rights. I have chosen women's land rights to highlight the complex and often contradictory legal landscape that has emerged for indigenous women as they become increasingly active in defining the legal systems under which they live. Their participation has become so important that some Mexican researchers (Hernández Castillo 2001; Sierra 2003) are now writing about what they call "indigenous feminism"—a form of feminism that attempts to protect ethnic rights and women's rights all at once, often by building alternative popular legal systems. Even though many people have counterposed ethnic or indigenous rights as collective and women's rights as individual, indigenous women activists do not see this dichotomy and emphasize that both ethnic and gender rights potentially bunch together collective and individual rights.

Some indigenous women have used the discourse of collective indigenous women's rights as a way to begin to counter losses, stated in terms of individual rights, that they have either already experienced or are likely to experience through the 1992 agrarian legislation. They feel that they are best able to defend their "individual" rights as women through being part of an ethnically or locally based collective; through this membership they seek equal rights to men in areas such as political leadership and decision making and access to land. They have had more influence on local indigenous rights than on national law, which can often undermine their collective rights in a way that leaves them with no material or political base. Some indigenous women have pursued strategies that revolve around staking claims to local indigenous rights that are not harmful to women, or strategies that involve alternative popular legal systems in the practice of indigenous rights. Through a case study from two indigenous communities in Chiapas that are attempting to consolidate local forms of justice and law that vary significantly from national law, I show how, in their struggles to be included in land rights, indigenous women are an important part of making Mexico's justice system more inclusive with regard to ethnicity and gender.

Is Mexico a Multicultural Nation? The San Andrés Accords and the 2001 National Legislation on Indigenous Rights

The Zapatista rebellion of 1994 initiated a nationwide process of reassessing the relationship between the Mexican state and indigenous peoples. There were two rounds of peace talks that ended optimistically in February 1996 with the signing of the San Andrés Accords by the Mexican government and the Zapatista National Liberation Army (Ejército Zapatista de Liberación Nacional, EZLN). The San Andrés Accords recognize the rights of indigenous peoples: "to develop their specific forms of social, cultural, political and economic organization"; "to obtain the recognition of their internal normative systems for regulation and sanction, insofar as they are not contrary to constitutional guarantees and human rights, especially those of women"; "to freely designate their representatives, within the community as well as in their municipal government bodies, as well as the leaders of their pueblos indígenas, in accordance with the institutions and traditions of each pueblo"; and "to promote and develop their languages and cultures, as well as their political, social, economic, religious, and cultural customs and traditions" (San Andrés Accords on Indigenous Rights and Culture 1999, 35). The Accords further specify that the Mexican Constitution should "guarantee the organization of their own elections or leadership selection processes within communities or pueblos indígenas," "recognize the procedures of cargo systems and other forms of organization, methods of designation of representatives, and decision making by assembly and through popular consultation," and "establish that municipal agents or other [local municipal] leaders be elected, or, when appropriate, named by the respective pueblos and communities" (ibid.).

The euphoria following the signing of the San Andrés Accords was short-lived, when it became evident that President Ernesto Zedillo's administration had no intention of implementing them. Not until 2001 did the Mexican Congress approve the so-called Indigenous Law, a greatly watered-down version of the original San Andrés Accords, which left most of the specifics as to how indigenous autonomy might be realized to individual state legislatures.

With regard to women's land rights, the Indigenous Law mirrors the 1992 agrarian legislation, which greatly limits women's rights. Where, under the 1971 Agrarian Law, ejido land rights were considered a family patrimony and wives and consensual partners were first in line to receive land use rights if male *ejidatarios* died, in the 1992 Agrarian Law decisions regarding individual parcelization and privatization of plots are made by the ejido assembly, not by families. Spouses and unmarried partners have no voice or vote in that process, as male ejidatarios may petition ejido assemblies to permit them to privatize and sell their plots or engage in joint ventures with their land. If a male ejidatario should decide to sell his parcel, his wife, unmarried partner, or children, have the right of first refusal—but only within thirty days of when the land is put up for sale. And most rural women do not have sufficient income to purchase land, should it be put up for sale by their husbands or partners (Stephen 1993).

Another change in agrarian legislation affecting women is that ejido rights need no longer stay within the family. Ejidatarios can bequeath the land to anyone they wish, and the heir has no obligation to support the ejidatario's dependents

(Deere and León 2001, 152; Baitenmann, this volume). As summarized by Carmen Diana Deere and Magdalena León (2001, 155): "With the end of land distribution by the state, and disintegration of family patrimony on the Mexican *ejidos*, women's access to land will largely depend on inheritance practices and on their ability to participate in the land market as buyers."

In some communities in Chiapas, where most nonprivate landholdings are in the form of ejidos, women's best chance of obtaining access to land is through emerging popular legal systems. Here, indigenous autonomy is being implemented outside state law, in the form of local indigenous and revolutionary law (such as the 1995 and 1996 Declarations of Autonomous Municipalities in Rebellion and the 2003 creation of Juntas of Good Government providing a regional structure of government and justice for the autonomous municipalities). The creation of rights at the margin is also gendered. By combining individual and collective rights and reconfiguring local governance structures, communities in Chiapas are providing new gendered models for how to create flexibility in local indigenous rights and governance structures that can give indigenous women more broadly defined land rights than those afforded them in current national legislation.

Indigenous Rights, Revolutionary Laws, and Gender Justice

From 1994 to the present, indigenous women have appealed to have their demands included in legal processes relating to indigenous rights. Women began by participating in sessions focused on indigenous women's rights as part of the negotiation of the San Andrés Accords. They were involved in a range of workshops and congresses, and by the mid-1990s had begun to create their own spaces within the two most important national indigenous rights organizations, the National Assembly for Autonomy (ANIPA) and the National Indigenous Congress (CNI). By 1997, women had created their own national network, the National Indigenous Women's Coordinating Council (CNMI) (Blackwell 2006). The creation of a national indigenous women's network, the ongoing participation of women in the two major national networks for indigenous rights, and the women's participation in international congresses have significantly elevated the voices and concerns of indigenous women in regional, national, and international political spaces.

In these varied political spaces, indigenous women have demanded citizenship rights in a variety of arenas—family, community, organization, and nation. They have attempted to integrate concerns of ethnicity and gender with nationalism and have pressed for a broader understanding of self-determination and autonomy. Although not without some degree of conflict (see Stephen 2001), indigenous women have by and large been successful in maintaining unity in their national and regional struggles (Blackwell 2006; Sierra 2002). These struggles include economic autonomy (access to and control over the means of production, including land), political autonomy (basic political rights), physical autonomy (the right to make decisions concerning their own bodies and the right to a life without violence), and sociocultural autonomy (the right to assert their identities as indigenous women) (Hernández Castillo 1997, 112).

For example, at the founding congress of the CNMI in Oaxaca, over seven hundred women representatives participated alongside a grassroots committee of women from the EZLN. They demanded the fulfillment of the San Andrés Accords, the demilitarization of indigenous zones of Mexico, multilingual and multicultural education programs, education for women, women's right to manage projects and resources aimed at them, reform of Article 4 of the Constitution to include equality between men and women and the recognition of a multiethnic society, parity for women in all representational bodies, and "a need to change [A]rticle 27 of the Constitution so that it enables women to have the right to inherit land through direct relationship and through the respect we have for Mother Earth and natural resources" (Gutiérrez and Palomo 2000, 70).

In documents produced by women in the CNI and ANIPA, as well as in the CNMI, the physical and psychological integrity of women's bodies and reproductive decision making were linked to the right to land, property, and participation in political decision making. Women in these organizational spaces demanded rights to land, but it became evident that indigenous land rights in general and those of indigenous women in particular would not be incorporated into national-level discussions of revolutionary laws. Indeed, the San Andrés Accords, the initial proposal for legislating the accords, and the 2001 Indigenous Law completely failed to address land rights in general, and women's land rights in particular, accepting instead the terms of the 1992 agrarian legislation.

The following example illustrates this point. In October 1996, the EZLN and the Comisión de Concordia y Pacificación, or COCOPA (the National Commission of Concord and Pacification), composed of representatives from Mexico's three leading political parties, announced that a joint commission had been formed to monitor the implementation of the San Andrés Accords. The COCOPA developed a legislative proposal endorsed by the EZLN, in which women's rights were stated as follows: "[Indigenous peoples] have the right . . . to apply their own normative systems in the regulation and solution of internal conflict, respecting individual rights, human rights, and the dignity and integrity of women." The proposal recognizes the right of indigenous peoples "to elect their authorities and exercise their own forms of internal government in accordance with their norms . . . guaranteeing the equal participation of women" (*La Jornada*, January 13, 1997). The draft thus subtly addresses the political participation of women where "traditionally" it has been overlooked, and also discourages internal forms of conflict resolution that do not respect women's rights. Land rights, however, are not addressed.

Analyzing the question of land rights in national-level discussions of indigenous women from 1994 to the present, one must conclude that the most promising political arena for this struggle is within the women's indigenous autonomy movement, and especially at the local level, where alternative popular legal systems and governance structures are challenging state law. One such place is in eastern Chiapas.

Women's Land Rights in La Realidad and Guadalupe Tepeyac: Zapatista Popular Law and Indigenous Autonomy

Just how much indigenous women understand about the 1992 agrarian legislation or the 2001 Indigenous Law and how these affect their rights to land varies greatly from one place to another. A related question is how much national laws actually matter at the local level, because local practices allow other avenues for women's access to land and/or because the local governance system has declared itself autonomous and set up its own rules for access to land, as in the Zapatista autonomous regions. There, women's engagement with land and resource rights is deeply informed by local and regional context. Women's relationship to land rights is mediated through local ethnic relationships and through belonging to a collectivity that serves as a basis for granting them rights that increasingly are declared equal to those of men. Local understandings of land rights are given meaning in daily life through the struggles to claim and maintain control of ejido land in the face of military occupation by the Mexican army and through alternative local legal systems, which in many cases have now coexisted for a decade with state law—a case of sustained interlegality.

The majority of land held in nonprivate status in Chiapas is in ejidos. In 1990, 1,405,025 people, or 43.7 percent of the state's total population, lived on approximately two thousand ejidos (Stephen 2002, 63; INEGI 1995, 3). Ejido formation has been an important and contentious process in the agrarian history of Chiapas, and it continues to be so today, as Zapatista ejidos challenge national law by asserting their own local indigenous laws and systems of governance.

The Tojolab'al communities of Guadalupe Tepeyac and La Realidad were formally constituted as ejidos in 1956 and 1966. Ejido members had migrated to the area a decade or more earlier. Most of the ejido founders had worked as sharecroppers for ranchers who lived at the outer edges of the Lacandon jungle. In hopes of a new beginning, they moved to national lands with the expectation of being able to make an independent living raising cattle, corn, beans, and coffee. Although women were among the pioneers who cleared the land, built houses, and worked harvesting coffee, very few were formally given ejidataria status (Stephen 2002, 110–111; Rovira 1997, 58). Women were seldom present at ejido assemblies, even though they worked the land alongside men during the coffee harvests and were in charge of small-scale commercialization.

Although a majority of those with formal ejido rights in these two communities were men from the time the ejidos were formed until the mid-1990s, women historically developed a sense of the land as belonging to their families and seem to have identified closely with the struggle to obtain land, keep it, and improve it.

For women like Comandanta Trinidad from the Zapatista ejido of Guadalupe Tepeyac, one's parents' transformation from peons who worked as sharecroppers to independent ejidatarios was of major significance. She remarked of the origins of her ejido: "We don't have a *patrón* now. We looked for a better life without a patrón and we found our land. We continued to be poor, but we had our products. When we would bring out products to Las Margaritas, they bought them at a very bad price. They told us, 'Your coffee is no good.' And because we were really poor, we sold it to them cheaply. . . . I decided to become a Zapatista so that our communities can improve" (Zúñiga and Bellinghausen 1997, 340–341; Stephen 2002, 103).

The statement by Comandanta Trinidad, and those of other EZLN women I have interviewed, suggest that these women see land as an integral part of their struggle for community improvement. Many women from these two communities were, in the early 1990s, EZLN *insurgentes* (trained soldiers living away from their communities in training camps), *milicianos* (mobile reservists who live in their communities, receive training, and participate in armed actions), or *bases de apoyo* (civilians who support Zapatismo, carry out Zapatista social programs in medicine, health, and agriculture, and provide material support for the EZLN). The Zapatista struggle for land includes keeping control of ejidos, expanding available land, and maintaining political control of ejido governance.

In Guadalupe Tepeyac and La Realidad, the traditional structure of governance has been the ejido, in conjunction with ten to fifteen years of participation in regional peasant organizations such as the Independent Federation of Agricultural Workers and Peasants (CIOAC), Ejido Union of the Jungle (Unión Ejidal de la Selva), and the collective association ARIC–UU (Asociación Rural de Interés Colectivo–Unión de Uniones).[6] By the time agrarian legislation was reformed in 1992, the EZLN was firmly entrenched in Guadalupe Tepeyac and La Realidad, and many of its supporters were women. Through the cover of a regional organization called the Independent National Peasant Alliance "Emiliano Zapata" (ANCIEZ), the EZLN held a rally in Ocosingo against the 1992 reforms to Article 27 and agrarian legislation. Four months later, the EZLN held another rally (see Stephen 2002, 237–238). During this time and afterward, ejidatarios in both communities discussed how to counter the 1992 agrarian reforms, as they discussed the formulation of new revolutionary laws for Zapatista communities. Men, women, and children attended the rallies and were also involved in community-wide discussions about the formulation of the new laws that came to form an alternative grassroots legal system. This alternative popular legal system had a much wider level of local participation in its formulation than had the 1992 agrarian reforms or the 2001 Indigenous Law.

As the governance structure of these communities changed to accommodate the secret presence of the EZLN, the local political culture began to change as well. In some communities, women were encouraged to speak up at secret meetings, to meet on their own, and to undertake important leadership roles. By the time the EZLN went public in 1994, the local political structure in La Realidad and Guadalupe Tepeyac had already been transformed with regard to gender and age roles. All men, women, and children were strongly encouraged to attend community meetings, and these were not over until everyone who wanted to had spoken. Women organized around specific tasks, including health, education, community defense, and food procurement.

After communities in Chiapas came under attack from the Mexican Army (and, in the case of Guadalupe Tepeyac, relocated for almost eight years, from 1995 to 2001), local gender roles for women came to include front-line confrontations with soldiers, communicating with reporters and foreigners about the urgent needs of the community, and traveling to San Andrés Larraínzar, San Cristóbal de las Casas, and elsewhere to support and protect EZLN delegations during peace talks, forums, and other events. They considered all these activities part and parcel of the efforts to protect ejido lands from military incursions. This context is key to understanding the perspective of women in Guadalupe Tepeyac and La Realidad on land rights and changes in local governance.

From the late 1980s until 1994, two parallel governing structures existed in these ejidos. The traditional ejido governance system coexisted with the clandestine structure of the EZLN. In one, women had little presence at assembly meetings. In the other, women were actively encouraged to take on leadership (see Stephen 2002, 135, 179–210).

At a broader level, those committed to the Zapatista struggle were engaging in a process of creating their own laws and their own system of land use, which in some cases challenged the established ejido structure. In late December 1993, the EZLN published a number of "revolutionary laws" in its underground newspaper *El Despertador Mexicano,* including the Revolutionary Agrarian Law and the Women's Revolutionary Law. Although the Women's Revolutionary Law has been widely analyzed with regard to its gendered implications, the Revolutionary Agrarian Law has received much less attention.

Revolutionary Agrarian Law

In order to establish a general law for land redistribution, the EZLN issued the Revolutionary Agrarian Law. Several characteristics make this law different from the 1992 agrarian reforms with regard to gender.

First, the law specifically mentions the rights of women, while the state's agrarian laws are only implicitly gender neutral—and, in practice, profoundly discriminatory:

First. This law is valid over the entire territory of Mexico, and is for the benefit of all poor peasants and farm workers in Mexico, regardless of their political affiliation, religious creed, sex, race, or color. . . .

Sixth. PRIMARY RIGHT of application [for expropriated land] belongs to the collectives of poor landless peasants and farm workers, men, women, and children, who duly verify not having land or [having] land of bad quality. . . . (Womack 1999, 253)

Second, women have the same obligations as men in terms of working the land. Land must be worked collectively and used to produce necessary foods, and may not be individually monopolized.

Fifth. The lands affected by this agrarian law will be redistributed to landless peasants and farmworkers who apply for it as COLLECTIVE PROPERTY for the formation of cooperatives, peasant societies, or farms and ranching production collectives. The land affected must be worked collectively. . . .

Eighth. Groups benefited by this Agrarian Law must dedicate themselves preferentially to the collective production of foods necessary for the Mexican people: corn, beans, rice, vegetables, and fruit, as well as animal husbandry for cattle, pigs, and horses and bee-keeping, and [to the production] of derivative products (milk, meat, eggs, etc.). . . .

Twelfth. Individual monopolization of land and means of production will not be permitted. (ibid., 253–254)

In practice, land expropriated by the EZLN has been available to women. Following the Zapatista rebellion, land invasions between January 1994 and the summer of 1996 resulted in the seizure of up to fifty thousand hectares (Stephen 1998, 19). In addition, a land trust run by the Ministry of Agrarian Reform in Chiapas negotiated two hundred and forty thousand hectares of land for fifty-eight thousand beneficiaries in a program allowing them to purchase the land (ibid.).

My discussions with men and women about land use rights, forms of production, and gender roles in Guadalupe Tepeyac (in 1994) and La Realidad (in 1995, 1996, and 1997), suggest a hybrid legal system melding the older ejido structure and the new revolutionary agrarian law that argues for collective production and women's access to land rights. This legal system can be viewed as both a revision to customary law and an emerging popular legal system that relates to national law (through ejidos). The Zapatista legal system reinterprets national and local law through a process that we might call an everyday form of state-building "from the fringes of the territorial state, by subaltern groups who

had formerly been excluded from participation in the national community"
(Nugent 1997, 308). Unlike the situation in the Chachapoyas region of Peru in the
1920s and 1930s described by David Nugent (1997)—where modern nationhood
equated with individual rights and private property, and economic development
was considered a form of liberation—in La Realidad and Guadalupe Tepeyac,
Zapatista laws insist on collective production and possession as a way of liberating
the community from the model of individual property rights and production
imposed by the 1992 reform to Article 27 (see Stephen 2002, 62–80). Ejidatarios
in these two communities see modern nationhood, as delivered through the
neoliberal economic model of the 1980s and 1990s, as having further marginalized them. Their strategy for being taken seriously and reintegrated comes
through alternative legal systems and state-building at the margins. Incorporating women into alternative legal and political structures that militate against
a neoliberal model has been an important and contentious part of the Zapatista
experience.

In 1994, Major Eliseo discussed with me the difficulties of getting both men
and women to convert to collective production. He also emphasized security
concerns.

LYNN STEPHEN: How is it, trying to convince people to change from an individual way of farming to a collective model?

MAJOR ELISEO: It is really hard. Think about what happens. They all have a lot of
individualism. They say, what is mine, is mine, I can't give it to someone
else. It is really hard to challenge this idea. We have to challenge our people
this way, even people in our own army, giving them the idea, showing them
what can happen with time. Part of the communities we have organized this
way because of the war. Because when it is time to go to war we can't have
one person here, and another person there and another person there.
Because that way they [the enemy] can enter very easily. We have people all
working in one place together so that there is better security. Any woman
can arrive to work and know that there will be people around. So we are car-
rying this idea out little by little. . . . In one ejido sometimes there would be
twenty people who would work collectively and the majority would be working individually. When they [the individual farmers] saw that it worked [the
collective] then another ten would join. And that is how the town was won.

LYNN STEPHEN: In the collective work that you are doing, are the women participating in agriculture? In planting?

MAJOR ELISEO: Women also participate. They have their own collective work.
Of course they are not working in the corn fields, but do other work. They
do vegetable farming collectively, bakeries, collectively. There are doing
small things, but they are learning. . . .

LYNN STEPHEN: And is this as difficult to implement as it is to get the men to work collectively?

MAJOR ELISEO: Yes, because the women have what we said—individualism. What they have they don't want to give to everyone else. But little by little this idea is changing. And finally people are convinced, the whole town is convinced. That's how it is. Little by little, but this takes time. It isn't going to happen overnight. . . . You have to keep trying various times in order to succeed. That's how it is. That is the way that we are fighting for the land.

My conversation with Major Eliseo suggested that the EZLN was attempting to implement certain parts of their Revolutionary Agrarian Law, particularly with respect to encouraging collective forms of production. What the conversation also reveals, however, is that collectivization was not just an economic strategy; it would keep people together in one place and provide safety in numbers. In addition, structuring ejido agriculture collectively served as an organizing strategy for the EZLN.

One other aspect of the conversation is worth noting. Although both women and men are organized collectively to the extent possible, according to Major Eliseo, there are differences in the type of collective work men and women do. According to him, women did not work in the cornfields, but did vegetable farming and worked in bakeries and other small scale projects. I do not know if Eliseo was referring to all areas or only one specific place; he did not tell me specifically where he was from. Later conversations with men and women from La Realidad suggest that women did go out to the fields and that some were also working planting corn and harvesting coffee. Gender roles can vary quite significantly from one Zapatista base community to another, or even within one community, particularly in relation to age. Perhaps because Guadalupe Tepeyac and La Realidad were early strongholds where men and women were socialized over a long period of time to Zapatista laws and thinking, they show more flexibility than elsewhere.[7] According to interviews I conducted in 1995–1997, women in La Realidad were involved in collective production projects focused on corn, vegetables, and animal production. Women worked together on a plot of land to produce food (this process of organization had in fact started before the 1994 rebellion). At the same time, ejidatarios and their families attempted to continue working their ejido lands as family units, but found it increasingly difficult, given the low-intensity war. Thus, changes in local understandings of land rights that might have allowed women to extend their use of land and perhaps be allocated more land were in part limited because of security concerns.

In the summer of 1996, women in La Realidad described to me their experiences of working together in collective agricultural projects. They described walking together to and from their field as a source of pleasure, but also of tension: they stayed together out of fear. After describing the collective projects, women also explained their attempts to continue growing coffee on their family's ejido plots. After the army's invasion in February 1995, the ejido land that had served as a refuge was difficult to access. María (a pseudonym) said the following:

> When the army came to take this community it was the ninth of February 1995, and we fled, we ran away. . . . We fled, we ran to our ejido land. We went to one side and settled there. Then the army came after us and screamed at us that we should return to our community, that they wouldn't do anything. They said they came for peace. They said they hadn't come to bother people. . . .
>
> . . . We didn't come back. But the next day we came back and we started to yell at them.
>
> We ran them out with all of the women. A group of women stood and we screamed at the army to leave, that they get out of here. The army doesn't belong here in our community. We are the owners here. We are in charge of the community. The army belongs in the city, in their barracks. . . .
>
> . . . We can't do our work. For example, we have coffee fields that are off this road. But we can't even walk there, because the Mexican army is going back and forth, watching us to see what we are doing to make sure we don't do anything. They say they won't do anything to us, but then they will come and they will betray us.

María's narrative gives us some insight into how she thinks about ejido land. She describes it as "our land," asserts "We are the owners here" and describes the major role that women played in removing the army from the community's lands. Her sense of collective ownership and use of the land is apparent. At the time, her everyday experience involved both working collectively with other women to produce corn and vegetables as well as attempts to check on the coffee fields her family holds through her husband's rights in the ejido. Although the land is formally registered in her husband's name as an ejidatario in the eyes of the Mexican government, in María's eyes the coffee fields belong to her as much as to him.

Conversations with men during this same trip revealed that most formally designated ejidatarios were men, and that land was still officially titled to men. Some men interviewed continued to state that, in the ejido of La Realidad, women gained rights to ejido land as widows if their husbands had been ejidatarios or as single mothers. While all men over the age of eighteen, whether single or married, could have access to ejido land, married women and single women without children over the age of eighteen could not, according to these ejidatarios. Women and some younger men, however, debated this interpretation. They emphasized women and men working together in collective agriculture, not individual ejido rights for men.

Because the EZLN has not dealt directly with government officials at the ejido level since 1994, there has been no process that would have allowed the community to officially change the designation of who has ejido rights. And it seems that there are still differences of interpretation within the community by generation and gender. For people who came of age in the Zapatista organizational and rebellion process between 1988 and the present, legal reality is more likely to be informed by Zapatista revolutionary law and legal practices then by Mexican national law. The communities of Guadalupe Tepeyac and La Realidad have been governed by Zapatista principles since the late 1980s, and probably longer. At thirty-five years of age in 1996, María had spent almost a decade of her life being socialized in the revolutionary ideology, laws, and political structures of the EZLN. For her, legal and political reality has most likely been defined by that experience.

Her community declared itself part of the autonomous municipality of San Pedro Michoacán in 1996. The consolidation of EZLN autonomous municipalities from 1996 to the present has involved: the demarcation of territory; the establishment and acceptance of a new normative framework; a series of rebellious actions that refuse to recognize governmental bodies; elections for and installation of parallel authorities and governments; and the creation of local-level governing structures in charge of policing, tax collection, and the civil registry (Burguete Cal y Mayor 2000). The consolidation of Zapatista autonomous municipalities and other units comes directly from the government's refusal to implement the 1996 San Andrés Accords that it signed. In communities like Guadalupe Tepeyac and La Realidad, this situation has triggered an ongoing process of establishing autonomous and parallel government institutions and processes that seek to implement the San Andrés Accords locally.

In August 2003, the Zapatistas announced the creation of five *caracoles* (literally "shells" but meaning "houses") as seats for five Juntas of Good Government. La Realidad is the site of one such junta. Each of the five juntas includes one or two delegates from each of the already existing autonomous councils in each zone. Currently there are thirty Zapatista Autonomous Municipalities in Rebellion feeding into the five juntas. The functions of the juntas include, among other things: monitoring projects and community works in Zapatista Autonomous Municipalities in Rebellion; monitoring the implementation of laws that, having been accepted by the communities, function within the jurisdiction of the Zapatista Autonomous Municipalities in Rebellion; caring for the Zapatista territory that they manage (Servicio Internacional para la Paz 2003). At the celebration for the new juntas in 2003, Tojolab'al Comandanta Esther— who addressed the Mexican Congress in 2001 urging it to implement the San Andrés Accords—captured the sentiment of other women and men who had decided to implement their own systems of government and justice, including the Revolutionary Agrarian Law. Addressing Mexico's indigenous peoples, Esther argued that

> now, we have to exercise our rights ourselves. We don't need to ask permission from anyone, especially politicians. . . . We call on you all to apply the San Andrés Accords. It's time to act and to apply indigenous peoples' autonomy all over the country. We don't need to ask for permission to form our autonomous municipalities. Just like we are doing and practicing—we don't ask for approval. (Comandanta Esther 2003)

In communities, such as La Realidad and Guadalupe Tepeyac, that have a tradition of ejido forms of government as well as a newer tradition as part of an Autonomous Municipality in Rebellion, gender roles and women's perceptions of their land rights are in flux. I found little evidence to suggest that women's experience and strategies are focused on obtaining individual use rights to ejido parcels. Because many, like María, have committed to creating an alternative system of agricultural production and use rights based on collective ownership and access, their emphasis is likely to continue to be on supporting a broader struggle for community land rights, and for their rights of access as women within that struggle. The primary vehicle they have identified for achieving their goals is the implementation of the San Andrés Accords at the national level by the Mexican government. In the meantime, their strategy is to live out the accords in their local communities. By adopting this strategy, women are fusing the collective struggle for ethnic rights (i.e., indigenous rights) to land and political control, with efforts to create individual rights for women that grant them equality with men.

Indigenous Women's Land Rights: Where To?

Indigenous women in Mexico are increasingly making themselves heard at local, regional, and national levels. In the 1990s, the combination of the new agrarian legislation and nonimplementation of the San Andrés Accords legally undermined women's rights to land and natural resources. At the same time, growing national movements for indigenous rights, the emergence of a national indigenous women's network, and local experimentation in integrating women into local forms of governance, communal land access, and systems of justice such as those highlighted above have created an optimistic juncture for expanding indigenous women's access to land. Indigenous rights organizing is likely to provide the most fruitful avenue for indigenous women to increase their access to land, rather than relying on changes in national legislation that might allow them to become private land owners. The fact that Mexico recognized multiculturalism at the same time that it implemented a neoliberal economic regime limited the material base for the reproduction of indigenous culture and surely limits possibilities for indigenous women as well (see Mattiace 2003b, 153–154); thus, although I do not doubt the importance of legislating the San Andrés Accords and reforming agrarian legislation to extend women's land rights in relation to ejido land, I believe that the kinds of experiences I describe in La Realidad are crucial to expanding women's access to land and natural resources.

The other lesson from the recent experience of the Zapatista autonomous municipalities in Chiapas is the importance of forging the exercise and practice of indigenous rights outside state control while at the same time continuing efforts to change the Constitution, the laws, and their regulation. The exercise of rights outside the control of the state is crucial to the everyday experience of those who seek them, such as the women discussed here. Situations of interlegality—of the coexistence of multiple systems of law—are quite common throughout history and can become important arenas of social change.

In many cases, constitutions and laws at federal and state levels are changed in response to a social movement in which persons are already defying the law and living their lives as if they already had the rights they seek (see Speed 2006 for another Chiapas example, and Sierra, this volume). Social movements demonstrate the importance of persistence and practice through time in making laws match reality. Both legal and social movement strategies involving the exercise of rights are important. Perhaps the Mexican state's resistance to legislating indigenous autonomy has ultimately helped to legitimize the practice of alternative popular legal systems.

The other reason to be optimistic in Mexico is the existence of a national indigenous women's network that is dedicated to getting women's rights enforced in the process of granting indigenous autonomy. This network provides a national sounding board for a wide range of local experiences and provides indigenous women leaders from different parts of Mexico with a chance to share and learn from one another's experiences while also working together to advance their cause at a national and international level. Through this network, pushing for collective ethnic rights and working to ensure women's equal rights within ethnically or locally based collectivities is a strategy being experimented with throughout Mexico (see Speed, Hernández Castillo, and Stephen 2006; Hernández Castillo 2002c). Land and natural resource use rights are fundamental for Mexico's indigenous women, and the staking of claims in these areas by women in the indigenous rights movement can provide an opening for all rural women to reclaim rights they lost in the 1990s, and perhaps even to expand them.

NOTES

1. Local indigenous legal systems are sometimes termed *usos y costumbres,* or "new" *usos y costumbres* as in the Zapatista Revolutionary Agrarian Law.

2. The 1992 agrarian legislation includes: the reform to Article 27 of the Mexican Constitution; the Agrarian Law and its (1993) regulations; the Forestry Law, the Law of

National Waters; and laws establishing or revamping the Office of the Agrarian Ombudsman (Procuraduría Agraria), the agrarian courts, and the National Agrarian Registry. It also includes the rules and regulations pertaining to the 1992 land titling program (see Baitenmann, this volume).

3. For a definition of ejidos, see Baitenmann, this volume. Other forms of rural land arrangements held in nonprivate or social tenancy are the agrarian communities (*comunidades agrarias*). This land constitutes a significant part of the holdings of indigenous communities and is based on historical claims, usually dating to pre-Columbian or colonial times. In many cases, these lands are known as *comunales* (communal lands). The 1992 agrarian legislation permits agrarian communities to turn into ejidos; once this occurs, land can then be individually parceled and privatized.

4. This "law" entails reforms to Articles 1, 2, 4, 18, and 115 of the Constitution (*Diario Oficial de la Federación*, August 14, 2001).

5. The San Andrés Accords were signed in February 1996 by the Mexican government and the EZLN. For an analysis of this complex process, see Hernández Navarro (1998).

6. See Stephen (2002, 126–145); Mattiace (2003a, 2003b); Leyva Solano (2003, 161–164); Leyva Solano and Ascencio Franco (1996).

7. Discussions with Márgara Millán in December 2003 revealed similarities concerning gender roles in La Realidad and in San Miguel Chiptic, where Millán has been conducting fieldwork for several years.

5

Indigenous Women, Law, and Custom

Gender Ideologies in the Practice of Justice

MARÍA TERESA SIERRA

In this chapter, I show how gender ideologies constitute disciplinary mechanisms in the form of rules and customs guiding social practices, limiting the possibilities for the emergence of new discourses about rights. The practice of justice and conflict resolution in indigenous regions offers us a space in which to analyze these processes, since it reveals how norms derived from different judicial systems—the state system and the indigenous system—shape social behavior and legitimate the subordination of women. What happens in the courts also enables us to reconstruct the strategies women have developed to challenge these models and ideologies and to redefine the relationship between them. I focus on the practice of justice in local and regional spaces of the Nahua communities of the Sierra Norte de Puebla. I seek to demonstrate, on the basis of legal interactions, how gender ideologies influence the alternatives available to indigenous women for settling controversies and containing violence. I briefly describe the indigenous organizations that exist in the region of Cuetzalan and the discourse of rights that these organizations are promoting, in order to document the changes, however small, that can contribute to the building of a plural justice embracing the principle of gender equity.[1]

The court is a place where a society's gender norms, values, and ideologies are revealed, for, in airing disputes before local authorities or mediators, people appeal to gender norms and thus shed light on the conflicts permeating the relationship between the sexes. As well as being spaces par excellence of legal discourse, courts are also spaces of performance (Turner 1986) and spaces of cultural production, where cultural meanings are activated and negotiated (Merry 1995). They are therefore privileged sites for the analysis of social practices and their representations.

Comparative research in different regions of Mexico reveals the high incidence of disputes brought to the indigenous authorities that involve women, as

well as the strategies employed to resolve such conflicts.[2] A significant proportion of the cases initiated by women concern conflicts within the household,
many involving physical and verbal violence. Women clearly see local judicial
institutions as important spaces in which to settle their disputes and negotiate
gender relations.[3] In most of the regions studied, the indigenous justice system
and its authorities continue to be the principal forum for dispute resolution,
but women are resorting more and more frequently to the state's judicial institutions when the local ones do not provide a solution to their problems.[4]

Indigenous Justice in Practice

In the Nahua region of Cuetzalan, the system of justice with which indigenous
women and men engage involves three main levels of judicial institutions: the
Court of the Justice of the Peace (Juzgado de Paz) in indigenous communities,
the municipal court in the town of Cuetzalan (Juzgado Menor Municipal), and,
to a lesser extent, the Court of First Instance (Juzgado de Primera Instancia) of
the state judicial district, located in the town of Zacapoaxtla. All these bodies
are part of the state judicial system. A recent addition is the Indigenous Court
(Juzgado Indígena) set up at municipal level in the town of Cuetzalan. This
court was established by the State of Puebla's Superior Court of Justice (Tribunal Superior de Justicia) in March 2002, in response to new federal policies
modernizing the legal system and recognizing cultural diversity. Set up as a new
instrument of mediation between the state and indigenous communities, the
court is run by indigenous authorities in accordance with the practice of indigenous law but under the aegis of the state's legal authorities. In Cuetzalan, the
Indigenous Court started to function in May 2002.[5]

At the time of this research (until 2001), the authority most frequently used
by the Nahua people, both women and men, was the justice of the peace. Next
in importance was the Auxiliary Public Prosecution Agency (Agencia Subalterna
del Ministerio Público) in the town of Cuetzalan, which, like the municipal
court, was an intermediate body between the community and district courts.
A significant number of cases that have not been resolved locally are brought to
these institutions, which serve as spaces of mediation between law and custom,
although the logic of positive law prevails. On the other hand, the district court
is ruled by a discourse of legality and there is no space for negotiation with
indigenous norms and customs.

In this study, I pay particular attention to the first two levels (the community and municipal courts), showing how indigenous women challenge and
negotiate with the justice system, and outlining the role played by gender ideologies;[6] I also illustrate how different discourses about gender, according to
which men's and women's behavior is judged, are reproduced in these judicial

spaces, and demonstrate the ability of these discourses to shape and convey cultural meanings.

Studying conflicts and their outcomes allows us to identify the arguments employed by indigenous authorities to clarify the obligations husband and wife have toward each other, and the need for them to conform to their assigned gender roles. In indigenous communities, judges generally try to arrive at negotiated settlements, not necessarily at just solutions, with the aim of restoring family relations and getting the parties to reconsider their actions. It is not the fact of violence itself that is questioned, but the abuse of violence and, above all, the failure to comply with gender roles. In the Cuetzalan region, many cases of this kind end up in the municipal courts. In other cases, women are seen as transgressing community norms, as when they are accused of taking lovers, spreading rumors, or failing to accept particular customs, and as a result they are criticized and pressured to answer accusations that may be based on gossip and slander.

In both community and state institutions of justice, women come up against norms and values, customs and laws, that reinforce the existing gender imperative, keeping them at a disadvantage. A number of studies have demonstrated how both law and custom subordinate women when they face the legal authorities of either the state or the community (Hernández Castillo 2002d; Martínez Corona and Mejía Flores 1997).[7] This perspective is not, however, enough to show how women try to negotiate and stake a claim to those legal spaces that do open up some limited options for women to restrain or mitigate violence. To document this process, we need to observe the spaces where justice is exercised, recording concrete interactions and reconstructing itineraries and narratives. This approach has enabled us to situate the meanings deployed by social actors— men and women—in their social and cultural context, so as to reconstruct gender roles and strategies in relation to justice without losing sight of the structural framework in which they develop (see Chenaut 2004; Sierra 1992, 2004; Vallejo Real 2004b).

Behind every judicial process there lies a series of prior, sometimes dramatic, events, such that the lawsuit is only one moment in a history of conflict that speaks to women's subordination in family, household, and community relations. The legitimation of custom contributes to this state of affairs. But the cases also reveal the structural poverty and marginalization that affect indigenous communities and foment violence, making it difficult for indigenous men and women to ensure their survival and thus begin to create new gender relations.

Indigenous Justice in the Community Courts

The main authorities responsible for the administration of justice in indigenous communities of the Sierra Norte are the justice of the peace, the auxiliary public prosecutor, and, to a much lesser extent, the president of the auxiliary council, the highest authority in the community. All three authorities are recognized by the state and, except for the president of the auxiliary council, who is elected by direct vote, are appointed by the state judicial authorities from a local shortlist. The shortlist is drawn up on the basis of proposals from the communities. Those whose names are put forward are men who have gained prestige as a result of their participation in community posts (*cargos*). The higher judicial authorities thus endorse local customary elections when they approve the pool. During the fieldwork period, the administration of justice by the communities themselves was of secondary importance as far as the state was concerned, and was not officially recognized as indigenous justice; the decisions of community authorities were not therefore recognized as valid judgments. A reform that came into force in January 2005 introduced an important change in this respect by conceding limited jurisdiction to indigenous justice.[8]

The justice imparted in the auxiliary councils and indigenous communities is interwoven with the state justice system by various means. It is in effect a subordinate system of justice. This means that the discourse of state law and rights has been incorporated as one more referent in conflict resolution, generating processes of mutual constitution between law and custom, that is, processes of interlegality (Santos 1987), but also generating clear tensions between them. Nonetheless, the cultural logics of indigenous justice prevail in the auxiliary councils and indigenous communities and make it different from state justice, especially as regards the meaning of agreements, the ways agreements are arrived at, and the type of judgment brought into play.[9] This system of justice is not, however, totally contrary to state justice. The ability of the Nahua authorities to settle disputes according to their own rules and customs depends on the local population's willingness to recognize their legitimacy, their styles of wielding power, and their relation with the municipal authorities. There are important differences among the different indigenous jurisdictions of Cuetzalan municipality, but it is clear that in general the indigenous authorities have been losing some of their power to impart justice.

A recurrent feature of indigenous justice is that trials are oral and can take a long time, drawing in household members and relatives, until an agreement is reached or a so-called act of conformity (*acta de conformidad*) signed. The signing of an act of conformity or written consent has become a custom for the residents and authorities of the communities, since it ensures the formality of the agreement (see González Montes, this volume). The act of conformity does not enjoy the same status at the municipal level, because the authorities—generally lawyers—consider that such written consents "have no legal force" (in the words of the auxiliary public prosecutor). In contrast to the state justice system, indigenous justice seeks to *hacer el balance,* "to make things balance out," reaching agreements that will satisfy all parties (Nader 1990, 59). This does not mean that the agreements will be harmonious, and some people benefit from them more than others. Dispute resolutions are in effect procedures where power relations are negotiated and reproduced, often hidden in agreements between parties and rituals reinforcing hierarchies and compromises, particularly within the household. Similarly, personal history is of fundamental importance during litigation, and can function either as a counterweight to potentially serious accusations or as a means to discredit the aggrieved party. In the case of women, this kind of consideration can mean that a woman's demands for justice are not regarded as legitimate if she is not considered to have behaved properly—for instance, if she is accused of going out of the house alone. This is an accusation which often features in malicious gossip, as in the case of an accusation of sexual harassment brought by the mother of a young girl in San Miguel, which was finally disallowed by the judge on the grounds that the child was "a great gossip" (*era muy platicadora*). According to a study on traditional Nahua justice by the Takachihualis Commission, in indigenous communities such as San Miguel Tzinacapan, physical punishments such as whippings or, for instance, exhibiting thieves with the stolen object so as to shame them, were also customary some years ago.[10] Offenses were punished differently according to whether they were committed by men or women: for example, in cases of adultery, men were punished with community work or prison, while women suffered corporal punishment (Comisión Takachihualis 1997). Today, these types of punishment have been abolished, as a result of social change as well as the influence of human rights organizations operating at the national and regional levels.

The kind of cases settled by the community-level justice of the peace deal with problems considered minor by the law. They can be classified as: offenses against neighbors and household members (rumor mongering, slander, assault, theft, "abduction of the bride" (*robo de la novia*), breach of promise, unpaid debts); offenses within the household (abuse, inheritance problems, insults, desertion, failure to recognize offspring), and offenses concerning land and property (boundary disputes, damage, etc.) (see also Vallejo Real 2004b). Some of these cases go beyond the community and end up before the state judicial institutions in Cuetzalan. Other, more serious, crimes, involving rape or murder, for example, are generally passed to the state authorities in the district court in Zacapoaxtla.

Indigenous Women and Gender Ideologies in the Administration of Justice

Indigenous women appear before judicial authorities to make a complaint, as accused parties, or as witnesses. Cases brought before the justice of the peace of the Nahua community and the municipal public prosecutor in Cuetzalan illustrate how indigenous law and state law both bring gender ideologies to bear on their evaluation of people's behavior, their understanding of hierarchies, and the limits they set on men's and women's actions in the communities (see Chenaut, this volume). Ideologies of this kind are revealed both in arguments based on custom and in the language of state law, without these necessarily contradicting each other. Recent reforms to the civil code have provided opportunities to recognize women's rights—in relation, for example, to domestic violence, contributions to running the household, and maintenance payments after divorce (*Periódico Oficial,* September 14, 1998).[11] The application of such laws tends, however, to remain at the discretion of the authorities. What prevail are, once again, gender ideologies that tend to discredit or play down women's demands, making it difficult for them to exercise their rights. Even so, within certain margins, some women develop strategies and, with varying degrees of success, manage to restrain violence and redefine their relationships.

Gendered Expectations and Obligations in the Indigenous Legal System: Slander, Rumors, and Violence

The complaint most frequently made by indigenous women is that of abuse. It usually results from an accumulation of previous conflicts and violent incidents that finally lead the woman to go to the authorities. In the context of patrivirilocal practices such as those of the Nahua, women are expected to move to the house of their husband's family when they marry, and therefore have to develop a relationship with their new family, especially their mother-in-law. This process is not always free from problems. It is precisely these tensions that lie behind some of the conflicts that reach the local court, and it is possible to see the strategies women use to negotiate separation from the mother-in-law's house and setting up independent accommodation (see also González Montes, this volume, and Varley, this volume). Sometimes the conflicts are not with the mother-in-law but with the sister-in-law or her brothers, as can be seen in comments such as the following:

SISTER-IN-LAW: Why did you come sticking your nose in here [in her house]?

MARÍA: Because I didn't know that I was going to come here; if you wanted it to be someone from around here you should have found a suitable wife for your brother.

The sister-in-law is complaining about María living in her house, revealing the bad relations between María and her new family. This exchange, and others like it, show that a custom rooted in the communities—that of running off with a partner and going to live with him in his parents' house—is a constant source of problems, especially if that decision is not acceptable to the woman's new family.

When quarrels escalate and someone decides to bring a complaint before the authorities, the parties are called to settle the dispute before the authorities.

A process of conciliation takes place, providing an opportunity to observe the renewal of norms and discourses about sex and gender. The advice offered by authorities to remind the parties of their assigned gender roles and responsibilities—for which judges rely on their own values and experiences— are especially revealing.

Case 1. Slander. A woman, Lupe, is accused of having a lover and of causing family problems with her husband and her son (Antonio), and there is the possibility that she will be ill-treated. For this reason, she decides to take the matter to the authorities. The judge calls in the people involved, including Pedro, the alleged lover. The session is held in the court at Yohualichan. During the session a series of value judgments and beliefs about gender relations, and also about the practice of community justice, emerge.

JUDGE: Secondly, you [addressing the son] have no call to be lacking in respect to your mamá, because she is your *mamá*. She is of the same blood as you. She has sacrificed herself to bring you up and now you are repaying her like this. . . . Even so, you could have said to her, "*Mamacita,* this is what I heard. I'm telling you [because] you know how you can resolve this. . . . I'm not telling my dad because you aren't doing anything." And your father must be feeling pain, because this is what your mother is doing while he goes to work. It's as if you yourself are ruining her. So that's a failure of trust. . . . And that's the way it has to be. For why should we be criticizing our fathers and our mothers? We know that they are the people who brought us up, and that's why I say to you, Antonio, that you have to give some cooperation here.[12]

In this case the authority is making use of his position to address the boy directly and criticize his behavior, saying that he must respect his mother and not accuse her without grounds, since by doing so he offends both her and his father. The direct, familiar style the judge uses to talk to the boy reveals one of the features of community justice, which is that it deals with people who know each other and are very often linked by family ties. The following exchange shows Lupe's effort to defend herself from the slander.

LUPE: So you're not telling me they really saw that he was grabbing me?

HUSBAND: Where they saw you . . . you were coming out of the woods. What were you doing there? If they saw you, let them say what they saw.

LUPE: I've done nothing; it's him who's making advances to me, and he's cross because I don't pay any attention to him, he's angry and so he's slandering me to my son. . . . If I were a widow, then I could let him do something, it's true, but I have a husband . . . and not even then. . . . Yes, if I were a widow I could be cuddling with someone, but having a husband, I can't.

This is how Lupe tries to explain the matter and avoid problems with her husband; she makes it clear, in the end, that she is not the one provoking the situation and tries in this way to recover her honor. Going to the authorities offers her an escape valve she can use to stop the conflict growing and to avoid possible aggression. In the opinion of indigenous women asked what they think about such situations, men see no need to justify themselves and do not tend to resort to the authorities to do so—evidence of important differences in gender roles that put women at a disadvantage compared with men.[13] Lupe's statement also reveals that widows are vulnerable: because they are alone they are considered "available" and are at risk of being approached by men, although at the same time it is accepted that widows may seek another partner.

Women who do not want to put up with aggression and rumors are therefore active users of legal institutions, and in one way or another they do find there some ways of challenging their subordination. The alternatives are limited, however, and gender imperatives define both the scope and the possibilities for action as single, married, or widowed women. Even within these limits women do manage to take steps to renegotiate their relations and above all to avoid reprisals, which can sometimes be very violent. In the case analyzed above, Lupe has to contend with both her husband and her son, who feels obliged to keep her under surveillance. In this case, the judge seeks to defuse the situation to prevent the husband's reacting to the rumors, which is why he speaks to the son in particular.

Violence is a recurring theme in the cases that women from the communities bring to their authorities—a violence usually fueled by alcohol and economic problems (see Chenaut, this volume). The violence can be physical or verbal and can be the product of accumulated tensions, generally within the household, until the woman finally decides to make it public (D'Aubeterrre Buznego 2000b). In the Nahua legal system, abuse is considered an offense only when it exceeds certain limits, since in this legal system it is men's prerogative to "correct" women. Some men display an attitude that can strike an observer as cynical, as they try to play down the impact of the blows they inflict on the grounds of jealously, drunkenness, or simply the belief that the woman belongs to them—a belief shared by village authorities and even the women themselves. For this reason, the aspect of the abuse that is questioned is not so much the man's right to correct his partner or the wife's perceived behavior, as the fact that his violence may be excessive. What follows is an example that reveals these ideologies.

Case 2. Domestic violence. This case concerns a charge of abuse brought to the community judge in San Miguel Tzinacapan by a woman, Rosa, who complains that her husband hits her and does not support her. She presents a complaint before the community authority and asks him to summon the husband.

In the record of proceedings it is obvious that Rosa is accusing her husband of continuous abuse and also of wanting to throw her out of the house because he has another woman. On one occasion he even tried to push her into a ravine, and at other times she lost consciousness under his blows. The husband presents himself before the judge and eventually accepts the accusation, but excuses himself on the grounds that he was drunk. They reach an agreement, recorded in a so-called act of conformity, which includes the following:

> Citizen José A. accepted the charges and said that it had all happened because he was drunk, but he commits himself, before this authority, not to beat his wife again or to abuse her physically or psychologically. Citizen Filomena Cantú de la Cruz says that she does not want her husband to complain that she has taken him to court about this every time he gets drunk, far less to try to hit her, because this frightens the children and she is not prepared to permit it. The judge asked José A. to abide by his commitment not to ill-treat his wife and to give up alcoholic drinks. If this problem happened again, he said, he would hand the case over directly to the district court in Zacapoaxtla without further notice.[14]

In this case, the critical situation of violence led the woman to denounce her husband. Generally the authorities summon a husband to warn him and demand that he change his attitude; the goal is to achieve an "arrangement" between the partners. The judge warns José that the case will be handed over to the district court of Zacapoaxtla if he continues to be violent, which means that he will face a trial; by doing this, the judge seeks to put pressure on José to behave better. Again, the case enables us to unpack the gender ideologies permeating the negotiations, which, although questioning the violence, do not deny the man's authority over the woman. Even under these conditions, the woman obtains a commitment made before the authorities from her husband, as a way of discouraging future aggression.

The Municipal Justice System: Law and Custom in Gender Ideologies

Many cases are transferred from the community to the municipal authorities in Cuetzalan, especially when the offenses are repeated and persistent or when the women are no longer confident that the case can be settled by their own authorities, because of bonds of friendship or family. Claims of abuse that reach the Cuetzalan municipal authorities tend to reflect the desire of women and their relatives to put a stop to the violence, and, if this is not possible, to ask as a last resort for a separation, for which they seek the backing of the state legal authorities. In the municipal courts of Cuetzalan the crimes most frequently denounced by indigenous women are assault, battery, and desertion. In these kinds of crimes, the aggressor is usually the woman's husband or partner, who tries to explain the arguments leading to the abuse as follows:

"He hit her because she hadn't cooked his food";

"Because he has another woman";

"Because he came home drunk";

"Because she asked him for money";

"Because she's useless to him now that she's ill";

"Out of jealousy [his or hers]";

"Because she's lazy."

On their side, these are some of the requests and comments the women make:

"He should be tried";

"He should be punished";

"She will leave the house, so that he won't hit her any more, and will go home to her parents";

"She will take her possessions and her children's documents and not go back to him";

"She asks that he leave her in peace at home with her children";

"He should pay for the medicines and medical attention and . . . he should be brought to justice";

"The authorities should give her and her children guarantees, and she asks for a definitive separation";

"He should recognize her children, if she is pregnant";

"He should pay her for the time she lived with him."

Sometimes in the municipal courts mestizo officials justify violence on the grounds that both men and women in indigenous communities are promiscuous and that this promiscuity is why the women do not carry out their domestic duties properly and the men are irresponsible. These opinions are used to discredit the complaints of indigenous women, even holding them responsible for provoking the attacks to which they have been subjected (Martínez Corona and Mejía Flores 1997). On occasion, however, the men are censured, especially when the aggression is blatant, and are threatened with imprisonment.

The state's judicial institutions are seen as more official spaces for resolving conflicts, even though people from the indigenous communities approach them with certain fears and misgivings that sometimes provoke cultural misunderstandings with legal implications. For example, I have seen several cases in which women have gone to the judicial authorities asking them to put pressure on the women's husbands to respect them and fulfill their commitments to their children, but without the women's necessarily wanting to separate from their husbands; separation, however, was the solution favored by the authority (Sierra 2004a).

State justice offers women opportunities to confront violence and seek alternative ways of negotiating household relations, but does not constitute a real challenge to the gender ideologies rooted in the communities, for the judicial authority shares the patriarchal vision of the family; indeed, such a view is often written into the laws themselves. Again, there is a tendency to play down claims of abuse and women's complaints about their partners in order to obtain agreement or a pardon from the woman, since, in the words of the auxiliary public prosecutor of Cuetzalan, the authorities "have an interest in protecting family unity"—a discourse similar to the one employed by the indigenous authorities. The officials also use legal discourse to discredit customs regarded as "savage," especially where women are concerned; they use such terms to talk about cases of incest, rape, or polygamous marriages, for example, with the intention of belittling indigenous people. Such incidents tend to be judged out of context and generalized as characteristic of indigenous groups.

In recent times, there has been an increase in indigenous women's claims for recognition of their children and for maintenance. Such claims are usually presented to the municipal authorities; the women appeal to the law, and sometimes the success of a claim entails going through a judicial process (involving expenses, time, and usually lawyers' fees). Few women succeed in obtaining the allowance via this route. Of three cases recorded in the proceedings of the Court of First Instance of Zacapoaxtla, only one was decided in favor of the woman, and even here it is not known whether the man was effectively obliged to pay the allowance. Nonetheless, recourse to the law plays an important part in pressuring the defendant to fulfill his commitments or discouraging him from separating from his wife.

For their part, women tend to be accused of deserting the home, adultery, theft, rumor mongering, slander, and slights against neighbors. Some of these claims get as far as the municipal court, particularly when a husband wants to put on record his wife's desertion of the home; this is often also a strategy to get custody of the children or to ensure that, if the wife is pregnant, the husband will not be legally responsible for the child. Although the law gives custody of children to the women, this provision is not always respected in practice, the decision tending to be at the discretion of the authorities. In several cases, it was the municipal authorities who decided who should take the elder children while the younger ones were generally left with the woman. This kind of solution is more in tune with the customs of the communities than with the stipulations of the civil code. In this way, too, gender inequity is enshrined in the law. Thus, when a woman finds herself enmeshed in accusations of adultery, she is faced with the threat of having her children taken away and of being driven from the family home—threats that do not apply equally to men who take another woman. In fact, polygamy (having more than one partner in the community, although not necessarily in the same house) is a common practice and is not always questioned, particularly if the man does his duty in regard to providing for both families. Nonetheless, many conflicts and disputes arise around polygamy, some taken to the state authorities.

Cases of rape provide similarly dramatic evidence of what happens to women who dare to denounce the crime and follow legal channels: these women suffer the full weight of exclusion and discrimination when faced with the agents of state justice. From what we could tell by analyzing court records in the district court of Zacapoaxtla, few cases of rape have ever been successfully prosecuted so as to result in a prison sentence. A large number of trials involving rape are left incomplete, and often the accused is released on grounds of insufficient evidence, which also shows how little importance is given to these cases. In yet other instances, the victim and her family find themselves in even more humiliating situations, forced to endure both racism and gender-based violence from the labyrinthine workings of the law and even from the agents of justice themselves. One example concerns a sixteen-year-old rape victim who was raped a second time by the legal doctor whose job it was to confirm that she had been raped. The crime went unpunished, despite the efforts of women's and human rights organizations to press criminal charges. I have documented elsewhere similar incidents that demonstrate women's structural disadvantage with regard to justice and show how both legal language and access to legal authorities reproduce dominant gender roles, leaving little space for negotiation, particularly when the offenses in question are serious and mestizos with power are involved (Sierra 1995, 2001). For this reason, it is important to highlight the role currently being played by the human rights organizations, which support people bringing legal cases, exposing irregularities, and forcing the judicial authorities to respect the law.

Indigenous Organizations and Women's Rights

In the Cuetzalan region, two important human rights groups are the indigenous human rights organization, Takachihualis, and the indigenous women's organization, Maseualsiuamej Mosenyolchicauanij. Together with other organizations, these play a central role in monitoring, following up, and defending the rights of indigenous men and women. Maseual (as they call themselves) play a particularly important role: with the support of mestizo women advisors, they have succeeded in ensuring that the indigenous women of the region know their rights and have recourse to legal and psychological support when abused. Another key group is the Indigenous Women's House (Casa de la Mujer Indígena, or CAMI), managed and run by indigenous women from a number of organizations and communities. CAMI was promoted by the National Commission for the Development of Indigenous Peoples (Comisión Nacional para el Desarrollo de los Pueblos Indígenas, or CDI), and has been taken over by indigenous women as a center offering psychological and health support and legal advice to women who are victims of domestic violence, as well as capacity-building workshops on rights issues, including masculinity. These organizations work tirelessly to promote a gender equity discourse derived from their own cultural frames of reference, throughout the Sierra Norte, using radio and other channels of communication. In this way, a discourse of women's rights is being established as a legitimate cultural and legal instrument offering new options for women. The strength of these organizations is clearly visible in their active participation in the new judicial and institutional spaces that have opened up in the municipality of Cuetzalan, spaces aimed at ensuring that women's rights are taken into account in the practice of justice.

Women's participation in the municipal Indigenous Court has given practical expression to the aspirations of both indigenous women's organizations and regional human rights organizations to build alternative forms of justice more in accord with local culture and more open to respect for women's rights. Important advances have been made in this area, as can be seen from the composition of the municipal Indigenous Court and from women's role as part of the council of the court. Women's participation at trials is making itself felt in the negotiations and agreements between the parties, which refer to both law and custom. However, the gender ideologies informing judicial practice, and entrenched mindsets at both local and regional levels, will continue to feature among the obstacles to progress in achieving deeper changes. It is to be hoped that the efforts of indigenous women to create projects promoting gender equity, together with the decision to participate in the struggles of their people, will lead them to defend projects such as the municipal Indigenous Court, which, despite its limitations, is seen as a collectively constructed alternative.

Conclusions

The gender ideologies revealed in the practice of justice in indigenous regions are evidence of the ideological constraints that reinforce a patriarchal vision of gender roles, defining hierarchies, power, and cultural values. These are essential elements of customary law and help define the behavior expected of Nahua women and men. The gender ideologies informing the practice of justice in both community and municipal institutions appear not so different from each other, even though the discourse of law is supposed to prevail in the latter and the language of custom in the former. What might appear contrasting juridical ideologies, legitimated through legal codes and the liberal rights discourse, on the one hand, or through appeals to tradition, on the other, are, in the end, parts of a cultural continuum that is oppressive to women. Nevertheless, women find in these institutions some tools with which to state their cases, build room for maneuver, and—to some extent—redefine their relations with others and contain violence.

It is significant that the community courts are the ones to which indigenous men and women generally take their cases, seeking negotiation and a warning to the offender rather than punishment or imprisonment. It is also clear that men and women of the indigenous communities turn to the state's judicial institutions, particularly those of the municipality, when matters become complicated and the community authorities are not seen as able to settle the case on their own. Taking a case to the state courts, however, is expensive: transport, paperwork, and ensuring the goodwill of the judicial authorities all cost money. People also have to deal with situations that they may find humiliating and offensive, such as encountering openly discriminatory attitudes toward them and having to speak Spanish. Moreover, the discourse of legality does not guarantee that the law will be applied, for the extent to which it is applied depends on the power relations in play and whether the claimants are strong enough to ensure that their rights are respected. The capacity to negotiate is not, however, distributed evenly and depends, for women, on the support that they can obtain from others in their pursuit of justice; in this respect, women's organizations and human rights organizations play a very important role. Recourse to the law and the claiming of rights open new spaces for challenging gender inequality inside and outside the communities, but do not question the basic structure of relations between women and men.

The socioeconomic changes affecting indigenous communities are also having an impact on gender relations, modifying family structures and the role of women in the household. Women are increasingly having to take on responsibility for household maintenance, especially when the men migrate and, sometimes, do not return. It is to be hoped that these changes will have an influence on gender ideologies, giving more power to women; however, such change does not come about of its own accord. Normative discourses continue to prevail, even when at odds with the new realities. At the same time, women are beginning to question these discourses—for instance, in matters concerning the subsistence allowance, divorce, inheritance, access to land, and shared participation in community cargos. The changes that are occurring are providing new opportunities, which many women have seized, pushing forward new practices and challenging male authority. These women are questioning deeply rooted customs that they see, in the words of indigenous women leaders, as "bad customs" that should be abolished or transformed. The experience of women leaders in Cuetzalan and other regions confirms what we observed concerning the practice of justice: the subordinate situation in which many women live in their communities is legitimized in models defining what is expected of a woman; but women themselves find alternatives for transforming certain customs that oppress them.

In the national context, the experiences of the Cuetzalan organizations serve as examples of how legal opportunities made available by the state can be used by indigenous groups without having to give up cultural and political demands as peoples. The creation of institutions such as the Indigenous Court in Cuetzalan, set up in response to a state initiative to recognize an indigenous jurisdiction, also entails a change in governance, as the authorities affirm their commitment to the constitutional mandate to recognize cultural diversity, however limited the scope of the reforms. Indigenous and human rights organizations will have to be alert to the potential for political manipulation of this recognition, but it has undoubtedly provided new options both within the communities and in their relations with the state. Legal discourse can also be used to resist the law itself (Lazarus-Black and Hirsch 1994). The questioning of certain oppressive customs also takes into account the innovative proposals that indigenous women are making in their struggle to find ways of living their lives with greater dignity without rejecting their cultural and ethnic heritage.

The demands of the indigenous women of Cuetzalan are consistent with the demands of many other indigenous women who, at local, regional, and national levels, are developing innovative proposals on how to think about diversity from a gender perspective without abandoning the struggle for collective rights. Local identities are being redefined in dialogue and tension with the state, in new transnational human rights discourses, and in demands for gender and cultural justice. These changes are helping women to imagine new ways of life in which they are also protagonists in their peoples' struggles and contribute to the practice of a multicultural form of justice. A legal anthropology with a gender perspective thus has to take into account varied positions on justice and diversity both within and outside indigenous communities, and to show how gender ideologies are expressed and become entrenched in state and indigenous law and in the practice of justice. To meet these challenges, we have to develop a critical analysis of legal practices, and question the idea that law and culture are homogeneous.

Translated by Mandy Macdonald.

NOTES

1. The *municipality* of Cuetzalan has a population of approximately thirty-five thousand people, of whom 70 percent are Nahua and the rest are of Totonac and mestizo origin. The mestizos are concentrated in the *town* of Cuetzalan. The municipality is located in the eastern part of the Sierra Norte de Puebla, and has eight auxiliary councils (Juntas Auxiliares), smaller population centers within the same municipality. In rural areas, many of these correspond to former Indian villages and indigenous communities.

2. The collaborative project Interculturality, Law, and Gender in Indigenous Regions was financed by the Consejo Nacional de Ciencia y Tecnología (CONACYT) (1998–2001). The project covered several regions of Mexico (see Sierra 2004d).

3. In a pioneering article, Laura Nader and Jane Collier (1978) demonstrate the persistent recourse to local courts by Zapotec and Maya women. The authors emphasize the need to consider the impact of socioeconomic conditions on the possibilities for legal change, since the creation of new rights does not in itself guarantee that the conditions needed for people to exercise those rights will be forthcoming.

4. This can be observed among the Nahuas of the Sierra Norte de Puebla (in Cuetzalan and Huauchinango) and in the Totonac region of Coyutla, Veracruz. It also occurs, to a lesser extent, among the Zinacantecos of Chiapas and the Mixtecs of Metlatónoc, Guerrero.

5. The Indigenous Courts were recognized as part of Puebla's judicial system in the revision in 2002 of the law defining the structure of the state's judicial system: Ley Orgánica del Poder Judicial del Estado 2002, art. 1. (For information on the various sorts of law in Mexico, see Zamora et al. 2004, 94).

6. I base this analysis on work we carried out in several auxiliary councils, as well as the municipal institutions of Cuetzalan, and especially the work in the Auxiliary Council of Yohualichan (Vallejo Real 2000, 2004b). I also refer to material obtained with the support of Korinta Maldonado, Adriana Terven, and Heber Morales.

7. Recent research in legal anthropology has demonstrated the disadvantages faced by indigenous women in both law and custom (Chenaut 1997, 1999; Hernández Castillo and Garza Caligaris 1995; Garza Caligaris 2002; Imberton Deneke 2002).

8. The reform in 2004 of the state's Code of Civil Procedures recognizes several alternative forms of access to justice, among them indigenous justice, which it defines as "based on recognition of the systems which have been used for this purpose within each ethnic group, in accordance with the usages, customs, traditions, and cultural values they have observed and accepted ancestrally" (Código de Procedimientos Civiles para el Estado Libre y Soberano de Puebla, 2004, art. 848). The research in this chapter was carried out before these legal changes took place, so I have not incorporated them into our analysis.

9. Research on justice in Zinacatán, Chiapas, by Jane Collier (1973, 2001) demonstrates convincingly both how cultural logics are constructed and how they differ from the logic of the state courts.

10. The Takachihualis Commission is an indigenous human rights organization based in the community of San Miguel Tzinacapan, Cuetzalan. As well as legal agency and accompaniment, the commission carried out research and documentation work on indigenous law and traditional justice.

11. Código Civil para el Estado Libre y Soberano de Puebla, 1985, arts. 291–292, 323–325, and 443, respectively. A reform to Article 454 made sexual intercourse against the wife's will, and violence against children of both or either of the spouses, grounds for divorce.

12. The excerpts quoted here have been translated from Náhuatl, via Spanish, into English.

13. Comments made by indigenous women from different parts of the country during a course on leadership at the Simone de Beauvoir Institute (ILSB), Mexico City, November 2004.

14. The act of conformity was consulted in the office of the court in San Miguel Tzinacapan, Cuetzalan. It was written in Spanish.

6

Indigenous Women and the Law

Prison as a Gendered Experience

VICTORIA CHENAUT

In the analysis of legal practices in multicultural societies, it is important to understand that indigenous law and state law do not constitute countervailing normative systems, self-contained and isolated from each other. As Santos has argued (1987, 297–298), what emerges in these contexts is a situation of "inter-legality," characterized by "different legal spaces superimposed, interpenetrated and mixed in our minds as much as in our actions." This implies that social actors can reference different normativities, which they use and manipulate, invoking both state law and local norms, depending upon the context and the interests in play. In this manner, the differentiated normativities that appear in situations of interlegality give rise among "consumers" of law to juridical practices that—given the existence of spaces of negotiation, exchange, conflict, and normative imbrication—are mutually shaped and constituted.

The functioning of indigenous law should not be seen as a harmonious field in which conflict and power relations within groups are absent. In fact, the case of indigenous women illustrates how gender hierarchies are expressed in social life. Numerous studies in Mexico have examined and debated this theme, even as organized indigenous women themselves question the gender inequality that exists in their communities. Thus, it has been noted that indigenous women live in situations of social and domestic violence that are generally related to male alcoholism and the sexual violence associated with it (Hernández Castillo 1998, 2002d; Sierra 2004a). It is important to bear in mind that these contexts can reproduce gender stereotypes that can actually create the conditions in which women are accused of certain crimes. Further, indigenous women find themselves marginalized, in structural socioeconomic terms. They live in conditions of extreme poverty and lack basic resources, circumstances that create the conditions via which the judicial system criminalizes them.

At the same time, one must recognize that the social construction of gender relations manifests in such a way that men display a higher incidence of violence than women, making criminality predominantly a masculine matter. Specialists in the field argue that it is men who commit the majority of crimes, but that there is a gender difference among offenders that remains stable across time, place, and culture. In general, men commit murder during fights or other violent encounters with other men, while the victims of female murderers are principally a woman's domestic partner or members of her family. Moreover, most victims of murder are men, even though the most frequent victims of certain crimes (such as domestic violence) are women (Fagan 2002).

The greater extent of masculine criminality is reflected in statistics on Mexico's prison population. In 1994, women represented 4 percent of the total incarcerated population in the country (Azaola Garrido and José Yacamán 1996, 18). A higher incidence of criminality among men than women appears a constant across countries, age groups, and historical periods, with the exception of crimes particular to women (especially prostitution, infanticide, and abortion) (Azaola Garrido 1998). Judicial statistics also reveal that men are more frequently accused than women of committing offenses and crimes. For example, in the late 1990s women represented only 9.9 percent of those charged with crimes who were subsequently sentenced by criminal courts in Mexico (INEGI 2000). According to those who have conducted research on this topic, the low incidence of female criminality can be explained in part by the fact that informal mechanisms of social control (school, family, church) are more effective with regard to women than to men (Azaola Garrido 1996a; Larrauri 1994).

The elements briefly highlighted in this introduction indicate that criminality is permeated by gender differences. For those interested in the problematic of indigenous women, these considerations compel several questions. How does the vulnerability produced by the poverty, marginalization, monolinguism, and illiteracy of indigenous women affect the social construction of criminality? To what extent does the imperative to identify the guilty lead agents of the state to charge indigenous women with crimes they did not commit? What are the social and cultural contexts in which indigenous women are charged with crimes? In what ways does the experience of incarceration affect them as women, both during and after their time in jail? How are these women perceived in their communities, in accordance with the local norms and sanctions that function as a system of informal control?

This chapter presents an initial reflection on these questions, focusing on the experiences of four Totonac women who were interviewed while imprisoned in Papantla, Veracruz (Chenaut 1999). These women, whose judicial files were also consulted, were jailed on charges of planning, complicity in, or instigation of murder, the most severe crime that can be committed by a human being and one sanctioned by lengthy incarceration. It is not my intention to judge their innocence or guilt, or to comment upon technical judicial matters, per se. Rather, the goal here is to understand these cases in their social and cultural dimensions, as other researchers have attempted to do in similar cases (see Azaola Garrido 1996a). In this context, it is important to bear in mind that legal disputes are both immersed in networks of social relations and culturally situated (Nader 1990), and that they take place in a particular historical context and within a specific set of power relations (Starr and Collier 1989).

The stories of these four rural, indigenous women, all of whom lived in poverty, constitute real personal and social dramas, in which one sees in play both the normative elements that regulate social life and the ways conflicting norms manifest themselves in the course of a legal dispute. In addition to the devastating significance that these events had for the personal lives of those affected, the term *social drama* (coined by V.W. Turner [1974]) is entirely appropriate for these legal cases because, over the course of the period in which the events evolved, they were characterized by: a public action that broke established norms; a crisis; an action involving formal or informal reparation (possibly including recourse to the legal system); and a resolution or consequences.

From a gender perspective, it is worth considering Elena Azaola Garrido's (1996a, 11) position that homicide is a "crime of gender" that permits one to examine how genders are socially constructed and the role differentiation they involve. Azaola Garrido argues that murder takes us to the limit of what society expects and manifests regarding the conduct of men and women in social life. This, in turn, leads us to ask what kinds of murder men and women commit, and whether it is possible to characterize the crime (and the resulting prison experience) by the gender of the person who committed it.

With these considerations in mind, this chapter divides into three parts. The first offers a brief characterization of the indigenous population interned in prisons in the state of Veracruz and, in particular, the female population in prison in Papantla. These data help establish the broad context in which one can characterize indigenous and female criminality in the region under study. The second section summarizes the case histories of the women accused of homicide. The third part compares the characteristics of the murders involved, taking two main elements as the narrative line: the accusatory mechanism that led to these women's incarceration, and the type of conflict in which the women were involved and the reasons for which they were accused of having committed a crime. One purpose of this study is to repay a portion of my debt to these women, who were "forgotten"[1] and marginalized from regional development, and into whose lives I suddenly appeared, asking them to tell their stories. More generally, the chapter contributes to a reflection on the relationships among gender, law, and interlegality in multicultural societies.

Finally, it is worth noting that the information presented here forms part of a broader investigation into the legal practices of Totonacs living in a multicultural region in the state of Veracruz, an area situated in the coastal lowlands of the Gulf of Mexico and the foothills of the Sierra Madre Oriental. The city of Papantla is the seat of the Papantla judicial district and the physical headquarters of the local Public Prosecution Agency (Agencia del Ministerio Público), the Public Prosecution Agency Specializing in Indigenous Affairs (Agencia del Ministerio Público Especializada en Asuntos de los Indígenas), the relevant civil and criminal courts, and the regional penitentiary, which houses the majority of those serving time for crimes committed in the eleven municipalities comprising this judicial district (Chenaut 2004).[2] The interviews I conducted with inmates from different municipalities in the Papantla district provided a broad perspective on the kinds of disputes that arise in the region and the way the indigenous population experiences the administration of justice.

The Totonac Population and Prison

The scanty information that exists concerning criminality among the indigenous peoples of the state of Veracruz indicates that in early 1997 there were a total of 772 indigenous men and women incarcerated in the state's jails. They represented 9.6 percent of the state's total inmate population. Disaggregating the data between those jailed for committing common crimes and those jailed for federal-jurisdiction crimes, a total of 674 men (97.4 percent) and 18 women (2.6 percent) were imprisoned for common crimes, and there were 53 men (66.2 percent) and 27 women (33.8 percent) imprisoned for federal offenses.[3] The higher proportion of women among those tried and convicted of federal crimes such as drug trafficking is striking, given that this is a form of criminality associated with the recent expansion of an activity based on networks of power going beyond indigenous regions. In 1999, 61.8 percent of all women sentenced in the federal district court in the state of Veracruz were charged with narcotics offenses (INEGI 2000). Drug trafficking has grown particularly rapidly in southern Veracruz, and indigenous people frequently serve as the "mules" who transport narcotics in small quantities in packages or cardboard boxes. They are often searched and arrested while traveling on public transportation— a pattern similar to that identified elsewhere in Mexico, and especially in Oaxaca, where Zapotec women are often recruited for this activity (Azaola Garrido 1996b; Azaola Garrido and José Yacamán 1996; Núñez Miranda 2004).

The crimes most frequently committed by the incarcerated indigenous population in the state of Veracruz are homicide and rape. In the late 1990s, the majority of these internees came from indigenous and peasant communities and were of low income and educational levels (Chenaut 1999). Prisoners of both sexes shared these common traits, indicating that the prison experience is constituted in a space in which those who are predominantly present are the poor, the marginalized, and victims of discrimination.

In a search for the principal elements of female criminality in the Papantla penitentiary, I profiled the cases of fourteen women interviewed in the course of field research conducted between 1996 and 1998. The majority were either Totanacs or women who came from rural families of indigenous origin and who had migrated to Papantla (twelve women), swelling the ranks of the city's urban proletariat and (in several cases) losing their command of their indigenous language. One internee was an ethnic Nahua from an area adjoining the Totonac region. All of the women had received very limited education. Two had been housewives before their arrest; the others were employed or self-employed: four as domestic servants, two as laundresses, three as street vendors, and one as a bilingual Nahua-Spanish teacher.[4] Nine of the women were mothers, with an average of four children each. Their average age was twenty-eight years.

It is useful to distinguish between the crime that these women were accused of committing (that is, the classification, by state law, of conduct considered illicit) and the motives involved (that is, the cause of the conflict that led to imprisonment, in which one can appreciate the importance of social relations with a high component of interpersonal violence). The crimes of which these women said they were accused included plotting, complicity in, or instigation of murder (five women);[5] assault and battery (two women); robbery (two women); and one case each of pimping, criminal endangerment, rape, committing bodily harm (*injurias y golpes*), rioting, and attack on the means of communication. In the majority of these cases the charge involved violence— domestic violence (four women) and violence in general (four women). In other cases, the reason for arrest was debt, robbery, political matters, a hidden pregnancy, and theft.[6]

What is striking is the privations that these women experience in daily prison life. In general, they are completely ignorant of the functioning of the legal system and the nature of the crime of which they were accused. They have no economic resources with which to cover the costs of the legal proceedings, in addition to the expense of caring for and maintaining their children—a burden that is especially great for women who have no domestic partner. Finally, these women are left unprotected not only by their lack of financial resources, but also by the absence of visitors, because most of their relatives live in rural communities and cannot afford to travel to Papantla. One of the women prisoners summarized the situation in which they find themselves with the following phrase: "We are like little animals, who were taken to jail and abandoned there."[7]

The information I have presented above appears to confirm what Pat Carlen (1992, 53) defines as the overarching traits of women who commit crimes and are imprisoned: "that women's crimes are, in the main, the crimes of the powerless; that women in prison are disproportionately from ethnic minority groups; and that a majority of women in prison have been in poverty for the greater part of their lives." That is, the lack of power, poverty, and membership

in a minority ethnic group define at least three central axes of female imprisonment. In the next section, we will observe how some of the social and cultural
specificities of this phenomenon are manifested in the state of Veracruz.

Gender and Personal Histories

This section begins with brief accounts of four women accused of murder who
were serving time in the Papantla penitentiary in the 1990s. The content of
these stories and information regarding the sequence of events that occurred
during the judicial process are based principally upon data in the women's case
files, with supplementary material from my interviews with the prisoners.
Needless to say, the names used in these accounts are not the persons' real
names.[8] There is no doubt about the effect of power exercised through the legal
process. As Foucault has noted (1975: x), what is expressed in judicial case files
is a relationship of power, "a battle among discourses and through discourses,"
that shows how institutions and juridical knowledge are deployed in social life.
But these files also permit one to appreciate the voices of social actors, whose
discourses and arguments are deployed in their capacity of accuser, accused, or
witness. The kaleidoscope of positions expressed in these records opens the
possibility of observing, via the law, actors' practices in their social lives.

Norma

Norma was born in a community in the Papantla highlands.[9] At the age of fifteen, she was arrested and jailed in the Papantla penitentiary, where she had
served three months at the time of interview. She was accused of having killed
a man who had been a patient of her *curandero* husband.[10] Her legal file forms
part of the complex prosecutorial case against her husband, who was accused of
using a machete to kill three men in a cornfield after leading them to believe he
would cure them. Norma was present when he killed the first of his victims.
Because she was below the age of full criminal responsibility, she was transferred to the juvenile detention center in Banderilla, Veracruz, and released six
months later. Her case is related to the practice of traditional medicine, which
is widely accepted in the Veracruz countryside.[11]

Micaela

Micaela also came from a community in the Papantla highlands. She was accused
of planning and participating in the murder of her husband, and was jailed
along with her father and twenty-one-year-old brother, who admitted having
committed the crime. At the time of her imprisonment, Micaela was twenty-six
years old and had three children, and she gave birth to a fourth child several
months after beginning her prison term. The murder took place in her parents'
home when her brother discovered the husband, who was drunk, beating

Micaela and strangled him. Like her father and brother, Micaela was sentenced to nineteen years in prison. On appeal, she and her father were absolved of responsibility because there was no evidence proving their legal responsibility for the crime, and her brother's sentence was reduced to ten years' imprisonment. Micaela was in jail for a total of eighteen months; her case is one involving male domestic violence.[12]

Felipa

Felipa comes from a community on the coastal plain of Veracruz. At the time she was jailed, she was thirty-one years old, had three children, and had been widowed for eight years. She is the only one of the four women discussed here who had been married in both civil and religious rites; the other three cohabited with their partners (*unión libre*). Her dwelling (as the case file notes, "a house with a palm roof and a dirt floor, surrounded by a fence of clay pots") was located on a parcel of land owned by her father-in-law, and so she was surrounded by members of her deceased husband's family. (According to the Totonacs' patrivirilocal residence patterns, they included her husband's parents and three of his brothers and their families.) Felipa was accused of killing the baby girl to whom, one day, she had given birth while working in the family cornfield (*milpa*). She left the baby's (strangled) body half-buried among stones and palm husks. Because she was a widow, Felipa had hidden her pregnancy from her relatives and neighbors. She was initially sentenced to nineteen years in jail, but on appeal her sentence was reduced to seventeen years and the charge was changed to simple homicide. Later, she appealed against her sentence, but her appeal was unsuccessful.[13] Felipa subsequently had another child while in prison. Her case is thus part of the problematic of love and sexual life.[14]

Rosa

Born on the coastal plain of Veracruz, at the age of fifty-four years Rosa was jailed, along with her twenty-eight-year-old son, for planning and participating in the murder of her husband, as well as for violating the laws related to burial and disinterment. Her husband left home one day in 1990 and, despite several attempts to locate him, was never seen again. Two years later, the case was reopened because it was discovered that he had been murdered by the curandero husband of Norma (see the first case summarized above), who claimed that Rosa had offered to pay him to kill her husband. Rosa and her son were detained two years after the murder, and each was sentenced to sixteen years in prison. They were absolved of the charges relating to burial and exhumation of the body, and on further appeal the son was freed because he could prove that he was not physically present at the time of the crime. However, the State Appellate Court (Tribunal Superior de Justicia del Estado) upheld Rosa's sentence, and her appeal to the federal appeals court was also unsuccessful. The son left jail after serving three years, and Rosa was freed on grounds of good conduct after having served eight years of her sentence. Her case arose in the context of a dispute over her husband's property (an ejido land parcel and a house in town), which one of her husband's female cousins had attempted to take from her.[15]

Murders Committed by Men

Of the four women whose cases I have reviewed, only Felipa actually committed the crime of murder (infanticide). Because infanticide is a crime generally committed by women, it is worth reviewing briefly the type of murders committed by men. In the case of the nine indigenous men interviewed in the Papantla penitentiary, it is noteworthy that (with the exception of one case of unintentional homicide involving a woman) the victims were all men killed in fights involving a machete, a knife, or a firearm. Alcohol was a factor in all of these disputes. In a couple of cases, the killing resulted from the assailant's attempt to protect the honor of his wife or female neighbor. Even though these indigenous men were just as poor and socioeconomically marginalized as the women, there were notable gender-related differences in the way the crimes occurred.

These data agree with the conclusions reached by Elena Azaola Garrido (1996a, 1998) and Abigail Fagan (2002), in the sense that there are differences in murders depending on the gender of the person committing the crime. Men's victims are generally not relatives, because the crime is typically committed in public areas like the street or a bar (cantina). In contrast, family and domestic life constitutes women's predominant sphere of action, and murder victims therefore tend to be closely related to the perpetrators.

Domestic Dynamics and Transgression

This section examines the family conflicts that resulted in homicide, the context in which the violation of norms became public, and the declarations made against the women accused of committing the crimes. In the case of Rosa, it is important to highlight the relationship she maintained throughout the judicial proceedings with her husband's first cousin, who made the formal accusation against her. In 1990, the cousin formally denounced Rosa before the public prosecutor, and she subsequently filed other papers expanding on her initial accusation. The documents suggest that the cousin accused Rosa of attempting to gain control over Rosa's partner's property on the grounds that he had no children from his previous relationships. (Because Rosa was not legally married, she had no legal rights over her partner's properties.) It is noteworthy, however, that Rosa's legal file shows that she had a seven-year-old daughter from her relationship with the man in question, and that this child was never considered a possible heir to her father's estate. The fact that Rosa had taken at least two of her four sons to live with her and her partner, and the fact that they were working the man's ejido parcel, were further indications to the cousin that Rosa had an interest in getting rid of her husband so that she could take over his property.

The prosecutor's office was not convinced of the veracity of these charges, but several months later Rosa and her son again found themselves in difficulty because Norma and a man accompanying her were arrested in Rosa's home (see the first case described above). The curandero husband managed to flee, but there was then a police investigation that found that he had killed three people, one of whom was Rosa's husband.

Both in her court testimony and in our interview, Rosa emphatically denied that she had instigated her husband's murder. What is clear from the case file is the dispute that existed over the man's property, and the fact that his first cousin considered herself a possible heir because he supposedly had no direct descendants. The fact that Rosa had cohabited with the man, and the fact that she had four adult sons who were interested in working his land, produced a conflict of interests that resulted in legal charges being filed against her. It is important to note in this context that there is a scarcity of cultivable land in this part of Veracruz, and that many family disputes arise from conflict over property ownership. Thus the charges against Rosa could have been motivated by a sense of jealousy over her control of (or the possibility that she might gain control over) the ejido parcel. Such considerations commonly motivate people in this area to try to manipulate the law in their favor.

The crime involving Micaela occurred in her parents' home, a thatch-roofed house with a dirt floor. She and her husband lived in Mexico City, where, like many Totonacs, they had migrated in search of work. Upon their return to the community, they lived for a time with Micaela's family, where problems quickly emerged because of her husband's violent conduct. On the night of the crime, he returned home drunk and demanded that Micaela give him something to eat. At the same time, he began to beat her. These actions were witnessed by Micaela's father, mother, and brother Joaquín, as well as by her three children. Joaquín defended his sister, and was also assaulted by his brother-in-law. The aunt of Micaela's husband heard the family fight, and she responded to the shouting by going to the house where the altercation was taking place. The aunt was denied entry, but she managed to see Joaquín beating his brother-in-law severely. The statement the aunt made to the prosecutor's office the following day was crucial in bringing about the arrest of Micaela, her father, and her brother. Micaela and her father emphatically denied having committed the crime, while her brother admitted that he had done so.

Additional family history came to light when Micaela was interviewed by the prison staff. She could not remember ever having a good relationship with her husband since the death of one of her children in Mexico City. Her husband blamed Micaela for the child's death, claiming that she had not given the child adequate care, and started to beat her.

In the middle of the fight described above, Joaquín asked Micaela for a cord with which to tie up his brother-in-law. However, the knots obstructed his breathing, and he died of strangulation. When I interviewed him, Joaquín described the events leading up to his brother-in-law's death:

> [That night] when I arrived, he had my sister. He was grabbing her by the hair and pulling her around by the hair. I couldn't stand for that; I had grown up with too much of that. . . . So I tell him, "Don't do that to my sister." . . . "No, I'm not going to let her go; what's it to you?" . . . Then he lets go of my sister and grabs me by the shirt . . ."[16]

Highlighting the information concerning Joaquín's intervention in the fight underscores the context of domestic violence in which the crime occurred. Joaquín indicates in his personal statement that he grew up witnessing domestic violence, first by his brothers against their girlfriends and wives, and then by his brother-in-law against his sister. At the same time, his actions tended to reproduce—and reinforce—gender roles that establish violence as more a male than a female prerogative. He responded to the situation with violence, and the spiral of violence ended in homicide.

In Felipa's story, the family conflict occurred in a context in which what was at stake was the honor and respectability of a widow who lived surrounded by her late husband's family. The facts of the case became notorious when some children found the body of a newborn baby in a cornfield. Thus began a series of deductions that rapidly cast suspicion on Felipa, especially her increase in weight (which she had attributed to simply becoming fatter or having diabetes) and the fact that on the day in question she had to lie down because she felt ill. At first, Felipa's in-laws told her parents (who lived in a nearby community) of what had happened, and it was her father who decided to inform the community authorities. This chain of events eventually led to her being formally charged with murder.

Nevertheless, in her personal story Felipa emphasized the role that the wives of her three brothers-in-law played in the formulation of criminal charges against her. She claimed that they were jealous of her because she obtained high-yielding corn crops and because she was the only one of them who had actually been formally married. In this regard, it is worthwhile noting the difference between the judicial record and her own account of how a criminal charge was specified against her: the latter stressed the role of her in-laws in sending her to jail. In her interview with the author, Felipa denied having committed murder ("the baby girl was stillborn," she said), and she shifted the focus of the conflict to her relationship with the wives of her brothers-in-law.

In her original statement to the police, Felipa acknowledged having had sexual relations with a man, and said that she had unsuccessfully taken herbal remedies to avoid getting pregnant. In this case, the judicial evidence points toward her guilt given that forensic doctors determined that the cause of her baby girl's death was asphyxiation by strangling. Of the four women's cases examined here, Felipa's is the only one in which the accused recognized in her police declaration that she had committed homicide. This particular crime was the consequence of Felipa's attempt, given that she was a widow, to prevent her family from learning about her pregnancy.

This case shows us the difficulty a single woman faces in dealing with a situation that affects her honor, faced with family and social sanctions. The fact that Felipa did not tell even her own mother that she was pregnant constitutes an act of negation that prefigured the subsequent drama. Indeed, when the baby girl's corpse was discovered and family members began to make accusations against her, Felipa argued "it must be La Llorona's child."[17] She thus broke not only the norms of state law (it is a crime to deprive someone of life) but also the norms of the community. On the day on which the baby's remains were found, Felipa's father told her, according to the case file, "You are going to go to jail. . . . Or you leave here and hit the road because you have shamed us." In rural communities, the breaking of codes of conduct concerning a woman's honor affects both the woman herself and her family members, aggravated in this case by the death of the baby.[18] Thus, in the dramatic moments in which the violation of norms became publicly known, Felipa's father presented her with a choice: going to jail, or leaving the community. In reality, he was telling her that her conduct had ostracized her from the community, and that her future now lay elsewhere. Her father's testimony, as well as Norma's testimony (examined below), constitute important points of reference for understanding both the situation of an indigenous woman who has committed a crime and her time in jail as a gendered experience.

Norma ended up being accused of a crime because she chose the wrong male partner, who, it turned out, abused his patients and used traditional medicine to settle personal vendettas. Throughout her case file, one finds evidence of popular belief in the benefits that this kind of medicine can provide. The fact that the man turned out to be a murderer does not invalidate the view that the crime was constructed on the basis of beliefs that are widely shared in the rural milieu. In fact, the relationships that he had with Norma (his partner) and Rosa (his patient) were central to the criminal case constructed against the two women. The first of them lived with the curandero, with whom she had fled her own community. This is a common practice in rural Mexico, but Norma's poor choice of partner placed her in a disadvantageous position vis-à-vis her family. Her father had filed charges against the curandero with judicial authorities in Papantla, demanding that the couple marry, but for some reason they never did, and continued living together for some months. Norma described in these terms the situation of domestic violence in which she found herself:

> He used to tell me "You are going to do what I tell you and nothing else," and that if I didn't do it he was going to kill me. Out of fear I had to obey him, because I preferred life to death.[19]

Given that her father was a respected man in her home community, and that being in jail shamed her family, Norma's father told her that he did not want her to return home when she got out of prison. Norma explained it as follows:

> He doesn't come [to the prison] because he is a respected man in the community. . . . It shames him for people to see him come here, and so he says "Why should I go and see her? She looked for trouble by not choosing better." He told me, straight out, "I'll help you, but I don't want you to come back home," because the possibility that I might return there embarrasses him. Everyone would be talking about me and about him. That's the way people are there; they notice everything, they talk, they make comments. . . . And he says, "If they talk about me now while you are here, what would they say if you were to return there when you get out? It's better that I help you and, once you get out, you take your own road, wherever that leads, because I don't want to see you at home again."
>
> It's just that everyone talks about him, saying that "Don Rubén's daughter is in jail" and that they never thought that would happen to one of his children. Sometimes, out of shame, he starts drinking and drinking, and sometimes he fights with my mother. But I say to my mother, "Don't pay any attention to him. I know that I am to blame, but, if I don't turn to the two of you, to whom can I turn? It's the two of you who should help me because I can't ask for help from anyone else." . . . And my mother says to me, "Your father is very upset with you, in the first place because he is your father, and if he doesn't feel anything for you, who is going to?" I say, "Yes, he is upset with me because I make other people feel awkward, and what did that make my father feel, embarrassment or hatred?" She responds, "Who knows? He says it's only anger, that he's going to help you, but that you shouldn't come back home." I tell her, "I've also thought about not going back there because, if they speak about me the way they do now, how are they going to talk about me then? They're going to treat me like chewing gum, chewing me over here, chewing me over there. It's better to be far away than to be close to you. Even though I feel badly about it, I'm going to have to resign myself to not seeing you. It's better that way, even though we can talk to each other sometimes just to stay in touch. It's better that way, though it's better for you than for me. Anyway, I've now lost the community's respect, and if I go

away it's better because then people won't see me and they'll talk about me less." If they see me, they're going to say, "Look, the jailbird's back," and other things that would upset me.

These comments show the importance that informal systems of social control have in rural communities, accentuating their accusatory mechanisms through gossip and rumors in the case of a woman who has been imprisoned. According to Norma's testimony, a woman in these circumstances loses her honor in the eyes of the community, and that has motivated both her father and herself to take the position that after her release from jail she should not return. Imposed and accepted ostracism of this kind is an indicator of the gender inequality with which generic roles are conceived regarding criminality and prison. Norma explained this in the following terms:

If a man falls, and falls again, he can still come out of it and go back home. But I don't think a woman can do that, because she is a woman. People talk more about a woman than a man. They don't talk so much about a man because he works. They would talk more about a woman because she is a woman. Most women speak ill of her, saying "Look at that woman who was in prison; she'd better not even come near here." They give a woman dirty looks, they begin to say nasty things to her, they talk about her behind her back. She might hear them, but she can't say anything back because she knows it's true. . . . My father came here once and he told me that he couldn't take me back into his home because I had left home. Now it was up to me to sort things out on my own. He said he would help me because he feels badly and because he's ashamed that I am here. However, once I walk back out through the prison gate, I should find my own way, wherever I'm best off and wherever I want to go.

Norma's words eloquently capture the differences between men and women's prison experiences. In one form or another, society expects that at some point in his life a man may go to jail, but his subsequent reintegration into society is not so difficult. The contrast with a woman's situation is obvious, because the gendered expectation is that a woman should not wind up in prison. When that happens, prison contaminates her; she can no longer be the same.

The fact that it would be impossible for her to return to the community where she was born and grew up obliged Norma to reflect on what she might do after she obtained her liberty:

Well, I wouldn't want to go back. [I would prefer to be] working somewhere distant from my family, where no one is scolding me and saying "Well, look, what did you do that for?" I am thinking about restarting my life on my own, valuing myself and respecting myself more, so that others respect me. . . . I have to recognize that life has dealt me a hard blow. I've now had that experience—a little nudge from God to see if I can stand up and not stumble again over the same rock. . . . Maybe someday my father will think again and say to me, "Come here." But my father says that I'm not going to get my act together. . . . He says that when I get out of here I'm going to the bad, or that I'm going to start working in bars. But I tell him, "No, I would like to get out soon to show [you] that isn't so, that I would like to help [you] in any way I can." If I'm going to help him, first I have to get out of here, and then we'll see what I do. Because here it's a world of expectations, and out there it's a world of realities. Here you have fantasies; out there you try to make them come true. But if not, then not.

It is in these terms that the association between prison and contamination is established. The prison experience places women in a position in which they are contaminated, inducing them to sexual promiscuity. Norma's words are an important testament to the gendered values that shape the construction of female criminality and the implications that the experience of being in prison has for women's lives.

One should add here that prisons are spaces of reclusion that have been designed on the basis of male necessities and problematics (Azaola Garrido 1998; Bodelón González 2003). The invisibility of women in the penitentiary system strengthens the gender roles that subordinate them. Women prisoners have fewer opportunities to work or to gain an education than do male inmates. They are, moreover, generally relegated to such tasks as cleaning, sewing, and mending. These considerations are important to the larger goals of this chapter because they indicate that prison life in itself reproduces gender roles. In other words, prison also produces gender.

Conclusion

This chapter began by recognizing that, in the social construction of criminality, delinquency is predominantly a male phenomenon. One goal here has been to highlight the relationship between the prison experience and gender roles, with particular reference to the case of indigenous women prisoners.

Taking into consideration the situation of interlegality in which these women live, the evidence presented here allows us to conclude that the conditions for their criminalization derive not only from structural circumstances of poverty, marginalization, and racism, but also from the gender inequalities that exist in indigenous communities. For these reasons, in certain extreme situations, conditions arise that lead to the incarceration of women. One of the most common such elements is the high incidence of violence, especially in the household sphere.

Another issue that arises from the material presented here is the fact that these women were detained for reasons generated within household dynamics.

The other people involved in these cases were close family members, and (with the exception of Norma's case) the principal charges and denunciations were made by in-laws. These facts reveal the existence of a certain degree of tension within indigenous families. It suggests, moreover, the prior failure of conciliatory mechanisms in both indigenous and state law, or perhaps that these alternative mechanisms were not made available to the individuals involved. One must also emphasize that the conflicts analyzed here were related to practices reflecting various aspects of social life: the use of traditional medicine (Norma), domestic violence (Micaela), honor and sexuality (Felipa), and conflicts over land (Rosa).

By reading legal files and appreciating the conflicting interests and positions of the parties involved, as well as the relationship established between the accuser and the accused, one sees in these cases how normative conflicts unfold in a situation of interlegality. One element is related to the sanctions—both formal and informal—mobilized to give course and direction to the accusations, which in these stories ended in the imprisonment of the accused. In this way, the dynamics of juridical practices and differentiated normative systems are imbricated and mutually constitutive, and both are informed by gender ideologies that subordinate women (see also Sierra, this volume). This suggests that in situations of interlegality there can be a correspondence between values and ideologies despite normative pluralism.

Among the things that stand out in the diverse testimonies given by indigenous prisoners are the references to the informal sanctions operating in their communities. These sanctions are based on moral codes of conduct, through which are transmitted evaluations and knowledge. The transgression of these codes, especially with regard to gender roles, is a source of shame not only for women but also for their families (as exemplified in the testimonies provided by the parents of Norma and Felipa). This constitutes a central dimension for understanding these cases. As Pitt-Rivers (1977) indicates, in this context "shame" is understood in reference to the community's moral values, rules of social interaction, and reputation.

But the gender inequality present in daily life in indigenous, rural communities can also cause these informal local sanctions to work against women found guilty of transgressions, as in the cases of Norma and Felipa. Indigenous women and men who go to jail for murder or some other serious crime transgress not only state law, but also the moral codes of the community. It can be much more difficult for women than for men to reinsert themselves into local life. Prison—associated with crime, dirtiness, and shame—so contaminates women that they can no longer be seen as their former selves. Although we must be cautious about generalizing on the basis of so few cases, Norma's testimony implies that the experience of being in prison affects men and women differently. Prison is, on this basis at least, a gendered experience. These initial reflections on the subject suggest that further research in rural and indigenous areas of Mexico should investigate in greater depth how both formal and informal sanctions affect the women and men accused of committing serious crimes and imprisoned. This task remains for future research in legal anthropology.

Translated by Kevin J. Middlebrook.

NOTES

1. This is an allusion to the title of Azaola Garrido and José Yacamán's book (1996), which refers both to the invisibility of imprisoned women in the criminal justice system and to their abandonment by their families.

2. Judicial districts cover several municipalities. Each municipality has a Public Prosecution Agency with responsibility for initiating criminal investigations, and a Justice of the Peace (Juzgado de Paz) responsible for dealing with minor matters. The Court of First Instance (Juzgado de Primera Instancia) of the judicial district handles more serious matters, including cases of murder and divorce. Judicial processes are conducted by written submission; there is no public oral testimony. In criminal proceedings, statements by the accused, accusers, and witnesses are of fundamental importance because they form the basis for the legal file (*expediente judicial*) and, thus, the judge's decision.

3. These statistics are taken from those compiled by the Instituto Nacional Indigenista (INI, now the National Commission for the Development of Indigenous Communities, or Comisión Nacional para el Desarrollo de los Pueblos Indígenas), Delegación Estatal Veracruz: Estadística de población penitenciaria general e indígena, Primer Trimestre 1997.

4. Two of the women interviewed provided no information concerning their prior employment.

5. One of those imprisoned for murder was not an indigenous woman, and her case was therefore excluded from the analysis.

6. One woman provided no information in this regard.

7. Azaola Garrido and José Yacamán (1996) heard similar testimonies in their study of incarcerated women in Mexico. See also Makowski Muchnik (1994, 1996).

8. Although the names of the individuals involved have been changed to protect their identity, the judicial records cited bear their actual identifying numbers.

9. The Papantla judicial district is located in a cultural area known as Totonacapan, consisting of two geographic zones: the Papantla highlands (the first foothills of the Sierra Madre Oriental) and the coastal plains bordering on the Gulf of Mexico (see Velázquez 1995). There is greater social marginality in the highlands than on the coast.

10. A curandero is someone who provides medical help without having an official medical license.

11. Author's interview with Norma, Papantla penitentiary, December 4, 1990; Court of First Instance of Papantla, file nos. 253/990, 185/992, and 208/992.

12. Author's interview with Micaela, her father, and her brother, Papantla penitentiary, October 4 and 9, 1997; Court of First Instance of Papantla, file no. 277/996.

13. She brought a petition for judicial review (*amparo*) to the federal appeal court. For a brief description of the amparo procedure, see Varley, this volume.

14. Author's interview with Felipa, Papantla penitentiary, October 7, 1997; Court of First Instance of Papantla, file no. 181/997.

15. Author's interviews with Rosa, Papantla penitentiary, May 14, 1996; February 19 and October 2, 1997; Court of First Instance of Papantla, file nos. 185/992, 253/990, and 208/992. See Chenaut (1999, 481–487) for a more detailed account of this case.

16. Author's interview with Joaquín, Papantla penitentiary, November 9, 1997.

17. The legend of La Llorona, "The Weeping Woman," tells of a woman who appears at midnight crying incessantly for her dead children. There are many versions of this popular legend, some of which suggest that it was she herself who murdered the children. In symbolic terms, Felipa took on the role of La Llorona.

18. The Totonacs are concerned about preserving the honor of their women. Even on the coastal plain, communities still conduct traditional marriage rituals to prove that the bride is a virgin. In the Papantla highlands, that custom is now dying out (Chenaut 1999).

19. This quotation, and those that follow, come from the author's interview with Norma, Papantla penitentiary, December 4, 1990.

PART THREE

Legal Constructions of Marriage and the Family

7

Domesticating the Law

ANN VARLEY

In the years after the Revolution's rewriting of Mexican family law, the judges of the nation's Supreme Court found themselves faced with deciding what constituted "the home" in divorce cases brought for abandonment of the marital home. In 1926, author and "emancipated woman" Antonieta Rivas Mercado sought to divorce her husband Albert Blair for abandonment. She initially won her case, but lost on appeal.[1] She then brought an *amparo* petition for review to the Supreme Court.[2] In 1930, the Court found against her. In doing so, it loftily dismissed the relevance of the home as material space: "The word 'abandonment,' in relation to the words 'marital home,' cannot refer only to the materiality of the house, of the dwelling which is inhabited, but, by a figure of language, the container is taken for the contained, that is to say, the dwelling which is inhabited for the spouse and children who inhabit it."[3] "Abandonment" meant neglect of one's marital obligations, such that someone still living in the marital home could have abandoned their spouse, though an absent spouse might not. Since Blair had continued to support his family, even though he neglected his "merely personal [obligations] towards his wife," his absence did not constitute grounds for divorce.[4]

This insistence on the insignificance of space can be read as an assertion of legal closure, of the power of legal rationality to house its own subjects and locate the relations between them in a conceptual landscape of its own making.

Legal closure has been challenged by critics who insist that law is social and political—not set apart, objective and autonomous, its authority unshakeable (Blomley 1994, 11). Critical scholars therefore reject conventional legal histories depicting law as either the heir of privileged normative values of the past or the result of progressive evolution, because they "subjugate the flux of historical contingency to the imperious logic of the Law" (ibid., 17). In Mexico, the authors of the new family laws introduced by the Revolution made very different claims about the historical status of their work, to the effect that it represented a radical break with past traditions, since the "transcendental political reforms" of the Revolution required the transformation of all other social institutions.[5] This chapter suggests that such claims should be received with the same caution as legal histories emphasizing continuity or evolution. In particular, scholars should be wary of the claim that the 1917 Law of Family Relations would introduce "modern ideas about equality"[6] into the family by abolishing the subjection of married women to their husband's authority, such that: "Husband and wife shall enjoy equal authority and respect in the home [*El marido y la mujer tendrán en el hogar autoridad y consideraciones iguales*]."[7] When the 1917 law was incorporated into the new civil code of 1928, the reforms were explicitly described as a response to "the feminist movement."[8] I argue, however, that the legislation and its subsequent interpretation by the Supreme Court perpetuated a structuring of marital obligations according to the belief that a man should protect his wife and a woman obey her husband, translated into a duty for husbands to provide a home and for wives to run it.[9]

In addition to rejecting the "historicity of social life," assertions of legal closure also reject its "spatiality" (Blomley and Bakan 1992, 669). As critical scholars have noted: "[T]he legal mentality is curiously acontextual, such that legal relations and obligations are frequently thought of . . . as existing in a purely conceptual space, with little recognition of their spatial heterogeneity or the local material contexts within which law is understood and contested" (ibid., 663–664). This chapter shows that Mexican family law has had difficulty in coming to terms with the home as the material context for marriage, leading some litigants in divorce cases to ridicule the lawyers' conclusions about the marital home. The discrepancy between everyday and legal logic arose because legislators had failed to take into account social and spatial heterogeneity in married couples' living arrangements.[10]

Critical and feminist approaches to theorizing law both draw on deconstruction, but Sara Ahmed (1998, 34) argues that deconstruction "is not *sufficient* for a feminist politics of the law." Drucilla Cornell (1992) combines deconstructive strategies with a reading of gender as system to show how, despite the continual restoration of the gender hierarchy, feminist legal reform is possible. Ahmed (1998, 33) picks up on Cornell's use of the notion of iterability to argue that rights are constantly reinvented as they are cited in judicial decisions, "and in that act of (re)constitution are subject to re-iteration and displacement." Legal discourse is not, in other words, "monolithic" (Lim 1996, 147). In Mexico, despite continued adherence to an ideology of masculine protection/provision and feminine obedience/service, changes have taken place in the judicial definition of what constitutes "the marital home"—changes that have operated to the advantage of women litigants.

Husbands Protect; Wives Obey

The 1884 civil code replaced by Venustiano Carranza's Law of Family Relations had summarized marital obligations in a short phrase: "The husband must protect the wife; she must obey him."[11] This formula was derived from the Napoleonic Code: "The husband owes protection to his wife; the wife, obedience to her husband."

Raquel Barceló (1997, 78) argues that Rousseau's views on the sexes shaped both the Napoleonic Code and the "letter from Melchor Ocampo" (Article 15 of the 1859 Law of Civil Marriage) that became part of Mexico's civil marriage ceremony:

> [T]he man, the gifts of whose sex are principally valor and force, should and will give the wife protection, food, and supervision, treating her always . . . with the magnanimity and generous benevolence that the strong owe to the weak. . . . The woman, the gifts of whose sex are self-denial, beauty, compassion, perspicacity, and tenderness, should and will give the husband obedience, thankfulness, assistance, consolation and counsel, treating him with the veneration owed to the person who supports and defends us.

The Napoleonic Code's definition of marital responsibilities has often been identified as the basis of *potestad marital,* a wife's legal subordination to her husband. Carmen Diana Deere and Magdalena León (2005) argue that its influence has been exaggerated, since potestad marital can be traced to medieval Spanish legal codes, which, like the French tradition, had their roots in Roman law. The phrase about protection and obedience nonetheless "captured the essence of the unequal relationship between man and wife" (ibid., 648). Its replacement by an assertion of domestic equality thus signaled the end of potestad marital, causing alarm among conservative commentators. One lawyer complained that "joint government [*cogobierno*]" of the family ran contrary to a universal need for strong leadership and would "break up the family group and give it yankee features" (Pallares 1923, quoted in Sánchez Medal 1979, 32–34).[12]

Family Law and Feminism

The 1928 Civil Code identified its family law reforms—mostly inherited from the Law of Family Relations—as a response to "the feminist movement" and the fact that "woman has ceased to be relegated exclusively to the home."[13] How convincing are these claims?

Reforms to the law on marriage were a key issue for middle-class women involved in the monthly *La mujer mexicana* before the Revolution, and scholars have linked the 1917 law to the two Feminist Congresses held in Yucatán in 1916, at which delegates called for the civil code to be reformed (Soto 1990; Macías

1982). Prominent feminist Hermila Galindo complained that "the wife has no rights whatsoever in the home . . . she lacks authority to draw up any contract. She cannot dispose of her personal property, or even administer it. . . . [A wife] lacks all authority over her children, and she has no right to intervene in their education" (Galindo 1916, quoted in Soto 1990, 10). The 1884 Civil Code had allowed women to make contracts or take part in litigation if they had their husband's permission; but the 1917 law authorized them to do so without his consent.

Sarah Buck (2000) observes that the 1928 legislation excluded aspects of the Law of Family Relations to which the Pan American Feminist Congress had objected in 1923. The president of the congress appealed to the legislators to repeal a number of articles on adultery, divorce, and a divorced woman's right to remarry but retain authority over her children. Several of the offending clauses were amended, lending support to the claim that the new legislation responded to feminist concerns.

Other aspects of the family law reforms are less easily attributed to feminist influences. One puzzle concerns the earliest of the reforms. At the end of 1914, Carranza issued a decree permitting remarriage after divorce.[14] Historians have not, however, identified divorce as a central concern of feminists at that time, and in fact the feminists gave it a mixed reception (Macías 1982; Soto 1990). Carranza could have been influenced by Hermila Galindo, who was working as his private secretary. Although Galindo later applauded the Carranza decree (Lau Jaiven and Ramos Escandón 1993, 263), there is apparently no record of her speaking out on divorce beforehand or being involved in drafting the document.

The decree seems to have been largely the work of Félix Palavicini, Carranza's director of education. It was even dubbed the Palavicini Law in Congress (*Diario de los Debates,* May 4, 1917). Palavicini suggests that he shared authorship with Carranza and José Natividad Macías. In his memoirs, he tells the story of how the three drafted the decree on board Carranza's train. At the time, the defeat of the Constitutionalist forces was predicted and it was rumored that Carranza would withdraw from Veracruz to Yucatán or even Cuba (Palavicini 1937, 246–249). It seems extraordinary that in these circumstances Carranza should have made divorce a priority. As Ramón Sánchez Medal (1974, 14) comments, moreover, "it had nothing do to with the political reforms announced in the original Plan de Guadalupe, nor the social reforms proposed by Carranza [in] 1913."

The preamble to the decree emphasized the unhappiness caused by preventing separated couples from remarrying and argued that the possibility of divorce would encourage the popular classes to marry rather than live together. Divorce would liberate middle-class women in unhappy marriages from dependence on the husband.[15] Carranza subsequently extended this claim to include working-class women (Soto 1990).

The possibility of more personal motivations also arises. Some sources report that Palavicini and other men close to Carranza pressured him to introduce the law because they were separated from their wives and wanted to marry their mistresses.[16] Palavicini (1937, 65, 70, 188) mentions family difficulties arising from his political activities in 1909–1914, and reports that he and two other members of Carranza's group found girl friends in Veracruz who they subsequently married on returning to Mexico City (ibid., 230); so there may well be some substance in this account.[17]

From Obedience to Housework

The authors of the Law of Family Relations claimed to be fulfilling Carranza's promise "to establish the family 'on more rational and just foundations.'"[18] It was "absurd" that, although the 1857 Constitution sought to invalidate any act undermining human liberty, women were deprived of their freedom and legally "incapacitated" by the marriage contract—hence the abolition of potestad marital.

The law has been described as a "firm step on the road to equality," but it also contained a number of deficiencies (Carreras Maldonado and Montero Duhalt 1975, 73). The authors reproduced word for word, for example, the 1884 pronouncement that a wife's adultery was always grounds for divorce whereas a husband's was not, except in certain limited circumstances.[19]

One article seemingly escaped criticism at the time but has since been castigated for betraying the pursuit of liberty and equality for married women (ibid.; Leret de Matheus 1975). Article 44 stipulated: "The wife is obliged to attend to all domestic matters; she will thus be especially responsible for the supervision and care of the children and the control and supervision of services in the home."[20]

This article seems to have been introduced in *direct response* to the loss of a wife's obligation to obey her husband, as can be seen by comparing the 1884 and 1917 legislation (Table 7.1). Article 192 of the 1884 Civil Code clearly becomes Article 43 in 1917, with the declaration of domestic equality replacing the phrase about protection and obedience. The other issues addressed in that article—the children's education and management of family property—remain the same.[21] The clauses before and after Article 192 can all be linked to corresponding entries in the 1917 law, even where modified. For example, Article 191, requiring the husband to provide for his wife's material needs, becomes Article 42, which now adds that he should meet all the costs of running the household.[22]

Comparing the two texts reveals no possible origin for Article 44 of the Law of Family Relations *other than* Article 192 of the 1884 code. The reference to domestic matters, *lo doméstico,* has apparently been lifted out to form the basis of the new article (where it becomes *los asuntos domésticos*). The article spells out what is meant by the "domestic matters" exempted from the principle of equality between the spouses.

I suggest that these new obligations for married women were a direct response to the replacement of "obedience" with "equality." Obedience, in effect,

---

TABLE 7.1.

Comparing the 1884 and 1917 Legislation

1884 Civil Code

Article 192: The husband must protect the wife; she must obey him, both in
domestic matters [*en lo doméstico*] and in the education of the children and
the management of the properties.

1917 Law of Family Relations

Article 43: Husband and wife shall enjoy equal authority and respect in the
home; therefore, they shall decide by mutual agreement on everything to
do with the education and upbringing of the children and the management
of their properties.

Article 44: The wife is obliged to attend to all domestic matters [*todos los
asuntos domésticos*]; she will thus be especially responsible for the
supervision and care of the children and the control and supervision of
services in the home [*del servicio del hogar*]. Consequently, only with
permission [*licencia*] from her husband can the wife commit herself to take
on personal services for an outsider, or take on a job, or exercise a
profession, or establish a business. The husband, in granting this
permission, should fix a precise period for it; for it shall otherwise be
considered to apply indefinitely, and the husband, in order to withdraw it,
should do so in writing to his wife, allowing two months' notice . . .

---

was translated into housework—or household management for women who
could afford servants. Although the legislators decreed that a wife need no
longer obey her husband, they were seemingly unwilling to lose the crucial
practical expression of that obedience.[23]

The legislators also went on to preclude the possibility that wives might
understand equal authority within the home to mean they could freely take
their services *outside* the home. Wives could take a job or start a business only
with their husband's formal permission (Table 7.1). The requirement for husbands to license their wives to enter into contracts or litigation had disappeared, but the same device was reintroduced to control wives wanting to work
outside the home. It seems there were limits that the legislators could not allow
women to cross.[24]

Judges, the Home, and Housework

Defining the Marital Home

The clauses concerning equal authority between spouses and a wife's responsibility for housework emphasized the home as the setting for marriage. The emphasis

was appropriate, given that men had previously regarded the home as the site of their absolute and unquestionable authority (García Peña 2006, 102, 237). The declaration that husbands and wives were to enjoy equal rights in the home could, however, be seen as drawing a line around the private sphere as the *only* space where women could expect equality with men. As it was only a few months since the Constitutional Congress had rejected female suffrage, the reforms could be interpreted as marking a public/private boundary.[25]

The home also made an appearance in the law on divorce (as it had since only separation was allowed). "Abandoning the marital home [*abandono del domicilio conyugal*]" was one of the grounds on which someone could bring a divorce case against a spouse.[26]

The way judges interpreted this clause shows how the understanding of marriage as an exchange of masculine protection for feminine obedience continued to shape their thinking. These terms do not appear in Supreme Court judgments, but I suggest they are still present in a translated form. The requirement that husbands provide for their wives translated "protection" into practical terms, and the requirement that a wife be responsible for running the home did the same for "obedience."

Judges had to decide what exactly constituted "the marital home." The legislators had apparently conceived of the home as a "container" for only *one* married couple. In reality, many Mexican homes housed more than one couple, given the practice of young wives being taken to live with their husband's parents, particularly widespread in rural areas or where people could not afford independent accommodation (Varley 2000b; González Montes, this volume; Sierra, this volume).[27] Could two "marital homes" occupy the same physical space? If the dwelling itself was not the issue, it should not have been a problem for couples to share accommodation, and in the 1930s and 1940s the marital home was regarded as "exist[ing] not only when the house is dedicated exclusively to use by a single married couple, but also when the spouses live with other people."[28] Starting in 1954, however, a series of rulings denied the existence of the marital home when couples depended on others for accommodation. In 1961, this latter interpretation was made obligatory for all lower courts (Table 7.2).[29]

From Equality to Autonomy

The judges who issued the 1954 ruling arrived at their position by considering the civil code articles stating that husband and wife enjoyed equal authority within the home and that running the home was the wife's responsibility.[30] However, the rulings leading to the 1961 thesis modified the way "authority" was interpreted: it became a question of autonomy rather than equality. Whereas the civil code depicted authority as something to which wife and husband were equally entitled, defining their relationship to each other, the concept now distinguished the space of the couple from the space of other people. Each couple

---

TABLE 7.2.

The 1961 *Tesis de Jurisprudencia* on the Marital Home

[The marital home] does not exist when the spouses live as *arrimados* in the
home of the parents, or of other relatives or third parties, in which the
spouses lack their own authority and freedom in the home [*autoridad
propia y libre disposición del hogar*], because they live in someone else's
house and lack their own home.

Source: *Semanario Judicial de la Federación, Apéndice 1917–2000*, Vol. IV (Materia
Civil: Jurisprudencia), Tesis 201: 165.

Note: Arrimados are people living with someone else.

---

was to have *autoridad propia* in the home (Table 7.2). Husband and wife are
treated as a unit, with their "own" *joint* authority over the home.

The word "propia" eventually entered the legislation, illustrating how legislation and adjudication are intertwined. The civil code was reformed in 1983 to
define the marital home as "the place chosen by mutual agreement by the
spouses, in which both enjoy their own authority and equal respect [*autoridad
propia e consideraciones iguales*]" (*Diario Oficial de la Federación,* December 27,
1983). The reference to "own authority" is ambiguous: it is unclear whether
"both" spouses are to have their own authority in relation to each other, or to
third parties (as was evidently intended in the Supreme Court thesis). "Equality," however, now serves only to qualify the notion of "respect."

Despite (or perhaps because of) this new definition of the marital home,
the courts continued to rule that there was no marital home when a couple was
sharing with others.[31]

Housework as a Right

The other basis for the 1961 thesis was the requirement that the wife be responsible for running the home. Analysis of the rulings shows that what was at issue was
the wife's obligation—interpreted as a "right"—to manage the home. If couples
shared accommodation, it was unclear *which* wife was to do so (Varley 2000b).

Sharing accommodation did not automatically deprive one of a marital
home. The key issue, the judges insisted, was the "autonomy and authority"
enjoyed by the couple[32]—and in particular by the wife, with regard to her
domestic responsibilities:

The existence of the marital home is not incompatible with living with
relatives of the wife or the husband, as is a frequent occurrence amongst
certain social classes in our country, providing that the wife can exercise

the rights granted to her by law, such that in the house or in the rooms to which the couple are restricted she should be the only one to give orders or take decisions about the work to be carried out within the home.[33]

How, though, was this autonomy to be demonstrated? If the husband's parents were living on the same property, there was a strong presumption that the younger couple lacked the desired autonomy.[34] The Court did not, for example, accept the existence of the marital home in two cases in which the couple shared a property with the husband's parents but lived in a separate structure.[35]

This did not mean, however, that couples in similar circumstances would necessarily be deemed homeless. The greater the physical separation between the areas occupied by each couple, the more likely the judges were to accept the existence of the marital home; but what mattered most were the arrangements concerning housework. Not content to rely on witness statements and cross-examination, the courts sometimes ordered physical inspection of the premises. This provided minutely detailed descriptions of the site: how many doors there were and whether they were numbered (using official municipal numbering or not); whether the rooms interconnected and who used which spaces; and how many kitchens and washstands (*lavaderos*, for laundry and crockery) there were.[36] In one case, the State of Oaxaca appeal court accepted the existence of the marital home on the basis of an inspection showing the physical independence of the couple's accommodation. The Supreme Court overturned this ruling, though, because "there is only one kitchen and one washstand, leading to the conclusion that the [wife] did not have exclusive rights [*disposición exclusiva*] over the kitchen, washstand and other parts of the house."[37]

The judges thus identified the existence of a marital home chiefly on the basis of whether the wife could exercise her "right" to run the home. Despite earlier insistence that the "materiality of the house" was irrelevant, the courts sought to evaluate social relations on the basis of the layout and amenities of the accommodation, and whether these would permit two wives to carry out housework independently.

The emphasis on housework persists even after the law had changed. In late 1974, in anticipation of International Women's Year and the United Nations Conference on Women (held in Mexico the following year), the article in question was repealed (*Diario Oficial de la Federación*, December 31, 1974).[38] The courts nonetheless continued to use the wife's responsibility for housework as a test for the existence of the marital home.[39] Other criteria could have been used: whether the husband gave his earnings to his wife or mother, for example.[40] Instead, the judges still focused on housework. This is evidence, I suggest, of the persistence of the belief that a wife's responsibility was to serve her husband by running the home, to obey him "en lo doméstico."

A Home of Their Own

What, however, of the husband's obligation to "protect," or provide for, his wife? The 1974 reforms also amended the clause making this a specifically masculine obligation (further testimony to the "paired" nature of the marital obligations discussed in this chapter); the spouses were now to distribute their marital responsibilities between themselves as they saw fit.

The cases analyzed are less explicit about what was expected of a husband, possibly because there was never a reference to "the marital home" in the article establishing his breadwinner role. Nonetheless, there is a clear underlying assumption that a husband should provide accommodation for his wife, ideally their *own* home.

One ruling found that who owned the property was not the issue.[41] Other cases suggest it was *an* issue, and an important one. The domestic independence desirable in a "proper" marriage ideally came from having the resources to be owner–occupiers. The wording of the 1961 thesis encouraged such interpretations, given its references to having one's "own" home and "*libre disposición* [literally, free disposition/disposal]" of the home (Table 7.2). There was a danger, as one husband argued, that only homeowners would be regarded as having a marital home[42]—when less than one-third of homes in Mexico's cities were owner-occupied (Gilbert and Varley 1991).

Some later rulings stipulated that couples should enjoy "rights in their own name to stay and govern [*derechos propios de permanencia y gobierno*]," a condition that seems difficult to satisfy *unless* they were owners.[43] Renting was not necessarily an acceptable alternative, if the landlord was a relative.[44] In one case the husband claimed he was renting a flat from his sister, who lived at the same address. The Court did not believe him but argued that, even if he were renting, it would only have weakened his case. Paying rent proved that the couple did not enjoy "the independence required in any marital home."[45]

The implicit emphasis on ownership seems to increase over time, especially in the late 1970s (by which time the proportion of homes that were owner–occupied had doubled: Gilbert and Varley 1991). The dwelling again figures, not only as a "container" for spouse and children, but as a witness to whether or not the couple could enjoy their "own authority."

Some of the husbands justified sharing on the grounds that they were too poor to afford independent accommodation.[46] In doing so, they probably drove the nail into the coffin of their own case. By their own admission, they lacked the resources to support a family "properly."

The husband's duty to protect his wife thus survived in the belief that he should provide her with a home. Her duty to obey him survived in translated form in the requirement that she undertake the running of that home. The home was the pivot of these reciprocal obligations. Without a home provided by the man and run by the woman, there was, it seems, no marriage worthy of the name.

The Litigants' Views: When Is a Home Not a Home?

It is not easy to distinguish the litigants' opinions from those of the lawyers. Sometimes, the language used surely has to be the lawyer's: for example, when one man claimed that "three days after the wedding, he indicated to his wife that as they were now united in marriage they would have to live together in a marital home in which they could fulfill their obligations."[47] At other times, the litigant's own voice seems to emerge more clearly, as when a woman argued that

> the house of my husband's parents cannot be our home, because I do not have the running of the house, as a wife, because in reality I do not know how much my husband earns, because I do not receive his salary and have lived only as a servant and an arrimada in the house of his parents. . . . My mother-in-law . . . controls everything, including my husband's salary.[48]

The wives did not reject the idea of being responsible for housework, providing that it was in their own home and not their in-laws'. This may have been a strategy to improve their chances of winning, but, whether or not they really liked being responsible for housework, they seem to have been genuinely offended by having to obey their mother-in-law's instructions about the home. Such a compulsion converted them, they protested, into mere servants (Varley 2000b). The wives therefore agreed with the judges about their right to have the authority to carry out domestic work independently. One woman complained, for instance, that "she had to undertake all her activities along with her in-laws, lacking the freedom and independence to carry out the household work."[49]

The husbands were mostly living in their parents' home and therefore found themselves on the defensive. This may account for the vigor with which some expressed themselves on the subject. These men contested the assumption that, to have the autonomy to sustain married life, they had to provide independent accommodation. A room of their own was all they needed:

> [T]his business of saying "arrimado" is very common among us Mexicans [es muy común en nosotros los mexicanos]. The couple virtually always lives with the man's family or the wife's family and this doesn't mean that they don't have a room of their own which is their marital home. I repeat, it is entirely normal [común y corriente] for couples to live on the property of relatives of the wife or the husband and set up their marital home there.[50]

A similarly incredulous response reads:

> [T]he fact that a son and his wife live with his parents is not sufficient reason to consider that there is no marital home; it would also be necessary to show that the spouses lived like hijos de familia in the parents' house, and that it is they who support the couple, or, what amounts to the same thing, that the wife lives as an arrimada with her in-laws; but if

> she lives an independent life with her husband, and he supports her, and
> they have their own things and solve their problems by themselves with-
> out interference by anyone else, not even their parents, even when they
> live in the same [house], it is obvious that the marital home does exist![51]

Another man argued that for his wife to have proved her case she would have
had to show:

> that [he] did not pay rent for the house; that it was the property of his
> parents; that he was dependent on them for food, clothing, etc.; and that
> the marital home was right next to their rooms.[52]

The husbands do not generally mention housework. One man who did so
sought only to show that his wife was neglecting her obligations: she did not
want "to live with me or offer me the services proper to her sex within the home
[*prestarme las atenciones propias de su sexo en el hogar*]."[53] The others may not have
thought housework important, or may have kept quiet because they knew they
were on shaky ground, given their domestic arrangements.

The men may have disagreed with the judges' position on the marital
home, and some seem to have found it absurd. They did not, however, disagree
about a husband's marital responsibilities. Some advanced alternative criteria
for judging how much independence the couple enjoyed, but these refine the
argument rather than counter the judges' assumptions. For a man to be "properly" married, he should ideally be providing for his family and maintaining a
degree of independence over the space occupied. Judges and litigants differed
only as to how easily that independence could be eroded by the husband's failure to acquire accommodation away from his relatives. For the husbands, this
(implicitly temporary) condition was excusable on economic grounds. For the
judges, it was not, if it meant that the wife was not free from her mother-in-
law's influence in running the home. Where the husband could not "protect"
her in this respect, the judges stepped in to do so in his place.

Conclusion

A year after losing her appeal to the Supreme Court, Antonieta Rivas Mercado
killed herself in Paris. The struggle with her husband, leading her to forge his
signature on her passport and smuggle their son out of Mexico, "certainly contributed to her suicide" (Franco 1989, 113).

The circumstances of the Rivas Mercado case are unusual in many respects,
other than her public prominence in the arts and politics. For one thing,
she sought to divorce her husband. In the cases reviewed, men initiating proceedings for divorce outnumbered women by three to one.[54] For another, the
couple had lived with *her* father, architect Antonio Rivas Mercado, and Antonieta
had effectively left Blair when she and her father went to Europe for a year; Blair
then left his father-in-law's house.[55] The "merely personal" attentions from her

husband about which the Supreme Court was so dismissive were in fact repellent to her (ibid.).

The case is also unusual in that the Court's position on the marital home meant that Rivas Mercado lost her case. More often, it favored the wife, such that the wife won the case more frequently than when the nature of the home was not a key issue in the final decision. In particular, once the judges started to rule that sharing with others meant there was no marital home, the only cases in which this did not favor the wife were where they deemed her proofs insufficient or where *she* had sought the divorce. Generally, the *wife* had left a home shared with her husband's parents, and he had tried to divorce her for abandonment, and the ruling prevented the divorce.[56]

These wives remained married to someone they presumably had no desire to live with. The reason for their opposition appears fairly clear: if found responsible for failure of the marriage, they would lose any right to financial support and possibly the custody of their children.[57] For husbands, the wife's leaving appears to have presented an opportunity to be free of the relationship without having to pay for freedom; but the Court's position on the home frustrated their plans.

These rulings cast the litigants, in some sense, into a no-man's-land, with no resolution to their marital problems (the very state from which Carranza had sought to liberate men and women by introducing absolute divorce). Given the gender ideology encapsulated in the definition of marital rights and responsibilities, it is ironic that husbands' failure to provide an independent home was sanctioned, not by divorce, but by the denial of divorce. There seems a lack of congruence between some aspects of family law and the mechanisms available to sanction noncompliance. The provider role is, nevertheless, more effectively policed than is the homemaker one: though abandoning one's family economically is a criminal offense as well as grounds for divorce, and spouses can seek court intervention to ensure financial support, there are no such sanctions for neglecting the housework.

These observations speak to what Nicholas Blomley (1994, 5) describes as "the indeterminacy and contingency of legal discourse." Feminist scholars' arguments about citationality, adjudication, and the possibility of displacement point in the same direction (Cornell 1992; Ahmed 1998). Despite the resilience of the gender system, changes in legal discourse that work to women's benefit are possible. In Mexico, claims that the Revolution's family law reforms sought to advance women's freedom and equality must be questioned in light of the simultaneous recodification of domestic power relations in the clause making newly "liberated" wives responsible for housework. The expectation that husbands protect and wives obey survived the abolition of potestad marital in translated form, as a duty for husbands to provide a home and wives to run it: there might be equality in an ideal home, but in everyday space someone had to do the housework. The gender ideology giving rise to this definition of marital obligations continues to inform judicial interpretation of family law to this day, despite the extension of gender equality in the legislation, *but* a significant change in the way judges interpreted "the marital home" took place in the 1950s without any modification to the articles on which the new position was based. It was this change that protected women who had left the home they shared with their husband and his relatives against being penalized for the failure of their marriage. Law is indeed a site of both resistance and change, "both empowering and disempowering" (Lim 1996, 127).

The gender outcomes of changes in legal discourse are not necessarily intentional. The change in judicial understandings of "the marital home" probably reflected social and cultural changes accompanying urbanization and the pursuit of modernization (Varley 2000b). This change may also have responded to women litigants' unhappiness with their living arrangements. Legal scholars have noted that "the space of the courtroom does provide the possibility . . . for a story to be told which otherwise would have been confined to the domestic sphere" (Lim 1996, 129). The cases reviewed in this chapter support this observation. Mexico's amparo suit has led the nation's most senior judges to study the stories of women who complained of being treated like a servant and humiliated or abused by their in-laws.[58] Is it possible that the judges' learning about those stories influenced their attitude to shared accommodation, even if only to confirm an opinion at which they had arrived by other means?

Unlike Antonieta Rivas Mercado, the women fighting these cases were not all from a privileged background, even though each had managed to pursue her case all the way through the court system. In approaching marriage as though it existed in an ideal space, legislators had failed to consider the class and geographical variations affecting the way couples organized their living space, finances, and domestic labor, and even the way they raised their children. For many Mexican couples, the domestic autonomy the judges prescribed as an essential condition for a proper marriage was a desirable but remote future possibility. Ironically, given the Supreme Court's dismissive attitude towards the "materiality of the house," judges sometimes had to turn to the material space of the home to establish whether or not couples actually enjoyed the autonomy that the law had taken for granted. The relations between law's subjects cannot, it seems, be contained in a purely figurative space.

NOTES

The research on which this chapter is based was supported by Research Grant R 000 23 6808, Economic and Social Research Council (UK).

1. Although she was originally granted a divorce, Rivas Mercado appealed, claiming that her husband owed her money, as he had failed to support the family for three years (a serious allegation: the 1917 Law of Family Relations made it a crime for a man to

abandon his family economically). Blair also appealed, denying his wife's accusations (Bradu 1991).

2. The juicio de amparo (suit of protection) is a unique institution providing judicial review of actions by public authorities. One type of amparo allows individuals to appeal directly to the Supreme Court or federal appeal courts (Tribunales Colegiados de Circuito, TCC) against decisions by lower courts (Baker 1971, xii–xiii, 175; Zamora et al. 2004, 258–274).

3. Archivo de la Suprema Corte de Justicia de la Nación: Amparo Directo (AD) 3697/28 (April 24, 1930). All case files quoted are from this archive.

4. In 1965, the Court ruled that providing economic support did *not* protect an absent husband: AD 2594/63 (April 28, 1965). By 1973 it still argued, however, that "material or physical abandonment of the family home" did not in itself constitute abandonment: AD 5856/72 (September 26, 1973).

5. Ley sobre Relaciones Familiares, 1917 (LRF), preamble.

6. Ibid.

7. LRF, art. 43.

8. Código Civil para el Distrito y Territorios Federales en Materia Común, y para toda la República en Materia Federal, 1928 (CC 1928), preamble.

9. I reviewed eighty amparo suits (filed from 1928 to 1997), including all those concerning the meaning of "abandonment of the marital home" as grounds for divorce. Wherever possible I consulted the case file (*expediente*), but in some cases only the published ruling was available. I omit personal names, except for the Rivas Mercado case.

10. One aspect of spatial heterogeneity on which I cannot elaborate here is the difference between the states' civil codes. I deal primarily with the Federal District code, but have checked arguments against local legislation where necessary.

11. Código Civil del Distrito Federal y Territorio de la Baja California, 1884 (CC 1984), art. 192.

12. The introduction of separate property as the default marital regime could also have fueled this alarm (see Deere, this volume), although measures were introduced to ensure that, in material terms, family unity was not undermined (Baitenmann, this volume).

13. CC 1928, preamble.

14. Decreto de 29 de diciembre de 1914 ("Ley de Divorcio," LD). Divorce had previously been limited to separation of bed and board, although between 1868 and 1904 there were at least five attempts to introduce absolute divorce (García Peña 2006, 113; López-Portillo y Rojas 1975, 330).

15. LD, preamble.

16. Historian Eugenia Meyer, interviewed by Shirlene Soto (1990, 158), and lawyer Ramón Sánchez Medal (1974, 1979) both name Palavicini and Luis Cabrera—who was "preoccupied by domestic difficulties" at the time (Palavicini 1937, 229).

17. The others were Gustavo Espinosa Mireles and Luis Manuel Rojas (who, Palavicini notes, was single). García Peña (2006, 256) criticizes the personal motivations theory as lacking empirical support, but overlooks Palavicini's own record of what does appear to have been his second marriage, as well as a sequence of events that does fit the theory.

18. LRF, preamble, referring to Carranza's speech to the Constitutional Congress.

19. LRF, art. 77. This glaring inequality was removed in 1928.

20. LRF, art. 44. The 1928 legislation was more succinct: "the supervision and care of household work shall be the concern of the wife" (*Estará a cargo de la mujer la dirección y cuidado de los trabajos del hogar*) (CC 1928, art. 168)—a wording reproduced in the legislation of most other states.

21. In 1917, wives gained the right to manage their own property and choose who should manage the joint property: LRF, arts. 45, 49. The 1917 clause thus referred to the *children's* property.

22. If a wife had assets or an income, she was to contribute up to one-half of household expenses, but unlike her husband she was not *obliged* to support the family: LRF, arts. 42 and 74.

23. Jorge Adame Goddard (2004, 113–114) has observed that, although Mexican legal scholars have not generally opposed the elimination of potestad marital, most have supported the retention of differing gender roles for husbands and wives, in the law on marriage.

24. The previous embargo on women making contracts appears to have prohibited their working without permission (unless they had a "commercial establishment"—CC 1884, arts. 198, 202). The restriction was removed in 1928, although it does not seem to have been the subject of feminist criticism.

25. The Constitutional Congress met in December 1916 and the Law of Family Relations was passed in April 1917.

26. LRF, art. 76. In the 1928 code, which came into force in 1932, the phrase was replaced by "*la separación de la casa conyugal*" (literally, separation from the marital house) (art. 267). Some states retained "abandono," as do published Supreme Court rulings.

27. In the cases reviewed, some of the husbands were professionals, military officers or businessmen; others worked for the state oil company or national railways, as small farmers or factory workers, or, in one case, as a mailman. Several were unemployed.

28. AD 2307/45 (July 9, 1945).

29. When the Supreme Court or federal appeal courts rule on the same point in five successive cases by a minimum majority of votes, the ruling becomes a *tesis de jurisprudencia,* binding on lower courts (Baker 1971, 256–263).

30. AD 3306/53 (March 4, 1954). In 1954, the requirement that a wife live with her husband was replaced by an obligation for spouses to live together "in the marital home" *Diario Oficial de la Federación,* January 9, 1954). However, it is difficult to see why this phrase should have triggered judicial opposition to shared accommodation when its appearances elsewhere in the legislation had not previously done so.

31. AD 166/88 (May 31, 1988) (TCC); AD 1277/89 (February 28, 1990) (TCC); AD 877/93 (January 4, 1994) (TCC).

32. AD 3711/72 (August 30, 1973).

33. AD 3306/53 (March 4, 1954).

34. AD 3711/72 (August 30, 1973).

35. AD 459/71 (October 1, 1971); AD 4512/76 (April 29, 1977).

36. AD 1385/77 (October 30, 1978).

37. AD 4512/76 (April 29, 1977).

38. The phrase "the running of the home [*manejo del hogar*]" was inserted into the article on authority within the home, reinstating the entire sequence of concepts found in CC

1884, art. 192. Some states kept the article making the wife responsible for running the home until much later—for example, Guanajuato (2000) and Michoacán (2004).

39. AD 98/77 (January 6, 1978); AD 1043/77 (March 13, 1978); AD 48/97 (February 28, 1997) (TCC). In AD 5906/78 (August 22, 1979), the ruling, referring explicitly to the Veracruz legislation, identified the wife's responsibility for housework as one of the criteria for existence of the marital home, although the state's civil code actually allowed the couple to decide how they divided responsibility for supporting and running the home: Código Civil para el Estado de Veracruz 1932, art. 103. On "the increasing importance of judicial precedent," see Zamora et al. (2004, 96–98).

40. AD 3306/53 (March 4, 1954). Legally, a wife had first call on her husband's earnings (CC 1928, art. 165).

41. AD 3688/76 (August 26, 1977). Two brothers occupied separate houses on a property owned, according to the wife, by their father. The Court found that there was a marital home, regardless of whose property it was. See also AD 142/80 (May 14, 1980) (TCC).

42. AD 4141/58 (June 4, 1959).

43. AD 459/71 (October 1, 1971); AD 1043/77 (March 13, 1978).

44. AD 1043/77 (March 13, 1978); AD 5906/78 (August 22, 1979).

45. AD 4688/71 (July 24, 1972).

46. AD 4141/58 (June 4, 1959); AD 3711/72 (August 30, 1973); AD 3688/76 (August 26, 1977).

47. AD 1796/73 (March 13, 1974).

48. AD 4512/76 (April 29, 1977).

49. AD 1385/77 (October 30, 1978).

50. AD 5906/78 (August 22, 1979).

51. AD 3574/62 (August 15, 1968). *Hijo de familia,* now a pejorative term for someone considered immature, was once the legal term for adults remaining subject to their father's authority.

52. AD 3711/72 (August 30, 1973).

53. AD 4423/70 (March 11, 1971).

54. Approximately one in three cases brought by the wife was for economic support from an absent husband.

55. AD 3697/28 (April 24, 1930).

56. In the cases reviewed, the district courts were much more likely than the Supreme Court to find in favor of the husband.

57. Several women seeking a divorce (whether or not they had originally initiated the case) appealed against rulings granting their husband a divorce and depriving them of economic support and/or custody: AD 5932/51 (December 3, 1954); AD 6752/57 (September 24, 1959); AD 1109/70 (October 19, 1972); AD 3378/72 (August 13, 1973); AD 1385/77 (October 30, 1978). The opportunity to get away from unloved (and often violent) husbands while maintaining a right to economic support accounts for divorce's being primarily a "feminine weapon" in the nineteenth century (García Peña 2006, 87); the introduction of absolute divorce appears to have reversed this pattern (Smith 2006).

58. Their stories are discussed in my earlier article on the subject (Varley 2000b). See also González Montes, this volume, and Sierra, this volume.

8

Conflictive Marriage and Separation
in a Rural Municipality in
Central Mexico, 1970–2000

SOLEDAD GONZÁLEZ MONTES

What options do married women have when they suffer from domestic violence and/or live in marital situations that they find oppressive or unsatisfactory? Research conducted in diverse ethnic and rural contexts in Mexico has found that a woman confronting these circumstances (whether formally married or in a common-law marriage) frequently abandons her home and seeks assistance from local judges in renegotiating her marital contract with the hope of improving her daily life.[1] In this chapter, I explore the interrelationship between these two forms of feminine agency and analyze the extent to which wives seeking changes in their marital relationship depend upon available family support and on the responses they receive from judicial authorities. Both arenas—the familial and the judicial—are not only fundamentally important for women's welfare, but they are also mutually constituted in multiple ways and subject to historical transformations.

Over the course of the period examined in this chapter, the conditions that permitted (or prevented) a wife to separate from her husband and to gain access to the local justice system changed in parallel with the transformation of women's role in the family and, more specifically, with the increase in their contribution to family income through wage labor undertaken outside the household.

The written records of the marital conflicts presented before local justices of the peace constitute an extraordinarily rich source of information concerning the actions of the parties in dispute, their points of view, the forms of judicial intervention involved, and the agreements reached. In addition, these documents provide insight into the protagonists' cultural representations with regard to gendered roles within marriage, authority in the family, the rights and obligations of family members, and some of the forms of control exercised by husbands. These materials, therefore, give us the opportunity of contrasting practices and representations that refer to family relations in general and the marital bond in particular.

The Context: The Construction of "the New Rurality" in Mexico

The neoliberal policies introduced in Mexico since the early 1980s have dramatically restructured regional economies: small- and medium-scale agricultural production has suffered a strong decline in relative economic value, and, as a consequence of deteriorating incomes, peasants have been forced to diversify their economic activities. Rural women have been compelled to find ways of contributing to the support of their households, just as their urban counterparts do, while the occupational structure underwent an extraordinarily rapid transformation. The result has been a notable feminization of the labor force in rural settings.

The municipality of Xalatlaco, the object of this study, exemplifies these processes exceptionally well. It is located in the southeastern part of the Valley of Toluca, in the state of Mexico; some three-quarters of its population was dedicated to agriculture in small family holdings in 1970, but by the year 2000 this proportion had fallen to less than one-fifth. By this latter date, almost half the economically active population was engaged in commerce and services, and more than one-third was employed in industry. Thus, over the course of three decades, and especially in the past ten years, there has been a radical shift toward a post-peasant economy in which women have an outstanding role.

Already by the 1960s, young single women in Xalatlaco had begun leaving their households to work as domestic employees, while married and older women sold foodstuffs and regional products in urban areas. When factories and clothing-assembly plants opened in nearby towns in the 1970s, many women (including married women) sought employment there. Women's entry into the labor force was not always free of conflict; some husbands had to give written permissions to their wives so they could work. These documents were legitimated by local municipal authorities, and copies can be found in the judicial records of the 1970s.[2]

Female participation in the economically active population at least doubled between 1970 and 2000, and women's earnings rapidly became an indispensable part of the family income. Other important changes accompanied the feminization of the labor force, including rising female educational levels, declining rates of fertility, and an increase in female-headed households.[3]

One important sociocultural change that took place in Xalatlaco, as well as in the surrounding region, was the apparent loss of indigenous identity that went hand in hand with the decline of Náhuatl as the dominant language. This shift was especially rapid after the early 1960s. Yet, even though people in the region no longer identify themselves as belonging to an ethnic group, many important aspects of family and community organization are very similar to those in areas that continue to be recognized as Indian. Particularly noteworthy in this respect are the practices regarding marriage and postmarital residence described in this chapter, which have a direct bearing on patterns of intrafamily conflicts. The very dense networks of exchanges, particularly those linked to public religious rituals, continue to demand the participation of families, and shape most of the social life of individuals.

As has been the case in most parts of the Mexican countryside, the reproduction of certain traditional forms of social organization is accompanied by the rapid adoption of globalized styles of consumption, particularly with regard to information and means of communication. The presence of televisions in rural households expanded notably after the late 1980s, and, since the second half of the 1990s, the use of the Internet has multiplied, as has the presence of video clubs and video games in the seat of municipal government (*cabecera municipal*), giving it an urban ambiance. These complex processes of continuity and change configure the new Mexican rurality, in which gender and generational relations, family organization, and ways of experiencing marriage are being redefined.

The Setting: The Justice of the Peace or Municipal Conciliator

Justices of the peace are based in the seats of municipal government and constitute the first level of state-imparted justice in Mexico. They hear cases involving infractions for which the penalty or fine does not exceed a certain number of minimum-wage-days, or for which the guilty party can be sentenced to no more than twenty-four hours in jail.[4] If the punishment for the infraction exceeds this amount, or if the crime is more serious (for instance, rape or homicide), then the case is forwarded to the Court of First Instance (Juzgado de Primera Instancia), the court for the local judicial district, which covers several municipalities. Studies of the local-level justice system indicate that justices of the peace routinely resort to the threat of sending the parties in dispute to the district court if they fail to come to an early agreement. This strategy of exerting pressure on the parties is usually successful, because people fear the additional cost in time and money in having to travel outside the home town.

Municipal justices of the peace are in charge of hearing the conflicts that arise in the course of daily life in small towns and rural communities, conflicts the resolution of which is vital if people are to continue living together. For this reason, the principal function of these judges has always been, as it continues to be, conciliation so that the disputing parties can reach an agreement, which is recorded in a so-called act of conformity, mutual agreement, or mutual respect and filed in the municipal court archives (see also Sierra, this volume). When an agreement is reached, the justice of the peace serves as witness, as do relatives accompanying the plaintiffs and the defendants. Relatives who accompany the disputants sign the agreement as guarantors (*fiadores*) who commit themselves to do everything possible to ensure that the agreement is respected.

Because the municipality of Xalatlaco is not large, recourse to a justice of the peace does not involve substantial journeys from hamlets to town. Nevertheless, women have not always had the same ease of access as men. As late as 1982, the municipal judge believed that women should not come before him unaccompanied, "because they're not responsible for themselves. If they are single, they should be accompanied by their parents, and if they are married, they should be accompanied by their husband or their parents as well." [5] In other words, this official (albeit not the law) did not view women as autonomous subjects who could fully exercise their rights as citizens. [6] The fact that until recently all women (except heads of households) had to be represented by a figure of superior authority constituted an important obstacle to their possibilities of seeking justice.

Another obstacle that women have frequently had to face is the unfavorable attitudes of judicial authorities, who until recently have always been male and more inclined to back husbands than wives. Local judges receive instructions from superior courts telling them to do all possible to maintain the integrity of the family, which in many cases leads them to minimize women's complaints or to try and dissuade the women from their demands in order to maintain family peace and harmony, even when the woman may be at physical risk from a husband who beats her (see also Sierra, this volume). [7] Thus, even if by law the court is open to all citizens, the gender bias that many judges display in imparting justice may discourage women and keep them out of the courtroom.

Historical studies that use as their source colonial and nineteenth-century court cases demonstrate that in different periods women did present themselves before judicial authorities, but in the majority of these cases they did so as victims, witnesses, or the accused. They usually did not come forward as plaintiffs, unless they did so as property owners whose rights were threatened. The women who appear in these older court records generally spoke to defend themselves against their husbands' accusations that they had abandoned their home, something they tried to justify in terms of the mistreatment to which they were subjected. In any case, the number of female plaintiffs was considerably fewer than the number of men seeking redress from the courts. [8]

Only at the end of the twentieth century was there in practice recognition (though, even then, not in all contexts) that women of legal age had the capacity to represent their own interests before judicial authorities in Xalatlaco. And it has only been recently that local authorities have started to show greater even-handedness with regard to women's demands than in the past. These two factors are fundamental when women ponder the decision as to whether or not to present their grievances before a court in expectation that they will be listened

to and that the judicial authority will seek to resolve the conflict that might be
in a way favorable to them.

Plaintiffs and Their Complaints

The principal source of information in this study is a set of 302 judicial documents dealing with marital conflicts brought to the municipal court of Xalatlaco
between 1970 and 2000 (all available cases for those years) (Table 8.1). The
increase in the number of cases during the last two decades of the twentieth
century reflects the increase (in absolute and relative terms) in the number of
women seeking an audience with the judge to state the reasons they have separated from their husband, leaving their conjugal home. They do so to anticipate
the accusations of their husband and to justify their conduct, to avoid any sug-
gestion that they have committed an offense by their actions (see below).

Although the monthly average of marital conflicts taken before the municipal court doubled between 1970 and 2000, it seems to have stabilized during
the 1990s. Throughout the period analyzed, the main issue involved in these
cases has been the wife's decision to return to live with her parents, leaving the
husband. Consistently, the records report that the wife is the person who abandons, not the husband. When testifying, husbands and wives blame each other
for failing to perform their duties as defined in terms of a traditional gendered
model of the sexual division of labor. Each tries to appear innocent and to justify his or her conduct—the strategy that parties in conflict normally adopt in all
judicial settings.[9]

What changes over time is who files a demand, and who is the first to make
statements concerning what happened. In the cases from 1970 to 1984, the husband or his parents were the ones who usually went before the judge to denounce
the fact that the wife had abandoned the conjugal home. Between 1990 and

TABLE 8.1
Marital Conflicts in Xalatlaco's Court Records, 1970–2000

	1970	1978	1980	1984	1990	2000
Total court records	30	37	25	53	75	82
Monthly average	2.5	3.1	2.1	3.2	5.7	5.4

Note: Grand total, 1970–2000: 302 court records.

2000, there were still large numbers of denunciations made by husbands, but a new phenomenon emerged: a notable increase in the proportion of plaintiffs who were women. These women went to court to anticipate their husbands doing so, to provide the judge with their own version of events and justify having left their husband.

Accusations by Husbands or Their Parents

The accusation that a husband most commonly makes against his wife is that she abandoned their home. It is likely that there are some instances in which the husband leaves that are not denounced before the court (and, therefore, not registered by judicial authorities).[10] Depositions made by husbands characteristically follow one or both of the following patterns: the husband states that he does not know why his wife left him because he gave her "no reason whatsoever" to do so; the husband accuses his wife of not having fulfilled her domestic obligations, of having been unfaithful, of having left the house without his permission, or of having disobeyed him in some other way.[11] Accusations of infidelity are also frequent and are often used by husbands to justify the use of physical violence.

Mistreatment Denounced by Wives

Throughout the period from 1970 to 2000, the denunciations made by women always focus on the same issues: the man's relatives (especially his mother) interfere in the couple's affairs; the husband does not give the wife sufficient funds to maintain the household; the husband inflicts physical violence upon her; the husband is alcoholic; the husband is involved with another woman. In many cases, women do not denounce just one circumstance but, rather, state at the same time that they have suffered from one or more (even all) of them.[12]

The intervention of in-laws in the couple's affairs is a characteristic feature of family organization in rural Mexico, where postmarital patrivirilocal residence is the norm, lasting for a period of several years.[13] This is when the majority of marital conflicts occur, often leading the wife to abandon the household because she fails to adapt to the situation and/or because she is suffering from physical abuse. Studies undertaken in other regions of the country have found a similar pattern.[14]

In Xalatlaco, marital life typically begins when a young woman goes to live with her boyfriend's family—a practice known as "the abduction of the bride" (el robo de la novia).[15] The man's parents then have the obligation of visiting the woman's parents, a few hours after she arrives at their home, to inform them of what has happened and to fix a date for civil and religious marriage ceremonies. Thus "the abduction of the bride" puts in motion a series of rituals intended to legitimate the union in the eyes of the community. Custom requires the intervention of both sets of parents and other family members, giving evidence that marriage is not so much an act of individual will as a series of exchanges between families.

The period between the moment when the couple begins living together and when they actually go through the marriage ceremonies varies in length, but it generally lasts less than a year and functions as a test period for the relationship. In particular, the situation is a trial for the new daughter-in-law, as she must adapt to conjugal life and the lifestyle of her in-laws. After the formal marriage rituals take place, the couple continues to live with the groom's family for a (variable) number of years, a number that has tended to diminish. The largest volume of intrafamily conflicts brought before the municipal judge arise during this period of living together as an extended family. Indeed, it is common that, a few months into the relationship, the young woman (often under the age of twenty years) regrets having left her parental home and returns to it. The husband and his parents then inform the judge that she has abandoned their home even though she may be pregnant or already have children, usually testifying that this occurred "for no reason whatsoever."

When the young woman is who testifies, she usually speaks of the difficulties she had with her husband's family. Documents frequently specify that women have conflicts with their mothers-in-law—who, according to women's statements found in judicial records, "always make life difficult for them," "instigate physical abuse by husbands," or "do not give them permission to visit their parents." [16] If the marriage has not yet been formalized, the document that registers the separation serves as a formal proof of the dissolution of the relationship, to prevent complications should one of the parties subsequently contest the matter.

Abandonment of the conjugal home is not, however, limited to young women during the initial period of their married life. There are numerous cases of older married women who have lived for many years with their in-laws and who state that they cannot bear continued cohabitation with them.[17] They, too, customarily justify their actions on the grounds that the husband's family interfered in the couple's life. On some occasions the difficulties of living with in-laws are further aggravated by the husband's physical abuse, his alcoholism, or his financial irresponsibility. In other cases, such as the following, the wife considers that the father-in-law has exceeded his authority over her as head of the household:

> A twenty-six-year-old woman, who began a common-law marriage twelve years ago and was married in a civil ceremony four years ago, denounces her husband for attacking her physically and verbally, for not working, and for being an alcoholic. They live with her in-laws, and her father-in-law has hit her on two occasions "without any right whatsoever." The father-in-law finally threw her out of the house, and she went to live in her sister's home, leaving behind her four children.[18]

When a wife perceives that the principal problem is life with her in-laws, abandoning the household is her main recourse to pressure her husband to build a separate home for her and her husband to live independently:

> Luisa and Felipe (a twenty-three-year-old worker), who were married ·in both civil and religious rites a year ago, declare that they have decided to separate because of problems deriving from the fact that they live with Felipe's parents. Luisa has returned to her parents' house, taking with her their two-month-old daughter, until Felipe builds their own home. Felipe will provide no money for her support, in view of the fact that all he earns will be destined to the construction of said house.[19]

Cohabitation with the wife's family (patriuxorilocal residence) is less common, given that few men accept it, since it means that the husband must submit to the authority of his in-laws, a situation considered entirely natural for married women but degrading for men. This living arrangement tends to be conflictive. The few cases of this kind that appear in the municipal court records involve men in special circumstances. For example, a twenty-year-old worker originally from Ensenada, Baja California, migrated to a neighboring town, married a woman from Xalatlaco, and went to live with her parents. The couple had constant difficulties and decided to separate until he built a house, for which the judge conceded a period of five months.[20] In another case, the couple went to live with the wife's parents because cohabitation with the husband's parents had proved so conflictive that it reached the point where the mother-in-law physically attacked her daughter-in-law.[21]

Blame for the husband's violence is, of course, always attributed to the other party. Usually wives are the ones who speak about this matter; husbands tend to remain silent on the topic, given that they are the ones who committed the actions in question. Husbands' depositions justify their behavior on the grounds that the wife failed to fulfill her obligations, went out without the man's permission, or exceeded such permission by arriving home late. The implicit message is that they resorted to violence as a means of disciplining their wives, and that this, according to prevailing family morals, is their rightful duty. Women, for their part, usually attribute physical violence committed against them to the consumption of alcohol. This view has the effect of diminishing the aggressor's responsibility for his conduct, given the widespread notion that a drunken person loses control over his actions.

Suspicions of infidelity and jealousies are also often the detonator for the more intense forms of violence committed by husbands, as in the following case.

> Tania, twenty-three years of age and married in a civil ceremony four years ago, accuses her husband of beating her at 6:00 A.M. The medical certificate issued by the local hospital and submitted as evidence attests

that she suffered first-degree injuries. The cause of her husband's anger was that on Saturday, February 5, she spoke briefly with a young man named Adolfo, who invited her to his engineering school graduation ceremony, while they were at a party at which they received an image of the Christ Child in the presence of family members, friends, and neighbors. . . . After they left the party and while she was asleep in their house at 6:00 A.M. yesterday morning, he grabbed her by the hair and threw her on the floor, kicking her. At 9:00 A.M. that same morning the complainant decided to take her son and go to her mother's house, where she will continue living until the problem with her husband is resolved.[22]

A Persistent Model of Conjugal Relations

Municipal court records reveal a notable continuity in cultural representations of men's and women's roles in marriage, linked to a traditional model of the sexual division of work and authority in the family. Overlooking the fact that during the last three decades women have been contributing to household finances a share almost equal to that of their husbands, court records from the year 2000 still state that wives are dedicated almost exclusively to domestic work, and no new definitions of marital relations have emerged. The following agreement, reached by a couple after an intense domestic conflict, illustrates this point:

Esperanza, a twenty-three-year-old nurse, and Julián, a twenty-four-year-old orchestra musician, were married in a civil ceremony a year and a half ago. They appear before the judge promising to solve their problems calmly. He promises to treat his wife more conscientiously and to speak to her in a civilized manner, without using any kind of abusive language. In the event that his wife does not obey him or does not do what he says she should do as his wife, Julián will go to her parents to inform them of what has happened. Esperanza is in agreement with what her husband declares, and she promises to behave like a true wife [como verdadera esposa]. In the event Julián does not keep his word, she will report what has happened to her mother-in-law. Before any situation gets out of hand, they jointly agree to discuss their problems with their relatives.[23]

The text reveals interesting contradictions. On the one hand, in the year 2000 the "true wife" was still obliged to obey her husband, and parents had the power to intervene in their children's marital affairs. On the other hand, couples have been embracing more modern notions of marital interaction, such as the idea that obedience should not be imposed by force and that civilized people avoid physical or verbal violence.

The next case underscores several fundamental elements in the exercise of authority within the family: the wife needs her husband's permission to leave the house, even to attend a social event in the company of her relatives; the parents intervene even though the couple is married and, therefore, legally emancipated; the in-laws urge the wife to put up with alcoholism and mistreatment by her husband (the notion that underlies this last injunction is that a wife is obliged to subordinate herself to her husband regardless of the situation). Here, the husband is the one to abandon the household, a much less frequent phenomenon than abandonment by the wife, and something that happens only when the couple is living independently or with the wife's parents.

> Esther is twenty-eight years old. She was married in a civil ceremony two and one-half years ago and has a daughter who is twenty months old. She declares that, from the time she married Raúl, she has had constant problems because he continually consumes alcohol and, when drunk, abuses her verbally and physically. Two days ago Raúl beat her because she accompanied her sisters and one of her brothers to a wedding, even though she had her husband's permission. Yesterday he again assaulted her and then took his clothes and left, returning later with his parents to take away the television set, the videocassette player, his clothing, and bank account documents. She and her daughter remained in the house where they had lived for three years. Her in-laws told Esther that she should put up with her husband.[24]

In Xalatlaco's family system, there is a common notion that parents not only can, but indeed should, intercede in their children's marriage (and even in their sex lives). The intervention is justified on the grounds that it will prevent marital problems from becoming extreme and ending in violence or separation. Parents are responsible for the good conduct of their children and for "correcting" their mistakes, thereby helping them solve conflicts and ensuring the continuity of the marriage—a practice that municipal judges readily accept.

Abandoning the Household, Separation, and Reconciliation

Abandoning the home is usually a female action, according to the municipal court records examined. For example, in the year 2000 there were forty-two wives who abandoned their household and only five husbands who did so. By leaving, the wife dramatically signals that she is no longer willing to continue living in a marital situation that she finds intolerable. However, for a woman to abandon her marital home, she must have somewhere to go. In a rural context, few women can live by themselves, not only because they lack sufficient financial resources to pay for their own housing, but because any woman living alone exposes herself to sexual harassment and gossip. For these reasons, support from a woman's parents is crucial. When her parents do not wish or are unable to take a woman back into their home, the option of separating from her husband is very difficult or simply unavailable. The following case exemplifies both the economic obstacles that a woman can face if she wishes to leave her husband and the young couple's dependence upon their parents.

Margarita, nineteen years of age, married and with completed secondary education, is employed as a worker [*obrera*]. Three years ago she married Antonio in a civil ceremony, and they have two children, aged four and two years. For the past seven months they have lived with Antonio's parents, where both began to work in his mother's sewing workshop. Antonio left this job to go to work in his father's workshop. He leaves the house at 7:00 A.M. and returns around 10:00 or 11:00 P.M. Margarita alleges that Antonio is romantically involved with one of his fellow workers, who has left hickies on his neck. Antonio gives Margarita 250 pesos each week in child support, but this amount is not sufficient. Margarita declares that she will continue living with her mother-in-law because she is working there to support her children.[25]

Why did Margarita go to the municipal judge if she was not going to take action against her husband? It is possible that she wanted to put on record her husband's infidelity and the insufficiency of the money he was giving her for child care in order to use the court file as antecedent and proof/justification when circumstances might be more propitious for abandoning her in-laws' household.

Many of the judicial files indicate that the wife had already abandoned her marital home on one or more occasions, suggesting a pattern of temporary separations with subsequent reconciliations.[26] Abandoning the household thus seems a strategy that wives use for exerting pressure so they can negotiate their return under better conditions. If the couple is legally married (in civil and religious ceremonies), there appears to be a greater effort to reestablish cohabitation than in cases of common-law marriage.

When negotiations are successful and reconciliation ensues, the couple goes before the judge to leave a record of their reunification in an Act of Conformity and Mutual Agreement, in which they state the new bases on which the marital relationship will be conducted. The acts filed in the year 2000 are not much different from those from the 1970s, with regard to the couple's stated commitments. The husband promises that he will never again mistreat his wife, that he will cease to be "irresponsible," and that he will establish an independent residence for his wife and children (if the conflict arose because they were living with his parents). For her part, the wife promises to fulfill her obligations and, above all, not to leave home again.

The judge functions as a witness to the agreements reached. In this role, he accepts the traditional gendered model of marital relations: the man will meet his obligations as provider, and the woman will fulfill her duties as a home-maker. If the woman has previously denounced physical mistreatment by her husband, she must forgive him. Indeed, some women who have filed formal charges against their spouse because of the physical injuries they have suffered have had to withdraw them to make the reconciliation possible.[27] The pressure to maintain the family unit falls upon these women. The judicial acts, however, record that both members of the couple seek reconciliation "for the good of their children under the legal age of consent [*menores hijos*]," underscoring their responsibility as parents.[28]

The cases in which a woman promises to return home despite having suffered repeated violence or actual physical injuries reveal the complexities of her position as wife, which leads her to have apparently contradictory attitudes. The action of abandoning her abusive husband and seeking recourse from judicial authorities emphasizes her capacity for agency and her determination to bring about a change in the marital relationship. Her return home, in contrast, clearly demonstrates the force of the cultural and social pressures upon her, which make definitive separation difficult or impossible. These pressures are also subjective, because women have internalized the cultural model in which a "good mother" is self-denying and sacrifices herself for her children. Women therefore assume that they are responsible for the integrity of the home and the family's well-being, values more important than their own physical safety and welfare.

Parents' Support for their Daughters and the Transformation of Judges' Responses

The court cases from Xalatlaco suggest that two processes have been particularly important in creating conditions that permit more women to abandon their marital home. On the one hand, there has been a change in women's relationship with their parents after marriage. On the other, municipal judges have stopped viewing household abandonment as an act that breaks the law, a view they had previously been inclined to.[29]

Increased support from parents for their married daughters is one of the most notable changes observed in the period from 1970 to 2000. It appears directly linked to the fact that, since the 1960s, more women have earned an income and have enjoyed greater decision-making power over how these resources are used. Various international studies have demonstrated that, when this occurs, children's (especially daughters') health and educational levels improve because their mothers use their incomes to invest in these areas.[30] I suggest that women also gain greater influence over the decision to help a daughter whose marriage fails.

Not only do parents permit their daughters to return to the family home, but now there are also cases in which, knowing their daughter is being mistreated, they go to her marital home and take her (and generally all her children as well) away to live with them. Occasionally, other family members (for example, the grandparents of the young abused wife) accompany the parents, thus constituting effective rescue teams to extract the wife, her children, and her belongings.

> Francisco is a thirty-five-year-old peasant with a primary education who lives in common-law marriage [en unión libre] with Julia. He informs the judge that, three days earlier, Julia's parents and grandparents arrived at their house with the purpose of taking away Julia and their children, and that they also carried away her belongings, some chairs, the kitchen blender, and the iron.[31]

> Néstor, a married thirty-four-year-old public employee, notifies the judge that his wife's father, uncle, mother, and brother arrived at their home, entered the dwelling, and removed all the furniture and clothing, as well as his wife and three children. They loaded everything into a pick-up truck and drove away. The brother filmed the removal of the household belongings as well as the presence of Néstor's parents, who were in the courtyard at the time.[32]

There is no evidence of this practice in previous decades. Woman usually used to escape while running errands—something that still occurs, especially in the case of younger women. Support from parents and relatives in a woman's effort to leave the marital home implies that she has maintained good communications with her family of origin. This contrasts with the old saying "You got married, you're stuck, and you have to put up with it [Te casaste, te amolaste, te tienes que aguantar]," which women born in the 1950s remember they were often told.

The second element that has been important for women who object to their marital situation is the role played by the local judiciary. Historical studies show that, until quite recently, there has been extraordinary continuity in the response of local authorities to women's abandonment of the home. During the colonial period, throughout the nineteenth century, and into the latter part of the twentieth century, judicial authorities issued orders for the capture of fugitive wives so that they could be returned to their husband.[33] A file in Xalatlaco's court archive from 1959 shows that a judge ordered a father to appear before the court because he had given protection to his daughter, sheltering her in his home, after she had fled the blows of her husband. The judge told the father that what he had done was a crime that could cost him three months in jail because "the father's authority [patria potestad] only lasts until children marry." The father was pressured to return his daughter to the person legitimately responsible for her (her husband) or go to jail. In another case, from November 1970, a municipal judge recommended the capture of a fugitive wife.

But in the municipal court files from subsequent years that were reviewed in the course of this study, I found no further cases of this kind.

Mexico's civil codes of 1870 and 1884 introduced the possibility of divorce understood as separation of bed and board, but required the judge to do everything possible to achieve reunification of a couple seeking divorce by mutual consent (Arrom 1985a, 311). The codes therefore established that judicially authorized separations were only temporary, for a period to be agreed before the judge, although at the end of this period couples could insist on remaining separate.[34] Until the end of the 1970s, Xalatlaco's judges continued routinely applying the practice of temporary separation in cases of major marital conflict in which the couple agreed to separate. In such instances, the judge authorized the "suspension" of the marital relationship for a period of thirty or forty-five days (during which time the wife could return to live with her parents) so that both members of the couple (especially the wife) could reeducate themselves with regard to their marital duties. This period of separation also would also permit the couple's respective parents to do everything possible to convince husband and wife to return to living together.

By the year 2000, the situation had changed. Xalatlaco's municipal judge accepted marital separations without establishing a definite time period, and set the amount of alimony (*pensiones alimenticias*) that the husband should provide to his wife for support of their children. Court records include numerous receipts for support payments made through judicial authorities.[35]

Thus, in the last three decades of the twentieth century, female abandonment of the marital home ceased being treated as though it were a criminal offense, an offense leading to the woman being returned to her husband against her wishes. Instead, it became a situation justified before the authorities as part of a process of establishing a legitimate right to separation. This represented a drastic change from the recent past.

Conclusion

Xalatlaco's judicial records show that from 1970 to 2000 there was great continuity both in the kinds of marital conflicts and in the arguments presented by men and women to the municipal court. What has changed are the way women, judges, and a woman's relatives respond to marital conflict. Also noteworthy is the persistence of a conservative discourse that preserves traditional gendered representations of the sexual division of labor and marital obligations, including the idea that the wife should obey her husband (see also Varley, this volume). The records examined for this study offer no indication that women questioned this discourse on its own terms, but they did so, in practice, by abandoning their marital home. Thus we find an evident contradiction between social representations and actual practices, and it would seem that in this terrain it is easier to take practical action than to change the discourse. The materials analyzed also suggest that it has become easier for women to bring their complaints to the municipal court.

Although there are instances throughout the historical record of women abandoning their household, the number of women who do so appears to have grown. As shifts have occurred in the occupational structure, and as wives have become an important source of economic support for the household, the model of masculine authority and household headship based on the husband's role as sole or principal provider for the family has entered into crisis. This transformation has inevitably altered women's expectations and aspirations with regard to marriage. Fewer women are willing to continue living in adverse situations, especially when they are victims of physical violence or experience excessive interference by in-laws in the couple's life.

The fact that the relatives of unhappy wives go in search of them, help them to leave the marital home, and provide somewhere to live when they no longer want to stay in an unsatisfactory situation opens a series of options rarely available in the 1970s. As in the past, in-laws play a central role in the lives of married women, but the intervention of women's own parents has emerged as a new resource. This process is reorienting the organization of the family by creating new domestic living arrangements and new forms of household composition, shifts that are reducing the family system's strongly patrilineal orientation and making it more bilateral.

It is worthwhile emphasizing that no court record examined for this study mentions that a woman abandoning her marital home thought of establishing herself independently. The women's dependence on parents or other relatives suggests that these women were not homeowners, and did not have sufficient economic resources to rent their own dwelling. In addition, they would certainly have encountered strong social pressure against living by themselves.

National statistics show that the increase in separations is not an exclusively urban phenomenon; it is also an observable tendency in Mexico's rural population (Ojeda 1986; Quilodrán 2000). The court records from Xalatlaco suggest that the phenomenon is due to the fact that women have reduced their level of tolerance for mistreatment, and expanded their capacity for taking action before the judicial authorities. In this respect, separations constitute a good indicator of women's power to negotiate and take decisions concerning the conditions of their marital life.

During the period under study, women's initiatives to separate from their husbands when suffering mistreatment have ceased to be viewed as transgressions; rather, they have become a right, albeit one with different meanings for men and for women. Although a woman may see separation as an advantageous option and a means of exerting pressure to improve the conditions of cohabitation, for a man it signifies a loss of authority over his wife. Moreover, separation questions the "right" of a husband to punish his wife physically to "discipline" her. These changes are taking place not only at the level of individual and local actions, but also at the level of national collective actions. Since the late 1990s, legislation adopted in most Mexican states has incorporated articles that define beatings as "domestic violence" and classified them as a crime—a fundamental change brought about by the national women's movement.[36]

Translated by Helga Baitenmann.

NOTES

1. See, for example, Collier (1973), Nader (1990), Martínez Corona and Mejía Flores (1997), Chenaut (2001a), D'Aubeterre Buznego (2000a).

2. The 1917 Law of Family Relations required women wishing to work outside the home to seek their husband's formal permission, but this requirement was withdrawn in subsequent legislation for the Federal District and other states.

3. National census data show that Xalatlaco's average number of live births per woman fell from 4.1 in 1970 to 2.7 in the year 2000. Approximately 7 percent of all households were female-headed in 1970; the figure rose to nearly 18 percent in 2000. Women's average age at first marriage rose from 19.3 years in 1970 to 21.2 years in 2000 (Dirección General de Estadística 1973; INEGI 2003).

4. On the nature and functions of the local courts, known in the State of Mexico as small claims courts (Juzgados de Cuantía Menor), see Ley Orgánica del Poder Judicial del Estado de México, 1995, arts. 78–87.

5. Interview with Juez Clemente Bobadilla Miranda, August 1982. The justice of the peace, who had only completed secondary education, was elected because he had the reputation in the community of being an honest person who did not engage in conflicts either with family members or with other persons.

6. The official was citing a principle that had disappeared from the law over sixty years earlier. Nineteenth-century civil codes had required wives to seek their husband's permission to take part in litigation, but this requirement did not appear in the 1917 Law of Family Relations or in subsequent legislation.

7. Martínez Corona and Mejía Flores (1997) describe a similar pattern in the Sierra Norte de Puebla, where judges had been instructed by their superiors to try to maintain family units at all costs.

8. See Taylor (1979), Kanter (1993), and Stern (1995) on the colonial period, and González Montes and Iracheta (1987) for 1890 to 1910.

9. For similar findings in other regions, see Collier (1973), Nader (1990), Martínez Corona and Mejía Flores (1997), and Chenaut (2001a).

10. The cases in which the husband leaves home generally involve situations in which the couple live with the wife's parents, or in which they live independently.

11. Chenaut (2001a) found the same male arguments in her study of a Veracruz community with a strong Totonac indigenous presence.

12. A typical package of grievances included intervention in the couple's affairs by the woman's in-laws, infidelity by her husband, her husband's lack of responsibility as a

provider, and his physical abuse of her. See, for example, Archivo del Juzgado Municipal de Xalatlaco (AJX), Acta Informativa, oficio (henceforth, of.) 112 (April 27, 2000).

13. Postmarital residence in the husband's family home is a widespread practice among Indian communities. For a review of the literature on marriage customs in contemporary indigenous Mexico, see González Montes (1999a).

14. Nutini (1968, 348), Collier (1973, 180, 190), and Chenaut (2001a) also find that this is the principal reason why the woman abandons her marital home in the regions they have studied.

15. For a discussion of the multiple meanings of "abduction of the bride," see D'Aubeterre Buznego (2003).

16. Actas de Conformidad y Mutuo Respeto that mention discord between mothers and daughters-in-law include: AJX of. 72 (March 8, 1990); unnumbered record (September 26, 1990); of. 103 (April 20, 1990); of. 104 (May 23, 1990); of. 106 (April 23, 1990); of. 110 (May 8, 1990); of. 146 (July 2, 1990); of. 247 (November 19, 1999).

17. Cases in which women abandoned their marital home because of disagreements with the in-laws with whom they resided include the following Actas Informativas: AJX of. 1 (January 2, 1990); of. 63 (March 5, 1990); of. 102 (April 20, 1990); of. 105 (April 23, 1990); of. 121 (April 30, 1990); of. 115 (May 16, 1990); of. 125 (May 28, 1990); of. 132 (June 11, 1990); of. 183 (August 31, 1990); of. 198 (August 28, 1990); of. 202 (October 11, 1999); of. 213 (October 13, 1999); of. 5 (January 6, 2000).

18. AJX, Acta Informativa, of. 54 (February 28, 2000).

19. AJX, Acta de Conformidad y Mutuo Respeto, of. 14 (March 8, 2000).

20. AJX, Acta Informativa, of. 92 (February 9, 1990); Acta de Mutuo Respeto, of. 77 (March 14, 1990).

21. AJX, Acta Informativa, of. 121 (May 11, 2000).

22. AJX, Acta Informativa, of. 32 (February 7, 2000).

23. AJX, Acta de Compromiso y Mutuo Respeto, of. 26 (July 4, 2000).

24. AJX, Acta Informativa, of. 103 (April 18, 2000).

25. AJX, Acta Informativa, of. 131 (May 23, 2000).

26. AJX, of. 77 (March 20, 2000) (a wife abandoned her marital home on six occasions but returned each time) and of. 232 (November 2, 1999) (after ten years of marriage and having two daughters, the wife, about to give birth for a third time, abandoned her household for a fifth time and went to her parents' house).

27. AJX, Acta de Conformidad y Mutuo Respeto, of. 9 (February 18, 2000).

28. For example, AJX, Acta de Conformidad y Mutuo Respeto, of. 12 (March 9, 2000).

29. Abandonment of the home has never been a criminal offense, although it is one of the grounds for "necessary" divorce, such that the spouse found guilty can be deprived of any right to economic support and can lose custody of the children. Article 74 of the 1917 Law of Family Relations made it a crime for a husband to leave his family without economic support, and economic abandonment of family members, including consensual partners, remains an offense in the State of Mexico and elsewhere (Código Penal del Estado de México, 2000, art. 217). The relationship between economic and physical abandonment has provoked debate or ambiguity at different levels of the judicial system: see Varley, this volume.

30. See for example several of the chapters in Blumberg (1991). Such findings are the basis on which institutions such as the World Bank support policies increasing women's access to income generation (World Bank 2001).

31. AJX, Acta Informativa, of. 251 (November 23, 1999).

32. AJX, Acta Informativa, of. 69 (March 4, 2000).

33. For the colonial period, see Kanter (1993); for the Porfiriato, see González Montes and Iracheta (1987).

34. Código Civil del Distrito Federal y Territorio de la Baja California, 1884 (CC 1984), art. 236.

35. This practice reflects the provisions to be made when couples agree to a divorce by mutual agreement, or "voluntary" divorce. When the couple has children, they are required to seek judicial approval and must draw up an agreement concerning living arrangements, maintenance payments for the spouse and children, custody of the children, and marital property (Código Civil del Estado de México 2002, art. 4.102). The judge may authorize a temporary separation before the divorce is finalized (art. 4.103). It appears that the justices of the peace in Xalatlaco treat this procedure as a *purely* temporary measure. Of twenty-one Actas de Conformidad y Mutuo Respeto examined for the year 2000, only three mention the possibility of the couple divorcing. Permanent separation may not lead to a formalized divorce because, among other reasons, there are costs, in both time and money, associated with such proceedings. Rural divorce rates remain low.

36. Código Penal del Estado de México, 2000, art. 218. This article criminalizes physical or moral violence within the family. The State of Mexico has also passed a law seeking to prevent family violence: Ley para la Prevención y Atención de la Violencia Familiar en el Estado de México, 2002.

9

The Archaeology of Gender in the New Agrarian Court Rulings

HELGA BAITENMANN

Scholars focusing on the intersection between law and gender tend to give attention to those aspects of the legal system that create and/or perpetuate hierarchical social relations based upon idealized notions of femininity, masculinity, and heteronormativity. In some instances, discrimination, unequal treatment, or power structures based upon naturalized conceptions of sexual difference are more or less explicit in laws, court procedures, jurisprudence, and so forth. In other contexts, the ideas that sustain a gendered asymmetry of rights and obligations are profoundly implicit; they can only be exposed by peeling away layers of constructed signification to reveal what Appignanesi and Garratt (1995, 80), in their discussion of Derrida's strategy of deconstruction, describe as "the underlayers of meaning."

The new court system created in conjunction with the 1992 constitutional reforms that ended Mexico's postrevolutionary agrarian reform project is a prime example of legal practices that are usually seemingly gender-neutral. For the most part, men and women use the new agrarian courts to settle disputes and validate their rights without being treated differently on the basis of sex or sexual preference. And yet the concepts employed in the present agrarian legal system—oftentimes created in the early twentieth century (or even earlier)—remain deeply gendered.[1]

This chapter analyzes the discourse found in a number of recent (1993–2004) agrarian district court rulings from the coffee-producing region of Central Veracruz, in order to identify a number of taken-for-granted concepts that gender present-day property rights, work, and daily life in rural Mexico. Specifically, it highlights some central constructs that underpin agrarian law, including the concepts of *ejidatario* (land reform beneficiary), agrarian family, and ejido parcel (land grant). In doing so, it makes two observations.

First, legal discourse and the language of daily life in the agrarian reform sector are mutually constituted. That is, these historical constructs are shared by all actors both inside the agrarian courtroom and outside (in rural communities throughout Mexico, in ejido assembly halls, in rural households, and so forth). Plaintiffs and defendants, judges and witnesses, court officials and court users, all employ the concept of ejidatario or ejidataria, talk about land parcels, and speak about an individual's positions within the family and how these positions shape her or his legal status in regard to land.

The second observation is that these shared, gendered concepts are deeply enduring. Indeed, they have persisted for almost a century, despite profound changes in the nature of the agrarian reform. Even after a major paradigm shift in 1992, in which the nature of agrarian property was altered in important ways, these early twentieth-century concepts surface again and again in present-day court hearings. These concepts are particularly likely to endure because they are difficult to discern.

The concluding section of this chapter takes up these two observations to challenge some of the analytical foundations of the study of law and gender as an academic subdiscipline.

The Agrarian Court System

Mexico's twentieth-century agrarian reform was one of the most wide-ranging and long-lasting in the nonsocialist world. To distribute land, the architects of the reform created a new body of law, a hierarchical administrative structure, and a series of intricate administrative practices that remained operational for over seven decades. Starting in 1915, what has come to be known as the postrevolutionary agrarian reform has been held together, bestowed coherence, and awarded permanence by its legal system, which operates in parallel with other legal frameworks such as mercantile, civil, penal, and labor law. Agrarian legislation—composed of hundreds of statutes, decrees, and regulations—became a distinct body of law practiced by a new cadre of legislators and jurists. To implement these laws, state planners constructed a multilevel administrative apparatus under the jurisdiction of the federal executive, with its own agencies at state and national levels and diverse administrative offices, consultative bodies, and archives. Between 1915 and 1992, this increasingly complex agrarian bureaucracy expropriated and redistributed over half of Mexico's total surface area to 3.5 million individuals and their families, organizing them into almost thirty thousand ejidos and agrarian communities (the land and labor arrangements that were the principal vehicles for land distribution) (Secretaría de la Reforma Agraria 1998, 313).[2]

In 1992, as many Latin American countries began to privatize their land reform sectors, the Mexican government amended Article 27 of the Constitution so as to cancel the state's historic commitment to land redistribution and to permit the gradual privatization of rural property. This shift in the role of the state toward the rural sector, and in the nature of agrarian property, was accompanied by: a series of laws that changed the nature of the postrevolutionary Mexican ejido; a thorough reorganization of the agrarian bureaucracy and the creation of an agrarian ombudsman (Procuraduría Agraria); the initiation of a large-scale land-titling program aimed at gradually privatizing the agrarian reform sector (the Programa de Certificación de Derechos Ejidales y Titulación de Solares Urbanos, or "Procede"); and the creation of a new agrarian court system composed of forty-nine individual agrarian district courts headed by a judge (Tribunales Unitarios Agrarios) and the Agrarian Supreme Court in Mexico City composed of five justices (Tribunal Superior Agrario). This new judicial system replaced the executive-controlled agrarian bureaucracy that had served as a proxy court system for the better part of the twentieth century (Chávez Padrón 2003). The new agrarian courts are one of the most important and least studied aspects of these post-1992 reforms.

The court cases analyzed in this chapter come from the agrarian district court in Central Veracruz.[3] Here, as in the more than one hundred thousand grievances filed across the country between 1992 and 1997 alone, the cases deal primarily with individual rights to ejido parcels. To speed up agrarian trials, rulings are based on oral statements made at a single hearing. The court secretary records oral statements verbatim, as well as the judge's deliberations and verdict (Zepeda Lecuona 1999, 9–49; Ochoa Pérez 1997–1998). This chapter focuses on a number of these statements to analyze the underlayers of gendered meaning of several key agrarian concepts.

Agrarian Citizenship

In 1999, Carmen Escalante sent a petition to the agrarian district court in Central Veracruz explaining that "she was resorting to the agrarian court to appeal for the recognition of her ejidataria status at the San Marcos de León ejido [*solicitando el reconocimiento de su calidad de ejidataria*]." She had acquired her ejido rights from her mother, an elderly member of the ejido. For the mother to transfer her ejido parcel to her daughter, agrarian law requires that she renounce her rights at the ejido's general assembly, where members periodically meet to discuss and vote on ejido matters. Here, the three-member ejido board (*comisariado ejidal*) first declared the rights "vacant" and, only then and with the assembly's concurrence, accepted the daughter as a new ejidataria (agrarian rights holder). The next step was for the daughter to take her case to the agrarian district court, in order for a judge to certify her rights. Her court hearing concluded (as many do) with the judge using the following formula: "Carmen Escalante Pérez's character as ejidataria of the population center San Marcos de León . . . is [hereby] recognized with all the rights and obligations that correspond to this species [*con todos los derechos y obligaciones correspondientes a los de su especie*]."[4]

What exactly does the legal term *species* mean in this context? In what ways are ejidatarios and ejidatarias different from other individuals? Does the fact that agrarian court rulings confirm women's agrarian rights mean that this category of rights holder is gender-neutral?

One way of analyzing the concept of ejidatario or ejidataria is by understanding it as a form of citizenship. In the early twentieth century, the post-revolutionary agrarian reform created a new rights-bearing individual (the agrarian rights beneficiary) who received a package of rights and obligations from the state different in content from the civil, labor, and political rights and obligations of other Mexican citizens at the time. For the most part, agrarian rights (like other forms of citizenship rights) were collectively endowed, but each person had to fulfill a number of requirements to be individually eligible. As with citizenship generally, there were a number of qualifications specified in agrarian law that agrarian rights holders had to fulfill—preconditions that have survived in agrarian thought for almost a century. For example, in the San Marcos de León court case, the judge certified the ejido assembly's agreement to allow the mother to pass on her agrarian rights to her daughter, but not before the daughter had demonstrated having the appropriate civil status to become a new agrarian rights holder—namely, being a Mexican national of legal age (or of any age, if in charge of a family) and a resident (*avecindada*) of the ejido in question.

Nationality is the most common form of citizenship restriction worldwide. Therefore, it is not surprising that the Decree of January 6, 1915, required land beneficiaries to be Mexican nationals.[5] Moreover, until 1992, they had to be Mexican-born, a requirement that excluded nationalized foreigners. Being of legal age, another common precondition for acquiring citizenship rights, has also been a long-standing category for inclusion in (or exclusion from) the Mexican agrarian reform. Like other forms of subjecthood, full membership in ejidos or agrarian communities has depended upon the attainment of legal age because (like marriage, military conscription, and electoral rights) agrarian rights are only granted to those considered old enough to fulfill certain roles. The Agrarian Regulatory Law (Reglamento Agrario) of 1922 established a minimum age of eighteen years, and the Agrarian Code of 1940 reduced the legal age to sixteen years (or younger, if the individual soliciting land had a family), where it remains today.

Residence is another common precondition for citizenship. However, whereas most nations consider residence to mean anywhere within the national territory, the Mexican agrarian reform restricts it to the town or community that originally solicited a land grant from the state. This is because, starting in 1915, the state recognized the collective rights of communities to demand and receive from the government enough land to satisfy the needs of their residents, and individuals could only claim rights as part of these communities. Moreover, when a community received rights to land (a precondition for individual agrarian rights), agrarian officials wanted to prevent the landless living in other towns from migrating to the land-endowed population centers to claim individual land rights as part of those communities. Therefore, during most of the agrarian reform period, a minimum residence of six months to one year in the endowed community was a prerequisite to obtaining individual land rights. After 1992, agrarian law became somewhat more flexible in this regard. The 1992 Agrarian Law states that the agrarian rights holder either has to be a resident of the ejido for at least a year prior to obtaining agrarian rights, or must fulfill the requirements found in the ejido's internal regulations.[6] This qualification gives ejido members some autonomy in determining whether outsiders will be incorporated into the ejido, or whether rights will be limited to ejido residents.

Understanding the status of ejidatario/a as a package of rights and obligations comparable to the concept of citizenship is helpful when trying to analyze its gendered nature, as we see in the cases that follow. Scholars have demonstrated that citizenship rights are historically constructed (Escalante Gonzalbo 1992; Lomnitz 2001, 58–80), always a matter of degree (Abel and Lewis 2002, 4–15), and profoundly gendered. Feminist scholars have long held that political theory, in both classical and present-day manifestations, conceives of citizenship in terms of the male citizen. Indeed, just as the liberal concept of citizenship took the male citizen as its model, the abstract individual with rights to land in Mexico (*"beneficiario"* first, "ejidatario" later) was conceived in male form. And, even though the 1971 Federal Agrarian Reform Law granted women equal rights to land, the post-1992 concept of agrarian citizenship is still based upon the notion of the heterosexual male citizen who heads the "agrarian family."[7]

The Agrarian Family

A year after Irineo Islas from the La Orduña ejido died intestate, his daughter, Teresa Islas, sued Guadalupe Hernández (relationship unknown) over an ejido parcel. She declared in court that she was entitled to inherit her father's agrarian rights because "she had lived with him in the same residence." Additionally, the agrarian district court documents include the names of two witnesses who stated that, indeed, "father and daughter had lived at the same domicile."[8] The judge ruled according to Article 18 of the 1992 Agrarian Law, which stipulates that when someone dies intestate the first person with the right to inherit is the spouse, followed by the common law partner (male or female), a descendant, an ascending relative, and, finally, someone who was unrelated by kinship but cohabited with and depended on the deceased. In this ranking order, Teresa Islas was entitled to inherit her father's parcel regardless of whether she lived with him in the same residence. Why did all the actors involved in the court case stress the fact that daughter and father resided in the same household?

Agrarian inheritance rules have always been, and still are, what gives content to the notion of agrarian family patrimony. Since its inception as a state project, agrarian inheritance has been a difficult concept to legislate because the ejido created by the Decree of January 6, 1915 was considered a temporary training ground to turn campesino and Indian agriculture into "efficient" family farms. It was not initially intended to survive the first generation of men who received land, much less the greater part of the twentieth century. Nevertheless, the laws enacted in 1925 introduced the idea of the agrarian testament (known as the succession list, and later refined in the 1934 Agrarian Code), which limited possible heirs to the ejidatario's wife or common-law partner (*la mujer del ejidatario*), his children, and persons of either sex who were part of the household (see Deere, this volume). The testamentary restrictions found in the 1934 Agrarian Code have survived to this day.[9] If an ejidatario or an ejidataria dies intestate (that is, without a will registered at a public notary, or a succession list registered at the National Agrarian Registry), the 1992 Agrarian Law stipulates the following inheritance sequence: spouse, common law partner, offspring, ascending relative, and then "a cualquier otra persona de las que dependan económicamente de él [any other person who depended economically on *him*]."[10]

Agrarian rights are linked historically to the concept of the agrarian family, the shape and content of which are often shaped by the state (see, for example, Collier, Rosaldo, and Yanagisako 1997, 71–81; Salles 1998, 279). For postrevolutionary Mexico, scholars have recently demonstrated that molding the family to fit certain ideals was central to the Mexican national project. Describing this project as the modernization or rationalization of patriarchy, a number of studies illustrate how government efforts were aimed at reconfiguring the domestic sphere.[11] The agrarian reform was precisely one of these efforts.

Agrarian law in twentieth-century Mexico was an unusual combination of nineteenth-century jurisprudence, revolutionary ideals (mainly urban and middle-class), and indigenous and peasant demands for the restitution of usurped lands. However, the legal scholars, politicians, and revolutionaries who played roles in the construction of the Mexican agrarian reform during the first decades of the twentieth century shared the ambition of changing the structure of land tenancy in favor of the creation of (nuclear) family farms (Baitenmann 1997, 294; Deere and León 2001, 3).

As in the case of postrevolutionary workers' rights, in which the minimum wage was intended to be the minimum required to support a nuclear family, an ejido parcel represented the minimum amount of land required to support the new agrarian family. Rules limiting the size of ejido parcels took into account the quality of land to determine how much was necessary for the head of family to support a household. Indeed, according to the 1920 Law of Ejidos, potential grantees were family heads who lacked enough land to earn twice the average daily wage (*jornal*) prevailing in the region. When agrarian officials and engineers went to the countryside to map and measure new ejido lands, the size of the land grant was directly related to the number of hectares needed for each land solicitor to support a family. By 1922, for example, the Agrarian Regulatory Law had established that the minimum individual grant had to measure three to five hectares if irrigated land, four to six hectares if rain-fed, and six to eight hectares in more arid environments.

This agrarian family had several characteristics. First, it was essentially a nuclear family, rather than an extended family (that is, a family embracing parents, children, and some dependents, often the elderly). Second, the agrarian family was a domestic group or household in that its members cohabitated (in contrast to an extended family living in several dwellings). Third, the individual receiving the parcel was the agrarian head of family.

The Agrarian Head of Family

In 1996, Felipe Campos, an ejidatario from La Orduña, died intestate. Both his widow, Amelia Conde, and his mother, María Ochoa, claimed the right to inherit his parcel. His widow argued that it was she who had been economically dependent upon her husband. In the end, Ochoa renounced her claim in favor of her daughter-in-law, by "confessing" that it was, indeed, Conde who had depended financially upon her husband, lived with him at the same residence, and worked the ejido parcel with which they supported themselves.[12] The district judge ruled in terms of Article 18 of the 1992 Agrarian Law, which stipulates that when someone dies intestate the first person with the right to inherit is the spouse or partner. In this ranking, Ochoa clearly stood behind her daughter-in-law. Nevertheless, the judge noted in his ruling that "the wife of the deceased had depended financially on her late husband," and that "both husband and wife had worked the land from which they supported themselves."[13]

If both husband and wife worked the ejido parcel, why did María Ochoa feel compelled to prove she was economically dependent on her late husband? If the judge acknowledged that both husband and wife worked the land that supported them, why did he automatically accept the widow's claim that she had been financially dependent on her husband? Why were they not equally financially dependent on each other?

The foundations of the postrevolutionary agrarian reform were laid at a time when the 1884 Civil Code was still in effect. The late-nineteenth-century civil codes "incorporated most of the colonial laws that . . . subjected wives and children to the paterfamilias's control" (Arrom 1985a, 305–306). And, just as the liberal civil codes empowered women only in default of the male spouse (ibid., 309), agrarian law recognized only widows and single women as heads of family who could enjoy agrarian rights.

This conception came directly from nineteenth-century jurisprudence on landed property. For example, the nineteenth-century liberal laws designed to privatize communal property decreed that land should be distributed among the "family heads" of each pueblo, including widows with children (Chassen-López 1994, 34). In postrevolutionary agrarian law, the 1920 Law of Ejidos explicitly employed the term *jefe de familia* (family head). If a man lived in the household, heads of family were automatically presumed to be male; women were considered heads of the agrarian family only if they were widows with children or single mothers—in other words, in the absence of a male.[14] In turn, all other household members (regardless of their roles in the family economy) were considered dependents of the head of the agrarian family.

This gendered concept was never fully shed in later legislation, not even in laws deemed more gender equal. For example, the 1971 Federal Agrarian Reform Law is famous for having given women equal rights to land. On closer inspection, however, this law only allowed women to become land grantees when new ejidos were distributed (or existing ones expanded). Had the law actually given women equal rights to land, it would have transformed the concept of agrarian family in such a way as to give wives and partners equal agrarian rights within already existing ejidos. In other words, all existing ejidatarios (and ejidatarias) would have had joint agrarian rights with a spouse or partner. This, in turn, would have allowed judges to develop jurisprudence on agrarian rights during separation and divorce cases (two situations entirely ignored by agrarian law).

More recently, the 1992 agrarian reforms also failed to give women equal rights. Activists in Mexico City pleaded with the architects of the reforms to preserve the concept of family patrimony (that is, the idea that land grants were intended to support a family).[15] However, what was needed was not more emphasis on family patrimony but rather a radical transformation of the concept. For example, scholars have noted that the Procede titling program could have recognized the dual-headed household and implemented a joint titling program within marriage and consensual unions (Deere and León 2001, 7–8, 187–188, 225–227, 338–340).[16]

Rural Housewives

In 1997, Plácida Tapia of the Tuzamapan ejido in Central Veracruz petitioned the agrarian district court to recognize her rights as an ejidataria based on her status as the heir of her late husband, a former agrarian rights holder. Her husband had registered Tapia as his successor at the National Agrarian Registry, the equivalent of registering a will or testament at a notary public. In addition, a representative of the ejido authorities supported Tapia's petition by identifying her as "the one who has possessed and cultivated the land parcel since before the death of the title holder, who had been ill and bedridden."[17]

In 2001, Zeferina González from the Zimpizahua ejido had recourse to the same district court to claim her right to inherit an ejido parcel from her mother, who had died intestate. In strictly legal terms, González had the right to inherit her mother's parcel because her two siblings agreed to give up their claims to the inheritance. As in other cases, all she had to prove was her nationality and age. Nevertheless, at the court hearing González thought it necessary to explain that it was she who tilled the land, and the judge reiterated this reasoning in his finding: ". . . because the plaintiff is in charge of working the parcel."[18]

Why was it necessary for these plaintiffs to claim (and for the judge to reiterate) that they worked the land they were already legally entitled to inherit? Why do most men claiming inheritance rights merely state that they possess the land, while women usually explain that they possess *and* work the land? Once again, plaintiffs, defendants, lawyers, witnesses, and judges in present-day agrarian court cases use concepts, particular to the Mexican postrevolutionary agrarian reform, that contain layers of gendered meaning.

There are two interrelated concepts at work in these cases. The first is the idea that individuals have rights to agrarian land parcels as long as they fulfill the obligation to work the land. Second, although it is taken for granted that men can work agricultural land, women—in the social imagination—have a more problematic relationship to agricultural work.

One of the early anarchist/socialist conceptions of the Mexican agrarian reform was that land was for the tiller. This meant that land beneficiaries had lifelong but conditional land use rights (*derecho condicionado de usufructo vitalicio* [Ibarra Mendivil 1989, 285]). From 1934 to 1992, not only did agriculturalists have the right to receive land from the state, but they also had the obligation to cultivate the land they were granted. Indeed, the 1934 Agrarian Code stipulated that land reform beneficiaries could lose their use-rights to ejido parcels if they left the land idle for two consecutive years. This idea worked well for men who had agrarian rights. However, if the agrarian rights holder was a woman, the situation became more complicated because women were not considered agriculturalists; women were mothers and housewives. One way of resolving this dilemma was to exempt women from personally working the parcel. To do this, the 1940 Agrarian Code stipulated that, although land beneficiaries could not hire salaried workers or engage in sharecropping agreements, women who supported families and were too busy with domestic chores and child care to work the land personally were exempted from doing so.

Scholars have noted that "irrespective of the amount of labor that rural women dedicate to agriculture—whether as unpaid family workers or as wage workers—agriculture in Latin America has been socially constructed as a male occupation" (Deere and León 2001, 102). In rural Mexico, women have long had to prove themselves agriculturalists in a context in which women's labor has been systematically characterized as household work. For example, in agrarian censuses from central Veracruz from 1917 to the 1970s, men's occupations included categories such as *carpintero* (carpenter), *jornalero* (day laborer), *agricultor* (agriculturalist), or often simply campesino. When it came to women, however, agrarian engineers and municipal authorities listed their occupation as *doméstica* or as engaged in domestic activities (*quehaceres domésticos*). In most censuses, "women" included all girls over the age of thirteen and all adult women.[19]

Scholars have also shown that there are many reasons why women's labor is not considered agriculture proper (not the right type of physical activity, not the right sequence of work hours, and so forth). As Heidi Tinsmann (2002, 35) argues in her study of the Chilean agrarian reform, "meanings attributed to male and female bodies . . . naturalized . . . gender divisions." This analysis is particularly valid for coffee cultivation—the main agricultural activity in many of the ejidos in Central Veracruz. At ejidos where coffee production is important, women, men, and often children harvest coffee cherries twice a year. Even though strength is required, because pickers must suspend from the shoulder or the waist baskets holding an average of twenty to twenty-five pounds of harvested berries, the picking of coffee cherries is perceived as feminized labor; it requires delicate handling (associated with women's hands) since only the ripe berries are chosen, leaving the unripe fruit to be picked later. Men are mostly in charge of weed- and pest-control measures, the application of fertilizer, and the pruning of coffee trees, activities that ostensibly require "the brawn and endurance" embodied by men (see Tinsman 2002, 35). Moreover, coffee picking is often not regarded as agriculture proper because, as seasonal work, it is not considered a permanent occupation.

If women in present-day court cases feel obliged to prove they are agriculturalists, it is because women's labor has been systematically characterized as household work in a system that attributed to land the moral obligation not to leave it idle. Land beneficiaries had to cultivate their ejido parcels to support the agrarian family. And, because the parcel was the mainstay of the *family* economy (large enough to support but one agrarian family unit), it could not be divided.

The Indivisibility of the Ejido Parcel

In the Tuzamapan ejido, two brothers fought over their late father's parcel because he had registered two different succession lists. At the district court hearing, the judge explained that the ejido's general assembly had been privy to the new will or testament: "In the ejido's general assembly, it was stated that . . . the ejidatario's last petition was substituted for his initial list."[20] As in civil law, the most recent agrarian succession list voids the former one(s). What is interesting in this case (and in many others) is that potential heirs, ejido assembly members, and judges have fully internalized the idea that ejido parcels are indivisible.[21] Only one of the two brothers could inherit agrarian land, because agrarian testamentary regulations prohibit the partitioning of ejido parcels.

If the initial philosophy behind the agrarian reform—giving all agricultural-ists a parcel of land to support their families—was potentially liberating for young men seeking independence from the authority of their fathers or grandfathers (i.e., from the family patriarch); this potential liberation nevertheless can only be seen as holding for the first generation. The fact that the ejido parcel is indivisible means that only one offspring can inherit it, turning one sibling into an ejidatario and all others into second-class ejido members (that is, ejido residents without agrarian rights). In this ranking system, women have often fared the worst. If it was unusual for women to receive land parcels from the state, it would be even less common for them to inherit agrarian rights ahead of their male siblings.[22]

Why were land parcels indivisible? As in so many cases, laws that discrimi-nate against women (or other categories based on gender or sexual preference) do not do so explicitly.

The early architects of Mexico's agrarian law agreed to define land grants as "family patrimony," to ensure that the land distributed to reform beneficiaries would not be sold or lost in mortgage. Rival factions during the 1910–1920 Revo-lution seemed to agree on the fundamental characteristics of the concept of family patrimony. For example, Pancho Villa's Agrarian Law of 1915 called for state governments to protect family patrimony by prohibiting land grants from being mortgaged or embargoed. Land would be registered as private property in the Public Property Registry, but it could only be passed on, by inheritance, to a member of the family (Ley General Agraria del Villismo 1915, quoted in Lemus García 1991, 226). Similarly, a decree issued by the state government of San Luis Potosí in April 1915 declared that land grant parcels could not be divided, alien-ated, mortgaged, or embargoed (Luna Arroyo and Alcérreca 1982, 599–601).

The idea that land grants were to be indivisible stemmed from two very dif-ferent philosophies of land ownership and family relations.

On the one hand, many of the Constitutionalists responsible for designing agrarian law in the second decade of the twentieth century believed (like many others thereafter) that the disentailment laws of 1856 had produced widespread landlessness and rural injustice, and that it was these conditions that led to rev-olution (Kourí 2002, 69). The new agrarian program of 1915 had to make sure that beneficiaries would not lose their granted or restituted land all over again, and it therefore imposed significant constraints on the disposition of property. The general idea that property (usually the home or a plot of land) could not be alienated was commonplace through most of Mexican history. In the Aztec *calpullis,* for example, individuals possessed only use rights to land, but these could be transmitted only by means of inheritance (Rincón Serrano 1980, 24); many colonial laws also restricted the transfer of Indian properties; land endowed to Indians by the Spanish crown was usually inalienable.[23]

The second line of thought had less to do with state protection over those deemed unable to manage private property, and more with reforms to civil law, specifically family relations. President Venustiano Carranza's 1917 Law of Family Relations, intended to bring "modern ideas about equality" into the family, abolished the subjection of married women to their husband's authority (see Varley, this volume). Possibly influenced by the 1862 Homestead Act in the United States, Article 284 of the Law of Family Relations also made the family home (and, in rural areas, the land accompanying it) inalienable and exempt from embargo. In the 1928 Civil Code, this principle was expanded into a formal set of rules making the home and a cultivable parcel of land inalienable "family patrimony" at the petition of a family member.

The same general concept was incorporated into Article 27 of the 1917 Constitution and remained valid until 1992. Although Article 27 established the principle of eminent domain by stating that land and water found within the limits of the national territory belonged "originally" to the nation, ownership over the land grant was vested in the community. Individuals acquired agrarian or social property rights, which included use-rights to a land parcel and to lands held in common (usually woods and pasture lands).[24] Both common and individual use-rights were considered agrarian family patrimony.

With the Agrarian Law of 1992, the rights to an ejido parcel and to lands held in common were divided into two separate rights, and each was given new meaning. Rights to individual parcels have been transformed into private rights (*derecho de propiedad en sí mismo*), which, under specified circumstances, allow individual holders to use or dispose of lands as they see fit (Pérez Castañeda 1995, 458–496). In the first phase of the land titling program, ejidatarios receive certificates of individual ownership and are entitled to sell land to other ejido members. The second phase of land privatization requires that a majority of ejido members vote to authorize unrestricted ownership, which would allow free market sales of ejido land (Hamilton 2002, 122). Thus, the new laws allow for ejidos to become fully privatized, although few have done so (in part to avoid property taxes).

What is striking is that the 1992 reforms did not alter the idea of the indivisibility of the parcel. Even though the post-1992 agrarian testamentary rules give individuals with registered testaments or succession lists testamentary freedom (the right to bequeath the ejido parcel to whomever he or she may choose), there is one important constraint that makes ejido land different from unrestricted private property. Although private property under the civil code can be distributed among several heirs, ejido parcels cannot be divided and must be bestowed as a single unit. Thus, bequeathed land parcels remain indivisible.

How did the architects of the 1992 reforms settle the contradiction between private and social property? When someone dies intestate and there are several offspring, parents and grandparents, or other individuals dependent upon the ejidatario or ejidataria and claiming inheritance rights, the claimants have three months in which to agree among themselves who will inherit the deceased's agrarian rights and the land parcel.[25] In the event that they do not reach an agreement, the courts can auction the agrarian right (parcel) and divide the profit among those who have inheritance rights.[26] Thus, although the profit from the transaction can be divided into parts, the land parcel itself remains undivided.

Reflections on Law and Gender

This exercise in peeling away layers of historically constructed signification is relevant for at least two reasons. First, the agrarian court system created in 1992 has become a key mechanism for resolving disputes and legally validating rights to land in rural (and parts of urban) Mexico. Since 1992, hundreds of thousands of individuals have resorted to the agrarian courts to settle disputes with neighbors and/or to validate their rights when the family's composition has changed (as in the case of deaths). For the most part, these individuals have not been overtly treated differently on the basis of sex or sexual preference. And yet Mexico's contemporary agrarian justice system is based upon profoundly gendered and gendering early-twentieth-century concepts (often with earlier roots) that shape social and property relations in important ways.

Apart from contributing to an understanding of the very real and material consequences that these gendered concepts have for many individuals and their families, this exercise advances debates about law and gender. Specifically, this chapter suggests that a gendered analysis of law cuts across one of the central dichotomies that shape most current sociological and historical analyses of the law—namely, the state–subject divide.

Studies that fall within the field of "law and society" (the study of law from a social science perspective) tend to rely on a putative opposition between the state (laws, courts, judges, and so forth) and society (custom, "the popular," indigenous communities, and so forth). Indeed, Douglas Hay defines the field as the "terrain where state law and folk law (however defined) meet" (2001, 415), while Carlos Aguirre and Ricardo Salvatore describe law as "a field of force, an arena of contestation, in which not only powerful but also marginal, subordinate, and previously neglected groups have a bearing" (2001, 10).

Although individuals litigating in Mexico's agrarian courts debate and fight for their rights to property in a hierarchical legal system in which judges embody the power of the state, all actors involved in the process take for granted concepts that fashion social relations, marital affairs, and family rights based upon naturalized conceptions of femininity, masculinity, and heteronormativity. This chapter suggests that law and gender studies must approach power relations less as a field of force where powerful and powerless negotiate, and more in terms of what it is that makes gendered concepts so enduring—and so taken for granted across classes and hierarchies.

In this context, legal anthropology has been particularly successful in understanding the complexity involved in the law/society dichotomy. Following Boaventura de Sousa Santos's pioneering work, many scholars in this field use concepts such as "interlegality" to describe not only the interconnectedness but also the mutual constitution of indigenous legal systems and national law (Sierra and Chenaut 2002, 157). However, it is more difficult to use this approach when the legal system under examination lacks an overt ethnic divide. Thus, rather than trying to mark out more clearly the boundary between state and society in cases in which there is no obvious ethnic (or state–indigenous) division, the current challenge for law and gender studies is to identify ways of traversing these apparently separate units of analysis and exploring how a framework of enduring common meaning—based on naturalized conceptions of femininity, masculinity, and heteronormativity—is actually constructed in specific contexts.

NOTES

I thank Victoria Chenaut, Ann Varley, and Kevin Middlebrook for their comments on a draft of this chapter. I also thank Carmen Diana Deere and Juan Carlos Pérez Castañeda for important discussions on inheritance rights.

1. For the same argument with regard to colonial law in later liberal legislation, see Owensby (2005, 43).
2. This chapter focuses on the ejido created through the land grant (*dotación*)—in particular, the parceled ejido (an ejido divided into separate parcels of agricultural land).
3. I reviewed fifty cases from the Tribunal Unitario Agrario del Trigésimo Primer Distrito del Estado de Veracruz filed between 1996 (date at which they began appearing with more frequency in the region) and 2004. Personal names given in reference to court rulings are fictitious. Subsquent references to individual cases are all from the same tribunal.
4. Juicio Agrario 470/99, San Marcos de León (Xico), Veracruz.
5. Decreto de 6 de enero de 1915, que declara nulas todas las enajenaciones de tierras, aguas y montes pertenecientes a los pueblos, otorgadas en contravención a lo dispuesto en la Ley de 25 de junio de 1856, preamble.
6. Ley Agraria, 1992, art. 15.
7. Beginning in 1971, anyone, male or female, could become a legal land beneficiary provided that he or she was over sixteen years of age (or younger, if he or she had a family) and fulfilled certain requirements, including being Mexican-born and working as an agriculturalist.
8. Juicio Agrario 410/97, La Orduña (Coatepec), Veracruz.
9. They were first reproduced in the 1940 Agrarian Code, which continued unmodified until 1971. Then they were incorporated into Article 81 of President Luis Echeverría's 1971 Federal Agrarian Reform Law. Here, testamentary restrictions were identical to those written almost fifty years earlier.
10. Ley Agraria, 1992, art. 18.
11. See, for example, Olcott (2005), Schell (2003), Vaughan (1997), and Varley (2000b).
12. Juicio Agrario 410/1997, La Orduña (Coatepec) Veracruz.
13. Ibid.

14. The 1921 *Circular 48* from the National Agrarian Commission specifically included single or widowed women with dependents in the category of agrarian family head (Hinojosa Villalobos 2000, 87–90).

15. Author's interview with Carlota Botey, Mexico City, August 2003.

16. According to Carmen Diana Deere and Magdalena León (2001, 183–85), such provisions were adopted in Brazil, Colombia, Costa Rica, Honduras, Nicaragua, and Guatemala, making the Mexican neoliberal reforms the most discriminatory in Latin America.

17. Juicio Agrario 177/98, Tuzamapan Orduña (Coatepec), Veracruz.

18. Juicio Agrario 211/2001, Zimpizahua (Coatepec), Veracruz.

19. I reviewed approximately forty censuses carried out between 1917 and the 1970s. None of the censuses listed women as coffee pickers, merchants, wage earners, or servants (Baitenmann 1997). The practice was not new, however. Heather Fowler-Salamini (1994, 60–61) shows how municipal census-takers during the Porfiriato (1876–1911) equated *jefes de familia* with male household heads and imposed a particular view of gender roles by allowing women only one occupational category, *doméstica* (housewife/homemaker).

20. Juicios Agrarios 316/2000 and 014/2001, Tuzamapan (Coatepec) Veracruz.

21. In practice, ejido lands have often been partitioned. Breaking rules, however, does not mean that individuals do not understand agrarian legislation. When land is fractioned, ejidatarios find ways of legalizing the transaction. For a different interpretation, see Nuijten (2003a).

22. Often, women siblings only inherited or received a parcel when the parent had purchased enough land throughout his or her life to bequeath land to all offspring. In these cases, individuals had either illegally purchased additional parcels or acquired private property outside the ejido.

23. See, for example, the colonial laws analyzed in Ots Capdequí (1941).

24. Rights over urban plots are a separate matter.

25. Ley Agraria, 1992, art. 18.

26. *Semanario Judicial de la Federación y su Gaceta*, Novena Época, vol. 15, February 2002: 932.

PART FOUR

Legal Reform and the Politics of Gender

10

Law and the Politics of Abortion

ADRIANA ORTIZ-ORTEGA

Abortion has been a crime in Mexico since colonial times. It still is, suggesting that reproductive freedom is as yet an unattained right for women. In this chapter, I argue that a gentlemen's agreement between church and state has shaped abortion politics in contemporary Mexico. This unspoken agreement has led to the state's compensating for the liberalization of abortion laws with secrecy and a failure to implement the legal options and services that could be available to women. From the 1970s, when the law on abortion began to be liberalized, until the present, reforms have remained buried in legal documents that only receive limited distribution among the judiciary (Ortiz-Ortega 2000).

As a result of this gentlemen's agreement, public hospitals have not been obliged to allow the abortions to which women are legally entitled under the "exceptional circumstances" clauses in Mexico's penal codes (Torres 1993). This remains the case even in states that have recently undergone changes in their abortion legislation. In addition, no efforts have been made to gather statistics about the incidence of (nonhospital) induced abortions to shed light on the practice as a public health problem. Neither public nor private hospitals distinguish between spontaneous and induced abortions when treating complications.[1] Abortion practices among women who have had induced abortions but suffer no complications and so do not require treatment remain off the record (Torres 1993).

The connections between the legal order and reproductive freedom are important because they contribute to the hardships women face when seeking to regulate their fertility. Legal reform alone is not, however, sufficient to effect real change. In this chapter, I explore the intimate relationship between the legal control of women's wombs and changes in the Mexican political system.

Mexico in the Latin American Context

In most Latin American countries, with the exception of Cuba and Puerto Rico, abortion is considered a crime. Nonetheless, a gradual tendency toward

TABLE 10.1

Legal Status of Abortion in Latin America

1. Completely banned: Chile, Nicaragua, and El Salvador

2. Permitted to save the woman's life: Brazil (R), Colombia, Guatemala, Honduras, Haiti, Paraguay, Panama (PA/R/F), Dominican Republic, and Venezuela.

3. Permitted for health reasons: Argentina (RM), Bolivia (R/I), Costa Rica, Ecuador (R/I, limited), Peru, and Uruguay (R)

4. Permitted for mental health reasons: Jamaica (PA)

5. No restrictions: Cuba* (PA) and Puerto Rico (PV)

Key:

SA   Husband's permission required
PA   Parental permission (father and mother) required for women under eighteen years of age
R   Abortion also permitted in cases of rape
I   Abortion also permitted in cases of incest
F   Abortion also permitted in cases of fetal impairment
RM   Abortion permitted in cases of rape, when the woman is mentally disabled
PV   Law does not limit pre-viability abortions
* Gestational limit of twelve weeks

Source: Rahman, Katzive, and Henshaw 1998; Htun 2003.

Note: In 2006, Nicaragua joined the countries outlawing abortion even where the mother's life is at risk.

decriminalization prevails and only three countries ban abortion completely (Table 10.1).

Although generally considered a crime throughout Latin America, abortion is permitted in certain circumstances (as indicated in Table 10.1). These do not automatically exempt a woman from all punishment, however, and they have to be supported by legal evidence. The logic behind the exemptions catalogued in Table 10.1 is that it is a woman's seeking an abortion of her own accord that marks the limit between what is permissible and what is condemned as criminal behavior.

In Mexico, the law on abortion varies from one state to another, although this fact is frequently overlooked in international reviews of abortion law. It is important to emphasize the great variation within Mexico, since parts of the country have what may be the most liberal abortion laws in Latin America, yet others are much more restrictive. Despite the relatively liberal position of parts of Mexico in comparison with other Latin American countries, it should not be assumed that easier access to abortion can be equated with a greater number of abortions practiced. The estimated rate of induced abortion in Mexico is among the lowest in Latin America, with one in every forty women aged between fifteen and forty-nine seeking an abortion (Allan Gutmacher Institute 1996, 1; Kulczycki 2003, 360).

The legislation on abortion in Mexico can be classified as advanced, intermediate, or conservative, based on the most permissive criterion for legal abortion recognized in each state. At least two criteria for legal abortion are considered in all states.[2]

1.   Advanced Legislation. In the penal code of approximately one-third of the states, no penalty is applied when continuing the pregnancy would present serious danger to the woman's health. Since this danger is not defined in more precise terms, the legislation in these states opens the door, to some extent, for women to seek an abortion for their own reasons or because of adverse circumstances they may face during pregnancy. Ten of the thirty-two states of Mexico fall into this category: Baja California Sur, the Federal District, Hidalgo, Jalisco, Michoacán, Nayarit, Nuevo León, Tamaulipas, Tlaxcala, and Zacatecas. In Yucatán, health comprises a justification for abortion only if the mother's life is in danger, but there is one additional, and unique, basis on which abortion can be carried out legally: in cases of severe and demonstrable poverty, if the woman already has at least three children.[3]

2.   Intermediate Legislation. In the eighteen states in this category, abortion is not prosecuted when the mother's life would otherwise be in danger. In addition, in nine of these states, abortion is also permitted in cases of fetal impairment, where there is medical evidence that the woman would otherwise produce a child with serious physical or mental health problems. The states in this more permissive category are Coahuila, Colima, Chiapas, State of México, Morelos, Oaxaca, Puebla, Quintana Roo, and Veracruz; the other nine are Aguascalientes, Baja California Norte, Campeche, Chihuahua, Durango, San Luís Potosí, Sinaloa, Sonora, and Tabasco.[4]

3.   Conservative Legislation. The three states grouped under this heading do not accept threats to the mother's life as sufficient grounds for abortion. Of the exceptional circumstances discussed under the previous headings, the state of Guerrero recognizes only the likelihood of a child being born with severe physical or mental health problems as a reason to withhold prosecution. Guanajuato and Querétaro have the most conservative legislation, accepting only rape and "carelessness" as bases for permitting abortion. (Carelessness is generally defined as *acción* or *conducta culposa*, or as *imprudencia*. However, the clause is sometimes worded so vaguely that it could be taken to mean the opposite of what the legislators undoubtedly intended—for example, *por culpa de la mujer embarazada*, in

Guerrero and Guanajuato. The actions in question are supposed to have been undertaken without any intention to terminate the pregnancy, if the woman is to escape penalty.)

The gradual inclusion of more circumstances under which abortion is permitted (see below) is evidence of a trend toward decriminalization. This progressive liberalization is often overlooked because the three most common criteria for allowing abortion without penalty are still rape, negligence/carelessness, and saving the life of the mother. In all cases, abortion after rape is legal.[5] Twenty-nine states allow abortion to avoid danger to the woman's life. Most do not penalize abortion brought about by the woman's carelessness.[6] Not surprisingly, women who are desperate to end a pregnancy resort to falling downstairs or beating their bellies, later claiming that these events were accidents. To avoid prosecution, however, the women require confirmation, from a doctor who has examined them, that they have not deliberately sought to provoke an abortion.

In one-third of the states, abortion after rape is permitted only during the first three months of pregnancy. The abortion practitioner usually has to obtain approval from a medical committee composed of at least two doctors. The purpose of this committee is to prevent doctors acting in "complicity" with women.

The penalty for a woman who aborts a fetus intentionally generally varies from one to five years in prison, depending on the legislation of the state in question. The penalty for medical personnel also differs from state to state, but usually ranges from one to eight years in jail. It may include cancellation of the license to practice. Additionally, in several states the legislation still allows sentences to be reduced when three conditions apply that together constitute what is known as *honoris causa* ("for the sake of honor"). These are: that the woman in question is of good reputation (*que no tenga mala fama*); that the pregnancy is the result of an extramarital relation; and that the woman has managed to conceal her pregnancy.[7] In these circumstances a substantial reduction in the sentence is permitted: for example, from six months to a year in place of one to five years.[8] Such is the variability in legislation on abortion, however, that this lesser sentence still exceeds the punishment for a woman practicing abortion illegally in the state of Tlaxcala (a fortnight to two months).

The Catholic Church and the Limits of Legal Reform

Mexico has the second largest Catholic population in the world (Kulczycki 2003). This, together with its geographic location next to the United States, plus the importance of its communications industry, make the country, in the eyes of the Catholic church, a crucial battleground for competing religious beliefs and moralities. The Catholic church in Mexico cannot be seen as a mere pressure group pushing an antiabortion agenda: it offers the state a crucial source of social and political support and thus contributes to maintaining social stability.

This is the case despite the fact that the Mexican state has long distanced itself from the church via legislation limiting religious influences on public life. The scope for promotion of sexual and reproductive rights is thus defined by the distance between, on the one hand, conservative religious agendas and, on the other, feminist, socialist, and gay activism, as well as the political openings secured by these social movements.

However, I would argue, the Mexican state is not so free from the influence of the Catholic church as might be expected. The church still influences which laws are passed and how they are worded—and also, more importantly, implemented. Given the uneasy relationship between church and state, sexual and reproductive rights constitute an arena in which the two test the limits of their power and influence. Legal reform and changes in public attitudes toward abortion are not therefore enough to secure change in this area. A thoroughgoing separation of church and state is required at all levels, along with the economic changes that would enable Mexicans to meet the costs incurred in securing full access to their sexual and reproductive rights.

The History of Abortion Reform and of Church–State Relations in Mexico

It is important to set the current situation concerning abortion law in historical context, since the influence of nineteenth-century thinking continues to be felt in Mexico's penal codes. Abortion has been prohibited since colonial times, when the Inquisition could sentence women accused of abortion to death (although there is no record of women actually being executed for this crime). Abortion was classified as a crime in the first systematic penal code for the Federal District, issued in 1871.[9]

I date the emergence of the gentlemen's agreement between church and state, making women's sexual and reproductive rights negotiable, to this period.[10] That abortion continued to be regarded as a crime indicates that the state was unwilling to reject Catholic morality completely. On the other hand, the influence of secular ideas led liberals to distinguish between born and unborn human life, and, hence, homicide or infanticide, on the one hand, and abortion, on the other. The 1871 Penal Code made intentional homicide a capital crime, and homicide committed in a fight received a penalty of ten years, almost double the penalty imposed on someone who deliberately caused a woman to abort by violent means.[11] The legislation specified a sentence for infanticide in honoris causa cases that was twice as harsh as that for abortion.[12] Since legal penalties reflect the value attributed to the juridical good they are intended to protect, it is clear that, in the nineteenth century, "the life of the product of conception was already considered to have lesser value than the life of a being already born" (de la Barreda Solórzano 1991, 81).

In contrast to Catholic morality (and today's legislation in three states), however, abortion was permitted when the mother's life was endangered. The liberal legislators thus came close to the recognition that humans must be born and engage in social interaction to become fully human.

In addition, abortion was penalized less severely in honoris causa cases. Women who were of "good reputation" and had concealed their pregnancy, the result of an illicit union, would only be sentenced to two years' imprisonment.[13] The absence of either of the first two conditions added an extra year each to the sentence. No such concessions were made in the case of a married woman aborting a fetus conceived within her marriage; she was to be sentenced to five years' imprisonment, whether or not she was of good reputation or had concealed her pregnancy.[14]

The honoris causa provisions again show that the value attributed to the life of the unborn child was not an absolute. Rather, it varied according to the extent to which male interests were affected, in the sense that damage to a woman's reputation was regarded as reflecting badly on her husband. Further, only women of "good reputation" were allowed this concession. It was denied to women regarded as "loose," including unmarried women who had not been able to conceal their pregnancy, prostitutes, and women living with men outside of marriage.[15]

The differences between Catholic ideology and the new criminal legislation did not mean, then, that the liberals condoned abortion. The minutes of the meetings in which the drafting committee discussed the code reveal the members talking about the fetus as a "child" and of the termination of a pregnancy as "an unthinkable action on the part of the woman."[16] Even their recognition of circumstances in which abortion should be legal underlined the fact that in all other cases it was seen as an act performed "without necessity."[17] Only if physically endangered would a woman be spared prosecution for abortion. The preservation of male honor acted as a mitigating circumstance, but women's own need to control their fertility did not.

The 1871 Penal Code remained in force until after the Mexican Revolution. In the aftermath of the Revolution a strong division emerged between political actors with a socialist agenda and Catholic activists angered by the exclusion of religion from public affairs and restrictions on religious education in the 1917 Constitution (Blancarte 1992). As anticlericalism and social confrontation grew, Catholic groups began to organize themselves to defend the interests of the church. The armed insurrection, the Movimiento Cristero (Movement in Defense of Christ), that emerged in 1926 did not enjoy the official endorsement of the Catholic hierarchy but received wide support from both clergy and laity in some parts of the country. Although the uprising failed to reverse the constitutional restrictions on the church, it enhanced its negotiating position, as both government and church learned that an autonomous ultraconservative movement could pose a threat to social order. The issue at stake was no longer the separation between church and state, but the contest for control of the souls of the Mexican people. President Plutarco Elías Calles created a new form of nationalism that preempted the radical potential of the Mexican Revolution (Meyer, Segovia, and Lajous 1978). In exchange, the church agreed to refrain from intervening in political parties and from related decision making. The bishops subsequently described the simultaneous conflict of interest and need for cooperation that characterized the relations between church and state as a modus vivendi (Blancarte 1992).[18]

In the 1930s, the state continued to rely on nationalism and anticlericalism as a unifying discourse, but proceeded to act more cautiously. When the country's criminal law was overhauled, the new 1931 Federal District Penal Code extended the circumstances in which no penalty would be applied to include abortion following rape.[19] The state refrained from further liberalization, however, at a time when the church was launching a worldwide offensive against the decriminalization of abortion.[20] Whereas in 1871 a woman's own desire to seek an abortion was characterized as an "unnecessary" act, the new Penal Code emphasized the "voluntary" nature of the act as the key to its criminal status.[21] A woman procuring an abortion was to receive six months to one year in prison, in honoris causa cases, one to five years in other cases.[22]

In the late 1930s, President Lázaro Cárdenas, often credited with the implementation of the Revolution's social program, reached a compromise with Catholic positions on the family and promoted pro-natalist policies in the name of modernization and development. Church and state united on an anticommunist platform that had the exaltation of motherhood at its core, while women were being incorporated into low-level government posts in the 1930s and 1940s. The lack of social support for impoverished mothers encouraged child abandonment, and adoption programs reinforced class-based understandings of motherhood (Blum 2006). Church and state shared a common opposition to the women's suffrage movement, which did not succeed in obtaining the vote for women, in national elections, until 1953. In this context, only socialist and communist voices still continued to call for the legalization of abortion.

The state's pro-natalist policies were not reversed until the early 1970s, at a time when a new wave of feminism was emerging and giving expression to women's wish to gain control of their fertility. Mexico pioneered the first family planning program in Latin America, leading the church to disagree publicly with the government position. The state sought to capitalize on women's need for birth control in ways that allowed it to expand contraceptive use and to offset the influence of the church. In 1974, Article 4 of the Constitution was reformed to include the statements "men and women are equal before the law" and "every person has the right to decide in a free, responsible and informed manner about the number and spacing of their children." Women did not need to seek permission from husband or church to obtain contraception from state clinics. At the same time, however, the reform added that "[the law] will protect the organization and development of the family."[23] This statement served to demonstrate to the church that the state still endorsed its support of traditional roles for women.

The state also sought to counter the accusations by feminists and the Left that its family planning campaigns were merely a response to the demands of the United States. The government declared that the new population policy did not endorse either the neo-Malthusianism of the United States or the Marxist interpretations of population growth promoted by the Soviet Union; instead, the government declared, it advocated an informed family planning model seeking to limit and space births (F. C. Turner 1974). This was part of President Luis Echeverría's effort to construct a nationalism that broke with anticommunism and to adopt a leading international role for Mexico.

The state was helped in its efforts to introduce family planning by internal divisions that had emerged within the Catholic Church with the rise of liberation theology, divisions leading to a critique of the church's endorsement of the subordination of women (Blancarte 1992). Since the government did not wish to antagonize the church, it retained an antiabortion rhetoric; nevertheless, abortion laws began to be liberalized, marking a significant change in the gentlemen's agreement between church and state. By the mid-1970s, several states permitted abortion in cases of fetal impairment (Acosta et al. 1976).[24]

Further liberalization of abortion would be associated with the broader changes resulting from the political reform of 1977, which allowed opposition parties to participate in public life for the first time since the Revolution. This period was also a critical one for the building of consensus within the feminist movement, as groups united around "voluntary motherhood" campaigns demanding access for women to safe and legal abortion. Feminists estimated that at least two million abortions were carried out in Mexico each year, despite the legal restrictions (Coalición de Mujeres Feministas 1977). They argued that the introduction of a constitutional right for women to limit the number of children they bore endorsed not only access to contraception but also the right to terminate an unwanted pregnancy.

After much debate, feminists decided to develop an alliance with the Mexican Communist Party and the Revolutionary Workers' Party to present a proposal for the legalization of abortion to the Chamber of Deputies. In the event, however, the Communist Party presented the voluntary motherhood bill on its own in 1980, excluding feminists from the political debate. Neither the dominant political party (the Institutional Revolutionary Party, PRI) nor the conservative National Action Party (PAN) supported the initiative and the bill was defeated.

The state understood, however, the radical potential of feminist mobilization in a context of growing demands for democratization and a shift in public opinion in favor of abortion. It therefore promoted liberalization of abortion laws, in a roundabout fashion. With presidential approval, top officials in the administration of José López Portillo suggested to state governors that reform of abortion legislation was desirable.[25] New criteria permitting abortion without prosecution were introduced in several states, and for the first time threats to the woman's health were recognized as grounds for abortion (i.e., the threshold was lowered from danger to a woman's life to serious but not necessarily life-threatening conditions).[26]

The political reform of 1977 also opened the way for the church to take on a more visible role in seeking to influence public opinion. Under the leadership of John Paul II, the conservative fractions of the church made advances. The archbishop of Mexico City, Corripio Ahumada, became an inspirational force in the establishment in 1978 of the Comité ProVida (the Mexican pro-life committee).[27] ProVida brings together a coalition of more than a hundred conservative organizations, many formed in the 1930s (Muro González 1991). ProVida and related organizations such as Vida y Familia (Life and Family) promote the establishment of abortion prevention clinics, sexual abstinence campaigns, and adoption services.

During the 1980s, the state continued to walk a tightrope between the potential for political mobilization around women's need for birth control, on the one hand, and conservative Catholic ideologies, on the other. The familiar corporatist bases for intervention gave way, however, to a neoliberal logic emphasizing the privatization of services and the reduction in state spending on social welfare programs. When penal code reforms for Mexico City were proposed in 1983, they initially included fetal impairment, economic adversity, and artificial insemination without consent as legal grounds for abortion, plus a more general decriminalization of abortion within the first trimester (Ortiz-Ortega 2000). The proposal was withdrawn after a public outcry orchestrated by the church. The economic and political difficulties facing the state made the government reluctant to face a fight over changes to the legislation in the nation's capital and largest city. The reform could have been interpreted as a victory for feminists, but its withdrawal signaled an unprecedented political achievement for the church. The government continued, nonetheless, to promote the liberalization of abortion as a purportedly local initiative. Between 1982 and 1988 several more states introduced fetal impairment or the need to protect the woman's health as grounds for legal abortion.[28] To minimize the possibility of conservative or church opposition hindering the process, these reforms were introduced surreptitiously. No mention of the modifications to the penal codes was made by state officials, and the new measures were given very limited dissemination in the national or local press. They were not communicated to public hospitals. Although the state neutralized the influence of the church in these cases, it paid the price of an inability to translate reforms into the provision of state services, or to provide public regulation of the private practice of abortion on public health grounds. Reform was limited to decriminalization in certain circumstances, because this was a low-cost strategy, in both economic and political terms.

By 1990, and with political transition underway, the most radical move yet was taken, a comprehensive liberalization of abortion in the state of Chiapas. The new penal code in the state of Chiapas permitted abortion in cases of contraceptive failure, both for couples and for single women. The church demanded the withdrawal of the measure, a few days after it was publicly announced, and won.[29] Feminists working with proponents of liberation theology to defend voluntary motherhood in Chiapas failed to obtain the support of the influential and liberal bishop of Chiapas, Samuel Ruiz. They believe that the Catholic hierarchy prevented Ruiz from getting involved (Fontanive and Damián 1994).

In 1991 some of the constitutional restrictions on church activities were removed, and diplomatic relations with the Vatican were renewed the following year. At the same time, the visibility of feminism grew during the 1990s, thanks to formation of several nongovernment organizations, to international funding, and to a strong international mobilization in favor of sexual and reproductive rights. Activists in Mexico were able to work with groups pursuing the same goals elsewhere: for example, Católicas por el Derecho a Decidir (Catholics for a Free Choice) (Marcos 1994).[30]

The state became more open to feminist influences in the 1990s. Feminists and nongovernment organizations joined the official delegations to the United Nations Conference on Population and Development in Cairo (1994) and the Fourth World Conference on Women in Beijing (1995). The Mexican government distanced itself from the position taken by the Vatican toward these events, and endorsed the resulting programs for action. Following the "Cairo+Five" review, Mexico enhanced its commitment to treating abortion complications as a public health problem. The government also transformed its family planning program into reproductive health programs with a more holistic approach, giving attention to quality of care and greater dissemination of information on contraception, for example.

The major political transition that occurred in the year 2000 marked a new stage in the gentlemen's agreement between church and state. The transition cannot be understood purely in terms of the success of an individual party, the PAN, but rather as the product of a complex series of considerations. Since the electorate perceived the PAN as the party with the greatest chance of winning elections for the presidency and Congress, it voted strategically to overcome the authoritarian rule of the PRI. Nonetheless, the result was that, for the first time, the conservative party was in power nationally.[31]

Shortly after the election, the PAN-dominated local congress in the state of Guanajuato voted to remove one of the two justifications for abortion allowed in the state's penal code, already one of the most conservative, by recriminalizing abortion after rape. The reform "was neither timely nor publicly supported"

(Lamas and Bissell 2000, 20), since it was less than a year since a rape case from the state of Baja California had received unprecedented media coverage when the thirteen-year-old victim, Paulina Ramírez Jacinto, was denied her legal right to an abortion by public authorities.[32] Realizing the strategic error of denying a right with wide public support, the national PAN leadership asked local legislators to withdraw the measure (Lamas and Bissell 2000, 17). The state governor vetoed the bill.

The Guanajuato initiative and the response of the Right to the "Paulina case" also backfired in the sense that these contributed to a liberalization of abortion in Mexico City (Lamas and Bissell 2000; Ubaldi Garcete 2004). After the failure of the 1983 initiative, the Federal District had been left with more restrictive legislation than many of the other states. Even before the Guanajuato reform was defeated, Rosario Robles, interim mayor of the Federal District, had introduced a bill making either threats to the woman's health or fetal impairment grounds for legal abortion. Despite opposition from the church and ProVida, the Robles Law was passed, as were bills introducing fetal impairment and various other grounds for abortion and introducing modifications to related legal procedures, in the state of Morelos. In both cases, the changing political landscape was significant: in Mexico City, the PRI now became an ally of the left-wing party in power, the Party of the Democratic Revolution (PRD), and in Morelos, the PRI and PRD combined to pass the liberalizing reforms before the newly elected PAN governor took power (ibid.).[33] In 2005, the state of Baja California Sur became the tenth to allow abortion in case of serious threats to the woman's health.

The PAN fought back by referring the Robles Law to the Supreme Court on the grounds that allowing abortion in cases of fetal impairment was unconstitutional. In January 2002, however, the Court dismissed the challenge. Following this event, antiabortion groups tried to burn down the first sexual and reproductive health clinic to offer legal abortions, in the state of Yucatán. Radical groups have gained access to public positions through which they advance the antiabortion agenda. For example, ProVida received public funding to open antiabortion clinics in Mexico City (*El Universal*, November 3, 2003).

From Law to Practice

Estimates of the number of induced abortions carried out each year vary widely. Figures in the order of five hundred thousand have been reported by several studies, but more than one source suggests the figure may be closer to one million (Kulczycki 2003, 359; Human Rights Watch 2006, 30). Despite the restrictions in even the most liberal legislation, however, few women are actually prosecuted. There is little information available, but the head of the Federal District Human Rights Commission reported that in 1988 only six women had been sentenced for the crime, and, in the following year, only two (de la Barreda Solórzano 1991).

The head of the forensic medical team in Guadalajara reported that in the last five months of 2005 ten women had been charged for illegal abortion (Human Rights Watch 2006, 34). Carlos Monsiváis's observation that Mexico has already achieved "moral decriminalisation" provides an apt assessment of the gap between the legal status of abortion and its prosecution (quoted in Lamas and Bissell 2000, 20). In practice, abortion is already, in this sense, socially accepted (GIRE 2006).

The injurious consequences of the legislation may, however, be detected not so much in the number of prosecutions but in the fact that women are failing to secure abortion in cases where they could legally seek a termination. A report by Human Rights Watch, *The Second Assault* (2006), documents how rape victims are denied access to their legal rights, suggesting that the Paulina case was only the tip of the iceberg. A social worker with a government agency in Yucatán reported seeing "dozens of underage rape victims suffer through unwanted pregnancies," and a nongovernment organization representative in the same state indicated that there were "a lot of cases of adolescents impregnated by family members" who were not told by investigating authorities that abortion was legal after rape (Human Rights Watch 2006, 37–39). The main reason women did not ask the authorities for an abortion was lack of information; many believe that even after rape abortion remains illegal (ibid., 38; Ehrenfeld 1999). The justice system and health services do not generally provide such information, in part because of personal opposition from officials, and procedures are often too slow for women to be able to obtain the abortion within the legal time limit (Human Rights Watch 2006, 39–49).

Five years after the Paulina case, there were still no guidelines requiring public health institutions to carry out legal abortions or regulating "conscientious objection" by public employees in Baja California (Ubaldi Garcete 2004).

Such evidence supports the argument that "the lack of normative instruments for the practice of [legal] abortion . . . leaves the woman unprotected," and that normative declarations are not enough without legal tools for their implementation (Pérez Duarte y Noroña 1993, 90). One consequence of the Baja California case is that such instruments are now beginning to appear. The new Penal Code for the Federal District requires doctors to provide accurate, objective information on the procedure, and the reforms to the legislation in Morelos instruct doctors to provide information without "in any way inducing the pregnant woman to avoid termination."[34] In addition, both the Federal District (in 2003) and Baja California Sur (in 2005) have reformed their general health codes, requiring public health institutions to provide legally permissible abortions free of charge (Human Rights Watch 2006, 32).

In these three jurisdictions, access is "more available than in states with no legal guidelines or procedures . . . [but] the existence of the formal procedures has not guaranteed unobstructed access to safe and legal abortion for all pregnant rape victims" (ibid., 52; Billings et al. 2002). Despite time limits imposed on public prosecutors and health authorities, procedures are still too complicated and officials ill-informed or uncooperative. Legal abortions are carried out in a largely "underground" fashion to avoid intimidation of those involved (Human Rights Watch 2006, 62).

Conclusion

Ever since abortion was made a crime in the 1871 Penal Code, its criminalization has been accompanied by a tendency toward liberalization. This shows that conservative religious influences do not dictate the law. Indeed, the liberalization of abortion represents an assertion by the state of its autonomy from the Catholic Church. The emergence of feminism and of a new population policy in the 1970s accelerated the liberalization of the legislation on abortion. Although the church has not succeeded in reversing the trend to liberalization, however, progressive forces have been unable to translate legal reforms into provision of public services. Thus, the greatest challenge facing the advocates of women's sexual and reproductive rights in Mexico is how to achieve the permanent institutionalization of the process of transformation that they have pioneered.

The coalition of actors in favor of legalizing abortion needs to expand. At present, it includes international population foundations, progressive lawyers, health workers, and radical members of the church willing to recognize the need for a fresh approach to abortion. The alliances between these groups are still relatively recent and do not necessarily translate into political pressure, permanent funding, or service provision.

In closing, it is important to note that there is no significant evidence that evangelical groups have made any difference to the balance of forces between church and state in relation to abortion in Mexico. Protestant evangelism mostly acts at the local level in certain states, and has no real political connections with the Catholic hierarchy; despite the conservative nature of many evangelical churches, religious conservatism has not created enduring alliances across faith traditions in Latin America (Htun 2003). This failure reflects one of the major weaknesses of antiabortion forces: their reluctance to accept values like diversity, tolerance, and respect for other beliefs. It is precisely this rigidity, however, that is propelling them to seek greater institutional power, and to resort to violence when thwarted.

NOTES

I thank Patricia Meza for her help in organizing the references and endnotes.

1. The only way to distinguish between spontaneous and induced abortions is by uncovering evidence of physical intervention, the presence of a foreign body, or information provided by the woman, by third parties such as family members, or by the individual who performed the abortion.

2. In Morelos, for example, these include danger to the mother's life, fetal impairment, particularly careless behavior on the woman's part, rape, or artificial insemination carried out without the woman's consent.

3. In the state of Hidalgo, poverty reduces the penalty imposed on a woman found guilty of abortion.

4. The Federal District and Yucatán also permit abortion in case of fetal impairment.

5. Apparently as an extension of the logic concerning rape, eleven states now also envisage artificial insemination without the woman's consent as legal grounds for abortion. It is not clear what exactly is meant by this provision.

6. The exceptions are Nuevo León, Chiapas, and Tabasco. Given that their legislation is more permissive in other respects, it is unclear whether the legislators intended to penalize abortions produced by carelessness or treated them as equivalent to spontaneous abortion.

7. These states are Aguascalientes, Campeche, Jalisco, Nayarit, Oaxaca, Puebla, Tamaulipas, Yucatán, and Zacatecas. In Durango, Hidalgo, and the state of Mexico, a reduction to avoid dishonor (*deshonra*) is permitted, but no definition is given. Honoris causa is gradually disappearing from the statutes; it was still to be found in virtually all penal codes in the mid-1960s (Porte Petit Candaudap 1966).

8. Hidalgo also permits the same reduction, from three months to two years rather than from one to three years, in cases of extreme poverty. Guerrero, Quintana Roo, and Coahuila also allow reduced sentences where one of a range of extenuating socioeconomic or medical circumstances applies.

9. Código Penal paral el Distrito Federal y Territorio de la Baja California sobre Delitos del Fuero Común, y para toda la República sobre Delitos contra la Federación, 1871 (CC 1871), Título Segundo: Delitos contra las personas, cometidos por particulares, Capítulo IX: Aborto.

10. Nineteenth-century liberalism was profoundly anticlerical. The 1857 Constitution and the reform laws instituted the separation of church and state and made religion a private matter. The church was denied legal recognition, priests could not exercise political rights, and no religious institution was allowed to acquire real estate or capital. Civil marriage was introduced in 1859.

11. CC 1871, arts. 561, 553, 576, respectively.

12. CC 1871, arts. 584, 573, respectively.

13. CC 1871, art. 573.

14. CC 1871, art. 574.

15. Antonio Martínez de Castro, 1871, Actas de deliberaciones de la Comisión del Código Penal. Documents in the collection of Luis de la Barreda Solórzano.

16. Ibid.

17. CC 1871, art. 569.

18. The term *modus vivendi* was first used by Pope Pío XI in relation to the agreements between church and state that ended the Cristero uprising in 1929.

19. When they in turn reformed their penal codes, most states followed the federal model (which also applied in Baja California and Quintana Roo). By the mid-1960s, however, neither Campeche nor Durango permitted abortion after rape, and the State of Mexico did not allow it to save the mother's life (Porte Petit Candaudap 1966, 228–235).

20. The 1930 papal encyclical *Casti Connubii* specifically condemned abortions practiced by married women for family planning purposes and those practiced for socioeconomic or eugenic reasons. This was at a time when some governments were starting

to liberalize abortion law: between 1920 and 1940, abortion was legalized in the Soviet Union, Iceland, Sweden, and Denmark.

21. Código Penal paral el Distrito Federal en Materia de Fuero Común, y para toda la República en Materia de Fuero Federal, 1931, art. 332.

22. According to legal scholar Antonio Moreno de P. (1994, 276), intention to obtain an abortion was also a crime. Evidence of a "woman's intention to kill the fetus" included the use of food, abortifacent potions, physical actions, tight dresses, dancing, horseback riding, and repeated intercourse, if any of these were undertaken "with the firm intention of provoking abortion" (ibid.). How intention was to be proven remains unclear.

23. Constitución Política de los Estados Unidos Mexicanos, 1917, art. 4.

24. The states in question, according to Acosta et al. (1976, 27), were Puebla, Chihuahua (where it is not now permitted), and Yucatán.

25. Interview with Alicia Elena Pérez Duarte y Noroña, May 1995.

26. Reforms were introduced to permit abortion in cases of fetal impairment in Oaxaca (1979), Quintana Roo (1979), and Veracruz (1980). Abortion was permitted to protect the woman's health in Tlaxcala (1980), Nuevo León (1981), Michoacán (1981), and Jalisco (1982). The possibility of a serious threat to the woman's health being considered as the basis for legal abortion had first been contemplated in a 1949 draft of reforms to the Federal District penal code (Porte Petit Candaudap 1966).

27. Most political actors I have interviewed believe that pro-life groups receive technical assistance and financial support from both the Mexican Catholic church and the headquarters of Vida Humana Internacional in Miami. Jorge Serrano Limón, then president of ProVida, acknowledged as much when interviewed (Ortiz-Ortega 1994a). As one source put it, "the [Mexican] movement is based in the U.S." (quoted in Haussman 2005, 133).

28. Coahuila (1983), Chiapas (1984), Colima (1985), Guerrero (1986), and Puebla (1986) permitted abortion in cases of fetal impairment. San Luis Potosí (1984) and Zacatecas (1986) allowed abortion to protect the woman's health. Yucatán introduced reforms concerning economic and health grounds for abortion in 1987.

29. The measure was temporarily suspended by a reform published in January 1991. The "temporary" substitute remains in force, permitting abortion in case of rape, threats to the mother's life, or fetal impairment.

30. Catholics for a Free Choice (1997) contends that there is more than one theologically and ethically defensible viewpoint on abortion within the Catholic tradition. Priests and theologians supporting the organization have been harassed by their superiors. In Mexico, Católicas por el Derecho a Decidir, founded in 1994, has a primarily lay membership and is seen as a radical grassroots group with no real influence on the Catholic hierarchy.

31. The PAN had for some years been gaining success in elections to state congresses and governorships. Local legislatures dominated by the PAN had tried to amend state constitutions to include a right to life from the moment of conception, in Chihuahua (1994), Baja California (1998), and Nuevo León (1999) (Kulczycki 2003). Only in Chihuahua were these initiatives successful. The influence of religious conservatism is felt not only within the PAN but also by all other parties, including the left-wing Party of the Democratic Revolution (PRD), which needed the support of the church during the period when it was consolidating its influence.

32. Although Paulina had an order from the state attorney's office to Mexicali General Hospital to carry out the abortion, the director claimed that, on principle, none of his

staff would perform the operation. Activist groups report: that the state's general attorney took the girl and her mother to visit a priest who explained that abortion was grounds for excommunication; that hospital staff exaggerated the risk of abortion to the family; and that ProVida activists were admitted to the hospital to pressure the girl. National and local church authorities supported these moves, condemning abortion under any circumstances (GIRE 2000; Poniatowska 2000; Lamas and Bissell 2000; Lamas 2001).

33. The governor threatened to veto this reform, but did not do so (Human Rights Watch 2006).

34. Nuevo Código Penal para el Distrito Federal 2002, art. 148. Codigo de Procedimientos Penales para el Estado Libre y Soberano de Morelos 1996, art. 141(bis).

11

Married Women's Property Rights in Mexico

A Comparative Latin American Perspective and Research Agenda

CARMEN DIANA DEERE

Mexico was a pioneer with respect to married women's property rights in Latin America, in a number of ways. In the nineteenth century, Mexico was the first country to offer couples a formal choice with respect to the marital regime governing marriage. Although, as in the colonial period, partial community property remained the default, after 1870 couples could also choose to marry under the separation-of-property regime. Moreover, after 1928 its partial-community-property regime became one of the most flexible in the region, giving couples a great deal of choice in terms of alternative arrangements regarding the ownership and management of marital property. Most notable from a feminist perspective is that, over the course of the twentieth century, Mexico led the way in instituting the legal figure of the dual-headed household, in which both husband and wife have equal rights to represent the household and manage its affairs.

With respect to inheritance, Mexico was also in the forefront in departing from the colonial legacy of forced heirs, introducing complete testamentary freedom in 1884. The nation remains one of the retrogrades, nonetheless, with respect to the inheritance rights of spouses under intestate succession. Over the course of the twentieth century, most Latin American countries gradually elevated the position of spouses, so that they would have at least equal rights to those of a child, and, in the absence of living children or parents, inherit all of the deceased's assets. In Mexico, if there are living children, the surviving spouse must prove economic need to inherit anything; moreover, in the absence of living children or parents of the deceased, the spouse must share the inheritance with the deceased's siblings.

The primary objective of this chapter is to analyze the similarities and dif-ferences in married women's property rights in Mexico in comparison to those in other Latin American countries. In analyzing the process of reform of marital and inheritance regimes, my interest is in discerning the extent to which these promote gender-progressive change. Specifically, I focus on whether these legal changes promote women's: economic autonomy (the capacity to make their own choices and decisions); bargaining power within the family (their ability to negotiate within marriage and influence outcomes); and fall-back position, or exit options, so that women can survive outside marriage.

Given the lack of comparative analysis until recently, and the notable lack of empirical work on these issues, the question of whether variations in marital and inheritance regimes make a difference in practice cannot yet be addressed. Draw-ing on recent advances in feminist theory, this paper suggests a series of proposi-tions that merit further research, and offers some tentative conclusions regarding married women's property rights in Mexico in a comparative perspective.

Marital Regimes and Their Reform

In colonial Hispanic America the default marital regime was partial community property (*gananciales*, the participation-in-profits regime).[1] There was a distinc-tion among three types of property: the husband's, the wife's, and the commu-nity (or common) property of the couple. The individual property consisted of what each spouse had owned prior to marriage, in addition to inheritances and donations received individually while married. Property purchased during the marriage from the income of either spouse constituted the common property (gananciales). The husband, as head of household, managed both the commu-nity property and his wife's (as well as his own) individual property. If the union ended, for whatever reason, the wife gained control over her own property as well as of half the gananciales.

The colonial marital regime was flexible, for couples could enter into prenup-tial agreements (*capitulaciones*) with respect to the ownership and management of any specific property or of their entire estates. Thus all property could remain individually owned (as in the separation-of-property regime) or be pooled (as in full community property). In practice few couples availed themselves of this flexi-bility (Deere and León 2005).

In the civil codes promulgated after Independence, most Latin American countries initially maintained partial community property as the default regime. Mexico in 1870 was the first country to innovate in this regard, offering separation of property as a formal option while maintaining partial community property as the default regime. During the period of the liberal revolutions in Central Amer-ica, Costa Rica (1887), El Salvador (1902), Nicaragua (1903), and Honduras (1906) went further, making separation of property the default (Deere and León 2005).

In 1917, with the Law of Family Relations, Mexico also adopted separation of property as the default, but this change lasted only a decade, until the promulgation of the 1928 Civil Code.

The main trend over the course of the twentieth century was for other Latin American countries to expand the number of marital property regimes that couples could choose among. As Table 11.1 shows, in most countries couples can now choose among two or three regimes, although the number of options has become less relevant since capitulaciones can also now be made anytime during the marriage. Nonetheless, this practice is not frequent, meaning that the most significant factor determining married women's property rights is usually the default regime.

TABLE 11.1.

Choice of Marital Regimes in Selected Latin American Countries

Country (Year)	Full community property	Participation in profits	Separation of property
Argentina (1968)		Yes (*)	
Bolivia (1988)		Yes (*)	Yes
Brazil (2002)	Yes	Yes (*)	Yes
Chile (2000)		Yes (*)	Yes
Colombia (1996)	Yes	Yes (*)	Yes
Costa Rica (1978)	Yes	Yes	Yes (*)
Ecuador (1989)		Yes (*)	
El Salvador (1994)	Yes (*)	Yes	Yes
Guatemala (1964)	Yes	Yes (*)	Yes
Honduras (1984)	Yes	Yes	Yes (*)
Mexico (1974)	Yes	Yes (*)	Yes
Nicaragua (1959)	Yes		Yes (*)
Peru (1984)		Yes (*)	Yes
Uruguay (1914)		Yes (*)	
Venezuela (1982)		Yes (*)	

Sources: Deere and León (2001, Table 2.3); for Argentina, Zamora (1969); Uruguay (1977); and Venezuela (1982).

Notes: Year refers to the last year the civil or family code was revised; (*) indicates the default regime.

With the exception of four Central American countries, partial community property remains the default. Only two significant changes took place in the last half of the twentieth century: Brazil in 1977 changed its default regime from full to partial community property; El Salvador in 1994 switched from separation of property to the full community property regime (Deere and León 2001).

Which marital regime is most favorable for women largely depends on the relative value of the assets that husband and wife bring to marriage, and on the probability that the husband will earn significantly higher levels of income than his wife. If, because of discriminatory inheritance practices, men are more likely to bring a larger patrimony to marriage and to earn more, then full community property will be the most favorable for women. It is also the most equitable, since it implicitly recognizes the domestic labor performed by wives. The partial-community-property regime does this, as well; however, should the union be dissolved, the full-community-property regime is more favorable to women since it would result in a larger transfer from husband to wife for services rendered.

By the same assumptions, the least favorable regime for women, particularly for poor women, is separation of property, for wives are less likely to bring any property to marriage. Moreover, if divorced or widowed, they have no claim on assets acquired by their husband during the marriage. Thus, for poor women, the separation-of-property regime greatly reduces the fall-back position and probably the women's bargaining power in marriage as well.

It is also crucial to consider whether women can manage assets during the marriage. Besides being a key measure of women's economic autonomy, control over property is particularly important if men and women have different spending preferences.[2] As noted earlier, in the colonial period the husband controlled both the common property and his wife's property. What was innovative about the adoption of separation of property as the default regime in Central America at the beginning of the twentieth century was that for the first time married women obtained the legal capacity to manage their own property without their husband's permission; that is, they acquired a similar legal capacity to that of single women.[3]

Thus, for married women of means, the separation-of-property regime considerably enhanced their economic autonomy and, potentially, their bargaining power. It may also have been beneficial for working-class women who earned independent wages, since such income was no longer subject to their husbands' control. It was probably most prejudicial to those who did not work outside the home; under the separation-of-property regime, housewives had no means of acquiring property during the marriage except through their husband's good will. Thus the extent to which the adoption of separation of property as the default regime in much of Central America was a gender-progressive reform largely depended upon a woman's class position. In its historical context, however, the adoption of this regime as the default in Central America represented the first major blow against potestad marital (the legal control of a husband over the property and person of his wife), and set an important precedent for the demands of the feminist movement.

Mexico's 1917 Law of Family Relations also established separation of property as the default, granting wives the right to administer their own property and to enter into contracts and suits, hence "removing the 'legitimate representation' that the male had with respect to the person and property of his wife" (Carreras Maldonado and Montero Duhalt 1975, 74). Moreover, this first successful reform to have reflected feminist influence was historic in establishing that husband and wife were to have "equal authority and consideration" in marriage. It formally established the goal of the dual-headed household, where both husband and wife represent the household and jointly manage its affairs, and provided that any common property could be administered jointly or by one spouse with the other's consent.

While Mexico's 1917 reform was a significant departure from the "protection and obedience" framework that had governed most nineteenth-century Latin American civil codes, it did not eradicate all elements of potestad marital (ibid., 73). Married women's right to contract was still limited, since they could only work outside the home with their husband's permission. In addition, while this code established that both spouses were to contribute economically, it assumed that men were the breadwinners and specifically charged women with responsibility for domestic labor. Also, wives were still required to live where their husband determined.

The 1928 Civil Code for the Federal District (subsequently replicated by many of the states) went further. The call for "equal authority and consideration" in marriage was strengthened, since wives were no longer required to obtain their husband's permission to work outside the home, accept an inheritance, or be the executor of a will.[4] This 1928 code gave couples considerable flexibility in designing their own marital regime. They could choose between the separation-of-property and the gananciales regime (termed *sociedad conyugal*) and were expected to make capitulaciones stipulating, along with which property was to constitute individual or common property, who in the family was to manage the common property.[5]

Outside of Mexico and Central America, reforms granting married women full legal personality and the right to manage their own property and community assets were slow and piecemeal. In some countries, such as Uruguay, female suffrage was achieved first; in others, married women's property and civil rights were achieved, as in Mexico, long before women obtained political rights (Deere and León 2001). Given the growing number of women in the labor force, the first wave of feminism in a number of South American countries focused on gaining married women's right to control their own incomes. Between 1916 and 1949, several countries gave married women the right to manage their own earned income and/or assets independently of their husbands, within the gananciales regime. These rights were usually abrogated once further reform gave both spouses the right to manage their own property and the shared right to manage the common property.

One of the main accomplishments of feminism has been the series of reforms that ended the primacy of husbands as legal household heads and instituted the dual-headed household, where both husband and wife represent the household and are jointly responsible for managing the common property. Only two countries, Mexico and Uruguay, attained this legal reform before the 1970s (Table 11.2).[6] In Mexico, achieving the dual-headed household was a piecemeal

TABLE 11.2.

The Dual-Headed Household and Recognition of Consensual Unions in Selected Latin American Countries

	Gender equality in household representation and management	Consensual unions recognized	Consensual unions granted same inheritance rights
Argentina	No	No	No
Bolivia	1972	1938	1938
Brazil	1988	1988	1994
Chile	No	No	No
Colombia	1974	1990	1990
Costa Rica	1973	1990	1995
Ecuador	1989	1982	1998
El Salvador	1994	1994	1994
Guatemala	1998	1964	1964
Honduras	1984	1984	1984
Mexico	1928	1974	1928*
Nicaragua	No	1987	1987
Peru	1984	1984	No
Uruguay	1946	No	No
Venezuela	1982	1982	1982

Sources: Deere and León (2001, Tables 2.1 and 2.4) and author's interviews; for Argentina, Zamora (1969); for Uruguay, Uruguay (1977); for Venezuela, Bocaranda Espinosa (1983) and Venezuela (1982).

* Only for women in consensual unions; in Mexico there is considerable variation by state in the recognition granted consensual unions.

process that began in 1917, was deepened in 1928, but was not completed until 1974. The 1974 reforms got rid of the sexism remaining in the civil code with respect to the gender division of labor in the home. Both spouses were made responsible for sustaining the household, according to their capacities. It was also made explicit that the rights and obligations of marriage were always equal, independently of the economic contribution of each spouse (*Diario Oficial de la Federación*, December 31, 1974).

A major impetus behind the reform of married women's property rights was the UN Convention on the Elimination of All Forms of Discrimination against Women. By 1990, this convention had been ratified by all Latin American countries and most had reformed their civil codes accordingly (Deere and León 2001). Nonetheless, Argentina, Chile, and Nicaragua have yet to grant husbands and wives equal rights in marriage, and stubbornly persistent aspects of potestad marital linger elsewhere.

Another accomplishment of the feminist movement has been the legal recognition of consensual unions. In some countries, these were first granted the protection of a marital regime and later, given similar inheritance rights (Table 11.2). Mexico is the exception, since women in consensual unions were granted inheritance rights a number of years before other benefits of a marital regime were extended to consensual partners.

The Reform of Inheritance Regimes

Under the Luso-Hispanic legal tradition, inheritance was bilateral, with all children, irrespective of sex, inheriting approximately equal shares of each parent's estate. Testamentary freedom was restricted to between one-fifth (Hispanic America) and one-third (Brazil) of an individual's estate, with the remainder divided into equal shares among the legitimate children.[7] If a parent died intestate, the entire estate was divided equally among the legitimate children.

Spouses generally did not inherit from each other unless the deceased left no living descendants, ascendants, siblings, or collateral kin. They could be beneficiaries, however, of the share of an estate that could be freely willed. The exclusion of spouses as automatic heirs was considered just, on the grounds that, under the prevailing marital property regimes, the surviving spouse was entitled to one-half of the common property. Under the partial-community-property regime, nonetheless, if the individual assets of the spouses were unequal in size and no significant gananciales had been accumulated, widows and widowers could potentially find themselves in a more disadvantageous position than the children.

During the nineteenth century, there were two major departures, in inheritance law, from the colonial tradition. The countries most influenced by liberalism—Mexico and those of Central America—introduced full testamentary freedom, and those in South America strengthened the inheritance rights of widows and widowers. The advocates of testamentary freedom in Central America considered it a desirable and logical consequence of private property, strengthening individual freedom and initiative (Deere and León 2005). In Mexico, the adoption of testamentary freedom in 1884 was quite controversial among jurists. Although advocates considered it necessary to promote a strong work ethic and encourage economic development, dissenters feared it would undermine the harmony of the family (Arrom 1985a).

Testamentary freedom was a dual-edged proposition for widows. On the one hand, it opened up the possibility of a husband's designating his wife as sole heir, leaving her with full ownership and control of their common property as well as of his individual property. It thus increased the probability that a widow would be able to consolidate ownership and control of the family business, land, and home, strengthening her economic autonomy. On the other hand, the possibility for a widow to inherit any of her husband's estate depended totally on his good will; she could also be totally disinherited.

South America followed a different trajectory. The civil codes inspired by the 1855 Chilean Civil Code gave a nod toward testamentary freedom, raising the share that an individual could will freely from one-fifth to one-quarter of an estate.[8] Brazil in 1907 followed this trend, increasing the share that could be freely willed from one-third to one-half of an estate. The dominant trend in Spanish America, however, was to strengthen the position of widow(er)s by requiring that, under certain conditions, they not be excluded as heirs.

The civil codes modeled after the 1855 Chilean Civil Code provided for a marital share (*porción conyugal*), an amount that depended upon the relative value of the individual estates of husband and wife. If these were unequal and the surviving spouse could prove economic necessity, the widow or widower could inherit a share equal to that of one child's, but usually not more than one-quarter of the estate. Thus, while the marital share afforded poor widows some protection, it was not designed to insure that they remain in control of the family farm or business, or even of the familial home (Deere and León 2001).

The most important change with respect to married women was that three South American countries added surviving spouses to the necessary heirs in the first order of succession, with equivalent rights to a child. Bolivia in 1830 and Argentina in 1869 excluded spouses from inheriting from the deceased's share of gananciales, but did elevate the surviving spouse to the first order with respect to the individual assets of the deceased. Venezuela's short-lived 1862 Civil Code provided for surviving spouses to share equally with the children in the inheritance of the deceased's individual assets and of his/her share of the gananciales (Deere and León 2005).

The addition of spouses to the first order of inheritance was a crucially important move in potentially strengthening the property rights of wives. If we assume that there is a male bias in inheritance and that men have greater income earning opportunities than women, the individual assets of husbands were probably greater than those of their wives. Thus the possibility for a widow to inherit along with the children from her husband's individual assets represented a potential shift in wealth accumulation, favoring married women. It also potentially strengthened the bargaining power of a widow in relation to control of the family farm or business, since her share was added to her half of the gananciales.

Even while, over the course of the twentieth century, most Latin American countries came to recognize the full property rights of married women, the reform of inheritance regimes lagged behind. The current challenge in terms of gender equity is to strengthen the inheritance rights of spouses. This has become a gender issue largely because of the growing gap in life expectancies between men and women, and a policy issue because of the probability that older widows will be living in poverty, particularly in rural areas (Deere and León 2001).

The inheritance rights of widows currently vary considerably in Latin America, but remain relatively unfavorable as compared to the privileged rights of children.[9] Table 11.3 distinguishes between those countries that provide for forced heirs and those with testamentary freedom. Among the former, the best practice is where the widow is included in the first order of inheritance, along with the children. This reform is relatively new, with Chile and Brazil only recently having so elevated the position of wives.[10] The widow is in a more favorable position in Bolivia and Peru than in Chile, Venezuela, or Brazil, where, besides sharing her husband's estate with the children, she must also share it with any surviving parents of the deceased. But from a social policy perspective, the inclusion of parents as well as the spouse among the forced heirs is probably a potential poverty alleviation measure that could favor older women.

With respect to the second order of inheritance (when the deceased has no living children or other descendants), only in Peru does the widow alone inherit the full restricted share (the *legítima*)— in this case, two-thirds of her husband's assets. In the other countries, she must divide this restricted share with the parents of the deceased. Widows are in the most unfavorable situation in Colombia and Ecuador, for if a woman's husband did not include her in his will, only if there are no living children is she eligible for a marital share from the husband's estate, and then only if she can prove economic need.

Turning to the countries with testamentary freedom, only two provide for a marital share for widows, a share that depends on the relative size of each spouse's estate and on whether the widow can demonstrate economic need. In Nicaragua and Honduras, the marital share is limited to one-quarter of the deceased's assets. In the other countries with full testamentary freedom, a widow and her dependent children may claim a pension (*alimentos*) from the heirs if excluded from a will. Widows in these countries who were married under the separation-of-property regime are potentially in the most precarious position

TABLE 11.3.

Inheritance Rights of Widows: Rules Governing Testaments
(year of latest reform of civil code)

Countries with Forced Heirs

1. Inclusion of widow in the first order of succession among the "forced heirs" (those who cannot be excluded from a will):

   a. with equal rights as children:
      Bolivia (1975): four-fifths to children and widow
      Peru (1984): two-thirds to children and widow

   b. with equal rights as children and parents of deceased:
      Chile (2000): three-quarters to children, widow, and parents
      Venezuela (1982) and Brazil (2002): half to children, widow, and parents

2. Inclusion of widow in the second order of succession (when there are no living descendents of the deceased):

   a. widow inherits the full restricted share [two-thirds]: Peru (1984)

   b. with equal rights as parents:
      Argentina (1968), Bolivia (1975): two-thirds to widow and parents
      Venezuela (1982), Chile (2000), Brazil (2002): half to widow and parents

3. Widow only eligible for *porción conyugal* (based on relative size of each spouse's estate and whether she can prove economic need): Colombia (1982), Ecuador (1970)

Countries with Testamentary Freedom

1. Subject to porción conyugal:
   Nicaragua (1903)
   Honduras (1906): maximum one-quarter of estate

2. Full testamentary freedom (subject to alimentos):
   Mexico (1884), Costa Rica (1887), El Salvador (1902), Guatemala (1933)

Sources: Constructed by the author from: Deere and León (2001); Zamora (1969); Venezuela (1982); Chile (2000); and Brazil (2002).

of all (and separation of property is the default regime in Costa Rica, Honduras, and Nicaragua).

The rules of succession demonstrate even more variation where the deceased dies intestate. Table 11.4 includes only the best- and worst-case scenarios for

TABLE 11.4.

Inheritance Rights of Widows: Rules If Deceased Dies Intestate

Best Case

1. Inclusion of the widow in the first order of inheritance with children:

   a. Widow guaranteed minimum of one-quarter of estate: Chile (2000)

   b. Widow and children have equal rights, by head: Bolivia (1975), Venezuela (1982), Peru (1984), Brazil (2002)

2. If no surviving children, inclusion of the widow in the second order of inheritance, along with the parents:

   a. Two-thirds of estate to widow, one-third to parents: Chile (2000)

   b. Deceased's estate to be shared equally, half each, by widow and parents: Honduras (1906), Nicaragua (1903), Ecuador (1949), Argentina (1968), Bolivia (1975), Venezuela (1982), Brazil (2002)

   c. Deceased's estate to be shared equally, by head, by widow and parents: El Salvador (1902), Guatemala (1986), Peru (1984)

Worst Case

1. In first order of inheritance, widow only entitled to porción conyugal (based on relative size of each spouse's assets and whether she can prove economic need):

   a. porción conyugal limited to a maximum share of one-quarter of estate: Ecuador (1860), Nicaragua (1903), Honduras (1906)

   b. porción conyugal limited to share equal to that of one child: Colombia (1873), Mexico (1928)

2. If no surviving children, widow and parents in second order of inheritance:

   a. half of estate to widow, half to parents: Nicaragua (1903), Honduras (1906), Mexico (1928), Ecuador (1949)

   b. one-quarter of estate to widow, three-quarters to parents: Colombia (1982)

3. If no surviving children or parents, widow and siblings of deceased in third order of inheritance:

   a. widow (two-thirds), siblings (one-third): Mexico (1928)

   b. widow (half), siblings (half): Nicaragua (1903), Honduras (1906), Colombia (1982)

Sources: Constructed from: Deere and León (2001); Venezuela (1982); Chile (2000); and Brazil (2002).

widows. The most favorable situation is again where widows are included in the first order of inheritance. Since the 2000 reforms in Chile, widows are guaranteed at least one-quarter of a husband's total assets. In other countries where widows are in the first order, they are entitled to a share of the estate equal to that of each child; thus, if there are more than three surviving children, the widow will be in a less favorable position in Bolivia, Venezuela, Peru, and Brazil than in Chile.

In most countries, if there are no surviving children, the widow is included in the second order of inheritance, along with the deceased's parents. As Table 11.4 shows, the most favorable situation for widows is again provided by Chile, where widows in such case are entitled to two-thirds of the estate, with only one-third accruing to the parents. The most frequent situation in this grouping is for the widow to be entitled to one-half of the estate. The least favorable situation is where the estate is shared equally, by head, between the widow and the parents if both of the latter survive the deceased (as is the law in El Salvador, Guatemala, and Peru).

The worst-case scenario for widows is in those countries where, in the first order of inheritance, they are entitled only to a marital share, and thus inherit along with the children only when they can prove economic need. Honduras, Nicaragua, and Ecuador limit this marital share to one-quarter of the estate (so that if there are only one or two surviving children, each would inherit more than the widow). In Colombia and Mexico, the marital share is equal to the share of each child.[11] If there are no surviving children, in Nicaragua, Honduras, Mexico, and Ecuador widows receive half of their husband's estate, with the other half accruing to the parents. In Colombia in this case widows only receive one-quarter of the estate.

In most countries, if there are no surviving children or parents, in the third order of succession the full estate passes to the widow. In Mexico, Nicaragua, Honduras, and Colombia, the widow is in a particularly unfavorable position, since she must share her husband's estate with his siblings.

This analysis is particularly important in terms of what it reveals about the probability of widows being able to maintain a controlling share of the family farm, business, or home. If any of these was acquired during the marriage (in the community property regimes), widows are guaranteed a controlling share only if they are in the first order of inheritance. If widows control over 50 percent of the assets, their bargaining power will be stronger, possibly allowing them to resist pressure to sell or divide the property.

Few countries have taken additional steps to protect the interest of widows, such as giving them the automatic right to remain in the familial home. In Peru and Brazil until recently, the right to remain in the home was conditional on widows refraining from remarriage. Moreover, in Brazil this privilege pertained only to women married under the full-community-property regime; since 2002, it applies irrespective of marital regime and is no longer conditioned by subsequent marital status.

In the period of agrarian reform in Latin America, the laws regarding inheritance of land distributed through the reforms were often more favorable to widows than were the prevailing civil codes (Deere and León 2001). In Mexico, whereas the civil code provided for full testamentary freedom, within the ejido sector from 1942 until the neoliberal reform of 1992, this right was constrained so that only the spouse, companion, or one son or daughter could inherit ejido rights (see also Baitenmann, this volume).[12] Moreover, if an ejidatario died intestate, the wife or companion was the automatic heir. This latter provision no doubt explains the relatively large share of women who have recently been granted secure rights on the ejidos: many inherited land from their husbands.[13] It also attests to the potential importance of public policy on inheritance in beginning to redress the gender asset gap in land ownership.

Unfortunately, few of the neoliberal land laws of the 1990s retained inheritance clauses favoring widows. Honduras is the exception: since 1991, widows are the automatic first heirs of land ceded by the state (Deere and León 2001). This is an important proactive measure for women, since, as seen in Tables 11.3 and 11.4, widows are in a particularly unfavorable situation in Honduras, a situation compounded by the fact that the default marital regime is that of separation of property.

In sum, legal reform to better the position of widows remains one of the most important challenges. Not only are widows one of the largest groups at risk in terms of poverty, but there is a growing literature demonstrating that ownership of assets is critical to enhancing their bargaining power over children and thus assuring the widows of some support in old age. Even where a widow is unlikely to manage agricultural production herself, land is critical to rural women as an asset to rent out or sharecrop or use as collateral. Moreover, since women are more likely than men to include daughters as heirs in the inheritance of land, strengthening the inheritance rights of widows should promote a culture of equality in inheritance (Deere and León 2001).

Research Issues

Civil code reform favoring gender equality over the last quarter of the twentieth century was usually advanced by the national women's offices constituted during this period. Although the feminist movement has been active, indeed crucial, in promoting reform, there often has been little follow-up in terms of disseminating women's property rights.[14] Most women in Latin America are unaware that they have a choice of marital regimes. It is generally assumed that the default is the only legal regime. Moreover, judges or civil functionaries rarely inquire as to a couple's preferences, or ask if they want a prenuptial agreement. This means that real options are only available to educated women who have some familiarity with their country's civil code.

A useful starting point for comparative research would be surveys aimed at measuring the degree to which women are aware of and understand their property rights.

The question of what difference the marital regime makes to women's accumulation of assets and well-being lends itself particularly well to comparative research. It would be useful to compare one or more of the countries where separation of property is still the default—Nicaragua, Honduras, Costa Rica—with Guatemala and/or Mexico. If my assumptions regarding unequal opportunities by gender are correct, then, if other factors (such as age, marital status, education, class) are held constant, women's accumulation of assets should be greater in the latter two. Further, bargaining theory would predict that women would play a larger role in household decision making in Mexico and Guatemala than in the other Central American countries.

Even though the most promising avenue for future research most likely will be comparative studies of countries with different marital regimes, it is nonetheless urgent to begin research at the national level in countries such as Mexico. The provisions for the sociedad conyugal in Mexico are flexible, if couples draw up a prenuptial agreement; but how often is this done, and what kinds of arrangements governing ownership and management of property are most common? In addition, the default is not very well understood. This question could perhaps be researched most readily through a study of divorce proceedings. Survey research could illuminate how well-known is the option of the separation-of-property regime, as well as the characteristics of women most likely to pursue it or insist upon a prenuptial agreement.

Another related topic requiring further research is the impact of the legal provisions supporting the dual-headed household. Mexico has the longest tradition of formal equality of rights within marriage, but it is probable that the dual-headed household remained a legal fiction until recent years. Even in countries where the legal change followed broader societal change with respect to gender roles, the lack of systematic public education on the subject may mean that it has had little impact in practice. The exception is with respect to state programs of land distribution and titling, where joint titling to couples was facilitated by the dual-headed household provision of the civil codes. Ironically, it was precisely in Mexico that the major land titling program of the 1990s ignored the rights of wives to joint titles of ejido land—what should have been their right under the civil code if such land was acquired during the marriage (Deere and León 2001).

Another topic worthy of further research is the impact of legal recognition of consensual unions. What happens in the event of separation? How does the outcome compare with the outcome in divorce settlements?

Turning to inheritance rights, we see there has been little research on the impact of full testamentary freedom on the position of widows. Has testamentary freedom favored children over widows? Has there been a tendency in favor of designating widows as the sole heir in response to the growing gender gap in life expectancies? Mexico offers a particularly interesting case for further study, since in ejidos the rules for inheritance differed from the civil code governing private landownership. Rights in the ejido could *only* be willed to one's spouse or companion or one child until 1992, whereas full testamentary freedom prevailed in the private sector. Widows were in a very different position with respect to intestate succession, with the spouse or companion being the forced heir in the ejido sector, but eligible only for a marital share of their spouse's assets under the civil code. Overall, we would expect widows to have a higher probability of inheriting land rights within the ejido sector.

Since the counterreform of 1992, testamentary freedom again prevails within the ejido sector, with the only restriction being that a testator may will land only to one heir. However, the difference with respect to intestate succession in the ejido and in the nonejido sectors remains: since the titling program required beneficiaries to file wills, one would expect intestate inheritance to be much less important than in the past. A study of 14,099 wills made out between 1993 and 1995 showed that testators on the ejidos were nearly equally divided among those designating their spouse as their sole heir versus those so designating a son (Valenzuela and Robles Berlanga 1996). It would be interesting to sample wills of landowners in the nonejido sector to see if a similar trend holds.

In general, little research has been done on inheritance patterns in Mexico (but see González Montes 1992) or in the Central American countries with full testamentary freedom. We know little about the propensity to make a will and how such a propensity differs by gender, class, or rural/urban residency, or of how these factors affect the bequeathal of property to wives versus children, and to daughters versus sons.

From a policy perspective, the most important research question regarding the property rights of married women is whether they fare better as widows under full testamentary freedom or under the system of forced heirs. This question could best be addressed by a comparative study of probate records in one of the countries where widows have the strongest inheritance rights (Bolivia, Peru, and Venezuela—and, recently, Chile and Brazil) with Mexico and/or one of the Central American countries. Comparisons will be complicated by the fact that countries follow such different provisions with respect to intestate inheritance. This is why the study of probate records should provide fuller information on inheritance outcomes than could the study of wills alone.

Detailed national studies of probate records will also be needed to answer such questions as the extent to which widows claim their marital share in countries where in theory they are able to do so. Similarly, research is needed on whether widows claim alimentos in countries such as Mexico, which provide for sustenance should a spouse needing support be excluded from a will.

Finally, a large share of the property of married women is acquired through inheritance; this is particularly true for rural women's acquisition of land (Deere and León 2003). In the Mexican ejido sector, 81 percent of women owners acquired land through inheritance compared with only 45 percent of the men (Procuraduría Agraria 1998). Further research is required on whether women are more likely to inherit land as daughters or widows, and on the factors that support an equitable division of property among children.

A number of trends supporting gender equity in the inheritance of land by children can be identified across Latin America (ibid.). For example, an increase in inheritance by daughters has been reported in regions where migration is more sex-balanced, with inheritance associated with a willingness to remain on the farm, caring for elderly parents. Inheritance by daughters is also associated with regions where peasant agriculture is in decline, and land is not only declining in economic value but also less a source of political power, undermining the previous logic of household reproduction that concentrated land on only one son. A tendency toward partible inheritance is also facilitated by smaller family size. But these propositions require further research.

Moreover, studies of property in the urban context, such as of housing, have only just begun (Varley 2000a; Varley and Blasco forthcoming). Since ownership of one's own home is as important to urban women as land is to rural women, this is an important avenue for future research. Such research will be crucial to further the study of the determinants of women's household bargaining power and economic autonomy.

Conclusion

Mexico has clearly been a pioneer with respect to married women's property rights in Latin America. It was one of the first countries, along with four in Central America, to give married women similar rights to those of single women regarding the administration of their own property. It went beyond the Central American countries that had adopted the separation-of-property regime at the beginning of the twentieth century, by establishing that any remaining common property could be potentially administered by either or both spouses. Moreover, in 1917 it was the first country to advance the goal of equality between husband and wife in marriage; establishing the legal basis for the dual-headed household, however, was an evolutionary process, and it was not until 1974 that all vestiges of potestad marital were removed.

The verdict is still out on whether the Mexican innovations in family law have promoted women's greater economic autonomy and bargaining power in marriage and how far these have been achieved compared with possible gains in other Latin American countries. There is still much to learn about how marital regimes play out in practice—for example, whether the flexibility allowed by Mexico's partial-community-property regime has been beneficial to wives, and, if so, whether they have been similarly beneficial across class positions and ethnic groups. Similarly, much remains to be investigated in terms of how testamentary freedom, as well as the wife's unfavorable position under interstate inheritance, have played out in practice.

The Mexican case demonstrates how civil law cannot be viewed in isolation from agrarian law. In the case of the ejidos, the disjuncture between civil and agrarian law presumably favored rural women for important periods of the twentieth century. The more favorable succession rules on the ejido (with restricted testamentary freedom and the priority given to wives in intestate succession) should have given women greater access to land than they had in the private agrarian sector; investigating this proposition should be high on the research agenda. The 1992 ejido reforms potentially worked in the opposite direction. By granting land rights to household heads in the process of individualization of land titling, Mexico struck a blow at the legal figure of the dual-headed household and violated one of the basic principles of the partial-community-property regime: that assets acquired during the marriage (except as inheritances) constitute the common property of the couple.

The Mexican case demonstrates that the gains in married women's property rights should not be taken for granted, but, rather, require eternal vigilance on the part of those committed to gender equality. Moreover, this case also demonstrates the importance of promoting legal literacy among women, so that they become aware of their rights, demand these in practice, and find themselves capable of defending them when they are challenged.

NOTES

1. Following Portugal, Brazil made the default full community property.
2. This proposition has been amply explored by feminist economists (Agarwal 1994; Deere and León 2001).
3. In Mexico, when the separation-of-property regime was initially introduced, restrictions were still maintained on married women's management of property. A wife could not sell her own real estate without her husband's permission, although the reverse did not apply (Arrom 1985a).
4. Código Civil para el Distrito y Territorios Federales en Materia Común, y para toda la República en Materia Federal, 1928 (CC 1928), arts. 169, 1655, and 1679.
5. CC 1928, arts. 178, 179.
6. In Uruguay, the 1946 Law on the Civil Rights of Women gave women the right to manage their own assets and income, and spouses shared rights concerning the location of the home, household expenses, and authority over children (Uruguay 1977, 390–392).
7. A testator could favor one child or descendant above others with as much as one-third of the reserved portion of the estate.

8. The civil codes of El Salvador (1859), Ecuador (1860), Venezuela (1862), Nicaragua (1867), and Colombia (1873) are all very similar to the 1855 Chilean code authored by Andrés Bello (Deere and León 2005).

9. The same rules apply to widowers, but, given the life expectancy gap, I assume that the surviving spouse is the wife. This analysis draws on Deere and León (2001) and the author's further study of the civil codes cited therein, especially those of Argentina, Uruguay, and Venezuela, together with the newly revised codes of Brazil and Chile.

10. Widows in Argentina are also in the first order of inheritance. However, the widow is excluded from a share of her husband's gananciales whenever there are living children and is therefore only entitled to an automatic share of her husband's individual assets.

11. In Mexico, the conditions for the marital share are as follows: "The surviving spouse, when there are also descendants, has the right of a child if he or she has no property, or if the property which such spouse holds at the death of the author of the succession is not equal to the share pertaining to each child." In this latter case, "the spouse shall be entitled to receive only what is necessary to make his or her property equal to said share" (CC 1928, arts. 1624, 1625).

12. Código Agrario, 1942, arts. 162, 163; Ley Federal de Reforma Agraria, 1971, arts. 81, 82; and communication from Juan Carlos Pérez Castañeda to Helga Baitenmann, July 2004.

13. According to a national survey of 516 ejidatarias in 1998, 43 percent were widows and 41 percent married, with the remainder single, divorced, or in consensual unions (Robles Berlanga et al. 2000, 47). As of 2002, women represented 22.4 percent of those receiving land during the titling process. They represented a much higher share of those receiving house plots than of those with full land rights (Beyer Esparza 2002; Deere and León 2005).

14. The feminist movement in the 1990s largely took up issues of representation, to the detriment of issues of redistribution, particularly women's property rights (Deere and León 2001). A blatant example of this neglect is the case of Brazil, where the civil code was reformed in 2002 without most feminists even being aware that this was pending (interviews by the author during 2000–2002). Luckily, the recent reforms expanded the range of marital regimes and improved the inheritance rights of wives.

AFTERWORD

Thinking about Gender and Law in Mexico

JANE F. COLLIER

The relationship between gender and law in Mexico has to be understood within the context of "bourgeois law," the legal concepts and practices that developed in eighteenth-century Europe. Although sometimes presented as a coherent set of ideas and practices, bourgeois law is a language of argument, riddled with contradictions (Fitzpatrick 1992; Kristeva 1991; Macpherson 1962). I will discuss some of these to consider their implications for gender justice in Mexico. I will repeat the obvious, but do so because generally accepted truths affect us most when they remain unexamined (Bourdieu 1977). I will restate what we all know but need to keep in mind when analyzing specific instances of law.

I borrowed Evgeny Pashukanis's (1978) term *bourgeois law* (rather than the term *liberal law*) because I want to emphasize historical connections between capitalism and legal systems in which "men" make laws to protect "the rights of man" (Collier, Maurer, and Suárez-Navaz 1995). The most important rights concern security of property and persons. When "men" demanded the right to create their own laws (rather than submit to laws of divinely ordained kings), they wanted to protect property owners' rights to use and dispose of properties without fear of physical violence (Macpherson 1962).

Feminists have long observed that the "rights of man" were, in fact, the rights of men (Pateman 1988). The *man* that eighteenth-century philosophers imagined was the owner of enough productive property to support himself and his dependents. Over time the category *man* has expanded, as workers, slaves, women, indigenous peoples, disabled people, etc., have demanded equal rights. But those who are not independent property-owning men continue to have difficulty realizing the promise of equality.

Because "equal rights" were articulated in opposition to monarchical status privileges, those who differ from "equal men" face the contradictory task of demanding both "special" and "equal" rights. Feminists demanding equal rights soon discovered that most women neither can nor want to be like the competitive, selfish, autonomous man of bourgeois law. Rather, women prefer family-friendly policies that allow mothers to participate in political and economic activities. Whereas women may enjoy equality as long as they forgo family responsibilities, many rightly resent men's ability to enjoy both family life and the independence granted those who "earn" their own way. Similarly, indigenous groups demanding equal rights find that their desire for cultural preservation may prevent their realizing "equality" based on European assumptions of personhood. Faced with having to demand "special" rights to avoid sanctions for being different, women and indigenous peoples appear to be arguing both for and against "equal" rights.

Children are women's problem. Because children need care, women can never realize the bourgeois ideal of the autonomous, rights-bearing man. Nor can they pay caretakers. Consequently, unpaid child-minders are usually condemned to economic dependence on someone who does earn money. The inventors of bourgeois law imagined that property owners would support the household dependents who lived and worked with them. But the idea that men would support dependents did not disappear when wages and salaries replaced property ownership as the basis of wealth. Drafters of the Universal Declaration of Human Rights assumed that working *men* would support their families when writing that "Everyone who works has the right to just and favorable remuneration ensuring for himself and his family an existence worthy of human dignity" (art. 23).

However tempting it may be to view laws protecting male-headed families as reflecting religious values, such laws are as integral to secular bourgeois law as are those mandating gender equality (chapters by Ortiz-Ortega, and Szasz, this volume). Both capitalism, which pays only for goods that enter the market, and bourgeois law, which grants equality only to autonomous individuals, must ensure that those who cannot support themselves are provided with food and shelter.[1] Religious groups may demand legal protection for male-headed households, but activists for secular causes such as fair wages and land reform also argue that workers and peasants also need resources to support their families (Baitenmann, this volume).

Bourgeois law commonly handles inequalities through two mechanisms—protecting individuals' right to choose, and emphasizing the public/private distinction. The central contradiction of capitalism, the class inequality that coexists with equal legal rights, is commonly portrayed as resulting from choices made by free individuals negotiating private contracts. Although propertyless individuals have to work for others or starve, and although markets are highly regulated, these facts are disguised by laws that protect workers' right to choose employment and by claims that markets are "free" from government controls.

Governments deal similarly with women's inequality: by protecting a woman's right to choose her husband, while refusing to interfere in "private" homes. Women's advocates have successfully obtained laws preventing forced marriages and criminalizing rape (although abductors and rapists may be pardoned if victims "freely" consent to marry them) (Szasz, this volume). Married women have also succeeded in obtaining legal rights to property and divorce that allow them to escape unwanted or failed marriages (Deere, this volume). Women's advocates have been less successful obtaining laws protecting women from domestic violence. States hesitate to interfere in "private" homes. States may offer battered wives protection if they leave home, but make it difficult for wives to stay away by refusing to help single mothers. States prefer to treat children as the private responsibility of parents, passing (easily evaded) laws requiring divorced men to pay child support.

When lawyers declare "there is no right without a remedy," they mean that rights have no effect unless those whose rights are violated have means of obtaining redress. Bourgeois legal institutions thus supply forums where individuals can appeal for justice. But rights are also meaningless if individuals cannot exercise them. The right to choose one's occupation has little effect if there are no jobs available. Similarly, laws decriminalizing abortion are meaningless if women lack access to clinics where the procedure can be performed (Ortiz-Ortega, this volume).

T. H. Marshall described three types of citizenship rights (1964). The first includes "the rights necessary for individual freedom—liberty of the person, freedom of speech, thought and faith, the right to own property and to conclude valid contracts, and the right to justice" (1964, 71). These are core rights that bourgeois states enforce through legal institutions and adequate remedies. Marshall's second type is the "political element": "the right to participate in the exercise of political power as a member of a body invested with political authority or as an elector of the members of such a body" (ibid., 72). Over time, the franchise—once limited to property owners—has expanded to include propertyless men, men of racial and ethnic minorities, and finally women, although people's ability to exercise political rights has varied over time and regime.

Marshall's third type are "social" rights: "the whole range from the right to a modicum of economic welfare and security to the right to share in the full social heritage and to live the life of a civilized being according to the standards prevailing in society" (ibid.). These are designed to help those who are not autonomous male property owners of the dominant ethnic group to enjoy equality of opportunity. The Universal Declaration of Human Rights of 1948 included many of these rights, and several states have tried to implement them. But debt crises and the triumph of neoliberal economics have caused most bourgeois states to retreat from social rights. Instead of providing health care, schools, and well-paying jobs, states now protect the "free" market that restricts benefits to those with money to pay. But the battle for social rights is far from over, especially given the promise of equal opportunity inherent in bourgeois law.

Although bourgeois law's contradiction of promising equality while privileging property owners was inherent in its inception, historical struggles determined specific outcomes. Mexico adopted the French version of the "rights of man," which assumes that men need rights to protect themselves from society (in contrast to the U.S. version, which assumes that men give up rights to enter society). Mexican feminists have thus been spared the battle between conflicting rights that plagues U.S. abortion debates. Instead of arguing over whether women must give up the right to choose or fetuses must give up the right to life, Mexican feminists can argue for safe abortions by referring to the rights that women and children need to participate in a just society (Ortiz-Ortega, this volume).

Because humans write laws, law can never be separated from politics (Fitzpatrick 1992). All attempts to analyze legal institutions carry political implications, even as the codes, decisions, documents, courts, and institutions that scholars analyze reflect outcomes of complex political maneuvers. Legal documents always contain multiple voices, even if ostensibly recording the knowledge of one person (Alonso, this volume). Similarly, court proceedings reflect the prejudices of their participants, even if general guidelines are prescribed by law. Legal forums can be analyzed as stages, where popular stereotypes about particular groups are affirmed or challenged. Most often, popular stereotypes prevail, as prosecutors, judges, and litigants share unspoken assumptions (see chapters by Alonso and Varley, this volume). But participants who challenge stereotypes, and scholars who publicize unspoken assumptions, can shift the balance of power by questioning accepted truths. Because studies of legal forums can never be neutral, whether challenging or supporting the status quo, scholars need to anticipate, and take responsibility for, the implications of their findings.

Following Laura Nader (1965), who urged anthropologists to study disputing processes rather than judicial decisions, I focused on litigant choices. Litigants obviously forum-shop, seeking forums where they will be respected and receive favorable judgments. But litigants consider other issues. When studying disputing processes in the highland Chiapas municipality of Zinacantan (1973), I found that people who took accusations of murder and rape to state judicial authorities were often less interested in justice than in disposing of a political enemy. Such accusations required state authorities to investigate, thus forcing a political opponent to flee or face incarceration. I also found that accused witches and adulteresses who initiated cases were less interested in punishing accusers than in avoiding being beaten or killed by kin and neighbors. When thinking about the many reasons why ejidatarios in Mexico have not taken advantage of the 1992 change in agrarian law to claim private ownership of ejido parcels (chapters by Baitenmann and Stephen, this volume), I have considered that one reason may be people's fear of antagonizing their relatives and neighbors.

Mexico, like many settler states, now faces demands for equality from indigenous groups. Although indigenous peoples have been fighting for rights since colonial times, recent international conventions and constitutional reforms (e.g., Convention 169 of the International Labor Organization, and the reform of Article 4 of the Mexican Constitution) have provided new weapons. Because they derive from bourgeois law, however, these weapons are two-edged. The discourse of rights can be, and has been, used against indigenous leaders by opponents who accuse them of violating the individual rights of community members (Speed and Collier 1999). The three types of legal practices most often criticized by opponents of indigenous rights—prosecutions for witchcraft, expulsion of religious dissidents, and oppression of women—all appear to violate the "civil" rights that Marshall characterized as required for individual freedom (1964, 71). Although there can be no doubt that some indigenous leaders have violated the human rights of individuals, the Mexican state is hardly innocent. The number of human rights violations perpetrated by state judicial and security forces far exceeds the number of those perpetrated by indigenous authorities.

Moreover, many apparent violations seem less problematic when viewed in context. For example, I found that Zinacantecos have a different understanding of social order than have Westerners (1973). Instead of assuming that selfish individuals need laws and enforcement mechanisms to live together in peace, Zinacantecos assume that, because people will inevitably fight with one another, authorities must always be available to help settle quarrels before someone is injured or killed.[2] As a result, Zinacanteco authorities are less concerned with determining guilt than with negotiating a settlement that allows disputants to make peace. When handling accusations of witchcraft, for example, Zinacanteco judges help disputants plan what the accused witch must do to convince fearful neighbors that they are no longer in danger. Although judges may appear to be punishing accused witches by forcing them to hold retraction ceremonies, even the accused recognize that ceremonies calm the angry hearts of those who want to kill them.

The two-edged nature of bourgeois law also puts indigenous women in the impossible situation of having to choose between women's rights and indigenous rights. When indigenous women argue for changing discriminatory customs, indigenous leaders can accuse them of siding with Western feminists against their own people. Should indigenous women fail to argue for changes, however, they continue to suffer oppressive customs even as they allow opponents of indigenous rights to use women's oppression as a justification for denying indigenous peoples the autonomy they crave. Given the impossible choice offered by bourgeois law, indigenous women who want both women's rights and indigenous rights must fight to speak for themselves. It is too easy for opponents to accuse them of being either mouthpieces for Western feminism or apologists for brutal men. Fortunately, indigenous women leaders are meeting this challenge (Hernandez Castillo 1997; Eber and Kovic 2003; chapters by González Montes, Sierra, and Stephen, this volume).

Indigenous women need a voice in determining the future of their communities because women's situation has changed. Customs that once seemed just are no longer so. In the 1960s, Zinacanteco men needed wives in order to become economically secure. Unmarriageable men had to emigrate, joining the shifting population of poor mestizos. Sensible men thus cared for their wives and children, and avoided becoming known for stinginess or brutality. At that time, most Zinacanteco families lived by farming corn for food and sale. Men's and women's roles appeared complementary, as the activities of both were required to maintain a household. By the 1990s, however, economic changes in Mexico had shifted the basis of wealth from household labor to ownership of capital resources, such as trucks, market stalls, and greenhouses (G. A. Collier 1990, 1999). Cash was the key to success, and men appeared to obtain cash through their own efforts. Although Zinacanteco women continued to work as hard or harder at household tasks, such tasks earned little money and so appeared valueless. Zinacanteco women thus became economic dependents of men. Although most Zinacanteco men continue to care for wives and children, men who brutalize or abandon their families no longer face exile and poverty. Indigenous women thus need a voice in political affairs if their communities are to craft institutions that ensure respect for everyone.

Mexico has experienced major economic and political shifts over the past forty years as the country participated in the international spread of "democracy" and neoliberal economics. As neoliberal economic policies, along with forced debt repayments, have starved the government of cash for funding social services, Mexico has been unable to placate groups suffering downward mobility. Faced with growing social unrest, the government has resorted to increased militarism combined with promises of democracy (Collier and Collier 2003). Both tactics have unfortunate consequences. Militarism can foster the violence it is supposed to prevent, and democracy can encourage "ethnic cleansing," as groups rid their communities of those who would vote against them.[3]

The spread of neoliberal economics has also created areas of ungovernability, since cash-starved governments cannot protect life and property. Some areas have dissolved into violence and anarchy, as armed groups or warlords fight for supremacy. In other areas, such as the Zapatista autonomous communities in Chiapas, people are experimenting with new forms of egalitarian and just societies (Stephen, this volume). Groups attempting to implement various forms of collective rights, however, face an uphill battle. Not only does the capitalist market starve them of resources, but states justify intervening in community affairs by claiming to protect the individual rights of citizens punished for violating collective agreements (Speed and Collier 1999).

States' retreat from social rights has also encouraged criminal activities. When states cut back social services and allow wages to fall, frustrated job seekers must still make a living. Young Zinacanteco men face a bleak future, given low prices for agricultural products and wages too low to support a family. The principal activities that pay enough money to buy trucks or greenhouses are illegal: stealing cars, dealing drugs, and transporting illegal immigrants from Central America. Both sexes suffer from the growth of illegal activities. Men die in gang wars, while women and children suffer increased violence and vulnerability to prostitution. Any analysis of gender and law in contemporary Mexico needs to explore not only the effects of formal and informal legal institutions, but also what goes on in the spaces that bourgeois law creates by defining these spaces as illegal. Because studies of illegal activities are dangerous, however, perhaps the best that scholars can do is to remember that analyses of legal activities provide only a partial picture of law's effects.

Although I have focused on the inequalities fostered by bourgeois law, it is important to remember that bourgeois law also provides a vision of the good society that motivates those fighting for social justice. Instead of either condemning or celebrating bourgeois law, we need to focus on the constraints and possibilities it offers. The ideals of "liberty, equality, and fraternity" are widely accepted. Today, no one would argue for bondage, inequality, or selfishness. But because individual freedom, equality of opportunity, and promoting the common good can be incompatible goals, it matters how issues are framed. Legal institutions provide important forums for negotiating competing claims, framing how issues will be defined and limiting possible outcomes. Whatever gender justice comes to mean, and however it may be realized (or not), legal institutions in Mexico and elsewhere will play a major role.

NOTES

1. Varley (this volume) analyzes the assumption by Mexican judges that married women must have a "home" to manage.
2. Chenaut (this volume) provides evidence that quarrels among kin in indigenous communities can lead to serious consequences if local authorities cannot help people to resolve their differences. Of the four women accused of homicide that Chenaut interviewed, three had been accused by family members.
3. The expulsion of supposed "Protestants" from the indigenous community of Chamula in Chiapas during the late 1980s is probably best understood as occurring when supporters of the ruling clique expelled those who were expected to vote against them in the upcoming election (Kovic 2005).

BIBLIOGRAPHY

Abel, Christopher, and Colin M. Lewis. 2002. Exclusion and engagement: A diagnosis of social policy in Latin America in the long run. In *Exclusion and engagement: Social policy in Latin America,* ed. Christopher Abel and Colin M. Lewis. London: Institute of Latin American Studies.

Acosta, Marieclaire, Flora Botton-Burlá, Lilia Domínguez, Isabel Molina, Adriana Novelo, and Kyra Núñez. 1976. *El aborto en México.* Mexico City: Fondo de Cultura Económica.

Adame Goddard, Jorge. 2004. *El matrimonio civil en México (1859–2000).* Mexico City: Universidad Nacional Autónoma de México (UNAM).

Agarwal, Bina. 1994. *A field of one's own: Gender and land rights in South Asia.* Cambridge: Cambridge University Press.

Aggleton, Peter, ed. 1998. *Men who sell sex: International perspectives on male prostitution and HIV/AIDS.* London: UCL Press.

Agosín, Marjorie, ed. 2001. *Women, gender, and human rights: A global perspective.* New Brunswick, NJ: Rutgers University Press.

Agostoni, Claudia, and Elisa Speckman Guerra, eds. 2001. *Modernidad, tradición y alteridad: La ciudad de México en el cambio de siglo (XIX–XX).* Mexico City: UNAM.

Aguirre, Carlos A., and Ricardo D. Salvatore. 2001. Introduction: Writing the history of law, crime, and punishment in Latin America. In Salvatore, Aguirre, and Joseph 2001.

Aguirre Beltrán, Gonzalo. 1953. *Formas de gobierno indígena.* Mexico City: Imprenta Universitaria.

Ahmed, Sara. 1998. *Differences that matter: Feminist theory and postmodernism.* Cambridge: Cambridge University Press.

Alan Guttmacher Institute. 1996. *An overview of clandestine abortion in Latin America.* New York: Alan Guttmacher Institute.

Alberro, Solange. 1979. Negros y mulatos en los documentos inquisitoriales: Rechazo e integración. In *El trabajo y los trabajadores en la historia de México / Labor and laborers through Mexican history,* ed. Elsa Cecilia Frost, Michael C. Meyer, and Josefina Zoraida Vázquez, with Lilia Díaz. Mexico City and Tucson: Colegio de México / University of Arizona Press.

———. 1980. Juan de Morga and Gertrudis de Escobar: Rebellious slaves. In *Struggle and survival in colonial America,* ed. David G. Sweet and Gary B. Nash. Berkeley and Los Angeles: University of California Press.

———. 1982. La sexualidad manipulada en Nueva España: Modalidades de recuperación y de adaptación frente a los tribunales eclesiásticos. In Seminario de Historia de las Mentalidades 1982.

Alberti Manzanares, Pilar. 2004. El discurso polifónico acerca de las mujeres indígenas en México: Académicas, gobierno e indígenas. In Pérez-Gil Romo and Ravelo Blancas 2004.

Alianza de Mujeres de México. 1953. *La situación jurídica de la mujer mexicana.* Mexico City: Estudios Jurídicos.

Alonso, Ana M. 1995a. Rationalizing patriarchy: Gender, domestic violence, and law in Mexico. *Identities: Global studies in culture and power* 2 (1–2): 29–47.

———. 1995b. *Thread of blood: Colonialism, revolution, and gender on Mexico's northern frontier.* Tucson: University of Arizona Press.

Alonso, Ana M., and María Teresa Koreck. 1999. Silences: "Hispanics," AIDS, and sexual practices. In *Culture, society, and sexuality: A reader,* ed. Richard G. Parker and Peter Aggleton. London: UCL Press.

Álvarez de Lara, Rosa María. 2002. Algunos comentarios sobre el reconocimiento de la costumbre y la discriminación de la mujer en la reciente reforma constitucional en materia indígena. In *Comentarios a la reforma constitucional en materia indígena,* ed. Miguel Carbonell and Karla Pérez Portilla. Mexico City: Instituto de Investigaciones Jurídicas, UNAM.

Appignanesi, Richard, and Chris Garratt. 1995. *Postmodernism for beginners.* Cambridge: Icon Books.

Aragón Salcido, María Inés. 2004. La paridad de género en el Código Electoral de Sonora: Una reforma suspendida. In Galeana 2004.

Archivo General de la Nación. 1912. *Procesos de indios idólatras e hechiceros.* Vol. 3 of *Publicaciones del Archivo General de la Nación.* Mexico City: Archivo General de la Nación.

Ariès, Philippe, and Georges Duby, eds. 1987. *A history of private life.* Vol. 1, *From pagan Rome to Byzantium,* ed. Paul Veyne. Trans. Arthur Goldhammer. Cambridge, MA: Harvard University Press, Belknap Press.

Ariza, Marina, and Orlandina de Oliveira, eds. 2004. *Imágenes de la familia en el cambio de siglo.* Mexico City: UNAM.

Arizpe, Lourdes. 1975. *Indígenas en la ciudad de México: El caso de las "Marías."* Mexico City: Secretaría de Educación Pública.

Arrom, Silvia Marina. 1976. *La mujer mexicana ante el divorcio eclesiástico (1800–1857).* Mexico City: Secretaría de Educación Pública.

———. 1985a. Changes in Mexican family law in the nineteenth century: The Civil Codes of 1870 and 1884. *Journal of Family History* 10 (3): 305–317.

———. 1985b. *The women of Mexico City, 1790–1857.* Stanford, CA: Stanford University Press.

Assies, Willem, Gemma van der Haar, and André Hoekema, eds. 1999. *El reto de la diversidad: Pueblos indígenas y reforma del estado en América Latina.* Zamora: Colegio de Michoacán.

Atondo Rodríguez, Ana María. 1986. De la perversión de la práctica a la perversión del discurso: La fornicación. In Ortega Noriega 1986.

———. 1992. *El amor venal y la condición femenina en el México colonial.* Mexico City: INAH.

Ávila Godoy, Clemente, and Eloisa Aguirre Angulo, eds. 1998. *Derechos y deberes de la mujer y la familia en el estado de Sonora.* Hermosillo: Gobierno del Estado de Sonora / Secretaría de Gobierno / Consejo Estatal de Población.

Ávila Osorio, Lidia. 1963. La capacidad jurídica de la mujer en el derecho agrario. BA thesis, UNAM.

Azaola Garrido, Elena. 1996a. *El delito de ser mujer. Hombres y mujeres homicidas en la ciudad de México: Historias de vida.* Mexico City: Centro de Investigaciones y Estudios Superiores en Antropología Social (CIESAS) / Plaza y Valdés.

———. 1996b. Les femmes autochtones incarcérées au Mexique. *Recherches Amérindiennes au Québec* 26 (3–4): 75–82.

———. 1998. Nuevas tendencias en la criminalidad femenina. In *Criminalidad y criminalización de la mujer en la región andina,* ed. Rosa del Olmo. Caracas: Nueva Sociedad.

Azaola Garrido, Elena, and Cristina José Yacamán. 1996. *Las mujeres olvidadas: Un estudio sobre la situación actual de las cárceles para mujeres en la República mexicana.* Mexico City: Colegio de México.

Baitenmann, Helga. 1997. Rural agency and state formation in postrevolutionary Mexico: The agrarian reform in Central Veracruz (1915–1992). PhD thesis, New School for Social Research.

———. 2000. Gender and agrarian rights in postrevolutionary Mexico. Paper delivered to Latin American Studies Association conference, Miami.

———. n.d. Gendered explorations of the state: Agrarian reform in twentieth-century Mexico. Institute for the Study of the Americas, University of London.

Baker, Richard D. 1971. *Judicial review in Mexico: A study of the Amparo suit.* Austin: University of Texas Press.

Bakhtin, Mikhail M. 1973. *Problems of Dostoevsky's poetics.* Trans. R. W. Rotsel. Ann Arbor, MI: Ardis.

———. 1981. *The dialogic imagination: Four essays.* Ed. Michael Holquist and trans. Caryl Emerson and Michael Holquist. Austin: University of Texas Press.

———. 1986. *Speech genres, and other late essays.* Ed. Caryl Emerson and Michael Holquist and trans. Vern W. McGee. Austin: University of Texas Press.

Banda, Fareda. 2005. *Women, law, and human rights: An African perspective.* Oxford: Hart Publications.

Barbieri, M. Teresita de. 1992. Algunas consideraciones para pensar la reforma al derecho de familia en México. In *Familias en transformación y códigos por transformar: Construyendo las propuestas políticas de las mujeres para el Código Civil,* ed. Ana Victoria Jiménez A. Mexico City: Grupo de Educación Popular con Mujeres AC.

Barbieri, M. Teresita de, and Gabriela Cano. 1990. Ni tanto ni tan poco: Las reformas penales relativas a la violencia sexual. *Debate Feminista* 1 (2): 345–356.

Barceló, Raquel. 1997. Hegemonía y conflicto en la ideología porfiriana sobre el papel de la mujer y la familia. In González Montes and Tuñón 1997.

Barreda Solórzano, Luis de la. 1991. *El delito de aborto: Una careta de buena conciencia.* Mexico City: Porrúa.

Barrera Bassols, Dalia, ed. 2000. *Mujeres, ciudadanía y poder.* Mexico City: Colegio de México.

Bedolla Guzmán, Epifanio. 1976. Los derechos de la mujer en las modificaciones del artículo 123 constitucional y su destino en el derecho social. BA thesis, UNAM.

Begné, Patricia. 1990. *La mujer en México: Su situación legal.* Mexico City: Trillas.

Behar, Ruth. 1987. Sex and sin, witchcraft and the devil in late-colonial Mexico. *American Ethnologist* 14 (1): 34–54.

———. 1989. Sexual witchcraft, colonialism, and women's powers: Views from the Mexican Inquisition. In Lavrin 1989b.

Bernal Gómez, Beatriz. 1984. La mujer y el cambio constitucional en México: El decreto de 31 de diciembre de 1974. In *Memoria del Tercer Congreso Nacional de Derecho Constitucional,* ed. Jorge Carpizo and Jorge Madrazo. Mexico City: UNAM.

Beyer Esparza, Jorge Edmundo. 2002. Mujer y tierra social: La experiencia mexicana y la insuficiencia de los mecanismos formales en la superación de la inequidad de género. Comment prepared for World Bank Regional Workshop on Land Issues in Latin America and the Caribbean, May 19–22, Pachuca, Mexico.

Bialostosky, Sara, ed. 2005. *Condición jurídica, política y social de la mujer en México.* Mexico City: Porrúa / UNAM.

Bialostosky, Sara, Beatriz Bernal, Marta Morineau Iduarte, Aurora Arnaiz Amigo, María Carreras Maldonado, Sara Montero Duhalt, Olga Hernández Espíndola, Elvia Arcelia

Quintana Adriano, Mercedes Fernández Bazavilvazo, Yolanda Frías Sánchez, and Guadalupe Belloc. 1975. *Condición jurídica de la mujer en México.* Mexico City: UNAM.

Billings, Deborah L., Claudia Moreno, Celia Ramos, Deyanira González de León, Rubén Ramírez, Leticia Villaseñor Martínez, and Mauricio Rivera Díaz. 2002. Constructing access to legal abortion services in Mexico City. *Reproductive Health Matters* 10 (19): 86–94.

Birgin, Haydée, ed. 2000. *El derecho en el género y el género en el derecho.* Buenos Aires: Biblos.

Blackwell, Maylei. 2006. Weaving in the spaces: Indigenous women's organizing and the politics of scale in Mexico. In Speed, Hernández Castillo, and Stephen 2006.

Blancarte, Roberto. 1992. *Historia de la iglesia católica en México.* Mexico City: Fondo de Cultura Económica / Colegio Mexiquense.

Bliss, Katherine. 2001. *Compromised positions: Prostitution, public health, and gender politics in revolutionary Mexico City.* University Park: Pennsylvania State University Press.

Blomley, Nicholas. 1994. *Law, space, and the geographies of power.* New York: Guilford Press.

Blomley, Nicholas, and Joel Bakan. 1992. Spacing out: Towards a critical geography of law. *Osgoode Hall Law Review* 30 (3): 661–690.

Blum, Ann S. 2004. Cleaning the revolutionary household: Domestic servants and public welfare in Mexico City, 1900–1935. *Journal of Women's History* 15 (4): 67–90.

———. 2006. Breaking and making families: Adoption and public welfare, 1938–1942. In Olcott, Vaughan, and Cano 2006.

Blumberg, Rae L., ed. 1991. *Gender, family, and economy: The triple overlap.* Newbury Park, CA: Sage.

Bocaranda Espinosa, Juan José. 1983. *La comunidad concubinaria en el Nuevo Código Civil de 1982.* Caracas: Principios.

Bodelón González, Encarna. 2003. Género y sistema penal: Los derechos de las mujeres en el sistema penal. In *Sistema penal y problemas sociales,* ed. Roberto Bergalli. Valencia: Tirant Lo Blanch.

Bonfil Sánchez, Paloma, and Raúl Marcó del Pont Lalli. 1999. *Las mujeres indígenas al final del milenio.* Mexico City: FNUAP / Comisión Nacional de la Mujer.

Bonfil Sánchez, Paloma, and Elvia Rosa Martínez Medrano, eds. 2003. *Diagnóstico de la discriminación hacia las mujeres indígenas.* Mexico City: Comisión Nacional para el Desarrollo de los Pueblos Indígenas.

Borah, Woodrow W. 1983. *Justice by insurance: The General Indian Court of colonial Mexico and the legal aides of the half-real.* Berkeley and Los Angeles: University of California Press.

Boswell, John. 1982–1983. Revolutions, universals, and sexual categories. *Salmagundi* 58–59: 84–113.

Bourdieu, Pierre. 1977. Outline of a theory of practice. Trans. Richard Nice. Cambridge: Cambridge University Press.

———.1991. *Language and symbolic power.* Ed. John B. Thompson and trans. Gino Raymond and Matthew Adamson. Cambridge MA: Harvard University Press.

Boyer, Richard E. 1989. Women, *la mala vida,* and the politics of marriage. In Lavrin 1989b.

———. 1995. *Lives of the bigamists: Marriage, family, and community in colonial Mexico.* Albuquerque: University of New Mexico Press.

———. 1998. Honor among plebeians: *mala sangre* and social reputation. In *The faces of honor in colonial Latin America: Sex, shame, and violence in colonial Latin America,* ed. Lyman L. Johnson and Sonya Lipsett-Rivera. Albuquerque: University of New Mexico Press.

Bozon, Michel, and Henri Leridon. 1993. Les constructions sociales de la sexualité. *Population* 48 (5): 1173–96.

Bradu, Fabienne. 1991. *Antonieta (1900–1931).* Mexico City: Fondo de Cultura Económica.

Brants, Chrisie. 1998. The fine art of regulated tolerance: Prostitution in Amsterdam. *Journal of Law and Society* 25 (4): 621–635.

Brazil. 2002. Lei No. 10.406, de 10 janeiro de 2002: Código Civil. http://www.senado.gov.br/sf/legislação/.

Bremauntz, Alberto. 1937. *El sufragio femenino desde el punto de vista constitucional.* Mexico City: Frente Socialista de Abogados.

Buck, Sarah A. 2000. *La ciudadana,* feminism, and conceptions of public and private in Mexico, 1923–1953. Paper presented at the conference of the Latin American Studies Association, Miami, March 16–18.

Buffington, Robert M. 2000. *Criminal and citizen in modern Mexico.* Lincoln: University of Nebraska Press.

Burguete Cal y Mayor, Aracely, ed. 2000. *Indigenous autonomy in Mexico.* Trans. Elaine Bolton. Copenhagen: International Work Group for Indigenous Affairs.

Cabal, Luisa, Mónica Roa, and Julieta Lemaitre, eds. 2001. *Cuerpo y derecho: Legislación y jurisprudencia en América latina.* Bogotá: Temis.

Cabal, Luisa, and Cristina Motta, eds. 2006. *Más allá del derecho: Justicia y género en América Latina.* Bogotá: Siglo del Hombre / Center for Reproductive Rights / Universidad de los Andes.

Calzadíaz Barrera, Alberto. 1975. *General Martín López, hijo militar de Pancho Villa: Anatomía de un guerrillero.* 2nd ed. Mexico City: Patria.

Cardaci, Dora. 2002. Visibilidad y protagonismo de las redes y ONG en el campo de la salud. In Gutiérrez Castañeda 2002b.

Carlen, Pat. 1992. Criminal women and criminal justice: The limits to, and potential of, feminist and left realist perspectives. In *Issues in realist criminology,* ed. Roger Matthews and Jock Young. London: Sage.

Carreras Maldonado, María, and Sara Montero Duhalt. 1975. La condición de la mujer en el derecho civil mexicano. In Bialostosky et al. 1975.

Castañeda, Carmen. 1989. *Violación, estupro y sexualidad: Nueva Galicia, 1790–1821.* Guadalajara: Hexágono.

Castro Gutiérrez, Felipe. 1998. Condición femenina y violencia conyugal entre los purépechas durante la época colonial. *Mexican Studies / Estudios Mexicanos* 14 (1): 5–21.

Castro Lučić, Milka, ed. 2000. *Actas del XII Congreso Internacional. Derecho consuetudinario y pluralismo legal: Desafíos en el tercer milenio.* Santiago: Universidad de Chile / Universidad de Tarapacá.

Catholics for a Free Choice. 1997. *Catholics and reproduction: A world view.* Washington, DC: Catholics for a Free Choice.

Caulfield, Sueann. 2001. The history of gender in the historiography of Latin America. *Hispanic American Historical Review* 81 (3–4): 449–490.

Centro Legal para Derechos Reproductivos y Políticas Públicas. 1997. Derechos reproductivos de la mujer en México: Un reporte sombra. http://www.crlp.org/pdf/sr_mex_1297_sp.pdf.

Chan-Tiberghien, Jennifer. 2004. *Gender and human rights politics in Japan: Global norms and domestic networks.* Stanford, CA: Stanford University Press.

Chassen-López, Francie R. 1994. Cheaper than machines: Women and agriculture in Porfirian Oaxaca, 1880–1911. In Fowler-Salamini and Vaughan 1994.

Chávez Padrón, Martha. 1956. La mujer y la reforma agraria. *Filosofía y Letras,* nos. 60–62: 235–244.

———. 2003. *Derecho procesal social agrario.* Mexico City: Porrúa.

Chenaut, Victoria. 1997. Honor y ley: La mujer totonaca en el conflicto judicial en la segunda mitad del siglo XIX. In González Montes and Tuñón 1997.

———. 1999. Honor, disputas y usos del derecho entre los totonacas del Distrito Judicial de Papantla. PhD thesis, Colegio de Michoacán.

———. 2001a. Disputas matrimoniales y cambio social en Coyutla, Veracruz (México). *Boletín Antropológico* (Universidad de Los Andes), no. 53: 293–312.

———. 2001b. Mujer y relaciones de género en la legislación veracruzana, 1896–1932. *Vetas* 3 (8):105–123.

———. 2002. El divorcio en la costa totonaca de Veracruz (1896–1932). *Antropología: Boletín Oficial del Instituto Nacional de Antropología e Historia*, no. 66: 70–80.

———. 2004. Prácticas jurídicas e interlegalidad entre los totonacas en el Distrito Judicial de Papantla, Veracruz. In Sierra 2004d.

Chenaut, Victoria, and María Teresa Sierra, eds. 1995. *Pueblos indígenas ante el derecho*. Mexico City: Centro Francés de Estudios Mexicanos y Centroamericanos / CIESAS.

Chile. 2000. *Código Civil: Edición Oficial*. Santiago: Jurídica de Chile.

Chiñas, Beverly. 1973. *The Isthmus Zapotecs: Women's roles in cultural context*. New York: Holt, Rinehart, and Winston.

CIMAC. See Comunicación e Información de la Mujer.

Clavero, Bartolomé. 1994. *Derecho indígena y cultura constitucional en América*. Mexico City: Siglo XXI.

Cline, Susan. 1986. *Colonial Culhuacan, 1580–1600: A social history of an Aztec town*. Albuquerque: University of New Mexico Press.

Cloete, Elsie. 2003. Specificities: An "eye" for an "I": Discipline and gossip. *Social Identities* 9 (3): 401–423.

Coalición de Mujeres Feministas. 1977. *La maternidad voluntaria y el derecho al aborto libre y gratuito*. Mexico City: Coalición de Mujeres Feministas.

Collier, George A. 1990. Seeking food and seeking money: Changing productive relations in a highland Mexican community. Discussion Paper 11, United Nations Research Institute for Social Development.

———. 1999. *Basta! Land and the Zapatista rebellion in Chiapas*. With Elizabeth Lowery Quaratiello. Rev. ed. Oakland, CA: Food First Books.

Collier, George A., and Jane F. Collier. 2003. The Zapatista rebellion in the context of globalization. In *The future of revolutions: Rethinking radical change in the age of globalization*, ed. John Foran. London: Zed Books.

Collier, Jane F. 1966. El noviazgo zinacanteco como transacción económica. In *Los zinacantecos: Un pueblo tzotzil de los altos de Chiapas*, ed. Evon Z. Vogt. Mexico City: Instituto Nacional Indigenista.

———. 1973. *Law and social change in Zinacantan*. Stanford, CA: Stanford University Press.

———. 2001. Dos modelos de justicia indígena en Chiapas, México: Una comparación de las visiones zinacanteca y del Estado. In *Costumbres, leyes y movimiento indio en Oaxaca y Chiapas*, ed. Lourdes de León Pasquel. Mexico City: CIESAS / Porrúa.

———. 2004. Cambio y continuidad en los procedimientos legales zinacantecos. In Sierra 2004d.

Collier, Jane F., Bill Maurer, and Liliana Suárez-Navaz. 1995. Sanctioned identities: Legal constructions of modern personhood. *Identities: Global studies in culture and power* 2 (1–2): 1–27.

Collier, Jane F., Michelle Z. Rosaldo, and Sylvia Yanagisako. 1997. Is there a family? New anthropological views. In *The gender/sexuality reader: Culture, history, political economy*, ed. Roger N. Lancaster and Micaela di Leonardo. New York: Routledge. (Orig. pub. 1981.)

Comandanta Esther. 2003. Palabras de la Comandanta Esther a los pueblos indios México. Oventik, Chiapas, August 9. http://palabra.ezln.org.mx/.

Comisión de Equidad y Género. See Mexico, Cámara de Diputados. Comisión de Equidad y Género.

Comisión Takachihualis. 1997. Investigación de la impartición de justicia tradicional. Comisión Takachihualis, Cuetzalan, Puebla.

Comunicación e Información de la Mujer. 2003. Promoverá *México Posible* ley federal para trabajo sexual. *Comunicación e Información de la Mujer,* June 23. http://www.cimacnoticias. com/noticias/03jun/03062304.html.

Congreso de la Unión. See Mexico, Congreso de la Unión.

Consentini, Francesco. 1930. *Declaración de los derechos y obligaciones de la mujer: Proyecto para la protección de la mujer y del hogar.* Mexico City: Cultura.

Córdova Plaza, Rosío. 2005. Vida en los márgenes: La experiencia corporal como anclaje identitario entre sexoservidores de la ciudad de Xalapa, Veracruz. *Cuicuilco,* no. 34: 217–238.

Cornell, Drucilla. 1992. The philosophy of the limit: Systems theory and feminist legal reform. In *Deconstruction and the possibility of justice,* ed. Drucilla Cornell, Michel Rosenfeld, and David Gray Carlson. New York: Routledge.

Cortés, María Elena. 1988. El matrimonio y la familia negra en las legislaciones civil y eclesiástica coloniales, siglos XVI–XIX. In Seminario de Historia de las Mentalidades 1988.

Craske, Nikki, and Maxine Molyneux, eds. 2002. *Gender and the politics of rights and democracy in Latin America.* Basingstoke, UK: Palgrave.

Cruz y F., Elodia. 1931. Los derechos políticos y la mujer en México. BA thesis, UNAM.

D'Aubeterre Buznego, María Eugenia. 2000a. *El pago de la novia: Matrimonio, vida conyugal y prácticas transnacionales en San Miguel Acuexcomac, Puebla.* Zamora: Colegio de Michoacán / Benemérita Universidad de Puebla.

———. 2000b. Mujeres indígenas campesinas y violencia sexual: Un estudio de caso en la Sierra Norte de Puebla. In *Salud reproductiva y sociedad: Resultados de investigación,* ed. Claudio Stern and Carlos Javier Echarri. Mexico City: Colegio de México.

———. 2003. Los múltiples significados de robarse la muchacha: El robo de la novia en un pueblo de migrantes del estado de Puebla. In Robichaux 2003.

Dávila Mendoza, Dora. 2005. *Hasta que la muerte nos separe: El divorcio eclesiástico en el arzobispado de México, 1702–1800.* Mexico City: Colegio de México / Universidad Iberoamericana / Universidad Católica Andrés Bello (Caracas).

Deere, Carmen Diana, and Magdalena León. 2001. *Empowering women: Land and property rights in Latin America.* Pittsburgh, PA: University of Pittsburgh Press.

———. 2003. The gender asset gap: Land in Latin America. *World Development* 31 (6): 925–947.

———. 2005. Liberalism and married women's property rights in nineteenth-century Latin America. *Hispanic American Historical Review* 85 (4): 627–678.

Delgado, Richard, and Jean Stefanancic. 2000. *Critical race theory: The cutting edge.* 2nd ed. Philadelphia: Temple University Press.

De los Reyes-Heredia, José Guillermo. 2004. Sodomy and society: Sexuality, gender, race, and class in colonial Mexico. PhD thesis, University of Pennsylvania.

Dirección General de Estadística. See Mexico, Secretaría de Industria y Comercio. Dirección General de Estadística.

Dore, Elizabeth. 2000. One step forward, two steps back: Gender and the state in the long nineteenth century. In Dore and Molyneux 2000.

Dore, Elizabeth, and Maxine Molyneux, eds. 2000. *Hidden histories of gender and the state in Latin America.* Durham, NC: Duke University Press.

Douglas, Mary. 1966. *Purity and danger: An analysis of the concepts of pollution and taboo.* London: Routledge and Kegan Paul.

Dowsett, Gary W. 2003. Sexual cultures, identities, and meanings of HIV–AIDS: Exploring diversity and commonalities. Paper presented at the World Congress of Sexology, Havana, Cuba, March 10–14.

Dueñas, Lina. 1980. La mujer en el derecho mexicano. BA thesis, UNAM.

Eber, Christine. 2002. *Buscando una nueva vida:* La liberación a través de la autonomía en San Pedro Chenalhó, 1970–1998. In *Tierra, libertad y autonomía: Impactos regionales del zapatismo en Chiapas,* ed. Shannan L. Mattiace, Rosalva Aída Hernández Castillo, and Jan Rus. Mexico City: CIESAS / Grupo Internacional de Trabajo sobre Asuntos Indígenas.

Eber, Christine, and Christine M. Kovic, eds. 2003. *Women of Chiapas: Making history in times of struggle and hope.* New York: Routledge.

Ehrenfeld, Noemí. 1999. Female adolescents at the crossroads: Sexuality, contraception and abortion in Mexico. In *Abortion in the developing world,* ed. Axel I. Mundigo and Cynthia Indriso. London: Zed Books.

Ejército Zapatista de Liberación Nacional. 1993. El despertador mexicano. EZLN, Chiapas.

Enciso Rojas, Dolores. 1982. Bígamos en el siglo XVIII. In Seminario de Historia de las Mentalidades 1982.

———. 1989. Desacato y apego a las pautas matrimoniales: Tres casos de poliandria del siglo XVIII. In Guzmán Vázquez and Martínez O. 1989b.

Enríquez Vidal, Rafael. 1938. La situación jurídica de la mujer en nuestra nueva legislación. BA thesis, UNAM.

Escalante Gonzalbo, Fernando. 1992. *Ciudadanos imaginarios: Memorial de los afanes y desventuras de la virtud, y apología del vicio triunfante en la República Mexicana: Tratado de moral pública.* Mexico City: Colegio de México.

Espinosa, Gisela. 2002. Los rezagos y los retos para el feminismo y los movimientos de mujeres. In Gutiérrez Castañeda 2002b.

Estrada Martínez, Rosa Isabel, and Gisela González Guerra, eds. 1995. *Tradiciones y costumbres jurídicas en comunidades indígenas de México,* Mexico City: Comisión Nacional de Derechos Humanos.

EZLN. See Ejército Zapatista de Liberación Nacional.

Facio, Alda, and Lorena Fries, eds. 1999. *Género y derecho.* Santiago: LOM / La Morada.

Fagan, Abigail A. 2002. Gender. In *Encyclopedia of crime and punishment,* ed. David Levinson. Thousand Oaks, CA: Sage.

Fernández Muñoz, Alma Clemencia. 1990. Los derechos de protección social de la mujer trabajadora en la ley positiva del estado mexicano. BA thesis, UNAM.

Figueroa, Juan Guillermo, Lucero Jiménez, and Olivia Tena, eds. 2006. *Ser padres, esposos e hijos: Prácticas y valoraciones de varones mexicanos.* Mexico City: Colegio de México.

Fitzpatrick, Peter. 1992. *The mythology of modern law.* London: Routledge.

Fontanive, Anita, and Diana Damián. 1994. Chiapas: Una mirada hacia atrás. In Ortiz-Ortega 1994b.

Foster, George M. 1967. *Tzintzuntzan: Mexican peasants in a changing world.* Boston, MA: Little, Brown.

Foucault, Michel. 1975. Foreword to *I, Pierre Rivière, having slaughtered my mother, my sister, and my brother . . . : A case of parricide in the 19th century,* ed. Michel Foucault and trans. Frank Jellinek. New York: Pantheon.

———. 1977 *Discipline and punish: The birth of the prison.* Trans. Alan Sheridan. New York: Pantheon.

———. 1978. *An introduction.* Vol. 1 of *The history of sexuality.* Trans. Robert Hurley. New York: Pantheon.

Fowler-Salamini, Heather. 1994. Gender, work, and coffee in Córdoba, Veracruz, 1850–1910. In Fowler-Salamini and Vaughan 1994.

Fowler-Salamini, Heather, and Mary Kay Vaughan, eds. 1994. *Women of the Mexican countryside, 1850–1990: Creating spaces, shaping transitions.* Tucson: University of Arizona Press.

Franco, Jean. 1989. *Plotting women: Gender and representation in Mexico.* New York: Columbia University Press.

French, William E. 1994. Rapto and estupro in Porfirian and revolutionary Chihuahua. Paper presented at the Reunión de Historiadores Mexicanos, Estadounidenses y Canadienses, Mexico City, October 27–29.

Freyermuth Enciso, Graciela. 2003. *Las mujeres de humo: Morir en Chenalhó. Género, etnia y generación, factores constitutivos del riesgo durante la maternidad.* Mexico City: CIESAS / Porrúa / Instituto Nacional de las Mujeres.

Gagnon, John H., and Richard G. Parker. 1995. Conceiving sexuality. In *Conceiving sexuality: Approaches to sex research in a postmodern world,* ed. Richard G. Parker and John H. Gagnon. New York: Routledge.

Galeana, Patricia, ed. 1998. *Mujer y constitución.* Mexico City: Federación Mexicana de Universitarias / UNAM.

———, ed. 2004. *Los derechos humanos de las mujeres en México.* Mexico City: Federación Mexicana de Universitarias / UNAM.

Gall, Olivia, and Rosalva Aída Hernández Castillo. 2004. La historia silenciada: El papel de las campesinas indígenas en la rebeliones coloniales y poscoloniales en Chiapas. In Pérez-Gil Romo and Ravelo Blancas 2004.

Gallo Campos, Karla. 2002. La perspectiva de género en el derecho. In *Juzgar con perspectiva de género: Manual para la aplicación en México de los tratados internacionales de protección de los derechos humanos de las mujeres y la niñez,* ed. Adán Moisés Aranda Godoy. Mexico City: Instituto Nacional de la Mujeres.

García Peña, Ana Lidia. 2004. Madres solteras, pobres y abandonadas: Ciudad de México, siglo XIX. *Historia Mexicana* 53 (3): 647–692.

———. 2006. *El fracaso del amor: Género e individualismo en el siglo XIX mexicano.* Colegio de México / UNAM.

Garza Caligaris, Anna María. 2002. *Género, interlegalidad y conflicto en San Pedro Chenalhó.* San Cristóbal de las Casas: Universidad Autónoma de Chiapas / UNAM.

Garza Carvajal, Federico. 2003. *Butterflies will burn: Prosecuting sodomites in early modern Spain and Mexico.* Austin: University of Texas Press.

Gastelum Gaxiola, María de los Angeles. 1987. *Agenda de derechos y obligaciones de la mujer.* Mexico City: Consejo Nacional de Población.

Gilbert, Alan G., and Ann Varley. 1991. *Landlord and tenant: Housing the poor in urban Mexico.* London: Routledge.

Gill, Christopher J. 2001. The intimate life of the family: Patriarchy and the liberal project in Yucatán, Mexico, 1860–1915. PhD thesis, Yale University.

Giraud, François. 1988. La reacción social ante la violación: Del discurso a la práctica (Nueva España, siglo XVIII). In Seminario de Historia de las Mentalidades 1988.

GIRE. See Grupo de Información en Reproducción Elegida.

Gobierno del Estado de México. 1992. *Derechos y deberes de la mujer.* Toluca: Gobierno del Estado de México.

Gómez González, Jesús. 1975. La mujer trabajadora en la legislación laboral. BA thesis, UNAM.

Gómez Lara, Cipriano. 1965. El delito de violación en el matrimonio. *Derecho Penal Contemporáneo* (UNAM), no. 6: 61–81.

Gómez Rivera, María Magdalena. 1994. La juridización de los indígenas ante la nación mexicana. In *Orden jurídico y control social*, ed. Diego Iturralde. Mexico City: Instituto Nacional Indigenista.

———, ed. 1997. *Derecho indígena*. Mexico City: Instituto Nacional Indigenista / Asociación Mexicana para las Naciones Unidas.

Gonzalbo Aizpuru, Pilar, ed. 1991. *Familias novohispanas: Siglos XVI al XIX*. Mexico City: Colegio de México.

———. 1998. *Familia y orden colonial*. Mexico City: Colegio de México.

Gonzalbo Aizpuru, Pilar, and Cecilia Rabell Romero, eds. 1996. *Familia y vida privada en la historia de Iberoamérica*. Mexico City: Colegio de México / UNAM.

González, Román. 2000. Necesarios cambios en la legislación de Veracruz en derechos sexuales y reproductivos. *Comunicación e Información de la Mujer*, September 6. http://www.cimac.org.mx/noticias/00sep/00090604.html.

González Ascencio, Gerardo. 1993. *La antesala de la justicia: La violación en los dominios del Ministerio Público*. Mexico City: Asociación Mexicana de Lucha contra la Violencia hacia las Mujeres AC (Covac).

González Ascencio, Gerardo, and Patricia Duarte Sánchez. 1996. *La violencia de género en México: Un obstáculo para la democracia y el desarrollo*. Mexico City: Universidad Autónoma Metropolitana-Azcapotzalco.

González de la Vega, Francisco. 1970. *Derecho penal mexicano: Los delitos*. 10th ed. Mexico City: Porrúa.

———. 1998. *Derecho penal mexicano: Los delitos*. 30th ed. Mexico City: Porrúa.

González de Pazos, Margarita. 1987. La mujer en la Constitución del 17. *Alegatos* (Universidad Autónoma Metropolitana-Azcapotzalco) no. 6: 45–51.

González Marmolejo, Jorge René. 1982. Curas solicitantes durante el siglo XVIII. In Seminario de Historia de las Mentalidades 1982.

González Montes, Soledad. 1988. La reproducción de la desigualdad entre los sexos: prácticas e ideología de la herencia en una comunidad campesina (Xalatlaco, Estado de México, 1920–1960). In *Las mujeres en el campo: Memoria de la Primera Reunión Nacional de Investigación sobre Mujeres Campesinas en México*, ed. Josefina Aranda Bezaury. Oaxaca: Universidad Autónoma Benito Juárez de Oaxaca.

———. 1992. Familias campesinas mexicanas en el siglo XX. PhD thesis, Universidad Complutense de Madrid.

———. 1998. La violencia doméstica y sus repercusiones en la salud reproductiva en una zona indígena (Cuetzalan, Puebla). In *Los silencios de la salud reproductiva: Violencia, sexualidad y derechos reproductivos*, ed. Asociación Mexicana de Población. Mexico City: Asociación Mexicana de Población / Fundación John D. y Catherine T. MacArthur.

———. 1999a. Las costumbres de matrimonio en el México indígena contemporáneo. In *México diverso y desigual: Enfoques sociodemográficos: Quinta reunión de investigación sociodemográfica en México*, Vol. 4, ed. Beatriz Figueroa Campos. Mexico: Colegio de México / Sociedad Mexicana de Demografía.

———. 1999b. Mujeres, trabajo y pobreza en el campo mexicano: Una revisión crítica de la bibliografía reciente. In *Las mujeres en la pobreza*, ed. Javier Alatorre, Gloria Careaga, Clara Jusidman, Vania Salles, Cecilia Talamante, and John Townsend. Mexico City: Grupo Interdisciplinario sobre Mujer, Trabajo y Pobreza (GIMTRAP) / Colegio de México.

González Montes, Soledad, and Pilar Iracheta. 1987. La violencia en la vida de las mujeres campesinas: El distrito de Tenango, 1880–1910. In Ramos Escandón et al. 1987.

González Montes, Soledad, and Vania Salles, eds. 1995. *Relaciones de género y transformaciones agrarias.* Mexico City: Colegio de México.

González Montes, Soledad, and Julia Tuñón, eds. 1997. *Familias y mujeres en México: Del modelo a la diversidad.* Mexico City: Colegio de México.

González Salazar, Gloria. 1969. Situación jurídica de la mujer en México. In *La mujer y los derechos sociales,* ed. Ifigenia M. de Navarrete. Mexico City: Oasis.

González Salazar, Guadalupe. 1989. *La mujer y la legislación duranguense.* Durango: Secretaría de Educación Pública.

Graue, Desiderio. 1965. Consideraciones sobre algunos aspectos jurídicos del régimen familiar en México. *Criminalia* 31 (7): 376–396.

Grupo de Información en Reproducción Elegida (GIRE). 2001. Paulina: En el nombre de la ley. GIRE, Mexico City.

———. 2006. ¿Por qué debe despenalizarse el aborto en México? GIRE, Mexico City.

Gruzinski, Serge. 1982. La conquista de los cuerpos (Cristianismo, alianza y sexualidad en el altiplano mexicano: siglo XVI). In Seminario de Historia de las Mentalidades 1982.

Guevara, María, and Patricia Begné, eds. 1993. *Presente y prospectiva de la mujer en Guanajuato.* Guanajuato: Universidad de Guanajuato / Asociación de Universitarias de Guanajuato.

Gutiérrez, Margarita, and Nellys Palomo. 2000. A woman's eye view of autonomy. In Burguete Cal y Mayor 2000.

Gutiérrez, Ramón A. 1991. *When Jesus came, the Corn Mothers went away: Marriage, sexuality, and power in New Mexico, 1500–1846.* Stanford, CA: Stanford University Press.

Gutiérrez Castañeda, Griselda. 2002a. Breves reflexiones sobre la historia de una incomodidad: O, de las encrucijadas, retrocesos y mutaciones teórico-políticos del feminismo en México. In Gutiérrez Castañeda 2002b.

———, ed. 2002b. *Feminismo en México: Revisión histórico-crítica del siglo que termina.* Mexico City: Programa Universitario de Estudios de Género, UNAM.

Guzmán Lazo, María Eugenia. 1957. Igualdad jurídica del hombre y la mujer. BA thesis, UNAM.

Guzmán Vázquez, Antonio, and Lourdes Martínez O. 1989a. Introducción. In Guzmán Vázquez and Martínez O. 1989b.

———, eds. 1989b. *Del dicho al hecho: Transgresiones y pautas culturales en la Nueva España.* Mexico City: INAH.

———, eds. 1992. *Amor y desamor: Vivencias de parejas en la sociedad novohispana.* Mexico City: INAH.

Hamilton, Sarah. 2002. Neoliberalism, gender, and property rights in rural Mexico. *Latin American Research Review* 37 (1): 119–143.

Haskett, Robert. 1997. Activist or adultress? The life and struggle of Doña Josefa María of Tepoztlan. In Schroeder, Wood, and Haskett 1997.

Haslip-Viera, Gabriel. 1996. *Crime and punishment in late colonial Mexico City, 1692–1810.* Albuquerque: University of New Mexico Press.

Haussman, Melissa. 2005. *Abortion politics in North America.* Boulder, CO: Lynne Rienner.

Hay, Douglas. 2001. Afterword: Law and society in comparative perspective. In Salvatore, Aguirre, and Joseph 2001.

Hernández, Adela. 1926. *Capacidad de la mujer para ser procuradora en juicio.* Mexico City: privately printed.

Hernández Bautista, Sergio Serafín. 1976. La mujer como sujeto de derechos agrarios en la Ley Federal de Reforma Agraria. BA thesis, UNAM.

Hernández Castillo, Rosalva Aída. 1997. Between hope and adversity: The struggle of organized women in Chiapas since the Zapatista rebellion. *Journal of Latin American Anthropology* 3 (1): 102–120.

————, ed. 1998. *La otra palabra: Mujeres y violencia en Chiapas, antes y después de Acteal.* Mexico City: CIESAS / Grupo de Mujeres de San Cristóbal / Centro de Investigación y Acción para la Mujer.

————. 2001. Entre el etnocentrismo feminista y el esencialismo étnico: Las mujeres indígenas y sus demandas de género. *Debate Feminista* 12 (24): 206–229.

————. 2002a. Género y ciudadanía diferenciada en México: Mujeres y hombres indígenas: reinventando la cultura y redefiniendo la nación. In *Ciudadanía, cultura política y reforma del estado en América Latina,* ed. Marco Antonio Calderón Mólgora, Willem Assies, and Ton Salman. Zamora: Colegio de Michoacán / Instituto Federal Electoral.

————. 2002b. ¿Guerra fratricida o estrategia etnocida? Las mujeres frente a la violencia política en Chiapas. In Jacorzynski 2002.

————. 2002c. Indigenous law and identity politics in Mexico: Indigenous men's and women's struggles for a multicultural nation. *PoLAR: Political and Legal Anthropology Review* 25 (1): 90–109.

————. 2002d. National law and indigenous customary law: The struggle for justice of indigenous women in Chiapas, Mexico. In Molyneux and Razavi 2002.

————. 2004. El derecho positivo y la costumbre jurídica: Las mujeres indígenas de Chiapas y su lucha por el acceso a la justicia. In Torres Falcón 2004.

Hernández Castillo, Rosalva Aída, and Anna María Garza Caligaris. 1995. En torno a la ley y la costumbre: Problemas de antropología legal y género en los Altos de Chiapas. In Estrada Martínez and González Guerra 1995.

Hernández Castillo, Rosalva Aída, and María Teresa Sierra. 2005. Repensar los derechos colectivos desde el género: Aportes de las mujeres indígenas al debate de la autonomía. In *La doble mirada: Voces e historias de mujeres indígenas latinoamericanas,* ed. Martha Sánchez Néstor. Mexico City: Fondo de Desarrollo de las Naciones Unidas para la Mujer / Instituto de Liderazgo Simone de Beauvoir.

Hernández Franco, Rosa Hilda. 2000. Desigualdad legal de la mujer ante el varón en el adulterio como causal de divorcio en el Código Civil para el estado de Durango. BA thesis, UNAM.

Hernández Navarro, Luis. 1998. Serpientes y escaleras: Los avatares de la reforma constitucional sobre derechos y cultura indígenas. In *Acuerdos de San Andrés,* ed. Luis Hernández Navarro and Ramón Vera Herrera. Mexico City: Era.

Hinojosa, Claudia. 2002. Gritos y susurros: Una historia sobre la presencia pública de las feministas lesbianas. In Gutiérrez Castañeda 2002b.

Hinojosa Villalobos, Luis Agustín. 2000. *Las sucesiones agrarias.* Puebla: OGS Editores.

Htun, Mala. 2003. *Sex and the state: Abortion, divorce, and the family under Latin American dictatorships and democracies.* New York: Cambridge University Press.

Human Rights Watch. 2006. *The second assault: Obstructing access to legal abortion after rape in Mexico.* New York: Human Rights Watch.

Ibarra Mendivil, Jorge Luis. 1989. *Propiedad agraria y sistema político en México.* Mexico City: Porrúa.

Imberton Deneke, Gracia María. 2002. *La* vergüenza: *Enfermedad y conflicto en una comunidad chol.* San Cristóbal de las Casas: UNAM.

INEGI. See Mexico, Instituto Nacional de Estadística, Geografía e Informática.

Instituto de Investigaciones Jurídicas, ed. 1994. *Derechos indígenas en la actualidad.* Mexico City: UNAM.

Instituto Francés de América Latina. 1983. *Violación: Un análisis feminista del discurso jurídico.* Mexico City: Instituto Francés de América Latina.

Jacorzynski, Witold, ed. 2002. *Estudios sobre la violencia: Teoría y práctica.* Mexico City: CIESAS / Porrúa.

Jastrow Becerra, M. Josefina. 1982. Los derechos humanos y la nacionalidad de la mujer casada. BA thesis, UNAM.

Jiménez Huerta, Mariano. 1968. *Derecho penal mexicano*. Vol. 3. Mexico City: Libros de México.

Kanter, Deborah E. 1993. Hijos del pueblo: Family, community, and gender in rural Mexico: The Toluca region, 1730–1830. PhD thesis, University of Virginia.

———. 1995. Native female land tenure and its decline in Mexico, 1750–1900. *Ethnohistory* 42 (4): 607–626.

Kardam, Nuket. 2005. *Turkey's engagement with global women's human rights.* Aldershot: Ashgate.

Kellogg, Susan. 1995. *Law and the transformation of Aztec culture, 1500–1700.* Norman: University of Oklahoma Press.

———. 1997. From parallel and equivalent to separate but unequal: Tenocha Mexica women, 1500–1700. In Schroeder, Wood, and Haskett 1997.

Knight, Alan. 1994. Popular culture and the revolutionary state in Mexico, 1910–1940. *Hispanic American Historical Review* 74 (3): 393–444.

Knop, Karen, ed. 2004. *Gender and human rights.* Oxford: Oxford University Press.

Kourí, Emilio H. 2002. Interpreting the expropriation of Indian pueblo lands in Porfirian Mexico: The unexamined legacies of Andrés Molina Enríquez. *Hispanic American Historical Review* 82 (1): 69–117.

Kovic, Christine M. 2005. *Mayan voices for human rights: Displaced Catholics in highland Chiapas.* Austin: University of Texas Press.

Kristeva, Julia. 1991. *Strangers to ourselves.* Trans. Leon S. Roudiez. New York: Columbia University Press.

Kulczycki, Andrzej. 2003. De eso no se habla: Aceptando el aborto en México. *Estudios Demográficos y Urbanos* 18 (2), no. 53: 353–386.

Kulick, Don. 1996. Causing a commotion: Public scandal as resistance among Brazilian transgendered prostitutes. *Anthropology Today* 12 (6): 3–7.

Kurczyn Villalobos, Patricia. 1975. Las condiciones laborales de las mujeres en los contratos colectivos. Mexico City: privately printed.

———. 1998. El constitucionalismo social frente a la reforma en el derecho del trabajo en México. *Boletín Mexicano de Derecho Comparado* 31 (92): 399–420.

———. 2000. *Derechos de las mujeres trabajadoras.* Mexico City: Cámara de Diputados / UNAM.

———. 2004. *Acoso sexual y discriminación por maternidad en el trabajo.* Mexico City: UNAM.

Kuznesof, Elizabeth Anne. 1992. The construction of gender in colonial Latin America. *Colonial Latin American Review* 1 (1–2): 253–270.

Lamas, Marta. 2001. *Política y reproducción: Aborto: La frontera del derecho a decidir.* Mexico City: Plaza y Janés.

———. 2002. Fragmentos de una autocrítica. In Gutiérrez Castañeda 2002b.

Lamas, Marta, and Sharon Bissell. 2000. Abortion and politics in Mexico: Context is all. *Reproductive Health Matters* 8 (16): 10–23.

Laqueur, Thomas W. 1990. *Making sex: Body and gender from the Greeks to Freud.* Cambridge, MA: Harvard University Press.

Larrauri, Elena. 1994. Control informal: Las penas de las mujeres . . . In *Mujeres, derecho penal y criminología,* ed. Elena Larrauri. Mexico City: Siglo XXI.

Lau Jaiven, Ana, and Carmen Ramos Escandón. 1993. *Mujeres y revolución, 1900–1917.* Mexico City: Instituto Nacional de Estudios Históricos de la Revolución Mexicana.

Lavrin, Asunción. 1978. In search of the colonial woman in Mexico: The seventeenth and eighteenth centuries. In *Latin American women: Historical perspectives,* ed. Asunción Lavrin. Westport: Greenwood Press.

——. 1989a. Introduction: The scenario, the actors, and the issues. In Lavrin 1989b.

——, ed. 1989b. *Sexuality and marriage in colonial Latin America.* Lincoln: University of Nebraska Press.

——. 1989c. Sexuality in colonial Mexico: A church dilemma. In Lavrin 1989b.

Lazarus-Black, Mindie, and Susan F. Hirsch, eds. 1994. *Contested states: Law, hegemony, and resistance.* New York: Routledge.

Legros, Monique. 1982. Acerca de un diálogo que no lo fue. In Seminario de Historia de las Mentalidades 1982.

Lemus García, Raúl. 1991. *Derecho agrario mexicano.* 7th ed. Mexico City: Porrúa.

Leret de Matheus, María Gabriela. 1975. *La mujer, una incapaz como el demente y el niño (según las leyes latinoamericanas).* Mexico City: Costa-Amic.

Lewis, Laura A. 1996. Colonialism and its contradictions: Indians, blacks, and social power in sixteenth and seventeenth century Mexico. *Journal of Historical Sociology* 9 (4): 410–431.

——. 2003. *Hall of mirrors: Power, witchcraft, and caste in colonial Mexico.* Durham, NC: Duke University Press.

Lewis, Oscar. 1960. *Tepoztlán, village in Mexico.* New York: Holt.

Leyva Solano, Xóchitl. 2003. Regional, communal, and organizational transformations in las Cañadas. In Rus, Hernández Castillo, and Mattiace 2003.

Leyva Solano, Xóchitl, and Gabriel Ascencio Franco. 1996. *Lacandonia al filo del agua.* Mexico City, San Cristóbal de las Casas, and Tuxtla Gutiérrez: CIESAS / UNAM / Universidad de Ciencias y Artes del Estado de Chiapas / Fondo de Cultura Económica.

Lim, Hilary. 1996. Mapping equity's place: Here be dragons. In *Feminist perspectives on the foundational subjects of law,* ed. Anne Bottomley. London: Cavendish.

Lim, Lin Lean, ed. 1988. *The sex sector: The economic and social bases of prostitution in Southeast Asia.* Geneva: International Labour Office

Lipsett-Rivera, Sonya. 1996. La violencia dentro de las familias formal e informal. In Gonzalbo Aizpuru and Rabell Romero 1996.

——. 2001. Marriage and family relations in Mexico during the transition from colony to nation. In *State and society in Spanish America during the age of revolution,* ed. Victor M. Uribe-Uran. Wilmington, DE: Scholarly Resources.

Lomnitz, Claudio. 2001. *Deep Mexico, silent Mexico: An anthropology of nationalism.* Minneapolis: University of Minnesota Press.

Loos, Eugene E., Susan Anderson, Dwight H. Day Jr., Paul C. Jordan, and J. Douglas Wingate, eds. 1999. *Glossary of linguistic terms.* In *LinguaLinks Library,* ed. SIL International. Version 4.0. Dallas, TX: SIL International. CD-ROM. Also available online at http://www.sil.org/linguistics/GlossaryOfLinguisticTerms/.

López-Portillo y Rojas, José. 1975. *Elevación y caída de Porfirio Díaz.* 2nd ed. Mexico City: Porrúa.

Lovera, Sara, and Nellys Palomo, eds. 1997. *Las alzadas.* Mexico City: Comunicación e Información de la Mujer AC / Convergencia Socialista.

Lozano Armendares, Teresa. 1987. *La criminalidad en la ciudad de México, 1800–1821.* Mexico City: UNAM.

Luna Arroyo, Antonio, and Luis G. Alcérreca. 1982. *Diccionario de derecho agrario mexicano.* Mexico City: Porrúa.

Macías, Anna. 1982. *Against all odds: The feminist movement in Mexico to 1940.* Westport, CT: Greenwood Press.

Macpherson, C. B. (Crawford Brough). 1962. *The political theory of possessive individualism: Hobbes to Locke.* Oxford: Clarendon Press.

Madrid Romero, Elvira. 2002. *La prevención del VIH/SIDA como práctica de la libertad entre trabajadoras y trabajadores sexuales.* Mexico City: Red Mexicana de Trabajo Sexual / Brigada Callejera de Apoyo a la Mujer "Elisa Martínez."

Makowski Muchnik, Sara E. 1994. Las flores del mal: Identidad y resistencia en cárceles de mujeres. Master's thesis, Facultad Latinoamericana de Ciencias Sociales, Mexico City.

———. 1996. Identidad y subjetividad en cárceles de mujeres. *Estudios Sociológicos* 14 (40): 53–73.

Mantilla López, Graciela. 1965. Los derechos agrarios de la mujer campesina. BA thesis, UNAM.

Marcos, Sylvia. 1994. Decidir abortar o no: Un derecho moral. In Ortiz-Ortega 1994b.

Margadant, Guillermo F. 1991. La familia en el derecho novohispano. In Gonzalbo Aizpuru 1991.

Marshall, T. H. (Thomas Humphrey). 1964. *Class, citizenship, and social development.* New York: Doubleday.

Martínez, Ernesto. 1983. *Guía legal de la mujer: Manual informativo para que el sexo débil conozca y defienda sus derechos, elaborado conforme a las leyes mexicanas vigentes.* Mexico City: Editores Asociados Mexicanos.

Martínez Corona, Beatriz, and Susana Mejía Flores. 1997. *Ideología y práctica en delitos cometidos contra mujeres: El sistema judicial y la violencia en una región indígena de Puebla, México.* Puebla: Colegio de Postgraduados, Campus Puebla.

Martínez Sánchez, Martín Alberto. 1996. La desigualdad jurídica entre el varón y la mujer contenida en el articulo 270 (efectos de la sentencia de divorcio) del Código Civil del Estado de México. BA thesis, UNAM.

Mattiace, Shannan L. 2003a. Regional renegotiations of space: Tojolabal ethnic identity in Las Margaritas, Chiapas. In Rus, Hernández Castillo, and Mattiace 2003.

———. 2003b. *To see with two eyes: Peasant activism and Indian autonomy in Chiapas, Mexico.* Albuquerque: University of New Mexico Press.

Mazadiego López, Xóchitl. 1966. Estudio sobre el trabajo de la mujer y su reglamentación. BA thesis, UNAM.

McKee Irwin, Robert, Edward J. McCaughan, Michelle Rocio Nasser, eds. 2003. *The famous 41: Sexuality and social control in Mexico, 1901.* Basingstoke, UK: Palgrave Macmillan.

McKnight, Kathryn Joy. 1999. Blasphemy as resistance: An African slave woman before the Mexican Inquisition. In *Women in the Inquisition: Spain and the New World,* ed. Mary E. Giles. Baltimore, MD: John Hopkins University Press.

Mehrotra, Aparna. 1998. *Gender and legislation in Latin America and the Caribbean.* New York: United Nations Development Program Regional Bureau for Latin America and the Caribbean. Published online at http://www.undp.org/rblac/gender/legislation/.

Mejía Flores, Susana, Rufina Edith Villa Hernández, and Cecilia Oyorzabal G. 2003. Violencia y justicia hacia la mujer nahua de Cuetzalan. In Bonfil Sánchez and Martínez Medrano 2003.

Mendiara, Irina. 2002. Modos de aparición: Imágenes travestis y representaciones deseables. *Studium,* no. 10. Online at http://www.studium.iar.unicamp.br/10/5.html.

Merry, Sally E. 1995. Gender violence and legally engendered selves. *Identities: Global studies in culture and power* 2 (1–2): 49–74.

———. 2006. *Human rights and gender violence: Translating international law into local justice.* Chicago: University of Chicago Press.

Mexico, Cámara de Diputados. Comisión de Equidad y Género. 2000. Memoria 1997–2000. Congreso de la Unión, Mexico City. http://www.cddhcu.gob.mx/camdip/ccdip/comlvii/cdip47.htm#MEMORIA.

Mexico, Congreso de la Unión. 1969. *Derechos de la mujer mexicana.* Mexico City: Congreso de la Unión.

Mexico, Instituto Nacional de Estadística, Geografía e Informática. 1995. *Chiapas. Datos por ejido y comunidad agraria: XI Censo General de Población y Vivienda, 1990, VII Censo Agropecuario, 1991.* Aguascalientes: INEGI.

———. 2000. *Estadísticas judiciales en materia penal: Cuaderno no. 8*. Aguascalientes: INEGI.

———. 2003. *Perfil sociodemográfico del Estado de México: XII Censo General de Población y Vivienda 2000*. Aguascalientes: INEGI.

Mexico, Secretaría de Industria y Comercio. Dirección General de Estadística. 1973. *IX Censo General de Población y Vivienda, 1970: Estado de México*. Mexico City: Secretaría de Industria y Comercio.

Mexico, Secretaría de la Reforma Agraria. 1988. *La transformación agraria: Origen, evolución, retos, testimonios*. 2nd ed. Mexico City: Secretaría de la Reforma Agraria.

Meyer, Lorenzo, Rafael Segovia, and Alejandra Lajous. 1978. *Los inicios de la institucionalización: La política del Maximato*. Vol. 12 of *Historia de la revolución mexicana*. Mexico City: Colegio de México.

Meza Escorza, Tania. 2006. Pugnan por una Ley de Identidad de Género. *Comunicación e Información de la Mujer*, July 26. http://www.cimacnoticias.com/site/06072604-Pugnan-por-una-Ley. 632.0.html

Miano Borruso, Marinella. 1999. Hombres, mujeres y muxe en la sociedad zapoteca del Istmo de Tehuantepec. PhD thesis, Escuela Nacional de Antropología e Historia, Mexico City.

Millán, Márgara. 1996. Las zapatistas de fin del milenio: Hacia políticas de autorepresentación de las mujeres indígenas. *Chiapas,* no. 3: 19–32.

Molyneux, Maxine. 1985. Mobilization without emancipation: Women's interests, the state, and revolution in Nicaragua. *Feminist Studies* 11 (2): 227–254.

———. 2001. *Women's movements in international perspective: Latin America and beyond*. Basingstoke, UK: Palgrave.

Molyneux, Maxine, and Shahra Razavi, eds. 2002. *Gender justice, development, and rights*. New York: Oxford University Press.

Montero Duhalt, Sara. 1984. *Derecho de familia*. Mexico City: Porrúa.

Morales Jurado, Alvaro. 1954. La mujer campesina mexicana. BA thesis, UNAM.

Moreno de P., Antonio. 1944. *Curso de derecho penal mexicano. Parte especial: Delitos en particular*. Mexico City: Jus.

Mummert, Gail, and Luis Alfonso Ramírez Carrillo, eds. 1998. *Rehaciendo las diferencias: Identidades de género en Michoacán y Yucatán*. Zamora and Mérida: Colegio de Michoacán / Universidad Autónoma de Yucatán.

Muñiz, Elsa, and Adriana Corona. 1996. Indigenismo y género: Violencia doméstica. *Nueva Antropología* 15 (49): 41–58.

Muñoz de Alba Medrano, Marcia. 1988. La condición jurídica de la mujer en la doctrina mexicana del siglo XIX. In *Memoria del Cuarto Congreso de Historia del Derecho Mexicano,* Vol. 2, ed. Beatriz Bernal Gómez. Mexico City: UNAM.

Muñozcano Skidmore, Dolores. 1995. Análisis del Código Penal en relación con los delitos de violación sexual, desde una perspective sociológica. In *Memoria de la Reunión Nacional sobre Derechos Humanos de la Mujer,* ed. Comisión Nacional de Derechos Humanos. Mexico City: Comisión Nacional de Derechos Humanos.

Muro González, Víctor Gabriel. 1991. Iglesia y movimientos sociales en México: 1972–1987. *Estudios Sociológicos* 9 (27): 541–556.

Nader, Laura. 1964a. An analysis of Zapotec law cases. *Ethnology* 3 (4): 404–419.

———. 1964b. *Talea and Juquila: A comparison of Zapotec social organization*. Berkeley and Los Angeles: University of California Press.

———, ed. 1965. The ethnography of law. Special issue, *American Anthropologist* 67 (6), pt. 2.

———. 1969. Styles of court procedure: To make the balance. In *Law in culture and society,* ed. Laura Nader. Chicago: Aldine.

———. 1990. *Harmony ideology: Justice and control in a Zapotec mountain village*. Stanford, CA: Stanford University Press.

Nader, Laura, and Jane F. Collier. 1978. Justice: a woman blindfolded? In *Women in the courts*, ed. Winnifred L. Hepperle and Laura Crites. Williamsburg, VA: National Center for State Courts.

Nader, Laura, and Duane Metzger. 1963. Conflict resolution in two Mexican communities. *American Anthropologist* 65 (3): 584–592.

Nash, June. 1972. Rhetoric of a Maya Indian court. *Estudios de Cultura Maya*, no. 8: 239–296.

Nieto Castillo, Santiago. 2001. Notas sobre igualdad, feminismo y derecho. *Boletín Mexicano de Derecho Comparado* 34 (102): 841–856.

Nugent, Daniel. 1993. *Spent cartridges of revolution: An anthropological history of Namiquipa, Chihuahua*. Chicago: University of Chicago Press.

Nugent, David. 1997. *Modernity at the edge of empire: State, individual, and nation in the northern Peruvian Andes, 1885–1935*. Stanford, CA: Stanford University Press.

Nuijten, Monique. 2003a. Family property and the limits of intervention: The Article 27 reforms and the PROCEDE programme in Mexico. *Development and Change* 34 (3): 475–497.

———. 2003b. *Power, community, and the state: The political anthropology of organisation in Mexico*. London: Pluto Press.

Núñez Becerra, Fernanda. 2002. *La prostitución y su represión en la ciudad de México (siglo XIX): Prácticas y representaciones*. Barcelona: Gedisa.

Núñez Miranda, Concepción. 2004. Mujeres en prisión: ¿Trasgresión u opresión? *Acervos: Boletín de los archivos y bibliotecas de Oaxaca*, no. 27: 65–72.

Nutini, Hugo G. 1968. *San Bernardino Contla: Marriage and family structure in a Tlaxcalan municipio*. Pittsburgh, PA: University of Pittsburgh Press.

Ochoa Flores, María del Carmen. 1968. Desarrollo social de la mujer mexicana. BA thesis, UNAM.

Ochoa Pérez, Verónica. 1997–1998. Sucesiones en materia agraria. *Estudios Agrarios* (Procuraduría Agraria), no. 9: 61–95.

Ojeda, Norma. 1986. Separación y divorcio en México: Una perspectiva demográfica. *Estudios Demográficos y Urbanos* I (2), no. 2: 227–265.

Olamendi Torres, Patricia, ed. 1998. *La mujer en la legislación mexicana*. 2 vols. Mexico City: Senado de la República.

Olcott, Jocelyn H., 2005. *Revolutionary women in postrevolutionary Mexico*. Durham, NC: Duke University Press.

Olcott, Jocelyn H., Mary Kay Vaughan, and Gabriela Cano, eds. 2006. *Sex in revolution: Gender, politics, and power in modern Mexico*. Durham, NC: Duke University Press.

Ortega Noriega, Sergio, ed. 1986. *De la santidad a la perversión: O de por qué no se cumplía la ley de Dios en la sociedad novohispana*. Mexico City: Grijalbo.

———. 1988. El discurso teológico de Santo Tomás de Aquino sobre el matrimonio, la familia y los comportamientos sexuales. In Seminario de Historia de las Mentalidades 1988.

———. 1989. Los téologos y la teología novohispana sobre el matrimonio, la familia y los comportamientos sexuales: Del Concilio de Trento al fin de la colonia. In Guzmán Vázquez and Martínez O. 1989b.

Ortega Ramos, Virginia. 1955. Protección a la mujer en el derecho del trabajo. BA thesis, UNAM.

Ortiz-Ortega, Adriana. 1994a. Entrevista con Jorge Serrano Limón. In Ortiz-Ortega 1994b.

———, ed. 1994b. *Razones y pasiones en torno al aborto: Una contribución al debate*. Mexico City: Population Council / EDAMEX

———. 2000. *Si los hombres se embarazaran, ¿el aborto sería legal? Las feministas ante la relación estado–iglesia católica en México (1871–2000)*. Mexico City: Population Council / EDAMEX.

Ots Capdequí, José María. 1941. *El estado español en las Indias*. Mexico City: Fondo de Cultura Económica.

Owensby, Brian P. 2005. How Juan and Leonor won their freedom: Litigation and liberty in seventeenth-century Mexico. *Hispanic American Historical Review* 85 (1): 39–79.

Palacios Escobar, Rita. 1977. La mujer campesina y la reforma agraria integral. BA thesis, UNAM.

Palavicini, Félix F. 1937. *Mi vida revolucionaria*. Mexico City: Botas.

Palmer, Colin A. 1976. *Slaves of the white God: Blacks in Mexico, 1570–1650*. Cambridge, MA: Harvard University Press.

Palomo, Nellys, Yolanda Castro, and Cristina Orci. 1997. Mujeres indígenas de Chiapas: Nuestros derechos, costumbres y tradiciones. In Lovera and Palomo 1997.

Parker, Richard G. 1993. The negotiation of difference: Male prostitution, bisexual behaviour, and HIV transmission. In *Sexuality, politics, and AIDS in Brazil: In another world?*, ed. Herbert Daniel and Richard G. Parker. London: Falmer Press.

Parnell, Philip C. 1988. *Escalating disputes: Social participation and change in the Oaxaca highlands*. Tucson: University of Arizona Press.

Pashukanis, Evgeny B. 1978. *Law and Marxism. A general theory*. Ed. Chris Arthur and trans. Barbara Einhorn. London: Ink Links. (Orig. pub. 1924.)

Pateman, Carole. 1988 *The sexual contract*. Stanford, CA: Stanford University Press.

Payán, Carlos, ed. 1975. *Los derechos de la mujer*. Mexico City: Consejo Nacional de Población.

Pedrero, María Ester. 1959. La condición jurídica de la mujer mexicana y sus conquistas en el derecho agrario. BA thesis, UNAM.

Penyak, Lee M. 1999. Safe harbors and compulsory custody: *Casas de depósito* in Mexico, 1750–1865. *Hispanic American Historical Review* 79 (1): 83–99.

Pérez, Emma M. 1988. Through her love and sweetness: Women, revolution, and reform in Yucatán, 1910–1918. PhD thesis, University of Californa–Los Angeles.

Pérez Carbajal y Campuzano, Hilda. 1975. Evolución histórica de los derechos familiares de la mujer. BA thesis, UNAM.

Pérez Castañeda, Juan Carlos. 1995. Las reformas a la legislación agraria en el marco de la propiedad territorial. In *El campo mexicano en el umbral del siglo XXI*, ed. Alejandro Encinas Rodríguez. Mexico City: Espasa Calpe.

Pérez Contreras, María de Montserrat. 2000. *Derechos de los homosexuales*. Mexico City: Cámara de Diputados / UNAM.

———. 2001. *Aspectos jurídicos de la violencia contra la mujer en México*. Mexico City: Porrúa.

———. 2004. *Discriminación de la mujer trabajadora: Fundamentos para la regulación del hostigamiento sexual laboral en México*. Mexico City: Porrúa.

Pérez Duarte y Noroña, Alicia Elena. 1993. *El aborto: Una lectura de derecho comparado*. Mexico City: Universidad Nacional Autónoma de México.

———. 1994. *Derecho de familia*. Mexico City: Fondo de Cultura Económica.

———, ed. 1995. *Marco legal de los derechos de la mujer en México*. Mexico City: Comité Coordinador para la Cuarta Conferencia Mundial sobre la Mujer / Consejo Nacional de Población / Fondo de Población de la Naciones Unidas.

———. 1997. La mujer y la familia indígenas en el contexto de la legislación. In *La condición de la mujer indígena y sus derechos fundamentales*, ed. Patricia Galeana. Mexico City: UNAM.

———. 2002. *Legislar con perspectiva de género: Evaluación legislativa en materia de derechos humanos de las mujeres, niñas y niños*. Mexico City: Instituto Nacional de las Mujeres.

Pérez-Gil Romo, Sara Elena, and Patricia Ravelo Blancas, eds. 2004. *Voces disidentes: Debates contemporáneos en los estudios de género en México.* Mexico City: Cámara de Diputados / CIESAS / Porrúa.

Pérez Guerrero, Faustino. 1976. La mujer en la reforma del derecho mexicano del trabajo. BA thesis, UNAM.

Pescador, Juan Javier. 1996. Del dicho al hecho: Uxoricidios en el México central, 1769–1820. In Gonzalbo Aizpuru and Rabell Romero 1996.

Petchesky, Rosalind P., and Karen Judd, eds. 2006. *Negotiating reproductive rights: Women's perspectives across countries and cultures.* 2nd. ed. London: Zed Books.

Piccato, Pablo. 2001. *City of suspects: Crime in Mexico City, 1900–1931.* Durham, NC: Duke University Press.

Pita Moreda, María Teresa. 1996. Conflictos familiares y tribunales de justicia a finales de la colonia: algunos casos novohispanos. In Gonzalbo Aizpuru and Rabell Romero 1996.

Pitt-Rivers, Julian A. 1977. *The fate of Shechem, or, the politics of sex: Essays in the anthropology of the Mediterranean.* Cambridge: Cambridge University Press.

Pizzigoni, Caterina. 2004. "Para que le sirva de castigo y al pueblo de ejemplo": El pecado de poligamia y la mujer indígena en el valle de Toluca (siglo XVIII). In *Las mujeres en la construcción de las sociedades iberoamericanas,* ed. Pilar Gonzalbo Aizpuru and Berta Ares Queija. Seville and Mexico City: Consejo Superior de Investigaciones Científicas / Colegio de México.

———. 2005. "Como frágil y miserable": Las mujeres nahuas del Valle de Toluca. In *El siglo XVIII: Entre tradición y cambio.* Vol. 3 of *Historia de la vida cotidiana en México,* ed. Pilar Gonzalbo Aizpuru. Mexico City: Colegio de México / Fondo de Cultura Económica.

Plummer, David. 2001. Policing manhood: New theories about the social significance of homophobia. In *Sexual positions: An Australian view,* ed. Carl Wood. Melbourne: Hill of Content / Collins.

Poniatowska, Elena. 2000. *Las mil y una . . . (la herida de Paulina).* Mexico City: Plaza y Janés.

Porte Petit Candaudap, Celestino. 1966. *Dogmática sobre los delitos contra la vida y la salud personal: Estudio comparativo con los códigos penales de las entidades federativas.* Mexico City: Jurídica Mexicana.

———. 1972. *Ensayo dogmático sobre el delito de estupro.* 2nd ed. Mexico City: Jurídica Mexicana.

Porter, Susie S. 2000. And that it is custom makes it law: Class conflict and gender ideology in the public sphere, Mexico City, 1880–1910. *Social Science History* 24 (1): 111–148.

Pretelín, Jesús. 2002. Entre cocteles y cotorreos: Prácticas homoeróticas en un cine porno del Puerto de Veracruz. BA thesis, Universidad Veracruzana.

Prieur, Annick. 1998. *Mema's house, Mexico City: On transvestites, queens, and machos.* Chicago: University of Chicago Press.

Procuraduría Agraria. 1998. *Los tratos agrarios en ejidos certificados.* Mexico City: Procuraduría Agraria.

Putnam, Laura, Sarah C. Chambers, and Sueann Caulfield. 2005. Introduction: Transformations in honor, status, and law over the long ninenteenth century. In *Honor, status, and law in modern Latin America,* ed. Sueann Caulfield, Sarah C. Chambers, and Laura Putnam. Durham, NC: Duke University Press.

Quilodrán, Julieta. 2000. Atisbos de cambios en la formación de las parejas conyugales a fines del milenio. *Papeles de Población* (Universidad Autónoma del Estado de México) 6 (25): 9–33.

Rahman, Anika, Laura Katzive, and Stanley K. Henshaw. 1998. A global review of laws on induced abortion, 1985–1997. *International Family Planning Perspectives* 24 (2): 56–64.

Ramos Escandón, Carmen. 1987. Señoritas porfirianas: Mujer e ideología en el México progresista, 1880–1910. In Ramos Encandón et al., 1987.

———. 2001a. Genaro García, historiador feminista de fin de siglo. *Signos Históricos,* no. 5: 87–107.

———. 2001b. Legislación y representación de género en la nación mexicana: La mujer y la familia en el discurso y la ley (1870–1890). In *Mujeres y naciones en América Latina: Problemas de inclusión y exclusión,* ed. Barbara Potthast and Eugenia Scarzanella. Frankfurt and Madrid: Vervuert / Iberoamericana.

———. 2001c. Mujeres positivas: Los retos de la modernidad en las relaciones de género y la construcción del parámetro femenino en el fin de siglo mexicano, 1880–1910. In Agostoni and Speckman Guerra 2001.

———. 2005. Cambio jurídico y jerarquía familiar en el México decimonónico: Género y generación en el control de la patria postestad. In *Análisis del cambio sociocultural,* ed. Magdalena Barros and Rosario Esteinou. Mexico City: CIESAS.

Ramos Escandón, Carmen, María de Jesús Rodríguez, Pilar Gonzalbo Aizpuru, François Giraud, Solange Alberro, Françoise Carner, Soledad González Montes, Pilar Iracheta, Jean Pierre Bastian, and Enriqueta Tuñón Pablos, eds. 1987. *Presencia y transparencia: La mujer en la historia de México.* Mexico City: Colegio de México.

Razavi, Shahra, ed. 2003. *Agrarian change, gender, and land rights.* Oxford: Blackwell.

Rincón Serrano, Romeo. 1980. *El ejido mexicano.* Mexico City: Centro Nacional de Investigaciones Agrarias.

Rivera-Garza, Cristina. 2001. The criminalization of the syphilitic body: Prostitutes, health crimes, and society in Mexico City, 1867–1930. In Salvatore, Aguirre, and Joseph 2001.

Robichaux, David, ed. 2003. *El matrimonio en Mesoamérica ayer y hoy: Unas miradas antropológicas.* Mexico City: Universidad Iberoamericana.

Robles Berlanga, Héctor M., Gloria Artís, Julieta Salazar, and Laura Muñoz. 2000. *. . . y ando yo también en el campo! Presencia de la mujer en el agro mexicano.* Mexico City: Procuraduría Agraria.

Rojas, Rosa, ed. 1999. *Chiapas: ¿Y las mujeres qué?* 3rd ed. Mexico City: La Correa Feminista.

Romo Chávez Mejía, Enriqueta. 1963. Reforma del Código Agrario en beneficio de la mujer campesina. BA thesis, UNAM.

Rovira, Guiomar. 1997. *Mujeres de maíz.* Mexico City: Era.

Rubio Goldsmith, Raquel. 1998. Civilization, barbarism, and norteña gardens. In *Making worlds: Gender, metaphor, materiality,* ed. Susan Hardy Aiken, Ann Brigham, Sallie A. Marston, and Penny Waterstone. Tucson: University of Arizona Press.

Rus, Jan, Rosalva Aída Hernández Castillo, and Shannan L. Mattiace, eds. 2003. *Mayan lives, Mayan utopias: The indigenous peoples of Chiapas and the Zapatista rebellion.* Lanham: Rowan and Littlefield.

Salles, Vania. 1998. Sobre grupos domésticos y las familias campesinas: Algo de teoría y método. In *La sociedad frente al mercado,* ed. María Tarrío García and Luciano Concheiro Bórquez. Mexico City: La Jornada / Universidad Autónoma Metropolitana-Xochimilco.

Salvatore, Ricardo D., Carlos A. Aguirre, and Gilbert M. Joseph, eds. 2001. *Crime and punishment in Latin America: Law and society since late colonial times.* Durham, NC: Duke University Press.

San Andrés Accords on Indigenous Rights and Culture. 1999. *San Andrés Accords on Indigenous Rights and Culture.* Trans. Lynn Stephen and Jonathan Fox. *Cultural Survival Quarterly* 23 (1): 33–38.

Sánchez Medal, Ramón. 1974. *El divorcio opcional.* Mexico City: Porrúa.

———. 1979. *Los grandes cambios en el derecho de familia en México.* Mexico City: Porrúa.

San Martín, Alma Celia. 2003. Policías de Veracruz extorsionan a sexoservidoras. *Comunicación e Información de la Mujer,* March 25. http://www.cimacnoticias.com/noticias/ 03mar/03032501.html.

Santos, Boaventura de Sousa. 1987. Law: A map of misreading: Toward a postmodern conception of law. *Journal of Law and Society* 14 (3): 279–302.

Scardaville, Michael C. 2000. (Hapsburg) law and (Bourbon) order: State authority, popular unrest, and the criminal justice system in Bourbon Mexico City. In *Reconstructing criminality in Latin America,* ed. Carlos A. Aguirre and Robert Buffington. Wilmington, DE: Scholarly Resources.

Schell, Patience A. 2003. *Church and state education in revolutionary Mexico City.* Tucson: University of Arizona Press.

Schroeder, Susan, Stephanie Wood, and Robert Haskett, eds. 1997. *Indian women of early Mexico.* Norman: University of Oklahoma Press.

Secretaría de la Reforma Agraria. See Mexico, Secretaría de la Reforma Agraria.

Seed, Patricia. 1988a. Marriage promises and the value of a woman's testimony in colonial Mexico. *Signs: Journal of Women in Culture and Society* 13 (2): 253–276.

———. 1988b. *To love, honor, and obey in colonial Mexico: Conflicts over marriage choice, 1574–1821.* Stanford, CA: Stanford University Press.

Seminario de Historia de las Mentalidades, ed. 1982. *Familia y sexualidad en Nueva España: Memoria del Primer Simposio de Historia de las Mentalidades.* Mexico City: Fondo de Cultura Económica.

———, ed. 1985. *La memoria y el olvido: Segundo Simposio de Historia de las Mentalidades.* Mexico City: INAH.

———, ed. 1988. *El placer de pecar y el afán de normar.* Mexico City: Joaquín Mortiz / INAH.

———, ed. 1994. *Comunidades domésticas en la sociedad novohispana: Formas de unión y transmisión cultural. Memoria del Cuarto Simposio de Historia de las Mentalidades.* Mexico City: INAH.

———, ed. 2000. *Vida cotidiana y cultural en el México virreinal: Antología.* Mexico City: INAH.

Sentíes, Yolanda, ed. 1984. *Los derechos de la mujer en la legislación mexicana.* Mexico City: Macció.

Servicio Internacional para la Paz. 2003. Resistance and autonomy: The creation of the Zapatista Juntas of Good Government. *SIPAZ Report* 8 (2): 1–6.

Shelton, Laura M. 2004. Families in the courtroom: Law, community, and gender in northwestern Mexico, 1800–1850. PhD thesis, University of Arizona.

Sierra, María Teresa. 1992. *Discurso, cultura y poder: El ejercicio discursivo de la autoridad en pueblos Hñähñús del Valle del Mezquital.* Mexico City and Pachuca: CIESAS / Gobierno del Estado de Hidalgo.

———. 1995. Indian rights and customary law in Mexico: A study of the Nahuas of the Sierra Norte de Puebla. *Law and Society Review* 29 (2): 227–254.

———. 1998. Autonomía y pluralismo jurídico: El debate mexicano. *América Indígena* 58 (1–2): 21–48.

———. 2000. Hay derechos humanos en Zacapoaxtla: Género, legalidad y derechos en la Sierra Norte de Puebla. In Castro Lučić 2000.

———. 2001. Human rights, gender, and ethnicity: Legal claims and anthropological challenges in Mexico. *PoLAR: Political and Legal Anthropology Review* 24 (2): 76–93.

———. 2002. The challenge to diversity in Mexico: Human rights, gender, and ethnicity. Working Paper 49, Max Planck Institute for Social Anthropology, Halle / Salle, Germany.

——. 2003. The rhetoric of diversity and the challenge of multiculturalism: The debate on human rights and indigenous jurisdiction in Mexico. Paper presented at the Annual Meeting of the American Anthropological Association, November 19–23, Chicago.

——. 2004a. Derecho indígena y mujeres: Viejas costumbres, nuevos derechos. In Pérez-Gil Romo and Ravelo Blancas 2004.

——. 2004b. Diálogos y prácticas interculturales: Derechos humanos, derechos de las mujeres y políticas de identidad. *Desacatos,* nos. 15–16: 126–147.

——. 2004c. Hacia una interpretación comprensiva de la relación entre justicia, derecho y género: Los procesos legales en regiones indígenas. In Sierra 2004d.

——, ed. 2004d. *Haciendo justicia: Interlegalidad, derecho y género en regiones indígenas.* Mexico City: CIESAS / Porrúa / Cámara de Diputados.

——. 2004e. Interlegalidad, justicia y derechos en la Sierra Norte de Puebla. In Sierra 2004d.

Sierra, Teresa, and Victoria Chenaut. 2002. Los debates recientes y actuales en la antropología jurídica. In *Antropología jurídica: Perspectivas socioculturales en el estudio del derecho,* ed. Esteban Krotz. Barcelona and Mexico City: Anthropos / Universidad Autónoma de México–Iztapalapa.

Smith, Stephanie J. 2006. If love enslaves, love be damned! Divorce and revolutionary state formation in Yucatán, Mexico. In Olcott, Vaughan, and Cano 2006.

Solís Cámara, Vicente. 1956. La condición jurídica de la mujer casada en México. BA thesis, UNAM.

Solís Marcin, Fernando. 1939. En defensa de la Ley de Divorcio vigente en el estado. BA thesis, Universidad de Yucatán.

Soria, Hilda. 2004. Busca iniciativa de Ley de Trabajo Sexual proteger derechos. *Comunicación e Información de la Mujer,* October 21. http://www.cimacnoticias.com/noticias/04oct/04102107.html.

Soto, Shirlene. 1990. *Emergence of the modern Mexican woman: Her participation in revolution and struggle for equality, 1910–1940.* Denver, CO: Arden Press.

Sousa, Lisa Mary. 1997. Women and crime in colonial Oaxaca: Evidence of complementary gender roles in Mixtec and Zapotec societies. In Schroeder, Wood, and Haskett 1997.

Speckman Guerra, Elisa. 2001. Las tablas de la ley en la era de la modernidad: Normas y valores en la legislación porfiriana. In Agostoni and Speckman Guerra 2001.

——. 2002. *Crimen y castigo: Legislación penal, interpretaciones de la criminalidad y administración de justicia (Ciudad de México, 1872–1910).* Mexico City: Colegio de México / UNAM.

Speed, Shannon. 2006. Rights at the intersection: Gender and ethnicity in neoliberal Mexico. In Speed, Hernández, and Stephen 2006.

Speed, Shannon, and Jane F. Collier. 1999. Limiting indigenous autonomy in Chiapas, Mexico: The state government's use of human rights. *Human Rights Quarterly* 22 (4): 877–905.

Speed, Shannon, Rosalva Aída Hernández Castillo, and Lynn Stephen, eds. 2006. *Dissident women: Gender and cultural politics in Chiapas.* Austin: University of Texas Press.

Spota Valencia, Alma L. 1967. *La igualdad jurídica de la mujer en México.* Mexico City: Porrúa.

Starr, June, and Jane F. Collier. 1989. Introduction: Dialogues in legal anthropology. In *History and power in the study of law: New directions in legal anthropology,* ed. June Starr and Jane F. Collier. Ithaca, NY: Cornell University Press.

Stavenhagen, Rodolfo. 1988. *Derecho indígena y derechos humanos en América Latina.* Mexico City: Instituto Interamericano de Derechos Humanos / Colegio de México.

——. 1992. Los derechos de los indígenas: Algunos problemas conceptuales. *Nueva Antropología* 13 (43): 83–99.

Stavenhagen, Rodolfo, and Diego Iturralde, eds. 1990. *Entre la ley y la costumbre: El derecho consuetudinario indígena en América Latina*. Mexico City: Instituto Indigenista Interamericano / Instituto Interamericano de Derechos Humanos.

Stephen, Lynn. 1993. Reconstructing the rural family: Ejidatario, ejidataria, and official views of ejido reform. Occasional Paper 4, Latin American Studies Consortium of New England, University of Connecticut.

———. 1997. *Women and social movements in Latin America: Power from below.* Austin: University of Texas Press.

———. 1998. The cultural and political dynamics of agrarian reform in Oaxaca and Chiapas. In *The future role of the ejido in rural Mexico,* ed. Richard Snyder and Gabriel Torres. La Jolla: University of California–San Diego.

———. 2001. Gender, citizenship, and the politics of identity. *Latin American Perspectives,* 28 (6): 54–69.

———. 2002. *Zapata lives! Histories and cultural politics in Southern Mexico.* Berkeley and Los Angeles: University of California Press.

Stern, Steve J. 1995. *The secret history of gender: Women, men, and power in late colonial Mexico.* Chapel Hill: University of North Carolina Press.

Talamantes, María Esther. 1956. La mujer y la política. *Filosofía y Letras,* nos. 60–62: 109–118.

Taylor, William B. 1979. *Drinking, homicide, and rebellion in colonial Mexican villages.* Stanford, CA: Stanford University Press.

Tinsman, Heidi. 2002. *Partners in conflict: The politics of gender, sexuality, and labor in the Chilean agrarian reform, 1950–1973.* Durham, NC: Duke University Press.

Torres, Indiana. 1993. Actitudes de los médicos ante el aborto. Research report, Population Council and GIRE, Mexico City.

Torres Falcón, Marta. 2003. Violencia de género: Un estado de la cuestión. *GénEros* (Universidad de Colima), no. 30: 17–25.

———, ed. 2004. *Violencia contra las mujeres en contextos urbanos y rurales.* Mexico City: Colegio de Mexico.

———, ed. 2005. *Nuevas maternidades y derechos reproductivos.* Mexico City: Colegio de México.

Torres Medina, Ricardo. 1997. *Derechos elementales de la mujer chihuahuense.* Chihuahua: Azar.

Toto Gutiérrez, Mireya. 2002. El feminismo en México y su impacto en el discurso jurídico. In Gutiérrez Castañeda 2002b.

Turner, Frederick C. 1974. *Responsible parenthood: The politics of Mexico's new population policies.* Washington: American Enterprise Institute for Public Policy Research.

Turner, Victor W. 1974. *Dramas, fields, and metaphors: Symbolic action in human society.* Ithaca, NY: Cornell University Press.

———. 1986. *The anthropology of performance.* New York: PAJ Publications.

Twinam, Ann. 1999. *Public lives, private secrets: Gender, honor, sexuality, and illegitimacy in colonial Spanish America.* Stanford, CA: Stanford University Press.

Ubaldi Garcete, Norma. 2004. Paulina cinco años después: Las deudas colectivas. In *Paulina: cinco años después,* ed. GIRE. Mexico City: GIRE.

Urrutia, Elena. 2002a. Estudios de la mujer: Antecedentes inmediatos a la creación del PIEM: Perspectivas y prioridades de los estudios de la mujer en México. In Urrutia 2002b.

———, ed. 2002b. *Estudios sobre las mujeres y las relaciones de género en México: Aportes desde diversas disciplinas.* Mexico City: Colegio de México.

Uruguay. 1977. *Código Civil de la República Oriental del Uruguay: Con las leyes y decretos que reforman y complementan su texto primitivo.* Montevideo: Barreiro y Ramos.

Valenzuela, Alejandra, and Héctor M. Robles Berlanga. 1996. Presencia de la mujer en el campo mexicano. *Estudios agrarios* (Procuraduría Agraria), no. 5: 31–63.

Vallejo Azuela, José. 1969. *Derechos de la mujer mexicana*. Mexico City: Herrerías.

Vallejo Real, Ivette Rossana. 2000. Mujeres *maseualmej* y usos de la legalidad: Conflictos genéricos en la Sierra Norte de Puebla. Master's thesis, CIESAS.

———. 2004a. Usos y escenificaciones de la legalidad ante litigios de violencia hacia la mujer *maseual* en Cuetzalan, Puebla. In Torres Falcón 2004.

———. 2004b. Relaciones de género, mujeres nahuas y usos de la legalidad en el municipio de Cuetzalan, Puebla. In Sierra 2004d.

Vance, Carol S. 1991. Anthropology rediscovers sexuality: A theoretical comment. *Social Science and Medicine* 33 (8): 875–884.

Varley, Ann. 2000a. De lo privado a lo público: Género, ilegalidad y legalización de la tenencia de la tierra urbana. *Estudios Demográficos y Urbanos* 15 (2), no. 44: 253–285.

———2000b. Women and the home in Mexican family law. In Dore and Molyneux 2000.

Varley, Ann, and Maribel Blasco. Forthcoming. Constructing gender and property rights in urban Mexico. In *Squatters or settlers: Rethinking ownership, occupation, and use in land law*, ed. Robert Home and Hilary Lynn. Oxford: Hart.

Vaughan, Mary Kay. 1997. *Cultural politics in revolution: Teachers, peasants, and schools in Mexico, 1930–1940*. Tucson: University of Arizona Press.

———. 2000. Modernizing patriarchy: State policies, rural households, and women in Mexico, 1930–1940. In Dore and Molyneux 2000.

Velázquez, Emilia. 1995. *Cuando los arrieros perdieron el camino: La conformación regional del Totonacapan*. Zamora: Colegio de Michoacán.

Venezuela, República de.1982. *Leyes nacionales: Código Civil de la República de Venezuela*. Caracas: Centauro.

Vidales Macouzet, Feliciano. 1938. ¿Limita el estado civil de casada a la capacidad para el ejercicio de derechos? BA thesis, UNAM.

Villa de Buentello, G. Sofía. 1921. *La mujer y la ley: Pequeña parte tomada de la obra en preparación, titulada "La esclava se levanta": Estudio importantísimo para la mujer que desee su emancipación y para el hombre amante del bien y la justicia*. Mexico City: privately printed.

Villafuerte García, María de Lourdes. 1989. Casar y compadrar cada uno con su igual: Casos de oposición al matrimonio en la ciudad de México, 1628–1634. In Guzmán Vázquez and Martínez O. 1989b.

Villa Hernández, Edith Rufina. 2003. La cultura indígena y los derechos de las mujeres. In Bonfil Sánchez and Martínez Medrano 2003.

Villa Rojas, Alfonso. 1945. *The Maya of East Central Quintana Roo*. Washington: Carnegie Institution of Washington.

Vogt, Evon Z. 1969. *Zinacantán: A Maya community in the highlands of Chiapas*. Cambridge, MA: Harvard University Press, Belknap Press.

Weeks, Jeffrey. 1986. *Sexuality*. Chichester: Ellis Horwood.

Wilets, James D. 1997. Conceptualizing private violence against sexual minorities as gendered violence: An international and comparative law perspective. *Albany Law Review* 60 (3): 989–1050.

Womack Jr., John.1999. *Rebellion in Chiapas: An historical reader*. New York: New Press.

Wood, Stephanie, and Robert Haskett. 1997. Concluding remarks. In Schroeder, Wood, and Haskett 1997.

World Bank 2001. *Engendering development through gender equality in rights, resources, and voice*. Washington and New York: World Bank / Oxford University Press.

World Conference on Human Rights. 1993. Vienna Declaration and Programme of Action. World Conference on Human Rights, Vienna, June 25. United Nations General Assembly Document A/CONF. 157/23.

Wrinkler, John J. 1990. *The constraints of desire: The anthropology of sex and gender in ancient Greece.* New York: Routledge.

Yee Verduzco, María de Jesús. 1975. Los derechos políticos de la mujer en México. BA thesis, UNAM.

Zamora, Antonio. 1969. *República Argentina: Código Civil con las notas de Vélez Sarsfield y las reformas dispuestas por las leyes 17711 y 17940. Textos ordenados y actualizados por Antonio Zamora.* Buenos Aires: Claridad.

Zamora, Stephen, José Ramón Cossío, Leonel Pereznieto, José Roldán-Xopa, and David Lopez. 2004. *Mexican Law.* Oxford: Oxford University Press.

Zepeda Lecuona, Guillermo R. 1999. La disputa por la tierra: Los tribunales agrarios en México. *Estudios Agrarios* (Procuraduría Agraria), no. 11: 9–49.

Zúñiga, Juan Antonio, and Herman Bellinghausen. 1997. Me hice zapatista para que mejoren nuestras comunidades: Trinidad. In Lovera and Palomo 1997.

NOTES ON CONTRIBUTORS

ANA M. ALONSO is an associate professor of anthropology at the University of Arizona. She was born in Havana, Cuba. Her great-great-uncle Manuel Márquez Sterling was an early supporter of feminism in Latin America. After receiving a BA from Wellesley College, she did graduate work in anthropology at the University of Chicago. Her first fieldwork was in Namiquipa, Chihuahua, Mexico, and this formed the basis for her book, *Thread of Blood: Gender, Colonialism, and Revolution on Mexico's Northern Frontier* (University of Arizona Press, 1995). Her work in Mexico has explored topics such as social memory, nationalism and ethnicity, and gender and law, as well as the Mexican Revolution. She is currently writing a book on Mexican museums and their role in the construction of national and ethnic identity. Her most recent fieldwork has been in Santa Ana, Oaxaca, Mexico.

HELGA BAITENMANN is an associate fellow of the Institute for the Study of the Americas, University of London. She received her PhD in anthropology at the New School for Social Research in 1998. Before moving to London, she taught and conducted research at the Colegio de la Frontera Norte (Tijuana). Her research has been supported by the Wenner Gren Foundation for Anthropological Research and the Ejido Reform Research Project at the Center for U.S.–Mexican Studies (UCSD). Among her most recent publications is "Blueprints of Governance: Agrarian Reform and State Formation in Postrevolutionary Mexico," *Journal of Latin American Studies* (forthcoming). She is currently preparing a book manuscript on the history of the agrarian reform in Mexico from a gendered perspective.

VICTORIA CHENAUT is a research professor at the Centro de Investigaciones y Estudios Superiores en Antropología Social (Xalapa, Mexico). A member of the Sistema Nacional de Investigadores (SNI), she has conducted fieldwork in the fishing communities of the Baja California Peninsula and in Yucatán, as well as in rural and indigenous communities in the states of Puebla, Quinta Roo, and Veracruz. Dr. Chenaut has published numerous book chapters and journal articles, and she is the author of *Aquellos que vuelan: Los totonacos en el siglo XIX* (CIESAS and Instituto Nacional Indigenista, 1995) and editor of *Procesos rurales e historia regional (Sierra y costa totonacas de Veracruz)* (CIESAS, 1996). Her research area is legal anthropology, and her topics include legal practices, justice, gender, and honor in multicultural societies.

JANE F. COLLIER is a professor emerita of anthropology at Stanford University. She is the author of *Law and Social Change in Zinacantan* (Stanford University Press, 1973), *Marriage and Inequality in Classless Societies* (Stanford University Press, 1988), and *From Duty to Desire: Remaking Families in a Spanish Village* (Princeton University Press, 1997). She is also coeditor with June Starr of *History and Power in the Study of Law* (Cornell University Press, 1989) and of two journal special issues, Law and Society in Southeast Asia (*Law and Society Review* 23 [3]) and Sanctioned Identities (*Identities* 2, [1–2]).

ROSÍO CÓRDOVA PLAZA is a researcher at the Instituto de Investigaciones Histórico-Sociales of Universidad Veracruzana, Mexico, and a member of the SNI. Dr. Cordova has extensive experience in anthropological research, focusing on gender, sexuality, family, migration, and peasant societies in central Veracruz. She has received the Gender Section Award "Helen I. Safa" for 2000 from the Latin American Studies Association and the 1996 Family Research Award given by the Universidad Nacional Autónoma de Mexico and Universidad Autónoma Metropolitana. Her publications include more than forty book chapters and journal articles, which have appeared in Mexico, Holland, France, Italy, Cuba, Spain, Brazil, Turkey, Costa Rica, and Poland. She is author of *Los peligros del cuerpo: Género y sexualidad en el centro de Veracruz* (2003), and is coeditor of *In God We Trust: Del campo mexicano al sueño americano* (forthcoming).

CARMEN DIANA DEERE is a professor of economics and the director of the Center for Latin American Studies at the University of Florida. Her PhD is in agricultural economics from the University of California, Berkeley. She is a past president of the Latin American Studies Association (LASA) and of the New England Council of Latin American Studies, and was a founding member and on the first executive board of the Latin American and Caribbean Economics Association (LACEA). Deere serves on numerous editorial boards, including those of *World Development* and *Feminist Economics.* Her most recent book (with Magdalena León) is *Empowering Women: Land and Property Rights in Latin America* (University of Pittsburgh Press, 2001), winner of the 2003 Bryce Wood Best Book Award of the Latin American Studies Association. During 2000, Deere was a Fulbright-Hays Scholar in Brazil. Her current research, in a project funded by the World Bank, is on the outcomes of women having land rights. She is also coediting a special issue of *Feminist Economics,* on women and the distribution of wealth.

SOLEDAD GONZÁLEZ MONTES has been a professor-researcher at the Interdisciplinary Women's Studies Program, El Colegio de México, since 1990. She holds a PhD in anthropology from the Universidad Complutense de Madrid, and has coordinated several research seminars and the collective books which have resulted from them: *Relaciones de género y transformaciones agrarias, Las mujeres y la salud, Las organizaciones no gubernamentales mexicanas y la salud reproductiva.* She is a member of the SNI and has written about gender relations in peasant and post-peasant families, inheritance, marriage, and motherhood. She has done research on domestic violence and reproductive health, and has sustained a permanent interest in peasant culture, in particular ritual feasts and dances. With Alejandro Patiño, she has coauthored a book on oral history, *Memoria campesina: La historia de Xalatlaco contada por su gente.*

MAXINE MOLYNEUX is a professor at the Institute for the Study of the Americas (ISA), University of London, where she teaches and writes in the fields of gender theory, political sociology, and development studies. As a comparative sociologist with a critical interest in socialist states, she is the author of monographs on the Ethiopian revolution and on South Yemen, as well as of articles on Cuba, Nicaragua, Eastern Europe, and the USSR. She was a cofounder of *Feminist Review* and acts as consultant to several UN agencies and NGOs. Since joining ISA in 1994, she has focused her research on issues of citizenship rights and rights-based approaches to development in Latin America. Her most recent books include *Hidden Histories of Gender and the State in Latin America*, edited with Elisabeth Dore (Duke University Press, 2000), *Gender and the Politics of Rights and Democracy in Latin America*, edited with Nikki Craske (Palgrave, 2002), and *Gender Justice, Development, and Rights,* edited with Shahra Razavi (Oxford University Press, 2002).

ADRIANA ORTIZ-ORTEGA has a PhD in political science (Yale University, 2001), and is presently head of the Interdisciplinary Women's Studies Program at El Colegio de México. She holds a Soros Fellowship at the Mailman School of Public Health, Columbia University. Ortiz-Ortega became a member of the SNI in 2002. She has been the recipient of several distinctions and fellowships from the Overseas Research Council, CONACYT, Wissenschaftskolleg zu Berlin, American Association of University Women, Population Council, and Open Society Institute, and from the Rockefeller, Ford, and MacArthur Foundations. She has taught at Yale University, El Colegio de México, and Rutgers University. Her most recent book is *Si los hombres se embarazaran, ¿el aborto sería legal?* (EDAMEX and Population Council, 2000).

MARÍA TERESA SIERRA is a research professor at CIESAS–Mexico City and member of the SNI, Level II. Her PhD dissertation (University of Paris, 1986) deals with the relationship among discourse, culture, and power in interethnic contexts. She has conducted research in several indigenous regions, including the Otomí region of the Valle del Mezquital and the Nahua region of the Sierra Norte de Puebla. Her current research interests include political and legal anthropology, ethnicity, gender, human rights, indigenous rights, and multiculturality. She has published several articles and five books, including *Haciendo justicia: Interlegalidad, derecho y género en regiones indígenas* (CIESAS and Porrúa, 2004), and, with R. Aída Hernández and Sarela Paz, *El Estado y los indígenas en los tiempos del PAN: Indigenismo, legalidad e identidad* (CIESAS, 2004). She has been part of a group of academics pioneering the study of indigenous law in Mexico and Latin America, and has coordinated a project on this topic.

LYNN STEPHEN is Distinguished Professor and chair of the Department of Anthropology at the University of Oregon. She is the author of four books, including *Zapotec Women* (University of Texas Press, 1991), *Hear My Testimony: María Teresa Tula, Human Rights Activist of El Salvador* (South End Press, 1994), *Women and Social Movements in Latin America: Power from Below* (University of Texas Press, 1997), and *Zapata Lives!: Histories and Cultural Politics in Southern Mexico* (University of California Press, 2002). She is the coeditor, with James W. Dow, of *Class, Politics, and Popular Religion in Mexico and Central America* (American Anthropological Association, 1990) and, with Matt Gutmann, Felix Matos Rodríguez, and Pat Zavella, of *Perspectives on Las Américas: A Reader in Culture, History, and Representation* (Blackwell Publishing, 2002). Lynn Stephen's research focuses on gender, ethnicity, political economy, social movements, human rights, migration, and nationalism in Latin America. She is currently working on two projects: a study on immigration and Mexican farmworkers in Oregon; and the role of cooperatives and global marketing on the political, labor, and gender identities of Zapotec women in southern Mexico. She is currently completing a manuscript, to be published with Duke University Press, *Cultural Difference and Globalization: Indigenous Migrants in the U.S. and Mexico.*

IVONNE SZASZ works as professor–researcher at El Colegio de México (Mexico City), where she coordinates the Reproductive Health and Society program. A member (level II) of the SNI since 1993, Dr. Szasz obtained a BA in law in 1972, MA in sociology in 1986, and a PhD in social sciences in 1990, and completed a postdoctoral study in 1992. She has published two books as author, four as editor and coeditor, more than thirty-five journal articles and book chapters; recently she coedited with Guadalupe Salas *Sexualidad, derechos humanos y ciudadanía: Diálogos en torno a un proyecto en construcción* (El Colegio de México, forthcoming), and with Susana Lerner *Salud reproductive y condiciones de vida en México* (El Colegio de México, forthcoming).

ANN VARLEY is Reader in Geography at University College London. Her research focuses on land and housing, and on gender relations and the urban household in Mexico. In both areas, her work has emphasized legal questions, especially land tenure regularization and family law concerning the home. Dr. Varley's books include *Landlord and Tenant: Housing the Poor in Urban Mexico* with Alan Gilbert (Routledge, 1991), and *Illegal Cities: Law and Urban Change in Developing Countries*, edited with Edésio Fernandes (Zed Books, 1998). She is currently writing a book on the meaning of home in Mexico. Her work has led to invitations to speak in Brazil and Spain (at the International Institute for the Sociology of Law) to legal scholars interested in urban space, and to audiences in Mexico, the United States, Denmark, France, Lesotho, Egypt, and Lebanon. She has held an individual residency at the Rockefeller Foundation Study Center, Bellagio, Italy.

INDEX

abortion, 31, 66, 234; and the Catholic church, 200–207, 209; criminalization of, 200–209 *passim*; and gender ideologies, 200, 202; liberalization of, 197, 200–209 *passim*; in Mexico, comparative legislation, 32, 197–199; and the "Paulina case," 207, 208, 211n32; and public health, 197, 199, 205–209, 211n26, 211n32, 233; and rape, 199–211 *passim*; and the "Robles Law," 207; and reproductive rights, 202–206; and state-level laws, 198–212 *passim*

Agrarian Code (1934), 185, 188

Agrarian Code (1940), 16, 183, 188, 193n9

Agrarian Law (1992), 93–100 *passim*, 107n2, 184–185, 187, 191, 229

Agrarian Law of Pancho Villa (1915), 190

Agrarian Ombudsman, Office of, 107n2, 182

agrarian reform, 181, 183–184, 186, 190, 191, 225; and agrarian communities, 2, 93, 108n3; and agrarian courts, 33, 107n2, 180, 182, 184, 187–189, 192; and the "agrarian family," 31, 95–96, 180, 184–187, 194n14; in Chile, 189; and ejidos, 2, 93, 95–108 *passim*, 132, 180–194 *passim*, 225, 229; and family patrimony, 95–96, 185, 187, 190–191; and gender ideologies, 31, 34, 95, 104, 184, 186–190, 192; and the land-titling program (Procede), 107n2, 182, 187, 227; and privatization, 93, 99, 102, 181–182, 187, 191–192, 225, 227, 229, 234; and property (use) rights, 31, 96, 97, 184–194 *passim*, 225, 227; women's legal status in, 95, 184, 187, 190, 193n7, 194n14, 194n22; women's role in, 98, 182, 187–188, 230n13; and the Zapatista National Liberation Army, 98–107

Agrarian Regulatory Law of 1922, 183, 186

Ahumada, Corripio (archbishop), 205

Alliance of Women in Mexico, 16, 38n29

armed forces, 25, 98, 100, 236

Aztecs, 190

"Cairo+Five" review, 206

Calles, Plutarco Elías, 203

Cárdenas, Lázaro, 203

Carranza, Venustiano, 12, 14, 148, 149

Catholic church, xii, 5, 33, 73; and abortion, 200–207, 209; and church-state relations, 200–207; and gender ideologies, x–xi, 60, 68

Católicas por el Derecho de Decidir, 206, 211n30

Civil Code (1870, Federal District and Federal), 10–11, 175, 214

Civil Code (1884, Federal District and Federal), 10–11, 14, 147–150, 175, 186, 213, 220, 222

Civil Code (1928, Federal District and Federal, pre-2000), xi, xii, 11, 15, 36, 146, 147, 151, 152, 190–191, 213–219 *passim*, 223

Civil Code (1928, Federal, post-2000), 36

Civil Code (1928, Federal District, post-2000), 36

civil codes, xii, 15–17, 32, 34, 35, 181, 183, 189, 225–229; elsewhere in Latin America, 10, 213–230 *passim*; Napoleonic, ix, x, 147; in the nineteenth century, 10–11, 14, 147–150, 175, 177n6, 186, 213, 214, 219–221; in Puebla, 114, 119; at the state level, 32, 34, 36, 39n33, 89; in State of Mexico, 179n35; in Veracruz, 12, 38n17, 161n39. *See also names of individual codes*

Coalition of Feminist Women, 18

Code of Civil Proceedings (Puebla), 124n8

Code of Penal Proceedings (Chihuahua), 50

Comandanta Esther, 105–106

Comité ProVida, 205, 207, 211n32, 212n32

Congress, 36, 148, 204, 206; and gender justice, 16, 19–20, 38n29; and indigenous rights, 93, 95, 105–106

Constitution of Mexico (1857), 149, 210n10

Constitution of Mexico (1917), 15, 76, 95, 88, 202; Article 4 of, 24, 76, 79, 89, 97, 203–204, 235; Article 27 of, 97, 99, 102, 107n2, 181, 191; Article 34 of, 16; and gender, xi, 17, 228

Constitutional Convention (1916–1917), 151, 160n25

courts: and acts of conformity, 112, 117, 164–165, 172–173; agrarian, 33, 107n2, 180, 182, 184, 187–189, 192; in the colonial era, 4–9; and gender ideologies, xii, xiii, 8–9, 29, 43, 44, 50, 109–121

courts (continued)
passim; hierarchies within, 28, 30–32,
   110–114, 117–120, 164, 182; and homicide, 4,
   8–9, 38n18, 49, 113, 126, 128, 131–133,
   140n2,164, 234; and indigenous affairs,
   6–8, 22, 26–31, 35, 109–124 *passim,* 140n2,
   161n56, 163–179 *passim,* 234–235; and marital conflicts, 117–120; men's role in, 3, 6, 7,
   22, 28, 113, 155–156, 166–167, 175, 181; in the
   nineteenth century, 4–5, 8–10, 13, 37n13,
   37n16, 165, 174, 185, 186; proceedings of,
   47–51, 55–57, 113–120, 122, 130, 140n2;
   records of, 4–8, 43, 46, 50–56 *passim,* 126,
   130, 133, 134, 139, 162, 164, 166, 170, 172; at
   the state level, 110, 131; women's role in,
   6–8, 28, 29, 109–120 *passim,* 146, 155, 162,
   165–177, 181, 182, 186–188. *See also names of
   individual courts*
Courts of First Instance, 49, 110, 113, 117, 119,
   120, 140n2, 161n56, 164

Decree of January 6 (1915), 183, 185, 190,
   193n5

Echeverría Álvarez, Luis, 17, 204
Edict of Policing and Government (Xalapa),
   79
ejidos. *See under* agrarian reform

family: and the "agrarian family," 31, 95–96,
   180, 184–187, 194n14; construction of, xi, 7,
   10, 12, 43–45, 50, 60, 61, 66–70 *passim,* 113,
   122, 145–161 *passim,* 203–204, 206, 210n20,
   232; and the law, xi, xii, 4, 7, 10–12, 18, 20,
   31, 44, 45, 50, 59, 64–73 *passim,* 76, 111, 119,
   145–161, 160n25, 177n2, 178n29, 191,
   215–217, 228, 232; and *patria potestad*
   (paternal authority), 10, 174; patrimony,
   54, 72. *See also* civil codes; marriage
Federal Agrarian Reform Law (1971), 12,
   38n28, 95, 184, 187, 193n9
Federal Appeals Courts, 131, 159n2, 160n29
Federal District Human Rights Commission,
   207
Federal Labor Law, 18, 20–21, 39n34, 79
Federal Law for Public Workers, 18
Federal Law to Prevent and Eliminate Discrimination, 76
feminism: and feminist movements, ix–xiii
   passim, 11–19 *passim,* 35, 62–63, 147, 148,
   187, 203, 204, 206, 209, 217–218, 225,
   230n14, 233, 234; and feminist scholarship, xii–xiv, 2, 15–20 *passim,* 60–61, 70,
   73, 94, 146, 157, 184, 188, 213, 214, 231–232;
   and the Left, xi, 17, 38n26, 204

Galindo, Hermila, 148
gender: ideologies of, 4, 5, 18, 33, 44–46,
   49–57 *passim,* 66–75 *passim,* 78–84
   passim, 109, 126, 134, 139, 173, 202; and
   legal anthropology, 3, 21–31, 123, 140; in
   prisons, 33, 127, 137–140; studies, 3, 18,
   20, 123
Gender and Equity Commissions, 19

gender justice, ix, xii, xiv, 231; campaigns for,
   16, 19–20, 121; and Congress, 16, 19–20,
   38n29; debates on, 1–2, 31; and international agreements, 19–20, 34–35; and the
   law, 18, 122, 214, 221, 229, 237
gossip, 52, 53, 55, 137, 171; and the law, 33, 43,
   46–50 *passim,* 54–57, 111, 113

heteronormativity, 1, 21, 34, 75, 77, 80, 82;
   definition of, 39n36. *See also* sexuality
Homestead Act (U.S.), 191
honor, 44; and gender ideologies, 45, 49, 53,
   54; in indigenous communities, 116,
   135–137, 139; and the law, 45, 56, 57; and
   sexuality, 66–67, 69
human rights: gendered conceptualizations
   of, xiii, 2–4, 19–20, 26, 27, 38n31, 121; promotion of, xiii, 19, 24–26, 28, 79, 88–89,
   96–97, 113, 120–124; violations of, 86–87,
   113, 120. *See also* gender justice; *names of
   individual organizations*
Human Rights Watch, 208

indigenous communities, 2, 93; *cargos* in, 112,
   122; and the courts, 6–8, 22, 26–31, 35,
   109–124 *passim,* 140n2, 161n56, 163–179
   passim, 234–235; crimes in, 132–140; and
   ethnic discrimination, 118, 119; and gender
   ideologies, 116, 119, 121, 125, 139, 141n18;
   and gender relations, 23, 111, 115–116; and
   indigenous identity, 93, 163–164; and
   international legal agreements, 24, 235;
   and the law, xiv, 22, 116, 121, 125; socioeconomic changes in, 122, 163–164; studies of,
   21–23. *See also* indigenous rights; indigenous women; *names of individual ethnic
   groups*
Indigenous Court, 110, 121, 123, 124n5
Indigenous Law, 93, 95, 97, 98, 100
indigenous rights: and Congress, 93, 95,
   105–106; promotion of, 22–27 *passim,* 93,
   96–98, 113, 120, 121, 124n10, 234–235;
   women's role in, 96–98. *See also* human
   rights; Indigenous Law
indigenous women: and the courts, 26,
   28–31, 35, 109; criminalization of, 31,
   125–141; demands by, 25–27, 39n47, 94–100
   passim, 106–107, 122, 123, 232, 235–236; and
   ethnic groups, 6–8, 22, 98, 105–106, 126,
   128, 129; and interlegality, 22–30 *passim,*
   93–94, 106, 127, 138–139; legal status of, 35,
   98, 122, 124n7; Nahua, 6–8, 114, 129; and
   poverty, 125, 127; as prisoners, 128–141;
   rights abuses of, 8, 120, 122; and rights
   movements, 25–27, 35, 96–97, 106–107,
   113, 120–121, 124n10; and the San Andrés
   Accords, 94, 96, 97, 105–107; and violence,
   25–27, 39n44, 109–116, 119, 125, 162; and
   the Zapatista National Liberation Army,
   97–106
Indigenous Women's House (CAMI),
   120–121
Institutional Revolutionary Party (PRI), 204,
   206, 207

interlegality, x, xiv, 28, 93, 98–100, 102, 107,
193; and agrarian law, 101; and the courts,
28–31, 110–114 passim, 118–124 passim; definition of, 26, 30, 112, 125; and gender, 29,
96, 109, 111, 119, 121–124, 139; and indigenous women, 22–30 passim, 93–94, 106,
127, 138–139; and state-level laws, 112
International Labor Organization, 24, 79, 235
International Women's Year, 17, 38n25, 153

John Paul II (pope), 205
judges, 47, 158, 162, 192; and gender ideologies, 29, 45, 165–166; role of, 16, 47–57 passim, 111, 115, 116, 140n2, 145, 164, 173–175,
181–189 passim, 192, 225–226; rulings by,
12, 20, 33, 34, 62, 151–159, 180, 187, 188
judicial review (amparo), 145, 158, 159n2
justices of the peace, 110, 111, 113, 118, 140n2,
164–165

Latin American Network of Legal Anthropology, 24
law: and citizenship, 31, 233; discourses on,
2, 45–47, 50–51, 56–57, 145, 146, 157; and
equality, x–xiv, 10–18 passim, 31, 76, 98,
106, 109, 147, 149, 150–152, 157–158, 187,
193n7, 203, 213, 217, 219, 225, 226, 228,
231–234, 237; and gender, x–xiv, 1–4, 13, 18,
26, 29–35, 43, 45, 59, 68, 72–73, 88, 93,
180–181, 190, 192, 219, 231; and gender ideologies, xi–xii, 2, 4, 8, 9, 11, 14, 26, 29–31,
34, 38n18, 96, 146–158 passim, 220–221, 231,
234; and justice, 45, 50, 56; and lawyers,
14–16, 28, 112, 146–147, 155; and legal scholarship, 3, 13–21; and practice, 34, 44
Law of Civil Marriage (1859), 147
Law of Family Relations (1917), 12, 160n25,
177n2, 178n29, 191, 215, 217, 228; discourse
analysis of, 146–151, 157–158; and feminist
movements, 11
Law of Social Assistance and Protection of
Boys and Girls (Veracruz), 77
Law on Prostitution and Social Prophylaxis
(Veracruz), 77–78, 87
legislation: colonial, x, 5–7, 9–11, 14, 31,
147–150, 175, 186, 190, 193n1, 194n23, 201,
203, 209, 213–222 passim, 231–237 passim;
Germanic and Anglo-Saxon, 72, 73; in the
nineteenth century, x, 10, 14, 31, 44, 71, 72,
177n6, 186–187, 193n1, 201, 210n10, 214,
219–220; Roman, ix, 71–72, 147; variation
by state, 13, 19, 32–36 passim, 39n33, 59–74
passim, 93, 160n38, 198–212 passim; Mexican, in comparative perspective, x–xiii,
10, 13, 19, 25, 31, 32, 44, 62, 197–199,
213–229, 229n6. See also civil codes; penal
codes; names of individual laws
López Portillo, José, 205

Macías, José Natividad, 148
marriage (legal and common-law): and "the
abduction of the bride" (robo de la novia),
167–168; as act of reparation, 47–56 passim, 63–70; and adultery, 4, 11–12, 25, 29,

36n2, 37n3, 44, 45, 56, 59, 70–72, 113,
119–120, 148, 149; conflicts in, 117–120,
132–134, 166–177; and divorce, 9, 12, 145–151
passim, 156–162 passim, 175, 178n29,
179n35, 216, 226, 233; and dual-headed
households, 213, 217–220, 226, 229; gender
ideologies of, 25, 146–158, 160, 160n23,
162, 166, 167, 170, 171, 175–177; and the
home, 31, 44, 145–161 passim, 168, 224–225;
and inheritance, 213, 219–225, 227–229,
230n10; and in-laws, 12, 22, 114, 134, 151,
155–158, 167–172, 177n12; and men's legal
status, 214, 218; and polygamy, 119–120;
and potestad marital, xi, 15, 147, 149, 157,
160n23, 216, 219, 228; and property rights,
11, 213–221, 225–229; and residence, 22, 25,
114, 131, 151–158, 160n26, 167–169, 178n13,
217; rights and obligations in, 9, 31,
37nn15–16, 145–162 passim; and women's
status, 11–15 passim, 37n14, 115, 147–158,
163, 169, 175–177, 217–218. See also family;
violence: domestic
Marxism, xi, 17, 23, 38n26, 204
Maseualsiuamej Mosenyolchicauanij, 120
Maximilian I (emperor), 77
men: as activists, 15–16; as fathers, 23, 29, 47,
48, 53; as heads of household, 71–72, 184,
186–187, 194n19, 232; as husbands, 25, 29,
51, 154–157, 159n4, 160n27; legal status of,
xi, xii, 10, 11, 14, 66, 95, 190, 220; and masculinity, 1, 43, 45, 47, 49, 82, 88, 121; in
prison, 126, 128, 132, 137, 139–140; widowed, 219, 220, 230n9. See also patriarchy
Metropolitan Autonomous University
(UAM), 20
Mexican Communist Party, 204
Mexican Feminist Movement, 18
Mexican Revolution (1910–1920), x, xi, 14, 16,
148; ideals of, 45, 203; impact of, 2, 51–52,
185, 202; and the law, 145, 190–191; and
women's rights, 11
minors: legal status of, 44; and rape, 8, 207,
208; and sexuality, 60–71 passim, 78,
79, 89
Mixtecs, 7
Movement in Defense of Christ, 202

Nahua, 123n1, 124n4, 163; and the courts,
6–8, 109, 110, 112; and gender ideology, 121;
and legal systems, 113, 116; and women's
roles, 6–8, 114, 129
National Action Party (PAN), 203–207
passim, 211n31
National Agrarian Registry (RAN), 107n2,
185, 187
National Assembly for Autonomy (ANIPA),
96, 97
National Autonomous University of Mexico
(UNAM), 15, 17, 21, 36
National Commission for the Development
of Indigenous Peoples (CDI), 121
National Commission of Concord and Pacification (COCOPA), 97
National Indigenous Congress (CNI), 96, 97

National Indigenous Women's Coordinating Council (CNMI), 96, 97
National Movement of Women, 18
1968 student movement, 17
North American Free Trade Agreement (NAFTA), 3

Palavicini, Félix, 148, 149, 159nn16–17
Party of the Democratic Revolution (PRD), 207, 211n31
patria potestad. See under family
patriarchy: in courts, 29, 119; generational dimensions of, 54, 190; in historical perspective, x–xii, xiv, 9–10, 44, 54, 71–72; in indigenous communities, 23, 29, 121; and state formation 185
peasant organizations, 99
Penal Code (1871, Federal District and Federal), 11, 44, 46, 56, 58n2, 201–203, 209, 210n15
Penal Code (1931, Federal District and Federal, pre-1999), 19, 20, 36, 62, 73, 203, 205
Penal Code (1931, Federal, post-1999), 36, 59–74 *passim*
Penal Code (1931, Federal District, 1999–2002), 36, 62, 74n4, 76, 77
Penal Code (2002, Federal District), 36, 59–74 *passim,* 208
penal codes, 15, 16, 30–33, 35, 38n17, 59–74 *passim,* 197, 201; in Chihuahua, 54, 211n24, 211n31; compared to civil codes, 64, 65; in the nineteenth century, 11, 44, 46, 56, 58n2, 201–203; and sexuality, 61–74; at the state level, 13, 32–35, 39n33, 58–74 *passim,* 77, 179n36, 199–200, 204–206, 210nn2–8, 210n19, 211nn24–31 *passim*; in State of Mexico, 178n29, 179n36; in Veracruz, 77–79. *See also names of individual codes*
prostitution. *See* sexual commerce
ProVida, 205, 207, 211n27, 212n32
Public Property Registry, 190
public prosecutors, 140n2; in Chihuahua, 48; and gender ideologies in prisons, 33, 126, 127, 132; and indigenous affairs, 110–113, 119, 123n1, 124n6, 128; in Puebla, 110–113, 119, 123n1, 124n6; in Veracruz, 127–133 *passim,* 138–140

Ramírez Jacinto, Paulina. *See* abortion: and the "Paulina" case
rape, 8, 129, 233; and abortion, 199–211 *passim*; and the courts, 8, 120, 164, 234; and *estupro* (statutory rape), 44–59 *passim,* 65–71 *passim*; and the law, xiii, 19, 55, 56, 58n10, 61–52; of minors, 8, 207, 208; *rapto* (abduction), 44, 54–59, 65, 69–71
Regulatory Law for the Practice of Prostitution (Federal District), 77
Revolutionary Agrarian Law, 100–107
Revolutionary Workers' Party, 204
Rivas Mercado, Antonieta, 145, 156–158
Robles, Rosario, 207
"Robles Law," 207
Rousseau, Jean-Jacques, 147

Ruiz García, Samuel (bishop), 206

San Andrés Accords on Indigenous Rights and Culture, 93, 95, 97, 105–106, 108n5; and women, 94, 96, 97, 105–107
San Cristóbal Women's Group, 25
sexual commerce, 70–71; criminalization of, 73, 75; and health risks, 87–88; history of, 77–79; by men, 80, 84, 90n23; and pimping, 71, 75, 78, 79, 87; regulation of, 77–79, 88; and transvestites, 75, 84–89 *passim*
sexual harassment, 171; and the courts, 28–29, 113; penalization of, 34–35, 61, 62, 68, 74n5; and sexual preference, 85–87; in the workplace, 21
sexuality: discourses of, 59–68 *passim,* 73n2, 77–88 *passim*; and discrimination, 1, 21, 35, 39n36, 75, 79–86, 88; and minors, 60–71 *passim,* 78, 79, 89; and reproductive rights, 202–206; and transsexuality 70–71, 75–76, 83–90
state formation, x, 101–102, 158; and gender, 44, 185; in the twentieth century, x, xi, 2, 5, 12, 202–204
Supreme Court, 32, 207; jurisprudence, 12, 16, 33–34, 145, 146, 151–161 *passim*

Takachihualis Commission, 113, 120, 124n10
Tojolab'al, 98, 105–106
Totonacs, 123n1, 124n4, 126–131, 133, 141n18

United Nations Conference on Population and Development (Cairo), 206
United Nations Convention on the Elimination of All Forms of Discrimination Against Women (CEDAW), 20, 219
United Nations World Conference on Women (Beijing), 206
United Nations World Conference on Women (Mexico City), 17, 153
Universal Declaration of Human Rights, 232, 233

Vida y Familia, 205
Villa de Buentello, Sofía, 15
violence, 3, 46, 56–57, 209, 231, 237; and the armed forces, 25, 98, 100, 236; domestic, xii–xiii, 2, 4, 7–8, 11, 25–27, 37n13, 44, 62, 94, 110–111, 116–119, 122–226 *passim,* 129, 131–139 *passim,* 161n57, 162, 167–174 *passim,* 177n12, 233, 237n2; and human rights, xiii, 2, 18–21, 72, 97; and indigenous women, 25–27, 39n44, 109–116, 119, 125, 162; and sexual preference, 75, 80–89 *passim. See also* rape
Violence Against Women Act (U.S.), 44

women: and criminality, 38n13, 126, 128, 129, 132; legal status of, xi–xiv, 9–19 *passim,* 38n31, 55, 57, 95, 148, 149, 160n21, 160n24, 165, 184, 187, 190, 187, 190, 193n7, 194n14, 194n22, 197, 214, 216–217, 220–226 *passim,* 229n3; and motherhood, xii, xiii, 11, 14, 25, 38n23, 104, 129, 173, 187, 188, 203, 204,

206, 232, 233; as prisoners, 33, 126, 128, 129, 137–140; and property, x, 31, 94–99 *passim*, 106–107, 159n12, 165, 213–221; and reproductive rights, 202–206; and suffrage, xi, 12, 15, 17, 203; widowed, 8–10, 104, 116, 186–187, 194n14, 216, 219–230 *passim*; and work, 23, 38n23, 45, 98, 103–104, 150–163 *passim*, 170–178 *passim*, 187–189, 216–217, 225, 236. *See also* indigenous women
Women's National Congress (Yucatán), 15
Women's Revolutionary Law, 26–27, 39nn46–47, 100

Zapatista National Liberation Army (EZLN), 3, 24, 26, 94–108 *passim*; and agrarian reform, 98–107; and autonomous municipalities, 29, 93, 98, 105, 106, 107, 236; gender roles in, 98–104; revolutionary laws of, 26–27, 39nn46–47, 96–107 *passim*; women's role in, 97–106. *See also* indigenous rights; San Andrés Accords on Indigenous Rights and Culture
Zapotecs, 7, 22, 128